NEWCOMER'S HANDBOOK®

Neighborhood GUiDE

Dallas-Fort Worth, Houston, and Austin

FIRST BOOKS®
6750 SW Franklin Street
Portland, OR 97223-2542
WWW.FIRSTBOOKS.COM
503.968.6777

Author: YuShan Chang

Editors: Linda Weinerman and Emily Horowitz

Proofreading: Linda Weinerman and Emily Horowitz

Design and production: Masha Shubin

Maps: Jim Miller/fennana design

Cover Photos © 2006: SoleilC (neighborhood), Valkeus (Texas flag), Cathleen Clapper (mother/daughter), Marilyn Nieves (father/son), Kris Hanke (man/dog), Tom Wald (couple/sunset)

ISBN-10: 0-912301-70-8
ISBN-13: 978-0-912301-70-9

Printed in the USA

Published by First Books, 6750 SW Franklin Street, Portland, OR 97223-2542, USA
tel 503 968 6777, www.firstbooks.com.

TABLE OF CONTENTS

INTRODUCTION 1

THE DALLAS–FORT WORTH METROPLEX 5

DALLAS 5
MAP OF DALLAS NEIGHBORHOODS 8
CENTRAL DALLAS 6
    Downtown 6
    Uptown Area 10
        Uptown 10
        Knox-Henderson 11
        Oak Lawn/Cedar Springs/Turtle Creek 11
EAST DALLAS 12
    Deep Ellum 12
    Old East Dallas 14
        Junius Heights 15
        Munger Place 15
        Vickery Place 15
        Belmont 15
        Swiss Avenue 16
        Wilson Historic District 16
        Greenville 16
        M Streets/Greenland Hills 17
        Cochran Heights 17
        Bryan Place 17
        Wilshire Heights 18
NORTHEAST DALLAS/WHITE ROCK LAKE 19
    Lakewood 20
    Lake Highlands 22
NORTH DALLAS 23
    Highland Park 23
    University Park 24
    Bluffview 26
    Preston Hollow 27
FAR NORTH DALLAS 28
    Northwood Hills and Spring Creek 29
    Prestonwood 30
SOUTHERN DALLAS 31
    Oak Cliff 31
    South Oak Cliff 35

SOUTH DALLAS 35
    The Cedars 36
    Fair Park/Exposition Park 36
SOUTHEAST DALLAS 38
    Pleasant Grove 38
    Scyene 38
SOUTHWEST DALLAS 39
MAP OF DALLAS–FORT WORTH REGION 42
EAST DALLAS SUBURBS 40
    Garland 40
    Mesquite 44
    Balch Springs 45
    Rowlett 46
    Sunnyvale 46
NORTH SUBURBS 47
    The Metrocrest 47
    Addison 47
    Farmers Branch 48
    Carrollton 49
    Coppell 50
    Richardson 51
    Collin County 52
    Plano 52
    Frisco 54
    McKinney/Fairview/Allen 55
    Denton County 56
    The Colony 56
    Lewisville 57
NORTHEAST SUBURBS 58
    Murphy/Wylie/Sachse 58
SOUTHWESTERN SUBURBS 59
    Duncanville/DeSoto/Cedar Hill/Lancaster 59
    Glenn Heights 61
MID-CITIES 61
    Irving 62
    Grand Prairie 63
    Tarrant County 64
    Arlington 64
    Dalworthington Gardens and Pantego 65
    Hurst, Euless, and Bedford (HEB) 66
    Flower Mound 68
    Grapevine 69
    Southlake 70
    Colleyville 71
    North Richland Hills/Richland Hills 71
    Keller 72

Watauga/Haltom City 73

FORT WORTH 74
MAP OF FORT WORTH NEIGHBORHOODS 76
DOWNTOWN 75
    Sundance Square.. 75
    West Seventh Street.. 78
WEST FORT WORTH 79
    Arlington Heights/Monticello/Crestwood and Como............. 79
      Arlington Heights/Monticello/Crestwood.......................... 79
      Como.. 80
    Rivercrest/Northcrest and Ridglea 81
      Rivercrest/Northcrest 81
      Ridglea.. 82
    City of Benbrook.. 83
    Ridgmar 85
    Westover Hills 86
    Western Hills, Las Vegas Trails, Westpoint/Westland, Lost
      Creek, Chapel Creek, Silver Ridge, and Tejas Trails............ 87
    Mira Vista/Meadows West/Cityview....................................... 88
    Westworth Village 89
    River Oaks 90
    White Settlement... 91
SOUTH FORT WORTH 92
    Fairmount, Ryan Place, and Mistletoe Heights/Berkeley Place...92
      Fairmount and Ryan Place.. 92
      Mistletoe Heights/Berkeley Place 93
    TCU Area and Surrounding Neighborhoods......................... 94
      Bluebonnet Hills.. 95
      Colonial/Bellaire... 96
      University Place and University West............................. 96
      Park Hill 97
      Tanglewood/Westcliff/Stonegate 97
      Overton 98
    Southwest Seminary/Wedgewood/Candleridge 99
      Southwest Seminary... 99
        Worth Heights, Rosemont, and Seminary.................... 99
      Wedgewood.. 100
      Candleridge... 100
EAST FORT WORTH 101
    Meadowbrook/Eastern Hills, Hampshire, Ryanwood/Carol
      Oaks, and Handley 101
      Hampshire and Meadowbrook/Eastern Hills 101
      Ryanwood/Carol Oaks 102
      Handley.. 102
    White Lake Hills, Woodhaven, and Brentwood Hills........... 103

White Lake Hills 103
Woodhaven 104
Brentwood Hills 104
John T. White/Sandybrook/Cobblestone Square, Cooke's
   Meadow, Sandy Oaks, and Bentley Village 105
   John T. White/Sandybrook/Cobblestone Square 105
   Cooke's Meadow and Sandy Oaks 106
   Bentley Village 106
   Eastchase 106
NORTH FORT WORTH 107
   Northside 107
   Riverside 108
   Rock Island/Samuels Avenue 109
   Far North Fort Worth 110
NORTHWEST FORT WORTH 111
   Sansom Park/Lake Worth 111
   Azle/Pelican Bay/Lakeside 112
SOUTH SUBURBS 113
   Crowley 113
   Johnson County 114
   Burleson 114
SOUTHEAST SUBURBS 115
   Forest Hill and Everman 115
   Mansfield 116
NORTH SUBURBS 116
   Haslet 116

HOUSTON 118
MAP OF HOUSTON NEIGHBORHOODS 120
INNER LOOP 119
   Downtown, Midtown, and the Wards 119
      Downtown 119
      Midtown 123
      The Wards 124
   Heights 126
   East Houston 127
   Montrose 130
   Bellaire, West University Place, Southside Place, and Old
      Braeswood 132
   Museum/Medical Center 135
      Rice University Area/Museum District/Texas Medical
         Center 135
      Medical Center and South Loop Area (Astrodome/
         Reliant Center) 136
      Braeswood Place 137

Stella Link/Linkwood..137
River Oaks/Upper Kirby/Greenway Plaza.........................138
  River Oaks...138
    Highland Village Area...138
  Upper Kirby...139
  Greenway Plaza Area...139
  Rice Military/Camp Logan/Crestwood.....................140
OUTER LOOP...142
  Uptown..142
    Tanglewood/Briargrove...143
  Westchase..144
  The Memorial Area..145
    The Villages...146
    Spring Valley...147
    Briar Forest...147
    Memorial West...148
    Spring Branch..148
  Katy...149
  Addicks/Barker...150
SOUTHWEST HOUSTON...151
  Meyerland..151
  Westbury..153
    Greater Fondren Southwest Area.............................153
    Glenshire...153
  Westwood/Harwin, Sharpstown, and Alief................154
    Westwood/Harwin..154
    Braeburn..155
    Sharpstown...155
    Alief...156
SOUTHWEST SUBURBS...158
MAP OF GREATER HOUSTON...160
  Fort Bend County..158
  Meadows Place and Stafford.....................................158
    Meadows Place...158
    Stafford..159
  Sugar Land...162
  Missouri City..163
    Oyster Creek..164
    Lake Olympia...164
    Sienna Plantation...164
  Richmond and Rosenberg..165
NORTHWEST HOUSTON..166
  Inwood Forest, Candlelight, Garden Oaks, and Oak Forest..167
    Inwood Forest..167
    Candlelight...167
    Garden Oaks and Oak Forest..................................168

Cypress Area..169
    Cypress...169
    Jersey Village...169
    Klein..170
    Champion Forest 170
    Gleannloch Farms...170
    Copperfield 171
    Fairfield 171
  Tomball...172
NORTH HOUSTON AND SURROUNDING COMMUNITIES 173
  Northline and Greenspoint..173
    Northline 173
    Greenspoint 174
  Aldine and Spring 175
    Aldine...175
    Spring...175
  Montgomery County 176
    Woodlands...176
    Shenandoah 177
NORTHEAST HOUSTON 178
    Humble 178
    Kingwood...179
    Atascocita..179
EAST OF HOUSTON 180
  Pasadena, Deer Park, and Baytown 180
    Pasadena..180
    Deer Park 181
    Baytown 181
  North Houston Ship Channel Area........................183
  La Porte/Bayshore 184
BAY AREA...185
    Clear Lake 186
GALVESTON COUNTY 189
    Kemah 189
    League City 190
    Galveston..191
    Texas City and La Marque 192
    Texas City...192
    La Marque..192
SOUTH OF HOUSTON 193
  Brazoria County 193
    Pearland 193
    Friendswood..194

AUSTIN 196

MAP OF AUSTIN..198
CENTRAL AUSTIN...197
   Downtown..197
   University Area and Hancock..200
      University Area...200
      Hancock..201
   Hyde Park..202
   Historic West Austin..203
      Old Enfield..203
      Pemberton Heights...204
      Old West Austin/Clarksville..204
      Bryker Woods...205
   Tarrytown..206
  West Central Austin...207
   Camp Mabry Area/Mt. Bonnell and Rosedale......................207
      Camp Mabry Area and Mt. Bonnell................................207
      Rosedale..207
   Allandale/Crestview/Brentwood...208
      Highland..209
WEST AUSTIN...210
   Travis Country, Barton Creek, and Riverplace.....................210
      Travis Country..210
      Barton Creek..210
      River Place..211
   Village of Bee Cave...212
   Westlake Hills and Rollingwood...213
SOUTHWEST AUSTIN...214
   Oak Hill..215
      Deer Park at Maple Run...216
      Sendera..216
      Circle C...216
   Outlying Communities...217
      Village of San Leanna...217
      Manchaca..217
EAST AUSTIN..217
      Riverside...218
   Delwood, Cherrywood, University Hills/Windsor Park........219
SOUTH AUSTIN..220
      Travis Heights/Bouldin..221
      Zilker and Barton Hills..222
FAR SOUTH AUSTIN...224
SOUTHEAST AUSTIN...225
      Onion Creek...226
NORTH AUSTIN..227
   Wells Branch/Scofield/Milwood/Walnut Creek.....................227
      Lamplight Village and Gracy Woods/Gracy Farms...........227

NORTHEAST AUSTIN 229
    Manor 229
    Harris Branch, Copperfield/North Oaks/Woodcliff 230
        Harris Branch 230
        Copperfield/North Oaks (Walnut Creek area)/Woodcliff . 230
    Pflugerville 232
NORTHWEST AUSTIN 232
    Balcones West/Cat Mountain/North Cat Mountain/
        Northwest Hills 233
    The Arboretum/Great Hills/Balcones/Spicewood Springs 233
FAR NORTHWEST AUSTIN 235
    Canyon Creek 235
    Avery Ranch 236
WILLIAMSON COUNTY 237
    Cedar Park and Leander 237
    Round Rock and Georgetown 239
LAKE SOUTH REGION 241
    Steiner Ranch, Lakeway, and Spicewood 241
LAKE NORTH REGION 242
    Volente, Lago Vista, and Jonestown 242

INDEX 245

INTRODUCTION

Texas is the second largest state in the United States, covering a diverse geographic area of mountains, beaches, hills, piney woods, prairies, lakes, deserts, brush, rivers, valleys, and swamps. Texas' name is derived from the Caddo Indian tribe word, "tejas," which means "friend." Indeed, the state motto is friendship, which is reflected in the amiable character of its residents.

Six flags have flown over the state of Texas (French, Spanish, Mexican, Texas, Confederate, and American), resulting in the blending of Spanish, Mexican, French, Southern, American, and frontier West cultures that have shaped the traditions and culture of Texas. Early French explorers established an unsuccessful post, Fort St. Louis, which was eventually taken over by the Spanish, who claimed Texas as a colony of Spain, known as New Spain. After Mexico's independence from Spain in 1821, Texas became the northern section of the Coahuila y Tejas state of Mexico. Unsatisfied with Mexican rule, the "Texians" fought for independence from Mexico and triumphed in 1826 against Mexican General Santa Anna at the Battle of San Jacinto. For nine years, Texas remained an independent country until it was admitted into the Union as the 28th state in 1845. However, the state seceded from the Union during the Civil War and joined the Confederate States of America. It was readmitted into the Union in 1870.

Texas is also known as the Lone Star State because of the single star on the Texas state flag. It is the second most populous state in the Union. Six Texas cities are in the top 25 most populous cities in the U.S. (Houston, San Antonio, Dallas, Fort Worth, Austin, and El Paso). Because of its size, Texas covers part of the American South and part of the American Southwest. The state shares characteristics of both these regions, but different cities may be more heavily influenced by one region, depending on their location. The state is in the central time zone, except for the far western tip where El Paso is located, which is in the mountain time zone.

Though there has been a growing interest in living inside the city, the majority of residents in the state's major cities live in suburbs, which are the fastest growing areas of the state. This can largely be attributed to the price of housing and quality of the school districts in the suburbs. Many of the new suburban communities are major developments in once-rural, unincorporated areas outside of municipalities. Suburbs in unincorporated areas receive their utilities through municipal utility districts ("MUD"), governmental entities specially formed to provide utilities to residents. MUDs are funded by a MUD tax, one of several other taxes that are levied on the homestead or make up a homeowner's property tax. Other taxes levied on the home may include county, school districts, cities, college districts, and hospital districts. The largest tax on a homeowner's property is typically the school district tax, which may be anywhere from $1,500 to well over $10,000 a year, depending on the value of the property. Therefore, while the property may be a bargain, buyers should research the annual school district and property tax on the home before purchasing.

An increasing population, road congestion, and environmental concerns have prompted many Texas cities to construct light rail lines and plan for other forms of public transportation. However, the preferred and most widely used form of transportation is still the personal vehicle. As a result, multi-lane freeways are part of the landscape of every major Texas city. As suburban sprawl causes cities to expand further outwards, rural roads known as FM (farm to market) and RM (ranch to market) roads have been incorporated into the new communities as local roads and freeways.

Freeways in metropolitan areas of Texas can be very confusing to non-locals. For example, there are two Interstate 35s, so knowing which one— I-35 East or I-35 West—will save drivers a lot of time and trouble. I-35 East runs north and south through Dallas, while I-35 West runs through Ft. Worth. In Houston, three major roads and highways encircle the city. The beltways, starting from inside the city, are Loop 610, Beltway 8/ Sam Houston Tollway, and Grand Parkway, which is not yet complete. One of the most common problems newcomers will encounter is the multiple names for one freeway. Stretches of freeways in major Texas cities are commonly referred to by their local name, which often pertains to a geographical location or was renamed in honor of a famous civic or political leader. This may confuse newcomers who are unaccustomed to the local freeway names, so below is a guide to navigating the state's major metropolitan freeways.

DALLAS

U.S. 75	north of downtown to McKinney	Central Expressway
I-635		LBJ Freeway
I-20		LBJ Freeway
Loop 12		Northwest Highway
Highway 183		Airport Freeway
I-35 East	south of downtown	R.L. Thornton Freeway South

I-30	east of downtown	R.L. Thornton Freeway South
I-35 East	north of downtown	Stemmons Freeway
I-30	west of downtown	Dallas–Ft. Worth Turnpike; Tom Landry Freeway
I-30		R.L. Thornton Freeway East
I-45		Julius Schepps
Spur 366		Woodall Rodgers Freeway
State Highway 289		Preston Road
State Highway 190		George Bush Turnpike; North Dallas Tollway
U.S. Highway 175		C.F. Hawn Freeway
U.S. Highway 67		Marvin D. Love Freeway
Spur 244		Northwest Highway

FORT WORTH

State Highway 121		Airport Freeway
I-30		East Freeway
I-30		West Freeway
I-820	west of I-35W	Jim Wright Freeway
I-820	east of I-35W	East Freeway North or South
I-820		Loop
U.S. Highway 377		Main Street
I-35W		North Freeway
I-35W		South Freeway
U.S. Highway 287		Mansfield Highway

HOUSTON

U.S. 59 South	south of downtown to Sugar Land	Southwest Freeway
U.S. 59 North	north of downtown to Kingwood	Eastex Freeway
I-10 West	west of downtown to Katy	Katy Freeway
I-10 East	east of downtown to Baytown	East Freeway
I-45 South	south of downtown to Galveston	Gulf Freeway
I-45 North	north of downtown to Conroe	North Freeway
U.S. 290 North	north of Memorial to Cypress	Northwest Freeway
State Highway (S.H.) 288	south of downtown to Pearland	South Freeway
Loop 610		The Loop
State Highway 99		Grand Parkway

THE DALLAS–FORT WORTH METROPLEX

The Dallas–Ft. Worth Metropolitan area is known as the Metroplex. It covers over 12,000 square miles, 12 counties, and several cities. Dallas and Ft. Worth are separated by approximately 30 miles, but are connected by several mid-size cities and small towns known collectively as the Mid-Cities.

The metropolitan area is located in north Texas on a prairie plain. The area has typical prairie weather: hot, dry summers and cold, icy winters. However, changes in the weather patterns in recent years have contributed to the area's severe drought, which has turned the verdant landscape yellow and fueled major grass fires. The Metroplex is also on the southern tip of Tornado Alley; in the spring, the winds pick up and tornados are not uncommon. Some communities have tornado sirens that alert residents to seek shelter. Residents are advised to tune into their local television or radio station for further instructions.

Dallas and Ft. Worth have always had a friendly rivalry. In the 1970s, the two cities decided to put their differences aside and collaborate on building a regional international airport, which would change the future of both cities. The construction of the Dallas/Ft. Worth International Airport and surrounding new highways led to the expansion and growth of the Metroplex. Towns around the new airport were especially impacted as many new companies moved near the airport, bringing jobs and revenue.

DALLAS

Dallas is also known as Big D, which is an appropriate nickname for a city famous for its many large-scale ventures and swaggering confidence. It has the largest concentration of corporate headquarters in Texas, the largest cowboy replica (52 ft.) in Big Tex, the most extravagant Christmas gifts on offer from Dallas-based Neiman-Marcus, and the largest metropolitan area in the state. The city's football team owner at one point even declared them "America's Team." The city has a maverick, pro-business attitude with a touch of flamboyance. It is an image-conscious town where scrappy individuals from nearby ranches and farms started with little and built empires.

To millions around the world, Dallas evokes images of oil millionaires, ranchers, and a mythical lifestyle popularized by the 1980s television drama of the same name. However, visitors to the city will quickly realize that there is much more to Dallas than the mostly exaggerated (and often inaccurate) images portrayed on television.

In fact, Dallas's economy is not centered around the oil and gas or the ranching industry. Instead, this city located on the rolling prairies of north central Texas has evolved from a trading post founded in 1841 on the Trinity River to an important financial, business, transportation, and high-tech center with diverse industries such as technology, airline, retail, healthcare, and food. After the World War II business boom and the opening of the Dallas/Ft. Worth International Airport, many businesses began opening or establishing headquarters in the area. Today, the Dallas metropolitan area is home to several major companies such as Southwest Airlines, Blockbuster, Kimberly-Clark Corporation, JC Penney, Texas Instruments, Nortel, Frito-Lay, Dr. Pepper, and Greyhound Bus Lines. Dallas is also a big sports town. It has all five major sports teams: football (Cowboys), basketball (Mavericks), baseball (Rangers), hockey (Stars), and soccer (Dallas FC).

Many people from around the United States and the world have been lured to the Dallas area by the economic opportunities provided by the numerous businesses and companies based in the city. A diverse population representing many nationalities can be found here, contributing to the growth of the city and its surrounding areas, as well as the development of suburbs and residential communities outside the city.

The Trinity River divides the city into two parts. The area north and east of the river contains the business district with skyscrapers, downtown office buildings, universities, city hall, medical center, art museums, and entertainment hot spots. Higher- to middle-income residential areas and luxury residences are generally located in this part of town. The area south and west of the river contains less affluent and lower-income residential communities. Traveling between the different sections of the city should be no problem because an expansive network of freeways connects the city to surrounding suburbs, towns, and Ft. Worth. In addition, the Dallas area has two forms of mass transportation operated by the Dallas Area Rapid Transit (DART): bus and light rail. However, the most reliable and most used form of transportation is still the personal vehicle.

CENTRAL DALLAS

DOWNTOWN

Boundaries: North: Woodall Rodgers Freeway; East: US-75; South: I-30; West: I-35E/US-77

There was a time when Downtown was strictly a business district that was deserted after business hours. Suggestions that people should live there would have probably elicited strange stares. However, times are slowly changing. Mirroring the national trend towards urban living and urban revitalization, several condominiums and apartment lofts have been constructed here in the past decade. Most of them are high-end luxury residences aimed at retired baby boomers who prefer the convenience of living in the city. The development has been in west Downtown, but a residential tower is planned for east Downtown, near the city's major train terminal and bus hub. There is hope that the construction of new residences on the east side of Downtown could spur other similar developments in an area currently filled primarily with warehouses and empty parking lots. Future residents of east Downtown will not have to travel very far for groceries. A daily Farmers Market on South Pearl Street offers shoppers row after row of festive, bright flowers, neatly displayed on the sidewalks, and fresh produce for sale under covered stalls.

In addition, the revival of Main Street has brought visitors Downtown after business hours and helped make it a place to not only work, but also to live and play. Several residential lofts have sprung up on Main Street alongside historic buildings, new restaurants, shops, and business offices, with several more under construction. For residents of Downtown, there are endless entertainment, dining, and shopping options. The Arts District, as the name implies, is where Dallas's art museums, symphony hall, theaters, performing arts center, and other arts-related activities are located. There is even a magnet high school for visual and performing arts (Booker T. Washington High School) here. Nearby is the West End, a historic turn-of-the-century district. This is Dallas's most famous entertainment district and a popular tourist spot. It contains many bars, clubs, shops, and restaurants. The West End is located directly south of the Victory community development, which is currently under construction. Also located downtown are Dallas City Hall, Dallas Convention Center, and the Aquarium and Zoological Garden.

Web Sites: www.downtowndallas.org, www.dallascityhall.com

Area Code: 214

Zip Codes: 75201, 75202, 75242

Post Offices: Downtown Dallas Station, 400 N Ervay St; Station C Station, 1100 Commerce St

Police Precinct: Dallas Police Department, www.dallaspolice.net, Central Division: 334 S Hall St, 214-670-4413

Emergency Hospital: Baylor Medical Center, www.baylorhealth.com, 3500 Gaston, 214-820-0011

Library: Erik Jonsson Central Library, www.dallaslibrary.org, 1515 Young St, 214-670-1400

Public Education: Dallas Independent School District, www.dallasisd.org, 3700 Ross Ave, 972-925-3700

Community Publications: *Dallas Morning News*, www.dallasnews.com; *Dallas Observer*, www.dallasobserver.com; *D Magazine*, www.dmagazine.com; *Dallas Business Journal*, www.bizjournals.com/dallas

Community Resources: City Hall, 1500 Marilla St, 214-670-4054; Greater Dallas Chamber of Commerce, www.dallaschamber.org, 700 N Pearl St, Ste 1200, 214-746-6600; Pike Recreation Center, 2807 Harry Hines Blvd, 214-670-1491; Farmers

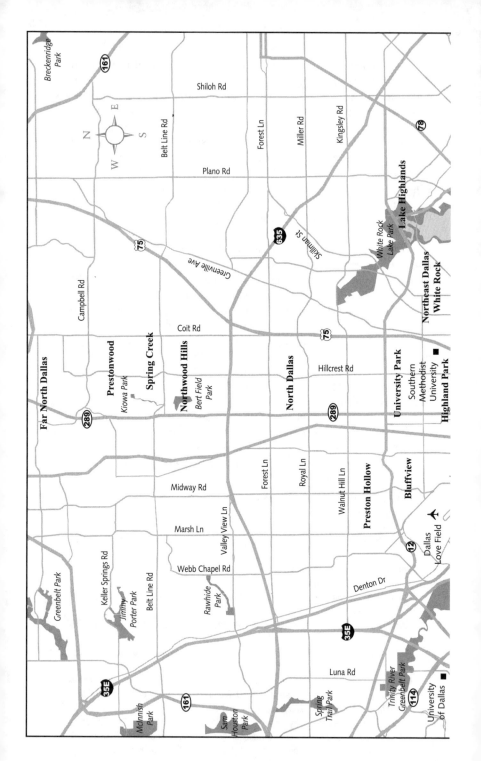

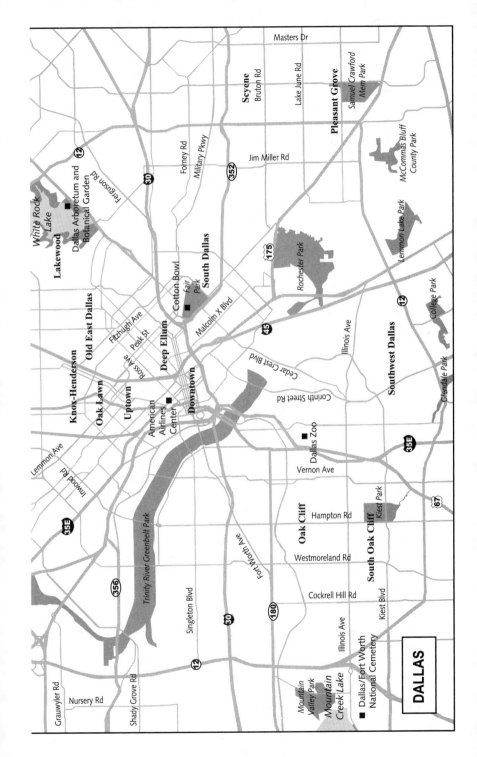

DALLAS

White Rock Lake
Lakewood
Dallas Arboretum and Botanical Garden
Ferguson Rd
12
30
Forney Rd
Military Pkwy
Jim Miller Rd
352
Masters Dr
Scyene
Bruton Rd
Lake June Rd
Pleasant Grove
Samuel Crawford Mem Park
McCommas Bluff County Park
Lemmon Lake Park
Cotton Bowl
Fair Park
South Dallas
Malcolm X Blvd
175
Rochester Park
45
Illinois Ave
Cedar Crest Blvd
College Park
12
Old East Dallas
Fitzhugh Ave
Peak St
Ross Ave
Deep Ellum
Southwest Dallas
Glendale Park
Knox-Henderson
Oak Lawn
Uptown
American Airlines Center
Downtown
Corinth Street Rd
Lemmon Ave
Inwood Rd
Dallas Zoo
Vernon Ave
35E
67
35E
Kiest Park
Oak Cliff
Hampton Rd
South Oak Cliff
356
Trinity River Greenbelt Park
Westmoreland Rd
Fort Worth Ave
Cockrell Hill Rd
Kiest Blvd
Singleton Blvd
30
180
Illinois Ave
12
Grauwyler Rd
Nursery Rd
Shady Grove Rd
Mountain Valley Park
Mountain Creek Lake
Dallas/Fort Worth National Cemetery

9

Market, www.dallasfarmersmarket.org, 1010 S Pearl St, 214-939-2808; Dallas Arts District, www.artsdistrict.org, 2100 Ross, LB 22, Ste 885, 214-953-1977

Public Transportation: Dallas Area Rapid Transit, www.dart.org; *Light Rail Blue and Red Line:* Union Station, West End, St. Paul (Arts District), Akard Station (Farmers Market); *Bus:* 1, 8, 11, 12, 19, 21, 24, 26, 29, 31, 35, 36, 37, 39, 42, 44, 46, 49, 50, 51, 52, 60, 63, 76, 161, 164, 165, 183, 185, 202, 204, 205, 210, 247; *Commuter Rail:* Trinity Railway Express: Union Station; *Regional Train:* Amtrak: Union Station

UPTOWN AREA

UPTOWN

Boundaries: (generally) North: Lemmon Ave at Turtle Creek Blvd; East: US-75; South: Woodall Rodgers Freeway; West: I-35

Uptown refers to the area between Downtown and the Oak Lawn neighborhood to the north. Though there are no clearly defined boundaries, in general it covers the area bordered by Stemmons Freeway (IH-35 east) on the west, North Central Freeway (US-75) on the east, Woodall Rodgers Freeway on the south, and Lemmon Avenue where it meets Turtle Creek on the north. Getting to, from, and around Uptown should be quite easy because it is served by light rail, buses, and streetcars. In addition, the city's only underground rail station is located in Uptown at Cityplace Station. Once a run-down and neglected part of Dallas, it is now one of the hottest zip codes in town. Uptown combines the old and the new with a charming historic neighborhood, modern residences, and glossy new shopping districts.

In the **State Thomas Historic District** on the southeast corner of Uptown is Dallas's most intact collection of late Victorian era homes in Italianate, Queen Anne, and Vernacular styles. The neighborhood's historic structures were in danger of vanishing until community and business leaders chose it to be one of the forerunners of the urban living model in the 1980s. Since then, Uptown has developed into a mixed-use commercial residential area with businesses; steel, glass, and concrete lofts; and upscale apartments gracing its leafy, tree-shaded streets. Stylish townhouses, brownstones, and condominiums can also be found beyond the red brick streets that are lined with outdoor cafes, art galleries, and fashionable shops.

For something newer, try the chic and trendy **West Village** at McKinney and Lemmon Avenue. This well-known shopping area has apartments and lofts above its unique shops, art boutiques, restaurants, bars, and cafes. Across from McKinney and the surrounding streets are many new townhomes and luxury apartments in various sizes and styles. West Village residents are spoiled with limitless entertainment options. A streetcar that stops in front of West Village runs down McKinney Avenue to destinations such as art galleries, Magnolia Theater art cinema, historical cemeteries, Dallas Theater Center, Dallas Children's Theater, the Symphony, Dallas Museum of Art, the Mavericks' basketball arena, and the popular West End entertainment district. The M-Line streetcar also stops at Cityplace Tower, located on a tree-lined boulevard in the Uptown neighborhood of **Cityplace**, near the intersection of US-75 and Haskell Avenue/Blackburn Street. The 43-story tower is one of several luxury residential high-rises in the area. There is an underground rail station located beneath the towers.

The urban living concept continues to grow as yet another mixed-use development is planned for the southwest side of Uptown bordering Woodall Rodgers Freeway and next to the West End entertainment district. **Victory Park** is an ambitious 75-acre development with high-rise apartments, condominium towers, a hotel, office space, streetfront retail shops, basketball/hockey arena, a park, and a community square. Completed in 2001, Phase I of the project featured the American Airlines Center, which houses the Dallas Mavericks basketball team and the NHL Dallas Stars hockey team. The rest of Victory Park is currently under construction. When the estimated $3 billion development is complete, all of Victory Park will be a wi-fi zone. A similar but smaller development is planned at International Center, a collection of office towers in Uptown.

KNOX-HENDERSON

Boundaries: North: US-75; Southeast: US-75; South: Fitzhugh Ave; West/Southwest: Highland Park city limits

One of Dallas's oldest shopping and entertainment districts, this neighborhood is named after Knox Street and Henderson Street, where the shops and restaurants are located. Several of the shops and eateries are housed in the original 1920s storefronts. Knox-Henderson is best known for dining. Many of Dallas's finest restaurants are located in this pedestrian area where people simply park their cars at one spot and walk around. The area was revitalized during the mid-1990s, when many luxury apartments and townhomes were built. The area off of Knox and Henderson Streets contains numerous brick and contemporary-style townhomes and a few apartments, which are the primary housing options here. Because this area is located just off US-75, residents have easy access to downtown Dallas.

OAK LAWN/CEDAR SPRINGS/TURTLE CREEK

Boundaries: North: Highland Park city limits; East: US-75; South: Lemmon Ave at Turtle Creek; West: IH-35

This neighborhood north of Uptown is surrounded by upscale condominiums, apartments, and duplexes that attract urban professionals. One of Dallas's well-to-do areas, it has many popular fine restaurants, bars, and clubs that are located mainly along Cedar Springs Road, which is the heart of **Oak Lawn**. The **Cedar Springs** area is home to one of Dallas's several gay and lesbian communities. It has housing options similar to Oak Lawn. Immediately north is another neighborhood with a sizable gay community, **Turtle Creek**. Named after a nearby creek, it is one of Dallas's most fashionable neighborhoods. It is perhaps best known for the iconic four-star luxury hotel Mansion on Turtle Creek, which is set on four acres of the winding tree-lined creek. Unlike Uptown and Oak Lawn, which are composed of apartments and townhomes, Turtle Creek has a variety of housing options. There are several luxury high-rises along Turtle Creek Boulevard as well as new expensive homes that have emerged in this secluded part of town. Turtle Creek has a romantic allure that is largely due to the natural beauty of the creek area. Young couples find this serene and enchanting backdrop a perfect place to pose for wedding photos. The creek, with its mini-waterfalls and rolling banks, meanders through the neighborhood along Turtle Creek Boulevard, which is lined with elegant mansions. In addition, luxury high-rises encircle the area. Off of Turtle Creek Boulevard, there are some apartments and new townhomes.

Web Sites: www.uptowndallas.net, www.westvil.com, www.dallascityhall.com
Area Code: 214
Zip Codes: 75219, 75204
Post Offices: Oaklawn Station, 2825 Oak Lawn; East Finance Station, 502 N Haskell
Police Precinct: Dallas Police Department, www.dallaspolice.net, Central Division: 334 S Hall St, 214-670-4413
Emergency Hospital: Baylor Medical Center, www.baylorhealth.com, 3500 Gaston Ave, 214-820-0111
Library: Dallas Public Library, www.dallaslibrary.org: Oak Lawn Branch, 4100 Cedar Springs Rd, 214-670-1359
Public Education: Dallas Independent School District, www.dallasisd.org, 3700 Ross, 972-925-3700
Community Publications: *Dallas Morning News*, www.dallasnews.com; *Dallas Voice*, www.dallasvoice.com; *Turtle Creek News*; *Dallas Observer*, www.dallasobserver. com
Community Resource: Dallas Recreation Center, Reverchon Center, 3505 Maple Ave, 214-670-7721
Public Transportation: McKinney Avenue Transit Authority, www.mata.org; Dallas Area Rapid Transit Authority, www.dart.org; *Light Rail Blue and Red Line*: Cityplace, Victory (special events only), Cedars Station; *Bus:* 8, 21, 26, 31, 36, 39, 44, 51, 183, 185, 409

EAST DALLAS

DEEP ELLUM

Boundaries: North: Good Latimer; East: Washington; South: Canton; West: I-45 (Julius Schepps)

Deep Ellum is a renovated warehouse district in east Dallas that was at one time a center for jazz and blues music and a thriving African-American community. The area fell into decline after the post–World War II growth of suburbs and was converted to a warehouse and industrial space in the 1960s and 1970s. The music has returned to this neighborhood where artists such as Bessie Smith and Leadbelly Ledbetter used to perform in the 1930s. Deep Ellum was redeveloped in the 1980s and early 1990s as a lively arts and entertainment district whose bars, nightclubs, and late-night restaurants are popular with young urban Dallasites. Dallas has several vibrant entertainment districts, but there is only one place where visitors and residents can see up-and-coming bands perform every night: Deep Ellum, Dallas's premier live music scene. At the height of its popularity, Deep Ellum often got crowded and had a carnival-like atmosphere on the weekends. Streets were frequently blocked off to vehicles, allowing pedestrians complete access to the roads. Luckily for residents who lived in the area, a car was not necessary to get home because shops and entertainment are all located within walking distance of the area's apartment lofts. Another benefit of living in Deep Ellum is its proximity to the downtown business district—only three blocks east of downtown means no more long commutes for those working there.

During the daytime, Deep Ellum is an urban village with unique shops, trendy clothing retailers, tattoo parlors, and other independently owned businesses. The neighborhood feels like a small community, which is the way developers envisioned it when they planned its redevelopment by purposely keeping the buildings to a minimum height, making the area pedestrian-friendly, and proudly declaring the area a no-mall zone. Street festivals that celebrate art, film, music, and the neighborhood are common. This young, alternative neighborhood has a counterculture edge that seems to be rebelling against society or the "norm." Graffiti covers the side of several buildings, but some of these are elaborate murals sanctioned by building owners for their artistic value and for advertisement purposes. Deep Ellum is a unique contrast to a city that is generally suburban and conservative in character.

However, the increase in crime and a downturn in the economy during the 1990s has slowed down business in the area. Many places have closed and it is not the thriving area it was in the 1990s. Competition from other new, trendy entertainment districts has also lured visitors away from Deep Ellum.

Web Sites: www.deepellumtx.com; www.dallascityhall.com
Area Code: 214
Zip Code: 75226
Post Office: Eastside Finance Station, 502 N Haskell
Police Precinct: Dallas Police Department, www.dallaspolice.net, 334 S Hall St, 214-670-4411
Emergency Hospital: Baylor University Medical Center at Dallas, www.baylorhealth.edu, 3500 Gaston Ave, 214-820-0111

Library: Dallas Public Library, www.dallaslibrary.org: J. Erik Jonsson Central Library Branch, 1515 Young St, 214-670-1400

Public Education: Dallas Independent School District, www.dallasisd.org, 3700 Ross Ave, 972-925-3700

Community Publications: *Dallas Observer*, www.dallasobserver.com; *Dallas Morning News*, www.dallasnews.com

Community Resource: City Hall, 1500 Marilla, 214-670-4054

Public Transportation: Dallas Area Rapid Transit, www.dart.org; *Bus*: Route 60 (Green)

OLD EAST DALLAS

Boundaries: North: Mockingbird Ln; East: Abrams Rd; Southeast: Gaston; South: I-30; West: US-75 (Central Expressway)

Old East Dallas is a collection of several historic neighborhoods east of downtown Dallas. Most of the homes were built over farmland in what was a rural area east of Dallas during the 1890s to 1930s. Some of these neighborhoods were part of the City of East Dallas, which was independent of Dallas until it was gradually annexed by the city. Most of the Old East Dallas neighborhoods were neglected and fell into decline after World War II. The area was rediscovered in the 1970s by young professionals looking for affordable housing near Downtown and historic preservationists interested in saving architectural gems. Thus, a historic preservation and neighborhood renewal movement took off. Diligent efforts by residents have paid off in some instances. The city has approved certain neighborhoods for historic or conservation district status, which allows residents to protect the historic characteristics of their neighborhood. An historic district requires the original structure to be preserved exactly as it was when first built, while a conservation district has less strict preservation requirements. Because of the community effort it takes to restore and preserve a historic neighborhood, most of the neighborhoods have an active neighborhood association. There is also the feeling of a close and friendly community.

Homes in Old East Dallas neighborhoods that have been fully restored generally start at around $200,000. There are also several that cost under $200,000. This may not seem like a bargain, but it is comparable to homes in surrounding areas and the suburbs. However, if you are willing to buy a neglected home that needs restoration or a few upgrades, then you may be able to find a home at an even better price. The homes in East Dallas come in a variety of sizes and styles. Some of the most common are prairie foursquare, Tudor, and Craftsman bungalow. A prairie foursquare has a simple box shape, four-room floor plan, and two and a half stories. Tudors are distinguished by their tall narrow windows, steep roofs, decorative chimneys, and cozy, romantic look. Craftsman bungalows have decorative braces, porches with square columns, low-pitched roofs, and stone chimneys.

Junius Heights

Homes in this neighborhood are mostly Craftsman and prairie-style bungalows that were built between 1910 and 1930 in what was then the eastern edge of town. The neighborhood is currently seeking recognition from the City of Dallas as a historic preservation district. It contains several historic landmarks such as the art deco Lakewood Theater, and Woodrow Wilson High School, which is noted for its Jacobean Revival architectural style by the National Trust for Historic Preservation, the State of Texas, and the City of Dallas. The high school is one of the many benefits of living in Junius Heights. It is an academically exemplary school that consistently produces a large number of National Merit Scholars and has educated several city mayors, business leaders, and two Heisman trophy winners. Woodrow Wilson High School also serves the East Dallas neighborhoods of Swiss Avenue, Mount Auburn, Lakewood, Munger Place, and Hollywood Heights.

Munger Place

The largest collection of prairie foursquares in the United States located on evenly spaced lots lie roughly between Junius Street on the north, Reiger Avenue on the south, Henderson Avenue on the east, and Fitzhugh Avenue on the west. This nationally recognized historic residential neighborhood was established in 1905 as an upscale development for high-class residents. To ensure its exclusivity and reputation as a fine neighborhood, developers Collett and Robert S. Munger stipulated that homes had to be two full stories and cost at least $2000. Many of the houses, which include styles other than prairie foursquare, have high 10-foot ceilings, large windows, and spacious rooms. During the Great Depression, several of these large homes were converted into apartments or boarding houses. Local artists and young professionals later moved into the area in the 1970s and began restoring the neighborhood. Residents pushed the city to recognize the neighborhood as a historic district. In 1980, Dallas established the Munger Place Historic District. Today, it is on the National Register of Historic Places.

Vickery Place

Established in 1900, Vickery Place is located about 4 miles from downtown Dallas. It consists of Craftsman bungalows and Tudor-style homes surrounded by large pecan trees. The neighborhood of approximately 1400 residents has applied for recognition by Dallas as a conservation district. The neighborhood lies between Belmont on the south, Goodwin on the north, US-75 on the west, and Greenville on the east. Street signs here are capped by lavender markers that say Vickery Place. There are several neighborhood bars and restaurants within walking or biking distance of the homes.

Belmont

The Belmont neighborhood is named after New York City subway developer and Belmont Stakes namesake August Belmont Jr., who bought the property in 1892. It was developed during the 1910s and 1920s into one of Dallas's most prestigious neighborhoods. Belmont is bounded by Greenville Avenue on the west, Skillman Avenue on the east, Llano Street on the north, and Belmont Street on the south, in an area shaded with large oak trees. A variety of architectural styles can be found in Belmont. Many decades later, it is still an attractive neighborhood for those seeking a beautiful home in a historic neighborhood conveniently located near downtown's businesses and the city's many entertainment districts.

Swiss Avenue

Perhaps Dallas's most famous historic residential neighborhood, the Swiss Avenue Historic District is also a popular tourist attraction. A walk down Swiss Avenue and it is easy to see why walking tours of this neighborhood are popular: impressive Victorian brick and stone mansions in a variety of architectural styles, including Tudor, prairie, and Georgian, hint of an era of wealth and elegance. Homes are set on well-manicured lawns lining the brick streets. During Christmastime, Swiss Avenue has one of the city's most colorful and best Christmas light displays.

Bordered by Skiles on the south, Good Latimer Expressway on the north, Live Oak Street on the east, and Gaston on the west, the Swiss Avenue neighborhood contains approximately 200 historic homes built in the early 20th century and was at one time part of Munger Place. The Meadows Foundation runs the 22-block district as a nonprofit organization. Designated a historic district in 1973, the district is on the National Register of Historic Places.

Wilson Historic District

The Wilson Historic District is run as a nonprofit community by the Meadows Foundation, which purchased the area as part of an urban renewal project in 1981. It uses many of the buildings as office space for its organization and other nonprofits. Surrounding it are luxury townhomes, condominiums, and lofts. The district, which is listed on the National Register of Historic Places, is within walking distance of entertainment, dining, and shopping.

Greenville

Greenville is named after an avenue that runs from LBJ Freeway (I-635) to Ross Avenue. Mockingbird Lane cuts through Greenville Avenue, dividing the neighborhood into Upper and Lower Greenville. Lower Greenville refers to the area north of Mockingbird Lane between Mockingbird and Ross. For decades, it has been a major Dallas entertainment district. The bars, restaurants, outdoor dining, nightclubs, funky shops, and vintage clothing stores are popular with Southern Methodist University students. It also features live entertainment. In this respect, Lower Greenville is more established than other popular nightspots such as Deep Ellum. As one of Dallas's oldest entertainment districts, it is set in a well-preserved historic 1920s neighborhood. Residences in this neighborhood consist of mainly townhomes and apartments. The area is popular with many Dallasites, except maybe the residents living immediately near the bars and clubs. There have been numerous complaints about parking, trash, noise, and general public disorder. Further up along Greenville Avenue, the entertainment district continues into Upper Greenville, which is between LBJ Freeway and Mockingbird Lane. In contrast to the historic ambience of Lower Greenville, this side of Greenville is a modern, commercial area with a mix of trendy and casual upscale shops and restaurants. Off of Greenville, there are many townhomes and some apartments. Many of the townhomes are new and designed in varying architectural styles. While Lower Greenville is popular with college students and bohemian types, Upper Greenville attracts an older, more sophisticated crowd of yuppies.

M Streets/Greenland Hills

Between Skillman Road on the east, Greenville Avenue on the west, McCommas Boulevard on the north, and Vanderbilt Avenue on the south, is a neighborhood whose streets all begin with the letter M. Thus, this area of Craftsman bungalows, Colonial, and Tudor houses is named the M Streets. This neighborhood is popular with young professionals looking for an affordable home near the downtown business district. A two-bedroom, one-bath, single-story home is available for as low as $125,000. However, these are usually older, small, plain homes on small, undecorated lots that would be perfect for some remodeling. For $50,000 more, there are larger homes with bigger yards and better landscaping. There are also larger homes on lots shaded by large oak and pecan trees from $250,000 to $750,000 for those looking for a grander home with fine historical architecture. Residents can be assured that the historic integrity of this neighborhood will be preserved for years to come because the City of Dallas has approved it as a historic conservation district.

Cochran Heights

This is a charming neighborhood with Victorian Revival and Tudor-style cottages ranging from $180,000 to $500,000. It is located conveniently near the Knox-Henderson dining and shopping district. In addition, the Katy pedestrian and biking trail is within walking distance. This heavily forested greenbelt is a beautiful and scenic place for a stroll.

Bryan Place

This neighborhood was formerly part of the City of East Dallas, which was annexed by Dallas in 1890. The actual Bryan Place is denoted by a place marker at its entrance. It is composed of a collection of homes that cover approximately four blocks. Homes are spaced closely together and face each other across cobblestone streets. The configuration of this neighborhood creates a small village atmosphere. The area immediately next to Bryan Place contains several recently constructed luxury apartments and condominiums that have a great view of the Dallas skyline. The townhomes are generally in the $300,000 range. More townhomes are planned or currently under construction. There are future plans to develop the City Lights entertainment district for this area. It will feature restaurants, bars, shops, and other retail businesses. One real estate agent speculates that the area's property values will really take off once City Lights is complete.

Wilshire Heights

This Lakewood area neighborhood contains over 900 Craftsman bungalows and period revival houses built during the 1930s. Unfortunately, many of the neighborhoods' historic homes have been torn down to make way for new, modern buildings. The city considers Wilshire Heights one of Dallas's endangered historic districts. Immediately to the south of it is another endangered historic district known as **Lakewood Heights**. While residents in other East Dallas neighborhoods treasure their historic homes, Lakewood Heights is on the forefront of a tearing and rebuilding trend. Buyers have been acquiring older small bungalows, bulldozing them, and building larger, more expensive homes on the lots.

Not all Old East Dallas homes in the Lakewood area are being torn down though. Some, such as **Hollywood/Santa Monica**, southeast of Lakewood Heights, are actually quite well-preserved and protected by active neighborhood associations. In fact, it has been designated a historical conservation district. This neighborhood is surrounded by pecan, crepe, myrtle, oak, and red bud trees, which provide a lush and leafy landscape. Approximately 800 mostly two- to three-bedroom stone or brick Tudor cottages lie between Grand Street to the east, Santa Fe on the west, Glasgow to the south, and the Sante Fe railroad on the north. Other architectural styles can also be seen in this area. Though smaller than some of the historic homes in other Old East Dallas neighborhoods, the homes in Hollywood/Santa Monica are noted for their stained glass windows, decorative chimneys, terraced lawns, elaborate stonework, and other fine details. The neighborhood rests on a bluff overlooking White Rock Creek, Samuell-Grand Park, and Tenison Memorial Golf Course. Homes are set on winding streets amidst hilly terrain and rocky creek beds. In addition, a golf course, country club, park, and recreational lake are located nearby. Hollywood/Santa Monica is a desirable neighborhood and has one of the fastest selling real estate markets in Old East Dallas. Homes range from $100,000 to $300,000.

Another nearby well-preserved historic district is **Gastonwood/Coronado Hills**, also known as the "C" streets. It features approximately 400 traditional and Tudor-style stone and brick homes built between 1920 and 1940 in the $100,000 to $300,000 price range. The homes here are distinguished by their high-gabled roofs, stonework, large masonry chimneys, and castle-like features. The prices are a bit high for the modest size of the homes, but they are still a good value for this location and are affordable for downtown professionals. Besides being close to downtown, it is next door to dining, shopping, and entertainment in Lower Greenville and Lakewood Village. This picturesque neighborhood is set in a heavily forested landscape and perfectly located between two beautiful recreational spots: Lakewood Country Club and White Rock Lake Park.

Web Sites: www.dallascityhall.com, www.mungerplace.com (Munger Place), www. vpna.org (Vickery Place), www.belmontna.org (Belmont), www.sahd.org (Swiss Avenue), www.mstreets.org (M Streets/Greenland Hills), www.cochranheights.com (Cochran Heights), www.hsmna.com (Hollywood/Santa Monica)

Area Code: 214

Zip Codes: 75246, 75204, 75226, 75206, 75214, 752131

Post Offices: Eastside Finance Station, 502 N Haskell Ave; Lakewood Station, 6120 Swiss Ave; Belmont Finance Station, 5650 Belmont; Vickery Station, 6640 Abrams Rd

Police Precincts: Dallas Police Department, www.dallaspolice.net: East Dallas Storefront, 4545 Bryan St, 214-670-5514; Hall Street Storefront, 1823 N Hall, 214-670-1794; Central Operations, 334 S Hall, 214-670-4413

Emergency Hospital: Baylor University Medical Center at Dallas, www.baylorhealth. edu, 3500 Gaston Ave, 214-820-0111

Library: Dallas Library, www.dallaslibrary.org: Lakewood Branch, 6121 Worth St; 214-670-1376

Public Education: Dallas Independent School District, www.dallasisd.org, 3700 Ross Ave, 972-925-3700

Community Publications: *Dallas Morning News*, www.dallasnews.com; *Dallas Observer*, www.dallasobserver.com; *D Magazine*, www.dmagazine; *Dallas Business Journal*, www.bizjournals.com/dallas

Community Resources: City Hall, 1500 Marilla St, 214-670-5708; Preservation Dallas, www.preservationdallas.org, 2922 Swiss Ave, 214-821-3290; Dallas Katy Trails, www.katytraildallas.org; Exall Recreation Center, 1355 Adair St, 214-670-7812; Samuell-Grand Recreation Center, 6200 E Grand, 214-670-1383; Ignacio Zaragoza Recreation Center, 4550 Worth, 214-670-7862

Public Transportation: Dallas Area Rapid Transit, www.dart.org; *Bus:* 1, 19, 21, 24, 36, 51, 60, 76, 409, 501, 503, 519, 768; *Light Rail: Blue and Red Line:* City Place Station, Mockingbird Station

NORTHEAST DALLAS/WHITE ROCK LAKE

For those who are seeking a quieter, more serene residence, but close to work downtown, the communities in northeast Dallas around White Rock Lake offer many options. This area features a combination of old and new homes from the moderately priced to the high end range. The neighborhoods in the White Rock area are generally lush with foliage and surrounded by towering trees. Many old, historic houses are set among majestic old trees. In some instances, it feels like living in the country. Beautiful natural landscape, excellent public schools, the variety of housing choices, and its proximity to the central business district make the Northeast Dallas/White Rock area a highly attractive part of Dallas. The major communities in this area border White Rock Lake—the largest lake in Dallas—and its adjoining park, which is a major benefit to living here. The lake is a popular recreational place for hiking, biking, walking, jogging, picnicking, fishing, sailing, and other outdoor activities. For nature lovers, there is also a bird watching area and a wetland inside the park. In addition, the Dallas Arboretum and Botanical Gardens are located on the lake.

LAKEWOOD

Boundaries: North: White Rock Lake Park; East: White Rock Lake; South: Gaston Ave; West: Abrams Rd

One of the largest communities in this area is Lakewood, a tranquil neighborhood in northeast Dallas that borders the western shores of White Rock Lake. This neighborhood is a quiet oasis within the city and ideal for those who like the city's convenience but could do without the stress and noise of big city life. Its distance from a major freeway contributes to this secluded, calm environment. It takes almost 10 to 15 minutes to reach a major freeway, but residents gladly trade easy freeway access for the benefits of a close community within a historic neighborhood. In fact, residents voted against light rail near its borders despite the economic boost it would bring to the area because it would intrude on their privacy. Instead, many residents opt to travel through residential streets for their commute to and from work downtown. Lakewood is popular with professionals who work downtown or in the Baylor Medical Center.

One of the main draws of residing in Lakewood is nearby White Rock Lake, a 1,015-acre, artificial freshwater lake, and its surrounding city park. After a hard day at work, residents can relax on the lake by watching the sun set, unwind with a walk or jog in the park, or take the dog for a walk at the dog park. Further away from the lake is an entertainment district with trendy restaurants, unique retail stores, one-of-a kind shops, bars, and cafes that surround the historic Lakewood Theater landmark, a restored art-deco movie palace established in the 1930s.

Lakewood offers a variety of housing options ranging from two-bedroom bungalows, duplexes, new townhomes, stately large homes along winding boulevards, fourplexes, small apartments, and quaint cottages set back from tree-shaded streets, to mansions on estates in a variety of styles and sizes from $130,000 to $800,000. With most of the homes built between 1900 and 1950, there are quite a number of historic homes in this community. This is a highly family-oriented community with civic pride and strong community activism. Lakewood students are zoned to Woodrow Wilson High School, perhaps Dallas

Independent School District's best-known high school because of its exemplary academic achievements and successful graduates. The area's quiet charm, good schools, and amenities have increased its property values in the past decades. The grandest neighborhood during the 1920s is still one of Dallas's most attractive.

Lakewood area neighborhoods include Casa Linda and Casa View. They are located across White Rock Lake, on its eastern shores. **Casa Linda** features winding, tree-lined streets in a heavily wooded area with brick and wood-frame single-family homes. Its beautiful environment and quality housing command hefty prices. A more affordable option is neighboring **Casa View**'s ranch-style homes, which are popular as starter homes. On the southern side of the lake sits the community of **Forest Hills**, aptly named because of the towering trees that cover its residential neighborhoods. The brick and stone houses set back on heavily wooded, usually estate-sized lots provide a forest-like, country setting. This wealthy neighborhood is situated along a wooded bluff. If Casa View is too simple and Forest Hills too upscale, then **Little Forest** offers something in between. Located south of Forest Hills, it features smaller wood-frame and brick cottages.

Web Site: www.dallascityhall.com
Area Code: 214
Zip Codes: 75214, 75218, 75228, 75238, 75231
Post Offices: Lakewood Station, 6120 Swiss Ave; White Rock Station, 1351 N Buckner; Northlake Finance Station, 10233 E NW Hwy, Ste 333
Police Precinct: Dallas Police Department, www.dallaspolice.net: Northeast Station, 9915 E NW Hwy, 214-670-4415
Emergency Hospitals: Baylor University Medical Center at Dallas, www.baylorhealth.edu, 3500 Gaston Ave, 214-820-0111; Doctor's Hospital Dallas, www.doctorshospitaldallas.com, 9330 Poppy Dr, #205 West, 214-324-6100; Presbyterian Hospital, www.presbyterianhospitalofdallas.org, 8200 Walnut Hill Ln, 214-345-6789; Humana Hospital, www.texashealth.org, 8624 Ferguson
Libraries: Dallas Library, www.dallaslibrary.org, Lakewood Branch, 6121 Worth St, 214-670-1376; Casa View Branch, 10355 Ferguson Rd, 214-670-8403; Skillman Southwestern Branch, 5707 Skillman, 214-670-6078
Public Education: Dallas Independent School District, www.dallasisd.org, 3700 Ross Ave, 972-925-3700
Community Publications: *Dallas Morning News*, www.dallasnews.com; *Dallas Observer*, www.dallasobserver.com; *D Magazine*, www.dmagazine; *Dallas Business Journal*, www.bizjournals.com/dallas
Community Resources: City Hall, 1500 Marilla St, 214-670-5708; Preservation Dallas, www.preservationdallas.org, 2922 Swiss Ave, 214-821-3290; Harry Stone Recreation Center, 2403 Millmar, 214-670-0949; Ridgewood/Belcher Recreation Center, 6818 Fisher Rd, 214-670-7115
Public Transportation: Dallas Area Rapid Transit, www.dart.org; *Bus:* 1, 60, 60F, 76, 60L, 60G, 164, 428, 466, 501, 506, 519, 569, 583, 768; *Light Rail: Blue Line*: White Rock Station, Lovers Ln Station

LAKE HIGHLANDS

Boundaries: North: Walnut St; East: Plano Rd; South: Northwest Hwy/ White Rock Lake Park; West: US-75/Fair Oaks Park

The other large community in this area is Lake Highlands, which borders the suburban cities of Richardson and Garland. Families and children come first in this community that feels more suburban than urban. While students in the other surrounding neighborhoods and communities in the White Rock Area attend the Dallas Independent School District, Lake Highlands is served by the excellent Richardson Independent School District, which has been recognized as one of the country's top public school systems. Lake Highlands is composed of over 50 neighborhoods and subdivisions. A listing of the neighborhoods can be found at www.lhaia.com. One of the most distinctive is the **Cloisters**. This neighborhood is located on the western shores of White Rock Lake north of Lakewood. It is one of the most attractive neighborhoods in Dallas with grand houses on slightly hilly terrain shaded by mature majestic oaks. These are magnificent homes, including huge lakefront estates. Others are houses set far back on beautifully landscaped lawns. More moderately priced homes built mostly in the 1960s and 1970s are located east of White Rock Lake in **Old Lake Highlands**. Portions of this neighborhood overlook White Rock Lake. Another neighborhood nearby is **Lochwood/Dixon Branch** located east of White Rock Lake, full of scenic creeks and greenbelts.

Web Site: www.dallascityhall.com

Area Code: 214

Zip Codes: 75238, 75243, 75231,

Post Offices: Lake Highlands Station, 10502 Markison; Richland Station, 9130 Markville

Police Precinct: Dallas Police Department, www.dallaspolice.net: Northeast Station, 9915 E Northwest Hwy, 214-670-4415

Emergency Hospitals: Baylor University Medical Center at Dallas, www.baylorhealth. edu, 3500 Gaston Ave, 214-820-0111; Doctor's Hospital Dallas, www. doctorshospital.com, 9330 Poppy Dr, #205 West, 214-324-6100; Presbyterian Hospital, 8200 Walnut Hill Ln, 214-345-6789; Humana Hospital, www.texashealth. org, 8624 Ferguson

Libraries: Dallas Public Library, www.dallaslibrary.org: Audelia Branch, 10045 Audleia Rd, 214-670-1350; Forest Green Branch, 9015 Forest Ln, 214-670-1335

Public Education: Dallas Independent School District, www.dallasisd.org, 3700 Ross Ave, 972-925-3700; Richardson Independent School District, www.richardson.k12. tx.us, 400 S Greenville, Richardson, 469-593-0000

Community Publications: *Dallas Morning News*, www.dallasnews.com; *Dallas Observer*, www.dallasobserver.com; *D Magazine*, www.dmagazine; *Dallas Business Journal*, www.bizjournals.com/dallas; *Lake Highlands People*, www. peoplenewspapers.com/lakehighlands.html

Community Resources: City Hall, 1500 Marilla St, 214-670-5708; Lake Highlands Area

Improvement Association, ww.lhaia.org, P.O. Box 741763, Dallas, 75374; Lake Highlands North Recreation Center, 9940 White Rock Trail, 214-670-7794
Public Transportation: Dallas Area Rapid Transit, www.dart.org; *Bus:* 569, 428, 374, 466SG, 372, 378, 380, 376, 519, 60L, 534, 551, 560, 583, 486, 410; *Light Rail: Blue Line:* White Rock Station, LBJ/Skillman Station, Forest Juniper Station

NORTH DALLAS

North Dallas neighborhoods are generally more established and wealthier than other parts of Dallas. North Dallas contains the city's most affluent areas and many of the most desirable neighborhoods. The city's two major medical centers are also located in this part of Dallas. In addition, it has several of the city's hot entertainment districts, fine dining, and good shops for people of various tastes, styles, and budgets. Located along I-30 and intersected by US-75 and the Dallas North Tollway, North Dallas residents have convenient access to the Downtown business district, the suburbs, and entertainment attractions throughout the Metroplex.

Prominent in North Dallas are the **Park Cities**, which consist of Highland Park and University Park, two independent cities that are adjacent to each other. They are located approximately 5–6 miles north of downtown Dallas and within easy access to shopping, entertainment, cultural centers, higher institutions of learning, a medical center, and the central business district. These two communities are often recognized as Dallas's wealthiest and most prestigious neighborhoods.

HIGHLAND PARK

Boundaries: North: University Park city limits; East: Abbott Ave; South: Dallas city limits; West: Dallas North Tollway

An island city with a population of 8842, Highland Park is home to the city's wealthy and socially elite. Coincidentally, the town's original planner, Wilbur David Cook, also planned the layout of another well-heeled town: Beverly Hills, California. The community's ritzy status is reflected in the luxury homes, estates, and mansions that grace the tree-lined streets. In the middle of the town is exclusive Dallas Country Club. Many of Dallas's old-money families live here and they tend to avoid excessive flaunting of money. Thus, homes here are tasteful and, unlike other wealthy areas of Dallas, more subtle in their displays of wealth. There are few, if any, ostentatious residences. In fact, some of the homes here can be described as low key. The area contains several new and older townhomes, as well as apartments. New and existing luxury condominiums can also be found in this neighborhood. Despite its high-class status, it often feels more like a quiet community with delightful neighborhood stores.

The area that is now Highland Park was originally a horse farm until it was purchased in 1907 by developers John S. Armstrong, Edgar L. Flippen, and Hugh E. Prather, Sr. for construction of a residential community. They named the new community Highland Park because of its higher elevation in comparison to the surrounding area and because development plans reserved 20% of the community for parks. Its beautiful parks, such as Lakeside Park, Fairfax Park, and Jester Park, are among the most distinctive and charming features of this neighborhood.

Highland Park also boasts its own upscale shopping center at Highland Park Village, near the country club. Built in 1931, this well-established shopping area is listed as a National Historic Landmark. The pedestrian shopping district is fashioned after a town square–inspired design and its buildings—beige-colored shops with red tile roofs—are based on the architecture of Spain, Mexico, and California. The district's cobblestone sidewalks, neatly trimmed trees, lush landscaping, and benches definitely create a village atmosphere.

Web Site: www.hptx.org
Area Code: 214
Zip Code: 75205
Post Office: University Dallas Station, 5606 Yale Blvd, Dallas
Police Precinct: Highland Park Department of Public Safety, 4700 Drexel Dr, Highland Park, 214-521-5000
Emergency Hospitals: Baylor Medical Center, www.baylorhealth.com, 3500 Gaston, Dallas, 214-820-0011; University of Texas Southwestern Medical Center, www3. utsouthwestern.edu, 5323 Harry Hines Blvd, Dallas, 214-683-3111
Library: Highland Park Library, www.hplibrary.info, 4700 Drexel Dr, Highland Park, 214-559-9400
Public Education: Highland Park Independent School District, www.hpisd.org, 7015 Westchester Dr, Dallas, 214-780-3000
Community Publications: Park Cities News, www.parkcitiesnews.com; Park Cities People, www.peoplenewspapers.com/parkcities.html; Dallas Morning News, www. dallasnews.com
Community Resources: Town Hall, 4700 Drexel Dr, Dallas, 214-521-4161; Park Cities YMCA, www.pcymca.org, 6000 Preston Rd, Dallas, 214-526-7293
Public Transportation: Dallas Area Rapid Transit, www.dart.org, 214-979-1111, Light Rail Red Line: Lover's Lane Station, Blue and Red Line: Mockingbird Station; Bus: 1, 569, 583, 768 (Express); Campbell Centre E-Shuttle: 21, 24, 501, 519; Dart on-call: Lakewood.

UNIVERSITY PARK

Boundaries: (roughly) North: Northwest Hwy; East: US-75; South: Highland Park and Dallas city limits; West: Dallas North Tollway

Directly north of Highland Park is the city of University Park. The city is named after its location next to Southern Methodist University ("SMU"), a private four-year university that was established in 1915. The area was originally a collection of homes around the university campus for the school's staff and professors. SMU provided residents with basic services such as utility, sewage, water, and sanitation. However, as the number of houses grew along with the population, the university could no longer supply the necessary basic services. The community offered to be annexed by neighboring Highland Park and then Dallas, which both rejected the proposal on account of the high cost of providing it with basic municipal services. Ironically, Dallas later wanted to annex University Park for tax purposes because of the area's high property values, but was defeated by University Park residents. The residents eventually voted to incorporate the area as a city in 1924.

This wealthy enclave of approximately 23,000 residents is surrounded by Dallas on the north, east, and west, and by the City of Highland Park on the south. It is primarily a residential community that is noted for its lovely parks, attractive homes, and beautiful churches. There is a significant college student population; students live in apartments and rental property near the SMU campus. Off of Lovers Lane, west of University Park, are numerous apartments and townhomes. Most of the complexes were built from the 1950s to 1980s, though there are a few recently renovated buildings. However, the area is mostly inhabited by homeowners (66.5%) who are at the higher end, if not the highest, of the income and education brackets. University Park residents do not have to travel very far for food or shopping. Snider Plaza, a shopping center in the heart of town at Hillcrest and Lovers Lane, offers a variety of retail stores and restaurants.

There is a strong sense of community here, perhaps partly due to the city's small geographic coverage (3.8 square miles). Like Highland Park, it has a quiet community atmosphere and a feeling of security. In addition, it is served by fine public schools. Not surprisingly, this well-established and desirable neighborhood was ranked Dallas's number one suburb by *D Magazine* in 2002 and 2004. These attractive features have increased or at least maintained University Park's high property values.

Web Site: www.uptexas.org

Area Code: 214

Zip Codes: 75205, 75206

Post Offices: Lovers Lane Station, 5111 Greenville, Dallas; University of Dallas Station, 5606 Yale Blvd, Dallas

Police Precinct: University Park Police Department, 3800 University Blvd, University Park, 214-987-5370

Emergency Hospitals: Baylor Medical Center, www.baylorhealth.com, 3500 Gaston, Dallas, 214-820-0011; University of Texas Southwestern Medical Center, www3.utsouthwestern.edu, 5323 Harry Hines Blvd, Dallas, 214-683-3111

Library: University Park Library, www.uplibrary.org, 6517 Hillcrest, Ste 110, University Park, 214-363-9095

Adult Education: Southern Methodist University, www.smu.edu, 6425 Boaz Ln, Dallas, 214-768-2000

Public Education: Highland Park Independent School District, www.hpisd.org, 7015 Westchester, Dallas, 214-780-3000

Community Publications: *Park Cities News,* www.parkcitiesnews.com; *Park Cities People,* www.peoplenewspapers.com/parkcities.html; *Dallas Morning News*
Community Resources: City Hall, 3800 University Blvd, University Park, 214-363-1644; Park Cities YMCA, www.pcymca.org, 6000 Preston Rd, Dallas, 214-526-7293
Public Transportation: Dallas Area Rapid Transit, www.dart.org, 214-979-1111, *Light Rail: Red Line:* Lover's Lane Station; *Bus:* 1, 21, 24, 501, 569, 583, 768 (Express)

BLUFFVIEW

Boundaries: North: Northwest Hwy; East: Inwood; South: Lovers Ln; West: Lemmon Ave

West of the Park Cities, near Bachman Creek and Dallas's second largest airport, Love Field, is a small, exclusive community hidden away from the stress and bustle of the city. It is hard to believe that this neighborhood is actually located minutes from Downtown because parts of it feel much more like the country with gently rolling hills, numerous mature trees, creeks, streams, and winding roads. The area's most distinctive and impressive feature is a 60-foot cliff above Bachman Creek, lending the name Bluffview to this area.

This small neighborhood is sandwiched between Park Cities and the nearby community of Preston Hollow. It is conveniently located near several major freeways, the Downtown business district, the wholesale apparel Trade Mart, and the University of Texas Southwestern Medical Center.

Bluffview is located on the site of a former 215-acre dairy farm, which was purchased by developers in 1924 to create a residential community. The architects hired to design the homes decided to preserve the area's many trees and scenic landscape, which resulted in some odd-shaped lots. In 1943, the City of Dallas finally annexed Bluffview after three years of disagreements between both parties.

It will be difficult to find two homes in this neighborhood that look alike because each Bluffview home has its own individual character and distinctive architectural style. There are small, single-story, plain brick homes on small, treeless lots next to charming country cottages and Tudor-style houses with porches and winding pathways surrounded by trees. There are also two-story homes and million-dollar estates. Some of the small, plain, two-bedroom, single-story homes on little parcels of land cost about $220,000, which is costly considering the size of the residence and the type of housing available for that price in other parts of Dallas. However, location, landscape, and proximity to good schools push up the value of all the homes in Bluffview. Buyers who want to get more square footage or extra rooms for the same amount they would pay for a home in Bluffview should head west of Bluebonnet/Midway Road into Northwest Bluffview. There is a bit more value for the money here, but there is not a significant difference in housing prices. Further along down the Northwest Freeway (Loop 12), going west, are some nice apartments just outside of the Bluffview neighborhood.

Web Site: www.dallascityhall.com
Area Code: 214
Zip Code: 75209
Post Office: Inwood Station, 7611 Inwood Rd
Police Precinct: Dallas Police Department, www.dallaspolice.net: Northwest Division, 9801 Harry Hines Blvd, 214-670-6178
Emergency Hospital: University of Texas Southwestern Medical Center, www3.utsouthwestern.edu, 5323 Harry Hines Blvd, 214-683-3111
Library: Dallas Public Library, www.dallaslibrary.org: Oak Lawn Branch, 4100 Cedar Springs Rd, 214-670-1359
Public Education: Dallas Independent School District, www.dallasisd.org, 3700 Ross Ave, 972-925-3700
Community Publications: *Bluffview People*, www.peoplenewspapers.com/bluffview.html; *Dallas Morning News*, dallasnews.com; *D Magazine*, www.dmagazine.com; *Dallas Observer*, www.dallasobserver.com
Community Resources: City Hall, 1500 Marilla St, 214-670-5111; Grauwyler Recreation Center, 7780 Harry Hines Blvd, 214-670-6303; Preservation Dallas, www.preservationdallas.org
Public Transportation: Dallas Area Rapid Transit, www.dart.org; *Bus:* 8, 31, 51, 428

PRESTON HOLLOW

Boundaries: North: I-635; East: US-75; South: Loop 12; West: Midway

Further north of the Park Cities, on the other side of Loop 12, is the attractive and prestigious community of Preston Hollow. Though only minutes from downtown Dallas, Preston Hollow's winding roads and mature trees provide an atmosphere akin to the tranquil isolation of a country setting. Many of Dallas's rich and notable inhabitants such as Ross Perot and Mavericks' owner Mark Cuban reside in this enclave of grand homes and magnificent mansions, many of which are set on sprawling estates with tennis courts, pools, and lavish grounds. The spacious lots on which most of the homes in this neighborhood are set provide peace and privacy for its residents. However, there are other housing options besides multimillion-dollar estates. The neighborhood contains a mixture of old homes constructed from the 1930s to recent homes built on the site of torn down, older residences. Homes may range anywhere from $200,000 to the millions. Styles include cottages built in the 1950s set in wooded areas and luxury condos located on Hillcrest. A string of condominiums can also be found along the Northwest Freeway around Preston Road in a commercial area of the neighborhood known as **Preston Center**.

This fine community is also matched by some of the finest private schools in the metropolitan area. Preston is home to well-regarded schools such as the private, all-boys' St. Mark's Academy and public Hillcrest High School. Ursuline Academy, all-girls' Hockaday, where the Bush twins went to high school, and Episcopal, are some other highly sought-after private schools.

The Dallas North Tollway runs through Preston Hollow and provides quick access for those who need to commute downtown for work. Preston Hollow is also conveniently located by Loop 12, US-75, and IH-635, which connect the community to arts and entertainment districts, fancy shopping centers, sports venues, and other attractions.

Web Site: www.dallascityhall.com

Area Code: 214

Zip Codes: 75225, 75229, 75230

Post Offices: Hamilton Park Station, 8135 Forest Ln; Preston Royal Finance Station, 5959 Royal Ln, Ste 539; Preston Station, 8604 Turtle Creek Blvd

Police Precinct: Dallas Police Department, www.dallaspolice.net: Central Station, 334 S Hall St, 214-670-4411

Emergency Hospital: Presbyterian Hospital of Dallas, www.texashealth.org, 8200 Walnut Hill Ln, 214-345-6789

Library: Preston Royal Branch: 5626 Royal Ln, 214-670-7128

Public Education: Dallas Independent School District, www.dallasisd.org, 3700 Ross Ave, 972-925-3700

Community Publications: *Preston Hollow People*, www.peoplenewspapers.com; *Dallas Morning News*, dallasnews.com; *D Magazine*, www.dmagazine.com; *Dallas Observer*, www.dallasobserver.com

Community Resources: City Hall, 1500 Marilla St, 214-670-5111; Churchill Recreation Center, 6906 Churchill Way, 214-670-6477; Walnut Hill Recreation Center, 10011 Midway Rd, 214-670-7112

Public Transportation: Dallas Area Rapid Transit, www.dart.org; *Bus:* 21, 36, 184,501, 503, 505, 506, 519, 567, 582, 702, 360, 567, 451, 488; *Light Rail: Red Line:* Walnut Hill Station and Park Lane Station

FAR NORTH DALLAS

For many decades, Far North Dallas was rural farmland where cotton and other cash crops grew. When the Dallas/Ft. Worth airport opened in the 1970s, it sparked development in the area as businesses began moving near the airport. New freeways were built to access the new airport, which brought further residential development. Since then, the growth has continued. Most of Dallas's economic development and expansion in the past three decades has been in the far north and northwest areas, especially the suburban cities that border Dallas.

Far North Dallas is a shopper's paradise with a wide choice of shopping locations. The most well-known shopping center is the Galleria, a four-story shoppers' mecca with an ice rink, hotel, restaurants, and stores ranging from Dillard's and other department stores to national retailer the Gap, to fine, high-end boutiques like Gucci and Louis Vuitton. Nearby is the well-established but less glamorous Valley View Mall. Those who are not satisfied with what Far North Dallas has to offer can head to the other shopping centers in the nearby suburbs of Addison, Plano, Carrollton, and Richardson.

NORTHWOOD HILLS AND SPRING CREEK

Boundaries: NORTHWOOD HILLS: North: Belt Line Rd; East: Coit Rd; South: LBJ Freeway (I-635); West: Preston Rd; SPRING CREEK: North: Arapaho; South: Belt Line; East: Coit Rd; West: Meandering Way

Between LBJ Freeway and the Belt Line is an older community built in the 1950s and 1960s. It was one of the first major housing developments in Far North Dallas. Unlike communities farther north, **Northwood Hills** developed in the 1950s, before the arrival of the Dallas/Ft. Worth airport or any major employers. At the time of its inception, it was a rural area with miles of cotton fields. Coit and Hillcrest, two major present-day thoroughfares, were nothing more than two-lane country roads. The main reason for placing a large-scale real estate development in such a remote area was the beauty of the surrounding landscape. Lovely trees, gently sloping hills, subtle curves and bends, a running stream, and an elevation above the surrounding land created a scenic place to construct luxury homes. Over 1000 single-family homes on spacious lots shaded by large oak trees make up this quiet neighborhood.

Many business executives and their families reside in Northwood Hills because of its location between Downtown and the major corporate headquarters in the northern suburbs. It is also ideally located just minutes from major shopping areas in the north and other Dallas attractions. The Northwood Hills neighborhood is served by highly regarded Richardson Independent School District.

The **Spring Creek** neighborhood to the north of Northwood Hills consists of mostly large one-story, ranch-style homes built in the 1960s. There are a few apartments and townhomes in the northeast corner of the neighborhood. However, Spring Creek is primarily a single-family residential place with a suburban-like appeal for families with children. It is covered by fully grown oak, elm, ash, and pecan trees in a quiet, relaxing environment. Two great recreational centers for families and kids are Fretz Park and the Spring Valley Athletic Association. Fretz Park is a community center offering art, dance, and other classes for children, adults, and senior citizens. It also provides yoga, tennis, and other activities, and there is a clubhouse for hosting events. Children looking for more can participate in soccer, basketball, and other sports leagues at the athletic association.

Web Sites: www.dallascityhall.com, www.northwoodhills.org
Area Code: 214
Zip Code: 75254
Post Office: Spring Valley Station, 13770 Noel Rd
Police Precinct: Dallas Police Department, www.dallaspolice.net: North Central Division, 6969 McCallum, 214-670-7253
Emergency Hospitals: RHD Memorial Medical Center, www.rhdmemorial, 7 Medical Pkwy, 972-247-1000; Presbyterian Hospital of Dallas, www.texashealth.org,

8200 Walnut Hill Ln, 214-345-6789; Medical City Hospital at Dallas, www.medicalcityhospital.com, 7777 Forest Ln, 972-566-7000

Library: Dallas Public Library, www.dallaslibrary.org: Fretz Park Branch, 6990 Belt Line Rd, 214-670-6420

Public Education: Dallas Independent School District, www.dallasisd.org, 3700 Ross Ave, 972-925-3700; Richardson Independent School District, www.richardson.k12.tx.us, 400 S Greenville Ave, Richardson, 469-593-0000

Community Publications: *Dallas Morning News*, dallasnews.com; *D Magazine*, www.dmagazine.com; *Dallas Observer*, www.dallasobserver.com

Community Resources: City Hall, 1500 Marilla St, 214-670-5111; Fretz Park, www.dalparis.com/fretz/home.html, 6950 Belt Line Rd, 214-670-6203; Spring Valley Athletic Association, www.svaa.org, 13650 TI Blvd, Ste 209, 972-238-9728; Walnut Hill Recreation Center, 1011 Midway Rd, 214-670-7112

Public Transportation: Dallas Area Rapid Transit, www.dart.org; *Bus:* 488, 463, 361, 400

PRESTONWOOD

Boundaries: North: President Bush Turnpike; East: Coit Rd; South: Belt Line Rd, West: Dallas North Tollway

The area north of Belt Line in far north Dallas is generally referred to as Prestonwood. It contains a mix of three- to four-bedroom homes ranging from $250,000 to $300,000 with large shaded yards. Residences here are mostly ranch-style homes and apartments. Though technically within the city, the area is more suburban than metropolitan in character with its malls, strip centers featuring recognizable chain stores, country clubs, and master-planned subdivisions. Prestonwood contains numerous subdivisions and neighborhoods, including **Preston Highlands, Preston Road Highlands, Prestonwood East, Prestonwood West, Prestonwood South, Prestonwood North, Prestonwood Estates West, Preston Hollow East, Preston Hollow North, Preston Trail** and **Preston Green.** However, there are plans to create an urban living center known as **Prestonwood Center** in the middle of the suburbs. This mixed-use development area will feature condominiums alongside retail space.

Part of Prestonwood extends beyond Dallas County into Collin County. It is located near the major corporate headquarters and shopping and entertainment districts of the north Dallas suburbs. With so many major employers and attractions in the surrounding suburbs, it can be difficult to distinguish whether Prestonwood is part of the city or just a suburb of neighboring Plano, Addison, and Carrollton.

Nearby is the **Bent Tree** neighborhood, tucked between Prestonwood on the east and south, the suburb of Plano to the north, and the suburbs of Addison and Carrollton to the west. This community is filled with modern homes and contemporary apartments that surround the exclusive Bent Tree Country Club and golf course.

Web Sites: www.dallascityhall.com, www.www.phha.org, www.prhha.org, www.
pehaweb.org, www.prestonwoodwesthoa.org, www.prestonwoodsouth.com, www.
prestonridgetrail.org

Area Codes: 972, 214

Zip Codes: 75248, 75254, 75287

Post Offices: Prestonwood Station, 5995 Summerside Dr; Bent Tree Station, 4475
Trinity Mills Rd

Police Precinct: North Central Division: 6969 McCallum, 214-670-7253

Emergency Hospitals: RHD Memorial Medical Center, www.rhdmemorial.com, 7
Medical Pkwy, 972-247-1000; Trinity Medical Center, www.trinitymedicalcenter.
com, 4343 N Josey Ln, Carrollton, 972-492-1010; Richardson Regional Medical
Center, www.richardsonregional.com, 401 W Campbell Rd, Richardson, 972-498-
4000

Library: Dallas Public Library, www.dallaslibrary.org: Fretz Park Branch, 6990 Belt Line
Rd, Dallas, 214-670-1335

Public Education: Dallas Independent School District, www.dallasisd.org, 3700 Ross
Ave, 972-925-3700; Richardson Independent School District, www.richardson.k12.
tx.us, 400 S Greenville Ave, Richardson, 469-593-0000

Community Publications: *Dallas Morning News*, dallasnews.com; *D Magazine*, www.
dmagazine.com; *Dallas Observer*, www.dallasobserver.com

Community Resources: City Hall, 1500 Marilla St, 214-670-5111; Fretz Park, www.
dalparis.com/fretz/home.html, 6950 Belt Line Rd, 214-670-6203; Timberglen
Recreation Center, 3810 Timberglen Rd, 972-306-1090

Public Transportation: Dallas Area Rapid Transit, www.dart.org; *Bus:* 451, 463, 562,
360, 361, 400, 551, 567; *Light Rail: Red Line:* Spring Valley Station

SOUTHERN DALLAS

OAK CLIFF

Boundaries: North: I-30; East: I-35; South: Illinois Ave; West:
Hampton

The southern half of Dallas, below IH-30, is generally less economically
developed than the northern portion of Dallas. With the exception of a
few pockets close to downtown and near IH-30 that have been revitalized,
the southern half of Dallas has a higher crime and poverty rate than the
northern half above IH-30. One of these pockets of revitalization is
within a large community below the Trinity River known as North Oak
Cliff. Though any neighborhood below the Trinity is generally known as
Oak Cliff, this is somewhat inaccurate because there are neighborhoods
and communities in that area that are not part of Oak Cliff, while some
areas that are part of Oak Cliff are referred to as **South Dallas**. This is
probably because Oak Cliff is such a large neighborhood with two areas,
north and south, that are more different than they are alike.

North Oak Cliff is, as the name implies, in the northern section of the Oak Cliff neighborhood. This area encompasses the original boundaries of Oak Cliff, known as Old Oak Cliff, which was originally an independent town separated by the Trinity River before it was annexed by Dallas in 1903. Many of the houses built at the turn of the century and up until the 1920s were finely constructed homes for the upper-middle class and the affluent. New housing developments continued to be constructed until as late as the 1950s. A post–World War II housing shortage resulted in some of the larger homes being subdivided into apartments. The area eventually fell into decline and was neglected until the 1980s when it became the target of revitalization and historic preservation for those interested in saving architecturally significant homes and by people looking for an affordable place to live closer to work downtown. One of the reasons North Oak Cliff is as popular today as it was in the early 20th century is the area's natural landscape. North Oak Cliff is an urban forest with rolling hills, creeks, and mature trees, creating a rustic atmosphere in some sections. It is composed of several neighborhoods with historic homes of various architectural styles and sizes, many of which are hidden urban oases.

One of these neighborhoods is **Lake Cliff**, which is named after the beautiful freshwater lake and park in the northern section of this area. Most of the homes here are of various sizes and were originally built between 1890 and 1930 in the Queen Anne, Colonial Revival, Neoclassical, Tudor, Prairie, and Craftsman styles. Prominent and wealthy citizens of the time built the grander homes that are scattered throughout the neighborhood. The City of Dallas has designated Lake Cliff the city's 15th historical district, which allows residents to protect historical structures. The revitalization of Lake Cliff continues with a mixed-use development known as **Oak Cliff Gateway** planned for construction on Lake Cliff. Lofts and condominiums ranging from $180,000 to $500,000, with a view of the downtown Dallas skyline, will overlook Lake Cliff. In fact, residents should be able to reach downtown in 15 minutes by walking over Zang Bridge. The surrounding areas will be updated with shops, restaurants, bars, and cafes. In addition, there are plans to construct a new medical center nearby.

To the west of Lake Cliff is **Kidd Springs**, which is named after a natural spring in the neighborhood. A beautiful park and recreation center that includes a basketball court, tennis court, mini lake, huge swimming pool, baseball diamond, and garden sits by the spring. The neighborhood has large Neoclassical, Prairie, Craftsman, Colonial Revival homes, one-story Victorian bungalows, and Tudor-styled houses. Kidd Springs developed in two phases. The first phase, known as the Miller-Stemmons addition, is located in the heart of the neighborhood and is on the National Register of Historic Neighborhoods. Kidd Springs also has some restored antique apartment complexes that are popular with young professionals who work downtown.

Next to Kidd Springs are two neighborhoods that have never gone out of style and are still among Dallas's most coveted: Kessler Park and Stevens Park. **Kessler Park** is an oddly-shaped neighborhood that stretches from Beckley on the east and encompasses Stevens Park Golf Course. The northern part of Kessler Park is a wooded residential area with gentle hills known as Kessler Park Estates. It has a mixture of brick, stone, and stucco cottages with arched porches and ranch-style and contemporary homes. However, it is most known for its Tudor and Spanish-style mansions on Colorado Blvd. Moving east, the hilly wooded terrain exposes chalk cliffs and streams that course through the area. The steep and winding streets, which mirror the area's topography, are lined with stone-cut houses and contemporary homes. On the opposite end of Kessler Park, Tudor cottages built in the 1930s and stone and brick ranch-style houses sit on a wooded bluff, overlooking creeks. The western side also has some interesting homes, such as a split-level home built into the hillside and a few large modern-style houses. Finally, at the southernmost part of this neighborhood are two-bedroom brick or stone cottages in Tudor, Colonial Revival, and ranch styles built in the late 1930s on tree-shaded yards along winding streets.

Kessler Park surrounds the Stevens Park Golf Course, which is located in the **Stevens Park** neighborhood. This area is a hilly urban forest that looks down onto downtown Dallas. The eastern part of this neighborhood, which borders the golf course, is a child-friendly neighborhood with unique play parks installed at the end of several blocks. Homes come in a variety of styles that range from small bungalows to large estates. The western part of Stevens Park features smaller one-story brick and stone houses, some of which are tucked against the edge of a cliff with views of the Dallas skyline.

At the center of North Oak Cliff is a group of preserved, intact, turn-of-the-century homes known as **Winnetka Heights**. The homes were constructed with the finest materials, no doubt contributing to the durable quality and good condition of the homes. When the area was originally developed as a prestigious suburb, several wealthy citizens built fancy, two-story, prairie-style homes. Later, bungalows and cottages were constructed. Dallas granted Winnetka Heights historic district status in 1991. It has also been approved by the state for the National Registry of Historic Places and for a Texas Historical Commission.

Far south, at the edge of North Oak Cliff, is the post–World War II development of **Wynnewood North**. It was built in the 1950s for middle- to upper-income families. It consists of mostly sprawling ranch-style houses on large lots shaded by massive oak trees with small lakes and creeks that meander through the area. Immediately south of it is the older development of Wynnewood Village, which has some large apartment complexes and a large strip shopping center on its eastern and southern end.

Several other neighborhoods in varying states of restoration and revitalization are located throughout North Oak Cliff, such as **L.O. Daniel Kings Highway Conservation District, Ruthmeade Place**, and **Sunset Hills**. Some of the other neighborhoods such as **Beverly Hills Addition** are country-setting places with beautiful natural landscapes. The neighborhood's Coombs Creek, with its banks covered by heavily wooded limestone and towering trees, provides a rural atmosphere. The neighborhood's beautiful landscape and convenient location have attracted builders, who in the 1990s started constructing two-story houses on the undeveloped parts of Beverly Hills. Today, it is a socially, ethnically, and racially diverse neighborhood. Other neighborhoods with charming houses that are set in similarly hilly, wooded areas with creeks meandering through them are **Dell, El Tivoli Place, Elmwood, Beckley Estates**, and **Ravinia Heights**.

One of North Oak Cliff's most famous districts is the **Bishop Arts District**. Formerly a busy trolley stop, it is now a dining and shopping district that is part of the revitalization success story. The independent shops and restaurants in this pedestrian-friendly section are housed in historic 1920s buildings. Unlike some other newly constructed pedestrian shopping areas, this one does not have a slick, pretentious feel to it. Part of its charm and allure are the old historic buildings and neighborhood, which provide an authentic atmosphere.

Web Sites: www.oakcliff.com, www.dallascityhall.com

Area Code: 214

Zip Codes: 75211, 75208, 75203

Post Offices: Station A Dallas Station, 515 Centre; Dallas Mpo Finance, 401 Dallas–Ft. Worth Tpke; Beverly Hills, 2202 S Cockrell Hill Rd

Police Precincts: Dallas Police Department, www.dallaspolice.net: Southwest Patrol Division, 4230 W Illinois Ave, 214-670-7470; North Bishop Storefront, 408 N Bishop Ave, 214-670-7519

Emergency Hospital: Methodist Medical Center – Dallas, www.methodisthealthsystem. org, 1441 N Beckley, 214-947-8181

Libraries: Dallas Public Library, www.dallaslibrary.org: North Oak Cliff Branch, 302 W Tenth St, 214-670-7555; Hampton-Illinois Branch, 2210 W Illinois Ave, 214-670-6746

Public Education: Dallas Independent School District, www.dallasisd.org, 3700 Ross Ave, 972-925-3700

Community Publications: *Dallas Morning News*, www.dallasnews.com; *Dallas Observer*, www.dallasobserver.com; *D Magazine*, www.dmagazine.com

Community Resources: City Hall, 1500 Marilla St, 214-670-5111; Old Oak Cliff Conservation League, http://ooccl.com, 972-606-3693; Kidd Springs Park, 711 W Canty, 214-670-7535; Beckley-Sauer Recreation Center, 114 W Hobson, 214-670-7595

Public Transportation: Dallas Area Rapid Transit, www.dart.org; *Light Rail: Red Line:* Hampton Station and Tyler/Vernon Station; *Bus:* 11, 19, 21, 42, 50P, 76, 206, 278, 405, 444, 453, 510, 522, 568

SOUTH OAK CLIFF

Boundaries: (approximately) North: Illinois Ave, East: Trinity River; South: I-20; West: Hampton Rd

Revitalization and economic development have bypassed South Oak Cliff, which has not fared as well as neighborhoods to the north. This is reflected in the area's higher poverty levels and high crime rate. There has been much discussion about the underdevelopment of South Oak Cliff, which some call South Dallas. Some efforts have been made to uplift the area, such as the $3 million renovation of the Cedars Crest Country Club, which was the site of the 1927 PGA tournament. Cedars Crest and the area around Kiest Park are some of the more recognizable neighborhoods within South Oak Cliff.

Web Site: www.dallascityhall.com

Area Code: 214

Zip Codes: 75237, 75211, 75216, 75203, 75233, 75224, 75216

Post Offices: Dr. Caesar A.W. Clark, Sr. Station, 1502 E Kiest Blvd; Station A Dallas Station, 515 Centre; Joe Pool Station, 5521 S Hampton Rd

Police Precincts: Dallas Police Department, www.dallaspolice.net: Southwest Patrol Division, 4230 West Illinois Ave, 214-670-7470; Brackins Village Storefront, 125 Monaghan Ct, 214-670-6739

Emergency Hospital: Methodist Charlton Medical Center, www.methodisthealthsystem. org, 3500 W Wheatland, 214-947-7777

Libraries: Dallas Public Library, www.dallaslibrary.org: Lancaster-Kiest Branch, 3039 S Lancaster Rd, 214-670-1952; Polk-Wisdom Branch, 7151 Library Ln, 214-670-1947

Public Education: Dallas Independent School District, www.dallasisd.org, 3700 Ross Ave, 972-925-3700

Community Publications: *Dallas Morning News*, www.dallasnews.com; *Dallas Observer*, www.dallasobserver.com; *D Magazine*, www.dmagazine.com

Community Resources: City Hall, 1500 Marilla St, 214-670-5111; Kiest Community Center and Park, 3080 S Hampton Rd, 214-670-1918; Cummings Recreation Center, 2900 Cummings, 214-670-6876; Eloise Lundy Recreation Center, 1229 Sabine, 214-970-6781; Tommie M. Allen Recreation Center, 7071 Bonnie View, 214-670-0986; Fruitdale Recreation Center, 4408 Vandervoort, 214-670-7600; J.C. Phelps Recreation Center, 3030 Tips Blvd, 214-670-7525; Singing Hills Recreation Center, 1909 Crouch Rd, 214-670-7550

Public Transportation: Dallas Area Rapid Transit, www.dart.org; *Light Rail: Red Line:* Westmoreland Station; *Blue Line:* Kiest Station and VA Medical Center Station; *Bus*: 1, 19AA, 21, 161, 405, 438, 441, 444, 445, 453, 466, 515, 522, 548, 549, 568, 574

SOUTH DALLAS

Boundaries: North: I-30; East: White Rock Creek; South: Trinity River; West: Trinity River

South Dallas is the area east of the Trinity River and below IH-30. It was once the center of the city's Jewish community. From the 1920s to 1950s, Jewish families began leaving the area for northern Dallas. During that time, parts of South Dallas became a major industrial and manufacturing center with several warehouses. African-American families moved into the area, but many also left for South Dallas suburbs after the warehouses and manufacturing plants closed in the 1970s. Since then it has been a low-income and underserved community. However, South Dallas has recently attracted the interest of developers because of its proximity to Downtown. New housing developments and businesses have moved into the neighborhoods, sparking urban revitalization. The residential developments attract mostly urban professionals who prefer to live close to work or, in some cases, people who work at home.

The Cedars
A neighborhood southeast of Downtown and just east of the Trinity River, the Cedars was the predominantly wealthy home to Dallas's Jewish community during the 1870s. During the early 1900s, it began to evolve into an industrial and commercial retail center. By the 1920s most of its residents had moved to North Dallas suburbs. Few of the Victorian-era homes are still standing today. In its place are highways and low-income housing. Until recently, Cedars had several vacant and abandoned buildings with many homeless people living in the vicinity. A major urban revitalization effort in the Cedars has led to the development of a light rail station and new townhomes and apartments. In the southern part of the neighborhood, on Lamar Street, there are several new businesses, bars, entertainment spots, and lofts.

Fair Park/Exposition Park
East of the Cedars are the Fair Park and Expo Park neighborhoods. Fair Park is an educational and recreational complex managed by the Dallas Parks and Recreation Center. It includes museums, a planetarium, an IMAX theater, an outdoor amphitheater, an aquarium, a music hall, and the Cotton Bowl football stadium. This popular tourist destination is recognized by the National Register of Historic Places for the Art Deco style of its original 1936 buildings. The surrounding neighborhoods also bear the same name as the complex. Once a middle-class neighborhood of mainly Jewish families, it is now primarily an African-American neighborhood. The area has been largely neglected since the Ford Motor plant closed in the 1970s. Fair Park is marked with overgrown yards, battered and faded signs, and dilapidated houses. Few retail stores or services operate here. However, there are signs of hope. Realizing the demand for intown housing, some enterprising development companies have converted several of the abandoned and empty buildings and warehouses in the area to residential lofts. Though located only two miles southeast of Downtown, traffic and parking may be a concern during the annual, three-week Texas State Fair, and also the Red River Shootout

football game between the Universities of Texas and Oklahoma. However, most of the lofts are not located immediately near the fairgrounds, so it should not be a problem for loft dwellers. There are also some attractive new duplexes currently under construction in the old neighborhoods north of Fair Park, where there have been some recent efforts to revitalize the area.

Lofts have also been converted from old warehouses in **Exposition Park** near Fair Park and Deep Ellum to the north. Several old, historic buildings have been upgraded for commercial use. Exposition Park is similar to Deep Ellum with its bohemian galleries, shops, video stores, and coffeehouses all within walking distance of the lofts. However, it is less known for its nightlife and is nowhere near as wild as Deep Ellum during party time.

South Boulevard/Park Row Historic District is a neighborhood of over 100 intact prairie, bungalow, and historical Revival-style homes built by the city's Jewish community from 1910 to 1935. It covers two streets and is centered around Temple Emanu-El, the neighborhood synagogue until 1957, when it moved to its current location on Hillcrest Road. South Boulevard/Park Row is listed on the National Register of Historic Places. However, this designation has not helped the preservation of these homes because no active community is present to enforce the regulations. In fact, it is considered one of Dallas's most endangered historic districts. Many of the homes are rotting, burned to the ground, or dilapidated. **Wheatley Place** is another historic district in South Dallas that is considered endangered. It features wood frame bungalows built between 1916 and the mid-1930s. Named for Phyllis Wheatley, an African-American poet from the 18th century, it was constructed as a neighborhood for African-Americans during segregation.

Web Site: www.dallascityhall.com

Area Code: 214

Zip Code: 75215

Post Office: Juanita Craft Station, 3055 Grand Ave

Police Precinct: Dallas Police Department, www.dallaspolice.net: Rhodes Terrace Storefront, 5715 Pilgrim Dr, 214-670-8572

Emergency Hospital: Baylor Medical Center, www.baylorhealth.edu, 3500 Gaston Ave, 214-820-2505

Library: Dallas Public Library, www.dallaslibrary.org, Martin L. King, Jr. Branch, 2922 Martin Luther King Blvd

Public Education: Dallas Independent School District, www.dallasisd.org, 3700 Ross Ave, 972-925-3700

Community Publications: *Dallas Morning News*, www.dallasnews.com; *Dallas Observer*, www.dallasobserver.com; *D Magazine*, www.dmagazine

Community Resources: City Hall, 1500 Marilla St, 214-670-5708; Rhoads Terrace Recreation Center, 5712 Pilgrim, 214-670-8527; Martin Luther King Recreation Center, 2922 M.L. King Dr, 214-670-8363; Mildred Dunn Recreation Center, 3322 Reed Ln, 214-670-8028; Exline Recreation Center, 2525 Pine St, 214-670-8121; Juanita J. Craft Recreation Center, 4500 Spring, 214-670-8391

Public Transportation: Dallas Area Rapid Transit: www.dart.org; *Bus:* 2, 12, 26, 35, 44, 46, 50, 409, 441, 444, 510, 515, 538; *Light Rail: Blue Line:* Morrell Station and Illinois Station; *Blue and Red Line:* Cedars Station and 8th & Corinth Station

SOUTHEAST DALLAS

PLEASANT GROVE

Boundaries: North: Bruton Rd; East: Cheyenne Rd; South: Trinity River; West: White Rock Creek

The residential neighborhood of Pleasant Grove is located eight miles from downtown in southeast central Dallas. It is named after the grove of cottonwood trees where the town's first school stood. The area's population increased dramatically during the post–World War II housing boom, but Pleasant Grove remained an unincorporated area outside of Dallas until the late 1940s. In 1954, Pleasant Grove Independent School District merged with Dallas Independent School District. By 1962, Dallas had incorporated all of Pleasant Grove. Dallas also slowly annexed other independent and unincorporated communities and areas around Pleasant Grove such as **Pleasant Mound, Urbandale/Parkdale**, and **Piedmont**. These areas are often lumped together under one name and are now considered part of Pleasant Grove. Urbandale/Parkdale features mainly brick ranch-style homes and 1950s/1960s-style stone homes. Piedmont homes are similar to Urbandale/Parkdale homes. The neighborhood is surrounded by hills and large pecan and oak trees. Pleasant Grove is a quiet neighborhood with single-family residential homes on tidy lawns.

Other neighborhoods in this part of Dallas worth taking a look at are:

- **Bruton Terrace/Riverway Terrace:** Affordable, newer custom homes near a large park, creek, and surrounded by plentiful trees.
- **Buckner Terrace/Everglade Park**: Homes built in the 1970s and 1980s and current new home construction.

SCYENE

Boundaries: North: Military Pkwy; East: North Master Dr; South: Bruton Rd; West: N Prairie Creek Rd

Further east, near the Dallas/Mesquite border, is the community of Scyene. Its name is derived from a misspelling of "Seine." It was originally called Thorpville and Prairie Creek. Established in 1854 as a small independent town, it never grew to more than 350 residents. As

Dallas grew, it eventually surrounded Scyene until it became just another Dallas neighborhood. The area is at the eastern edge of Dallas and like large parts of Southeast Dallas is surrounded by semi-rural undeveloped land with a few small single-family neighborhoods. However, there has been an increase in residential development since the 1980s. Nearby neighborhoods where many residential homes are located include **Fireside and Seagoville.**

Web Sites: www.dallascityhall.com, www.seagoville.us

Area Code: 214

Zip Codes: 75227, 75217

Post Offices: Parkdale Station, 7720 Military Pkwy; Pleasant Grove Station, 350 S Buckner Blvd

Police Precinct: Dallas Police Department, www.dallaspolice.net: Lake June Storefront, 10325 Lake June Rd, 214-670-8032

Emergency Hospital: Baylor Medical Center, www.baylorhealth.edu, 3500 Gaston Ave, 214-820-2505

Libraries: Dallas Public Library, www.dallaslibrary.org: Skyline Branch, 6006 Everglade Rd, 214-670-0938; Pleasant Grove Branch, 1125 S Buckner Blvd, 214-670-0965

Public Education: Dallas Independent School District, www.dallasid.org, 3700 Ross Ave, 972-925-3700

Community Publications: *Dallas Morning News*, www.dallasnews.com; *Dallas Observer*, www.dallasobserver.com; *D Magazine*, www.dmagazine

Community Resources: City Hall, 1500 Marilla St, 214-670-5708; Southeast Dallas Chamber of Commerce, www.sedcc.org, 1515 S Buckner Blvd, Ste 351, 214-398-9590; Pleasant Oaks Recreation Center, 8701 Greenmound, 214-670-0945; Umphress Recreation Center, 7615 Umphress, 214-670-0956

Public Transportation: Dallas Area Rapid Transit, www.dart.org; *Bus*: 37, 11, 11S, 475, 118, 466, 283, 50, 165B

SOUTHWEST DALLAS

Boundaries: North: I-30; East: Hampton; South: I-20; West: Loop 12

Southwest Dallas is a largely undeveloped area with beautiful scenery and a few neighborhoods sprinkled throughout it. One of the neighborhoods in this area is actually a small independent city known as **Cockrell Hill**. The island city covers only 0.6 square miles and has a population of approximately 4500 people. The town's population is largely working class Hispanics with a median income close to $33,000. The median house value is about $55,000. Cockrell Hill has its own city government and police force, but is served by the Dallas Independent School District. There have been rumors of mismanagement by the city government in recent years, but there are no known plans for Dallas to annex it. Further to its west is another neighborhood, **Arcadia Park**, which has similar social, economic, and racial demographics to Cockrell Hill. Its western side borders the City of Grand Prairie, while the western end borders an undeveloped part of Dallas. Arcadia Park is often lumped together with Oak Cliff, but was actually an independent community until Dallas annexed it. Below Arcadia and to the west of Cockrell Hill is the **Mountain View** neighborhood and below it is **Red Bird**. Mountain View and Red Bird are located near large undeveloped areas, but low land prices and proximity to Grand Prairie, major highways, and Joe Pool Lake have attracted recent commercial and residential development. Housing options include newly constructed homes, older single-family residences, apartments, and trailer parks. Both neighborhoods are near the Dallas city border and are surrounded by impressive landscape. Major employers here include the Dallas Community College, Red Bird Industrial Park, and Mountain View Industrial Park.

Web Sites: www.dallascityhall.org; www.cockrell-hill.tx.us
Area Code: 214
Zip Code: 75211
Post Office: Beverly Hills Station, 2202 S Cockrell Hill Rd
Police Departments: Dallas Police Department, www.dallaspolice.net: Southwest Patrol Division, 4230 W Illinois Ave; Cockrell Hill Police Department, www.cchpd.com, 4125 W Clarendon, 214-339-4141
Emergency Hospitals: Dallas Southwest Medical Center, www3.utsouthwestern.edu, 2929 S Hampton Rd, 214-330-4611; Methodist Charlton Medical Center, www.methodisthealthsystem.org, 3500 W Wheatland Rd
Libraries: Dallas Public Library, www.dallaslibrary.org, Arcadia Park Branch, 1302 N Justin Ave, 214-670-6446; Cockrell Hill Public Library, 4125 W Clarendon
Public Education: Dallas Independent School District, www.dallasisd.org, 3700 Ross Ave, 972-925-3700
Community Publications: *Dallas Morning News*, www.dallasnews.com; *Dallas Observer*, www.dallasobserver.com; *D Magazine*, www.dmagazine.com
Community Resources: Dallas City Hall, 1500 Marilla St, 214-670-5111; Cockrell City Hall, 4125 W Clarendon; Arcadia Recreation Center, 5420 N Arcadia, 214-670-1909; Martin Weiss Recreation Center, 1111 Martindell, 214-670-1919
Public Transportation: Dallas Area Rapid Transit, www.dart.org; *Bus:* 50, 76, 404, 444, 549

EAST DALLAS SUBURBS

GARLAND

When settlers from the Peters Colony arrived in the area that is now Garland, they found a prairie with few trees but acres of wildflowers. A community with cotton as the primary cash crop soon developed and was incorporated in 1891. For decades, Garland continued as a small town on the outskirts of Dallas. It formed its own electric and water utility company in the 1920s, which it still operates as a business. Like the other surrounding suburbs, it experienced a post–World War II population boom. The town today has over 215,000 residents. It has a relatively young and diverse population (53% white, 26% Hispanic, and 12% African-American). Garland is a largely industrial town with Raytheon as one of the biggest employers.

Housing in Garland is a real bargain, especially compared to Dallas and even the other suburbs. The average house value is $70,000, which is one of the lowest of the Dallas suburbs. The Rose Hill neighborhood in southeast Garland near Audubon Park has three-bedroom houses that go for under $100,000. In addition, there are apartments and several master-planned communities that offer very affordable housing. Rose Hill was a separate community that was settled as early as 1853, but was annexed by Garland in the 1970s. Nearby is Lake Ray Hubbard, which provides boating, fishing, water sports, and other fun recreational activities. Some of the newer lakeside neighborhoods near the Eastern Hills Country Club in the **Centerville** neighborhood have starting home prices that range from $170,000 up to $400,000. Newer, more expensive development is located around the **Naaman** neighborhood in northeast Garland.

For those seeking something more upscale, recently constructed golf course communities next to public Firewheel Golf Course feature expensive, brick Georgian homes with their own amenities. One of the main attractions in Garland, directly across from the golf course, is Firewheel Town Center, an open air shopping center designed like an old town Main Street. However, this faux main street houses major chain stores and national retailers instead of authentic mom-and-pop businesses. On the other side of the President George Bush Tollway is another attraction, Spring Creek Forest Preserve. Many of the residences are located near such natural treasures and attractions. The **Duck Creek Greenbelt**, where ducks can often be seen along the creek, offers several such communities.

Richardson
Bordering the eastern and northern boundaries of Garland is the suburb of Richardson, large portions of which are next to Dallas. For more information on Richardson, please refer to North Suburbs.

Web Site: www.ci.garland.tx.us
Area Codes: 972, 469
Zip Codes: 75040, 75041, 75042, 75043, 75044
Post Offices: Garland Station, 1000 W Walnut St; North Garland Station, 2346 Belt Line Rd; Kingsley Station, 3260 Saturn Rd; South Garland Station, 501 E Oates Rd
Police Department: Garland Police Department, 1891 Forest Ln, 972-485-4840
Emergency Hospitals: Baylor Medical Center of Garland, www.baylorhealth.com, 2300 Marie Curie Blvd, 972-487-5000; Leland Medical Plaza, 2696 W Walnut, 972-276-7116
Libraries: Nicholson Memorial Library System: Central Library, 625 Austin St, Garland, 972-205-2500; North Garland Branch, 3845 N Garland Ave, Garland, 972-208-2802; Ridgewood Branch Library, 120 W Kingsley Rd (at S First St), Garland, 972-205-2580; South Garland Branch, 4845 Broadway Blvd (at Oates Rd), Garland,

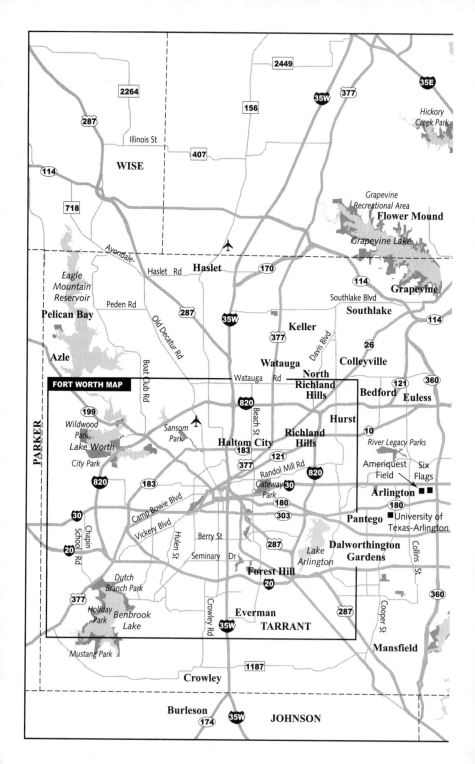

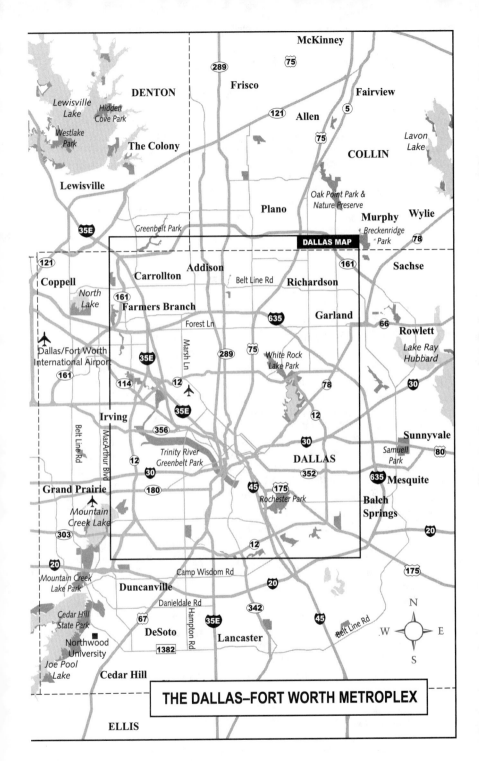

THE DALLAS–FORT WORTH METROPLEX

972-205-3920; Walnut Creek Branch Library, 3319 Edgewood Dr (off Jupiter Rd), Garland, 972-205-2586

Public Education: Garland Independent School District, www.garlandisd.net, 501 S Jupiter Rd, Garland, 972-494-8201; Dallas Independent School District, www. dallasisd.org, 3700 Ross Ave, Dallas, 972-925-3700 (small portions of southwest Garland); Richardson Independent School District, www.richardson.k12.tx.us, 400 S Greenville Ave, Richardson (small portions of northern Garland)

Community Publications: *Dallas Morning News*, (Garland Edition), www.dallasnews. com; *Garland News Weekly*

Community Resources: City Hall, 200 N Fifth St, 972-205-2000; Garland Chamber of Commerce, www.garlandchamber.com, 914 S Garland Ave, 972-272-7551

Public Transportation: Dallas Area Rapid Transit, www.dart.org; *Bus:* 377, 378, 380, 400, 463, 486, 513, 557, 566, 571; *Light Rail: Blue Line:* Forest/Jupiter Station and Downtown Garland Station

MESQUITE

Two events have led to the growth of Mesquite in the last half-century. First, a post–World War II housing boom led to the building of subdivisions in this town. Second and more influential was the expansion of IH-75, which connected Mesquite with neighboring towns and Dallas. Mesquite is a down-to-earth town with a distinctly Southwestern character. It is not shy about displaying its small town agricultural heritage. This suburb, which bills itself as the Rodeo Capital of Texas, is probably best known for the annual professional Mesquite Championship Rodeo held from April through September.

Mesquite is a major retail center and industrial, manufacturing hub that attracts people from the surrounding towns. Most famous of the retail areas is the city's "Rows of Texas," a series of restaurants, retailers, and rodeo-related entertainment, which are divided into Retail Row, Restaurant Row, and Rodeo Row. This commercial development along I-635 consists of mostly a series of chain restaurants. The largest component of the retail district is the giant Town East Mall.

The city offers many new master-planned communities and housing developments that are available at relatively affordable prices. House prices here are similar to Garland, with homes ranging from $90,000 to 250,000.

Major manufacturers and distributors such as UPS and Tyco are attracted to Mesquite's location along U.S. Interstates I-20 and I-30, Texas State Highway 352, and U.S. Highway 80, which provide easy access to the Dallas/Ft. Worth airport and the surrounding communities. Many of these businesses are located in Mesquite's Industrial Park, which is a major source of employment for the community.

Web Site: www.cityofmesquite.com
Area Code: 972
Zip Codes: 75149, 75150, 75180, 75181
Post Offices: Mesquite Station, 120 E Grubb Dr; North Mesquite Finance Station, 3501 Gus Thomasson Rd, Ste 35; Balch Springs Station, 3400 Hickory Tree Rd

Police Department: Mesquite Police Department, 711 N Galloway Ave, 972-216-6261
Emergency Hospitals: The Medical Center of Mesquite, www.medicalcenterofmesquite. com, 1011 N Galloway Ave, 214-320-7000; Mesquite Community Hospital, www. mchtx.com, 3500 Interstate 30, 972-698-3300
Library: Mesquite Public Library: Main Branch, 300 West Grubb Dr, 972-216-6220; North Branch, 2600 Oates Dr, 972-681-0465
Public Education: Mesquite Independent School District, www.mesquiteisd.org, 405 E Davis St, Mesquite, 972-288-6411; Dallas Independent School District, www. dallasisd.org, 3700 Ross Ave, Dallas, 972-925-3700 (small portions); Forney Independent School District, www.forney-isd.org, 600 S Bois d'Arc, Forney, 972-564-4055 (minuscule portions in Kaufman County)
Community Publication: *The Mesquite News*
Community Resources: City Hall, 711 N Galloway Ave; Municipal Center, 1515 N Galloway Ave, 972-288-7711, Mesquite Chamber of Commerce, www. mesquitechamber.com, 617 N Ebrite, 972-285-0211; Mesquite Championship Rodeo, www.mesquiterodeo.com, 1818 Rodeo Dr, 972-285-8777
Public Transportation: Mesquite Transportation for the Elderly and Disabled (MTED) curb to curb service

BALCH SPRINGS

Located south of Mesquite and 12 miles southeast of Downtown Dallas, the city of Balch Springs is one of the most rural and least developed of the eastern Dallas suburbs. Those who choose to live here can find a good deal. Large oak trees, huge lots, affordable new homes, and a short commute to work make it an attractive alternative to the other more popular suburbs. The city has numerous parks and recreational facilities for families to spend some quality time. Balch Springs is a rural area with a young and racially diverse population.

Web Site: www.ci.balch-springs.tx.us
Area Codes: 972, 469
Zip Code: 75180
Post Office: Balch Springs Station, 3400 Hickory Tree Rd, Mesquite
Police Precinct: Balch Springs Police Department, 12500 Elam Rd, Balch Springs, 972-557-6011
Emergency Hospitals: The Medical Center of Mesquite, www.medicalcenterofmesquite. com, 1011 N Galloway Ave, Mesquite, 214-320-7000; Mesquite Community Hospital, www.mchtx.com, 3500 Interstate 30, Mesquite, 972-698-3300
Library: Balch Springs Public Library, 12450 Elam Rd, Balch Springs, 972-913-3000
Adult Education: Eastfield College (Dallas Community College), www.efc.dccd.edu, 3737 Motley Dr, Mesquite, 972-860-7100
Public Education: Dallas Independent School District, www.dallasisd.org, 3700 Ross Ave, 214-841-4941 (southwest Balch Springs); Mesquite Independent School District, www.mesquiteisd.org, 405 E Davis St, Mesquite, 972-288-6411
Community Resources: City Hall, 3117 Hickory Tree Rd, Balch Springs, 972-557-6070; Balch Springs Chamber of Commerce, www.balchspringschamber.org, P.O. Box 800095, Balch Springs, 75180, 972-557-0988

ROWLETT

This quiet and laid-back community is located along the shores of Lake Ray Hubbard, an artificial recreational lake created to supply Dallas with water. The construction of the lake attracted new residents to the area in the 1970s and greatly increased the town's population. Though the average home price in Rowlett is $142,000, it is possible to get a three-bedroom house with less than 2000 square feet for under $100,000. The town has the atmosphere of a small, summer lakeside town with plenty of outdoor activities available for residents. Golfing, hiking, boating, sailing, fishing, and swimming are just some of the activities residents can enjoy. Especially outstanding is that Rowlett's Parks and Recreation Department operates a wonderful family-oriented water park known as the Wet Zone.

Web Site: ci.rowlett.tx.us/
Area Codes: 972, 469
Zip Codes: 75088, 75089
Post Office: Rowlett Station, 416 Enterprise Dr, Rowlett
Police Department: Rowlett Police Department, www.rowlettpolice.org, 4401 Rowlett Rd, Rowlett, 972-412-6200
Emergency Hospital: Lake Pointe Medical Center, www.lakepointemedical.com, 6800 Scenic Dr, Rowlett, 972-412-2273
Library: Rowlett Public Library, www.rowlett.lib.tx.us, 3900 Main St, Rowlett, 972-412-6161
Public Education: Garland Independent School District, www.garlandisd.net, 501 S Jupiter Rd, Garland, 972-494-8201 (serves Dallas County portion); Rockwall Independent School District, www.rockwallisd.com, 1050 Williams St, Rockwall, 972-771-0605 (Rockwall County portion)
Community Publication: *Lakeshore Times*
Community Resources: City Hall, 4000 Main St, 972-412-6100; Rowlett Chamber of Commerce, www.rowlettchamber.com, 3910 Main St, 972-475-3200
Public Transportation: Dallas Area Rapid Transit, www.dart.org; *Bus:* 207, 412, 557; *DART On-Call East Rowlett* (neighborhood shuttle service)

SUNNYVALE

Sunnyvale was incorporated in 1953 when several small farm communities merged to form the town. This quiet rural town with its beautiful landscape and location along Lake Ray Hubbard seems more like a place for a vacation home than a suburb of Dallas. This is an upscale community where homes typically start at $150,000. Located 15 miles east of Dallas, it has a little over 3000 residents. The bigger towns of Garland and Mesquite are nearby for shopping, entertainment, and other conveniences.

Web Site: www.townofsunnyvale.org
Area Codes: 972, 469
Zip Code: 75182
Post Office: Mesquite Station, 120 E Grubb Dr, Mesquite
Police: Dallas County Sheriff–Allman Substation, 537 Long Creek Rd, Sunnyvale, 972-226-4606

Emergency Hospitals: The Medical Center of Mesquite, www.medicalcenterofmesquite. com, 1011 N Galloway Ave, Mesquite, 214-320-7000; Mesquite Community Hospital, www.mchtx.com, 3500 Interstate 30, Mesquite, 972-698-3300, Lake Pointe Medical Center, www.lakepointemedical.com, 6800 Scenic Dr, Rowlett, 972-412-2273

Library: Sunnyvale Public Library, 402 Tower Pl, Sunnyvale, 972-226-4491

Public Education: Sunnyvale Independent School District, www.sunnyvaleisd.com, 417 E Tripp Rd, Sunnyvale, 972-226-7601

Community Resources: City Hall, 127 Collins Rd, Sunnyvale, 972-226-7177; Sunnyvale Chamber of Commerce, www.sunnyvalechamber.org, 317 Hwy 80 E, Sunnyvale, 469-583-0726

NORTH SUBURBS

A few decades ago, the area that is now the northern suburbs of Dallas was mostly undeveloped land with some small towns. Since then, it has experienced explosive growth for a combination of reasons. The construction of the Dallas/Ft. Worth International Airport and major interstate highways into the area has contributed to the area's development. Many major corporations are headquartered here, employing thousands of residents. Most importantly, young families can find an affordable home in a good public school district. These Dallas suburbs are quickly growing into considerable cities and towns of their own. The communities here are prime examples of exurbs, family-oriented developments on the fringes of a major city. Because Dallas, like most other major Texas cities, is not confined by any other urban area or geographical limitation that would curb its expansion, new communities continue to develop farther and farther away from it.

THE METROCREST

The four cities that are near or border Dallas and make up part of its northern suburbs are collectively known as the Metrocrest. These four cities are Addison, Farmers Branch, Coppell, and Carrollton. The Metrocrest cities share cultural, economic, and social ties that are the equivalent of a mini-metropolitan community.

ADDISON

Addison is a suburb next door to the far northwestern part of Dallas where Dallas residents go for food, entertainment, and work. For many decades it was a small town at the edge of Dallas. When the town approved the sale of individual servings of alcoholic beverages, in 1975, it increased the number of restaurants and businesses in Addison. Since most of north Dallas and the nearby suburbs are dry, which means there is a ban on the sale of alcohol, Addison's restaurants are popular with residents of these areas. The town covers only 4.5 square miles, but has over 150 restaurants. Addison has also used its tax rate to attract businesses, including the corporate headquarters of Pizza Hut, Mary Kay Cosmetics, and CompUSA.

Addison's initiatives have resulted in explosive growth of the town. Before the 1970s, it had a population of 535 residents, which grew to over 5000 in the 1980s and over 8000 in the 1990s. The town has 14,166 residents, but during the daytime its population swells to approximately 100,000 because many of the people who work and play in Addison are commuters from Dallas. Currently, Addison has over 1500 single-family homes and townhomes and 21 apartment complexes ranging from $100,000 to the millions. However, the town is planning on adding more with recently approved plans to construct a condominium complex at Addison Circle, the town center. The town center was conceived in the 1990s when the town decided to move away from the sprawling suburban model and create a mixed-use development where residents could work, play, and live. As a result, the town created a highly lauded and award-winning urban area within the suburbs. Addison Circle has European-style apartments and townhomes, pedestrian-friendly streets, and a commercial business section.

Addison residents go to public schools in the Dallas Independent School District or the Carrollton-Farmers Branch Independent School District. Another option is to attend the town's two private schools: Greenhill and Trinity Christian Academy.

Web Site: www.ci.addison.tx.us
Area Code: 972
Zip Code: 75001
Post Office: Addison Station, 4900 Airport Pkwy
Police Precincts: Addison Police Department: Main Station, 4799 Airport Pkwy, 972-450-7100; Addison Circle Station, 4943 Addison Circle, 972-392-1731; Brookhaven Club Station, 14362 Marsh Ln, 972-243-5135
Emergency Hospital: RHD Memorial Medical Center–North Dallas, www.rhdmemorial.com, 7 Medical Pkwy, Farmers Branch, 972-247-1000
Library: Farmers Branch Manske Library, 13613 Webb Chapel Rd, Farmers Branch, 972-247-2511
Public Education: Carrollton-Farmers Branch Independent School District, www.cfbisd.edu, 1445 N Perry Rd, Carrollton, 972-968-6100; Dallas Independent School District, www.dallasisd.org, 3700 Ross Ave, Dallas, 972-925-3700
Community Publications: *Addison Times Chronicle; Metrocrest News*
Community Resources: Town Hall, 5300 Belt Line Rd, Dallas, 972-450-7001; Addison Airport, 16051 Addison Rd, Ste 220, Addison, 972-392-4851; Metrocrest Chamber of Commerce, www.metrocrestchamber.com, 1204 Metrocrest Dr, Carrollton, 972-416-6600
Public Transportation: Dallas Area Rapid Transit, www.dart.org; *Bus:* 31, 36, 183, 205, 333, 341, 344, 350, 361, 400, 463, 488, 562

FARMERS BRANCH

Farmers Branch is located southwest of Addison and northwest of Dallas. Formerly known as Mustang Branch, it was renamed Farmers Branch for its rich farm soil. The area was heavily advertised for settlement to the populations in Europe and the eastern United States during the 19th century. The city is nothing like the small farm town of the past. Instead of growing crops, the city is sprouting office towers. It is a major business district with 88 corporate headquarters and 38 Fortune 500 companies based here. Most of these companies are located along the Platinum Corridor, a 15-mile stretch of office towers along the Dallas North Tollway that extends from IH-635 to State Highway 121. In addition, many other businesses are located in business parks along I-635 (LBJ Freeway), which makes up the city's southern border. As a result, its daytime population of approximately 85,000 is more than triple the number of actual residents (about 26,900).

The city offers apartments, condominiums, and single-family residential homes. Homes in Farmers Branch range from $120,000 to $800,000. Many of the residences are new construction, though there are older neighborhoods, such as Branch Crossing, which are being targeted for revitalization by the city. This suburb has a diverse population with a large Hispanic community (37%).

Web Site: www.ci.farmers-branch.tx.us

Area Code: 972

Zip Codes: 75234, 75244

Post Office: Farmers Branch Station, 13904 Josey Ln, Farmers Branch

Police Department: Farmers Branch Police Department, 3723 Valley View Ln, Farmers Branch, 972-484-3620

Emergency Hospital: RHD Memorial Medical Center – North Dallas, www.rhdmemorial. com, 7 Medical Pkwy, Farmers Branch, 972-247-1000

Library: Manske Library, 13613 Webb Chapel, Farmers Branch, 972-247-2511

Adult Education: Brookhaven College (Dallas Community College), www. brookhavencollege.edu, 3939 Valley View Ln, Farmers Branch, 972-860-4700; Dallas Christian College, www.dallas.edu, 2700 Christian Pkwy, Dallas, 1-800-688-1029

Public Education: Carrollton-Farmers Branch Independent School District, www.cfbisd. edu, 1445 N Perry Rd, Carrollton, 972-968-6100

Community Publications: *Farmers Branch Times Chronicle, Metrocrest News*

Community Resources: City Hall, 13000 William Dodson Pkwy, Farmers Branch, 972-247-3131; Farmers Branch Chamber of Commerce, www.fbchamber.com, 12875 Josey Ln, Ste 150, Farmers Branch, 972-243-8966; Metrocrest Chamber of Commerce, www.metrocrestchamber.com, 1204 Metrocrest Dr, Carrollton, 972-416-6600

Public Transportation: Dallas Area Rapid Transit, www.dart.org; *Bus*: Park and Ride: 185, 204, 247, 331, 400, 486; Regular Routes: 205, 183, 218, 44R, 44B, 36V, 31, 234, 210, 463

CARROLLTON

The City of Carrollton is a former small farming town that was incorporated in 1913. Today, it is a city known for its suburban convenience and business-friendly environment. Many distribution centers and call centers for major companies like Budget Rent-A-Car Reservation, Chrysler, and Ford Motor Parts Distribution are located here. Despite its suburban status, Carrollton still has a small town atmosphere. Employment opportunities and a strong public school system have contributed to its growth, which is one of the fastest in Texas. Houses in Carrollton are a bargain. The average home price is approximately $170,000, with the low end starting at $50,000 and the high end at $750,000. New home construction and new community development continue to be strong, with more homes being built every year.

Web Site: www.ci.carrollton.tx.us
Area Code: 972
Zip Codes: 75006, 75007, 75010
Post Offices: Carrollton Station, 2030 E Jackson Rd; Rosemead Station, 3755 N Josey Ln
Police Department: Carrollton Police Department, 2025 E Jackson Rd, 972-466-3256
Emergency Hospital: Trinity Medical Center, www.trinitymedicalcenter.com, 4343 N Josey Ln, Carrollton, 972-492-1010
Libraries: Carrollton Public Library: Hebron and Josey Branch, 4220 N Josey Ln, 972-466-4800; Josey Ranch Lake Branch, 1700 Keller Springs Rd, 972-466-4800
Public Education: Carrollton-Farmers Branch Independent School District, www.cfbisd.edu, 1445 N Perry Rd, Carrollton, 972-968-6100
Community Publications: *Carrollton Chronicle, Metrocrest News*
Community Resources: City Hall, 1945 E Jackson Rd, Carrollton, 972-466-3000; MetroCrest Chamber of Commerce, www.metrocrestchamber.com, 1204 Metrocrest Dr, Carrollton, 972-416-6600
Public Transportation: Dallas Area Rapid Transit, www.dart.org; *Bus:* Park and Ride: 204, 333, 344; Regular Routes: 185, 331, 400

COPPELL

Coppell is a wealthy bedroom community located west of Carrollton and Farmers Branch, directly north of the Dallas/Ft. Worth airport. Though it was incorporated in 1955, the area was settled by farmers as early as the 1830s. Previously known as Gibbs, the name was changed to Coppell in 1890. This is a tight community of 36,000 residents; with its small town atmosphere, low crime rate, and a high school reputed for its quality academics, people find Coppell an ideal place to raise a family. The average home costs about $230,000. There are also townhomes, condos, and duplexes available from $67,000 to $363,000.

Web Site: www.ci.coppell.tx.us
Area Code: 972
Zip Code: 75019
Post Office: Coppell Station, 450 S Denton Tap Rd, Coppell
Police Department: Coppell Police Department, 130 Town Center, Coppell, 972-304-3610
Emergency Hospitals: Medical Center of Lewisville, www.lewisvillemedical.com, 500 W Main St, Lewisville, 972-420-1000; Las Colinas Medical Center, www.

lascolinasmedical.com, 6800 N MacArthur Blvd, Irving, 972-969-2000; Baylor Medical Center at Grapevine, www.baylorhealth.com, 1650 W College, Grapevine, 817-481-1588

Library: William T. Cozby Public Library, 177 N Heartz Rd, 972-304-3655

Public Education: Coppell Independent School District, www.coppellisd.com, 200 S Denton Tap Rd, Coppell, 214-496-6000; Carrollton-Farmers Branch Independent School District, www.cfbisd.edu, 1445 N Perry Rd, Carrollton, 972-968-6100

Community Publication: *Coppell Gazette*

Community Resources: Coppell City Hall, 255 Pkwy Blvd, Coppell, 972-304-3669; Coppell Family YMCA, 146 Town Center Blvd, Coppell, 972-393-5121; Senior Adult Services, www.senioradultservices.org, 1111 W Belt Line Rd, Ste 110, Carrollton, 972-242-4464

RICHARDSON

Richardson is located partly in Dallas County and partly in Collin County. This suburban city is well-known for its excellent public school system and the Telecom Corridor, a 3-mile long strip along the North Central Expressway (US-75) that includes over 5000 technology companies. The Telecom Corridor contains 25 million square feet of office space, housing major technology companies such as Nortel, Ericsson, Alcatel, Southwestern Bell Communications, Samsung Electronics, and EDS. It employs about 70,000 people and has provided much of Richardson's growth. The town was originally a pioneer settlement and remained a quiet prairie town until the 1950s. In the following decades, electronic manufacturing companies replaced the cotton fields. The area became a bedroom community of Dallas, but with the growth of its economy, Richardson soon developed into a sizable city. The town's high-tech industry has attracted skilled workers from all over the United States and even the world. In fact, approximately 19% of Richardson's population is foreign-born.

Richardson's school district is well-known in the area for its excellent academic reputation and has become a highly desirable place for parents to send their children. The town has traditionally supported and emphasized education. The University of Texas at Dallas and Texas A&M Research Center are both located in western Richardson, near the Dallas border. In addition, many of its residents are skilled high-tech workers, with advanced college degrees.

Richardson is composed of several neighborhoods, many of which have an active neighborhood association. For a listing of all the Richardson neighborhood associations and their web sites visit the city's web site. Eastern Richardson, near the Plano border, contains newer housing developments with recently built, master-planned communities. The city also has more established neighborhoods such as Richardson Heights, which features 50-year-old homes, and Highland Terrace with its single-story homes surrounded by large trees.

In the southern part of town is **Buckingham**, a 159-acre former semi-rural residential enclave housing 102 residents that Richardson annexed in 1996. Richardson grew and eventually surrounded the town. Developers bought out the existing homes and converted them into apartments, supermarkets, liquor stores, and strip malls.

Web Site: www.cor.net

Area Codes: 972, 469

Zip Codes: 75080, 75081, 75082

Post Offices: Richardson Station, 433 Belle Grove Dr; Promenade Station, 400 N Coit Rd, Ste 1975; Huffhines Park Station, 1206 Apollo Rd

Police Department: Richardson Police Department, 140 N Greenville Ave, Richardson, 972-744-4800

Emergency Hospital: Richardson Regional Medical Center, www.richardsonregional. com, 401 W Campbell Rd, Richardson, 972-498-4000

Library: Richardson Public Library, 900 Civic Center Dr, 972-744-4350

Adult Education: University of Texas at Dallas, www.utdallas.edu, 800 W Campbell Rd, Richardson, 972-883-2111

Public Education: Richardson Independent School District, www.richardson.k12.tx.us, 400 S Greenville Ave, 469-593-0000

Community Publications: *Mercury* (University of Texas at Dallas), www.utdmercury. com

Community Resources: City Hall, 411 W Arapaho, 972-744-4100; Richardson Chamber of Commerce, www.telecomcorridor.com, 411 Belle Grove Dr, 972-792-2800

Public Transportation: Dallas Area Rapid Transit, www.dart.org, 214-979-1111; *Light Rail: Red Line:* Arapaho Center Station; *Bus:* Park and Ride: 234, 360, 361, 372, 400, 562, 571; *Dart On-Call:* Richardson

COLLIN COUNTY

PLANO

Plano is a thriving, affluent suburb approximately 20 miles north of downtown Dallas in Collin County. The area was settled in the mid-19th century, mainly by pioneers from Kentucky and Tennessee, and incorporated in 1873. Settlers who mistakenly believed that "plano" was the Spanish word for plain named it Plano because of the area's plain, flat, prairie landscape. Previously a small rural farming and ranching community with 17,872 residents, it experienced explosive growth between the 1970s and 1980s, when its population ballooned to 72,000. However, it was still a remote suburb with unpaved roads, farmland, and grazing livestock up until the 1980s. During the next decade, the population doubled and continued to grow. By 2000, it had over 220,000 residents. Plano has grown so much that it would be more accurate to describe it as a major city instead of as a Dallas suburb. Its growth can largely be attributed to the presence of major companies such as Dr. Pepper, EDS, Frito-Lay, JC Penney, and several other major employers. In addition, relatively affordable housing, a good public school district, and its proximity to Dallas have made it attractive to a diverse population.

However, to most people, Plano is synonymous with suburban living because it is the largest Dallas suburb and a typical model suburb. There are neatly divided subdivisions and master-planned communities with houses that have uniform brick exteriors. Homes are located in quiet neighborhoods that are served by nearby strip malls and convenient shopping. Plano is primarily for families looking for a quiet, safe neighborhood to raise children. Homes here range from the relatively affordable to the extravagant. They can cost under $100,000 at the low end and top out at $8.5 million. However, the average Plano home costs $250,000. Residential property here includes single-family homes, townhomes, and condominiums. Eastern Plano has smaller and older homes. Farther west and north, the homes get bigger and are more expensive. Plano is known for flashy McMansions, of which there are quite a few. Deserved or not, the city has somewhat of a reputation for keeping up appearances.

Even as recently as ten years ago, Plano was considered the far edge of the Dallas area. Plano has changed tremendously in the last 30 years and continues to transform itself. The most recent project was the construction of a transit-oriented complex in the historic downtown area in southern Plano. It is located along the Light Rail line near the Plano-Richardson border. The mixed-use development replaced strip shopping centers, parking lots, vacant land, and office parks that were in the area. This convenient, pedestrian-friendly development combines apartment lofts, restaurants, retail, and office space in a compact environment near public transportation. Like Addison, Plano has created an urban area within the suburbs.

Web Site: www.planotx.org
Area Codes: 972, 469
Zip Codes: 75023, 75024, 75025, 75074, 75075, 75093, 75094
Post Offices: Downtown Station, 1112 18th St; Wildcat Station, 2901 W Parker Rd; Plano Station, 1200 Jupiter Rd; Coit Station, 3400 Coit Rd; Northwest Plano Station, 3905 Hedgcoxe Rd
Police Department: Plano Police Department, www.planopolice.org, 909 14th St, 972-941-2135
Emergency Hospitals: Medical Center of Plano, www.medicalcenterofplano.com, 3901 W 15th St, 972-596-6800; Presbyterian Hospital of Plano, www.presbyplano.org, 6200 W Parker Rd, 972-981-8000
Libraries: Plano Library, www.planolibrary.org: Gladys Harrington Branch, 1501 18th St, 972-941-7175; L.E.R. Schimelpfenig Branch, 5024 Custer Rd, 972-769-4200; W.O. Haggard, Jr. Branch, 2501 Coit Rd, 972-769-4250; Maribelle M. Davis Branch, 7501-B Independence Pkwy, 972-208-8000; Christopher A. Parr Branch, 6200 Windhaven Pkwy, 972-769-4300
Adult Education: Collin County Community College, www.ccccd.edu: Courtyard Center Campus, 4800 Preston Park Blvd, 972-985-3790
Public Education: Plano Independent School District, www.pisd.edu, 2700 W 15th St, Plano, 469-752-8100

Community Publications: *Plano Daily Star Courier, Plano Morning News Collin County Edition, Inside Collin County Business, Plano Profile*

Community Resources: City Hall, 1520 Ave K, 972-941-7000; Plano Chamber of Commerce, www.planocc.org, 1200 E 15th St, 972-424-7547; Plano Homeowners Council, www.planohomeowner.org

Public Transportation: Dallas Area Rapid Transit, www.dart.org, 214-979-1111; *Light Rail: Red Line:* Bush Tpke Station, Richardson Station, Downtown Plano Station, Plano Station, Parker Rd Station; *Bus:* 210, 316, 350, 451, 564, 760, 360, 564, 566, 234, 410, 570

FRISCO

Lying mostly within Collin County, at the Denton County line, Frisco is one of the fastest growing suburbs in the Dallas area. Between 2000 and 2004, Frisco doubled in size from over 30,000 residents to more than 70,000. A major reason for its tremendous growth is its location near the fast growing suburb of Plano. Just across from southern Frisco near the Plano border are several corporate headquarters, which serve as major employers for both suburbs. Frisco has attracted several retailers and businesses, such as IKEA, along with its residential growth. The population is young upper-middle-income families in their early 30s who seek a safe, quiet, and affordable place to live. The average Frisco home costs about $240,000. At the high end of the housing market are exclusive gated communities like Stonebriar Park in west Frisco. The development features elegant European-style designs ranging from $550,000 to the millions.

Frisco is named after the St. Louis–San Francisco Railway, which led to the development of the town. This suburb about 30 miles north of Dallas has grown greatly, from a town of 2000, in the last 25 years. It is an example of the many exurbs in the Dallas area. One of the things that distinguishes Frisco from the other exurbs is the array of sporting options available. It is home to a minor league baseball team and a professional soccer team. The Dallas Stars of the National Hockey League practice here and it is the future home of an indoor football team. Most unique are the Superdrome, a large velodrome, and the Canyons, an indoor climbing facility for all ages. In addition, there are facilities nearby for golfing, hiking, walking, and fishing.

Web Site: www.ci.frisco.tx.us

Area Codes: 972, 469

Zip Codes: 75034, 75035

Post Office: Frisco Station, 8700 Stonebrook Pkwy, Frisco

Police Departments: Frisco Police Department: Police Administration, 8750 McKinney Rd, #500, 972-335-5502; Criminal Investigation and Community Services, 8680 Main St, Ste 50341E, 972-335-5603

Emergency Hospitals: Presbyterian Hospital of Plano, www.presbyplano.org, 6200 W Parker Rd, Plano, 972-981-8000; Presbyterian Hospital of Allen, www.texashealth.org, 1105 Central Expy, Allen, 972-747-1000

Library: Frisco Public Library, www.friscolibrary.com, 8750 McKinney Rd, Ste #200, 972-335-5510

Adult Education: Collin County Community College – Preston Ridge Campus, www.cccd.edu, 9700 Wade Blvd, Frisco, 972-377-1790

Public Education: Frisco Independent School District, www.friscoisd.org, 6942 Maple St, 469-633-6000

Community Publications: *Frisco Enterprise*; *Frisco Style Magazine*, www.friscostyle.com

Community Resources: Frisco City Hall, 6891 Main St, 972-335-5555; Frisco Chamber of Commerce, www.friscochamber.com, 6843 Main St, 972-335-9522; EDS Superdrome, www.superdrome.com, 9700 Wade Blvd, 972-731-1100

MCKINNEY/FAIRVIEW/ALLEN

McKinney is the most northern suburb of Dallas. Its development is mostly due to the growth of the surrounding suburbs of Dallas. Unlike some of the suburbs farther south, McKinney still has a rural, small town feel. Surrounded by beautiful natural landscape and historical buildings, it has a charming atmosphere. McKinney is also a popular weekend getaway for residents of the Metroplex who want to relax at a bed and breakfast, play golf, or just visit a historic town. Its historic downtown is popular for shopping, dining, and entertainment.

The town has many charming historic Victorian homes that can vary from $95,000 to almost $1 million. The typical McKinney home usually costs between $140,000 and $525,000. There are single-family homes, condos, new construction, Victorian homes, golf course communities, luxury homes, farmland, horse property, and historic homes.

Fairview is a hidden find located between Frisco and McKinney. This is a charming small town committed to a high quality of life within a quiet, country setting. Its motto is "Keeping it Country," and it certainly has been successful in promoting that ambience. There are numerous horse farms in the area with rolling hills, meandering creeks, and wooded areas. However, some parts feel more like an exclusive neighborhood for middle-aged, affluent people than one of the numerous family-oriented suburbs in the Metroplex. In fact, some communities are restricted to adults only. Homes are typically large and on large lots. Fairview is a wealthy community, whose homes typically range from $200,000 to over a million dollars.

Allen is located between Plano and McKinney. Younger, more family-oriented, and less upscale than Fairview, it is another one of the rapidly growing northern Dallas residential communities. It attracts young to middle-aged professionals who work in the computer, technology, and communications industries in Plano, Richardson, and North Dallas.

Two other small communities to consider in this area are **Prosper** and **Parker,** where there has been a rash of recent new home construction.

Web Sites: www.mckinneytexas.org, www.fairviewtexas.org, www.cityofallen.org

Area Codes: 972, 469, 214

Zip Codes: 75070, 75069, 75002, 75013

Post Offices: McKinney Station, 550 N Central Expy, McKinney; Allen Station, 304 W Boyd Dr, Allen

Police Departments: McKinney Police Department, www.mckinneypolice.org, 130 S Chestnut St, McKinney, 972-547-7600; Fairview Police Department, 500 S State Hwy 5, Fairview, 972-562-0522; Allen Police Department, 205 W McDermott Dr, Allen, 214-509-4200

Emergency Hospitals: North Central Medical Center, www.ncentralmedical.com, 4500 Medical Center Dr, McKinney, 972-547-8000; Presbyterian Hospital of Allen, www.presbyallen.org, 1105 Central Expy, Allen, 972-747-1000

Libraries: McKinney Memorial Public Library, 101 E Hunt St, McKinney, 972-547-7323; Allen Public Library, 300 N Allen Dr, Allen, 972-727-0190

Adult Education: Collin County Community College – Central Park Campus, www.cccd.edu, 2200 W University Dr, McKinney, 972-548-6790; Collin County Community College at Allen, www.cccd.edu, 300 Rivercrest Blvd, Allen, 972-377-1060

Public Education: McKinney Independent School District, www.mckinneyisd.net, 1 Duvall St, McKinney, 469-742-4000 (serves McKinney and Fairview); Frisco Independent School District, www.friscoisd.org, 6942 Maple St, Frisco, 469-633-6000 (serves McKinney); Lovejoy Independent School District, www.lovejoyisd.net, 259 Country Club Rd, Allen, 972-562-5077 (serves Fairview); Allen Independent School District, www.allenisd.org, 601 E Main St, Allen, 972-727-0511 (serves Allen and Fairview)

Community Publications: *McKinney Courier-Gazette*, www.courier-gazette.com; *McKinney Messenger*, *Allen American*, www.allenamerican.com

Community Resources: McKinney Chamber of Commerce, www.mckinneytx.org, 1650 West Virginia St, #110, McKinney, 972-542-0163; McKinney City Hall, 222 N Tennessee, McKinney, 972-547-7000; Fairview Town Hall, 500 S State Hwy 5, McKinney, 972-562-0522; Allen City Hall, 305 Century Pkwy, Allen, 214-509-4100; Allen Chamber of Commerce, www.allenchamber.com, 210 W McDermott Dr, Allen, 972-727-5585

DENTON COUNTY

The Colony

In 1972, developers Jacobs & Fox Company envisioned an ideal city located far from Dallas. Since the growth and development of north Dallas, The Colony is no longer an isolated community removed from the troubles of the big city. Suburban sprawl has surrounded The Colony with Frisco to the east and Lewisville to the west. At times, this has led to problems, including a lawsuit with Frisco in the 1980s regarding annexation of land and boundary issues.

Because of its location by Lake Lewisville, The Colony is nicknamed the City by the Lake. It is ideally located along Texas State Highway 121, which connects to major employers in Plano such as JC Penney, Frito Lay, Dr. Pepper, and EDS. Additionally, it is only 15 miles from Dallas and a few minutes from the Dallas/Ft. Worth airport.

Lewisville

Lewisville is a Dallas–Ft. Worth suburb centrally located 26 miles from Dallas, 34 miles from Ft. Worth, and 10 miles from the Dallas/Ft. Worth airport. It straddles Dallas and Denton counties and is adjacent to The Colony. Located between two beautiful recreational lakes, Lake Lewisville and Lake Grapevine, it is also a popular vacation destination. Numerous outdoor activities such as golfing, boating, fishing, and other water sports are readily available on Lake Lewisville. Before the construction of IH-35, which runs through Lewisville, its population was less than 1000. With the completion of the freeway, the Dallas/Ft. Worth airport, and the economic development of north Dallas, Lewisville's popularity and population have increased to over 70,000 residents. Despite the growth, it still has a small town feel. The town's biggest employer is Xerox, but tourism is also a large industry. Lewisville offers an almost equal number of single-family residences and multi-family units. Homes range from $140,000 to $300,000.

Communities around Lewisville Lake and Lake Dallas, above Lewisville, include **Oak Point, Lakewood Village, Shady Shores, Corinth, Hickory Creek, Highland Village, Double Oak, Lake Dallas, Little Elm, Corinth, Copper Canyon, Copperas, and Hackberry.** The Lake Dallas and Lewisville area is somewhat far from Dallas, but it is a feasible option for those working in the northern suburbs.

Web Sites: www.cityoflewisville.com, www.ci.the-colony.tx.us/

Area Codes: 972, 469

Zip Codes: 75056, 75057, 75067, 75077

Post Offices: Old Town Finance Station, 320 S Charles St, Lewisville; Lewisville Station, 194 Civic Cir, Lewisville; The Colony Station, 5200 S Colony Blvd, The Colony

Police Departments: Lewisville Police Department, 184 N Valley Pkwy, Lewisville, 972-219-3600; The Colony Police Department, www.thecolonypd.org, 5151 N Colony Blvd, The Colony, 972-625-1887

Emergency Hospitals: Medical Center of Lewisville, www.lewisvillemedical.com, 500 W Main St, Lewisville, 972-420-1000; North Central Medical Center, www.ncentralmedical.com, 4500 Medical Center Dr, McKinney, 972-547-8000

Libraries: Lewisville Public Library, 1197 W Main, Lewisville, 972-219-3570; The Colony Public Library, 6800 Main St, The Colony, 972-625-1900

Public Education: Lewisville Independent School District, www.lisd.net, 1800 Timber Creek Rd, Flower Mound, 972-539-1551 (serves The Colony and Lewisville); Coppell Independent School District, www.coppellisd.com, 200 S Denton Tap Rd, Coppell, 214-496-6000 (serves small portions of Lewisville)

Community Publication: *Lewisville Leader*, www.lewisvilleleader.com

Community Resources: Lewisville City Hall, 151 W Church St, Lewisville, 972-219-3400; www.visitlewisville.com; Lewisville Area Chamber of Commerce, www.lewisville-chamber.org, 551 N Valley Pkwy, Lewisville, 972-436-9571; The Colony Town Hall, 6800 Main St, The Colony, 972-625-1756; The Colony Chamber of Commerce, www.thecolonychamber.com, 6900 Main St, The Colony, 972-625-4916

NORTHEAST SUBURBS

MURPHY/WYLIE/SACHSE

Located northeast of Dallas in Collin, Rockwall, and Dallas counties are three fast-growing suburbs that are gaining from the economic growth of their neighbors. All are former small rural towns that still have plenty of country charm. Bordering Richardson and Garland and Plano on its eastern border is the small town of **Murphy**, which covers only 3.8 square miles. Despite the development of several new subdivisions, Murphy is committed to preserving the rural atmosphere. Murphy homes range from $140,000 to $529,000. Immediately west of Murphy is the larger town of **Wylie**, located near Lake Lavon, a popular recreational lake. Wylie offers more affordable single-family residential housing starting as low as $70,000 to $400,000. However, the average home prices do not differ that much from the Murphy housing market. The most affordable housing, though, can be found in **Sachse**, where the average home price is $85,000. Homes at the higher range of the market cost about $200,000. Sachse is a quiet, friendly community, which is near the conveniences of Garland's Firewheel Center and golf course, Lake Lavon, and Lake Ray Hubbard.

Web Sites: www.murphytx.org, www.ci.wylie.tx.us, www.cityofsachse.com

Area Code: 972

Zip Codes: 75094, 75098, 75048

Post Office: Wylie Station, 940 W FM 544, Wylie

Police Departments: City of Murphy Police Department, 206 N Murphy Rd, Murphy, 972-468-4200; Wylie Police Department, 2000 Hwy 78 N, #300, Wylie, 972-442-8170; Sachse Police Department, 3815 Sachse Rd, Sachse, 972-495-2005

Emergency Hospital: Bariatric Care of Wylie, 801 S Hwy 78, Wylie, 972-429-8000

Libraries: Rita and Truett Smith Public Library, 800 Thomas St, Wylie, 972-442-7566; Sachse Public Library, 3815 Sachse Rd, Ste C, Sachse, 972-530-8966

Public Education: Wylie Independent School District, www.wylieisd.net, 951 S Ballard Ave, Wylie, 972-429-3000 (Murphy, Wylie, Sachse); Garland Independent School District, www.garlandisd.net, 720 Stadium Dr, Garland, 972-494-8201 (Sachse); Plano Independent School District, www.pisd.edu, 2700 W 15th St, Plano, 469-752-8100 (Murphy)

Community Publications: *The Wylie News*; *Murphy Messenger*, www.murphymessenger.com; *Murphy Monitor*, www.murphymonitor.com

Community Resources: Murphy City Hall, 206 N Murphy Rd, Murphy, 972-468-4000; Murphy Chamber of Commerce, www.murphychamber.org, P.O. Box 941864, Murphy, 75094, 972-384-1002; Wylie City Hall, 2000 Hwy 78 N, Wylie, 972-442-8100; Wylie Chamber of Commerce, www.wyliechamber.org, 108A W Marble, Wylie, 972-442-2804; Sachse City Hall, 5560 Hwy 78, Sachse, 972-495-1212; Sachse Chamber of Commerce, www.sachsechamber.com, 5941 Hwy 78, Sachse, 972-496-1212

SOUTHWESTERN SUBURBS

DUNCANVILLE/DESOTO/CEDAR HILL/LANCASTER

The four cities that make up Dallas's southwestern suburbs share a similar topography, economic base, and demographics. They are located among southwestern Dallas County's gently rolling hills and woods, which provide a scenic and relaxing atmosphere. These suburbs have attracted a significant middle-class African-American population, many of whom left South Dallas many years ago for employment, better public schools, and the safer environment of the suburbs. Because of their location near major interstates and airports, these suburban cities have attracted manufacturers and distribution companies who are among the towns' major, if not primary, employers.

Duncanville calls itself the City of Champions because its high school sports teams have won many state championships. It is a family-oriented community that offers many housing options. On the high end, there are recently constructed custom homes and large million-dollar country estates. There are also plenty of more affordable homes in the mid-$100 thousand range in quiet neighborhoods for those seeking something less extravagant. Buyers seeking more cosmopolitan surroundings should consider Main Station, where residential lofts are located above retail stores. This mixed-use development is part of the new urbanism concept that is a popular nationwide trend and has already spread to northern Dallas suburbs. In addition, the city has a new townhouse project that is underway. For the more mature population, a new, gated, senior living community is expected to be ready in 2008. Located along I-20, Duncanville residents and businesses have convenient access to Dallas and parts beyond. This is one of the reasons why so many manufacturing and distribution parks are located here. The Duncanville Industrial Park houses approximately 80 companies that employ over 2000 people. Near the city limits is Redbird Industrial Park, which employs over 30,000 people.

Next door to Duncanville and also bordering I-20 is **DeSoto**. It is surrounded by the natural beauty of the hills, trees, and creeks. The city has a friendly, small town atmosphere that is accentuated by its low crime rate. The city's new Town Center helps promote the small town feel and community ties. Built in the 1990s on a former strip center, it serves as a town anchor for community gatherings and recreational activities. It includes City Hall, a recreation center, the public library, a civic center, an outdoor amphitheater, a conference center, a theater, the chamber of commerce, and a visitor information center. The average home price here is similar to those in Duncanville. The wooded areas feature more expensive homes. Also like Duncanville, DeSoto has industrial parks, such as Eagle Business and Industrial Park, which house several manufacturing companies and distribution centers.

Named for the miles of cedar trees that cover its hills, **Cedar Hill** has a quiet country charm. Instead of a mall, it has a historic district that provides plenty of shopping options. A new pedestrian retail center modeled as a lifestyle center will open in 2008. Cedar Hill sits on some of the highest hills in all of the southwestern suburbs, which provide parts of the city a view of the open spaces and hills below. Cedar Hill also overlooks Joe Pool Lake, a sparkling recreational lake popular for boating, fishing, sailing, and other water sports. The city's average home prices are lower than in Duncanville and DeSoto. Like all the other southwestern suburbs, Cedar Hill has an industrial park, known as Cedar Hill Business Park.

The least populated and least developed suburb, **Lancaster** offers views of hills, open fields, creeks, and the woods. It is a family-oriented community that has an even more small town, country setting than Cedar Hill. The heart of this community is the Lancaster Town Square. It contains charming streetfront, one-of-a-kind retail shops. Lancaster has a collection of lovely Victorian, Queen Anne, and prairie-style historic homes near its historic district. These homes, combined with its historic town square, provide some old-time nostalgia. The average Lancaster home costs somewhere between the price of homes in Duncanville/DeSoto and the Cedar Hill homebuying price range.

Web Sites: www.ci.duncanville.tx.us, www.ci.desoto.tx.us, www.cedarhilltxgov.org, www.ci.lancaster.tx.us

Area Codes: 214, 972, 469

Zip Codes: 75104, 75115, 75116, 75134, 75137, 75138, 75146

Post Offices: Duncanville Station, 711 S Cedar Ridge Dr, Duncanville; DeSoto Station, 229 S Hampton, DeSoto; Cedar Hill Station, 475 E FM 1382, Cedar Hill; Lancaster Station, 200 N State St, Lancaster

Police Departments: Duncanville Police Department, 203 E Wheatland Rd, Duncanville, 972-780-5038; DeSoto Police Department, 714 E Belt Line Rd, DeSoto, 469-658-3000; Cedar Hill Police Department, 601 E Belt Line Rd, Cedar Hill, 972-230-5053; Lancaster Police Department, 1501 N Dallas Ave, Lancaster, 972-227-4006

Emergency Hospitals: Margaret Jonsson Charlton Methodist Hospital, 3500 W Wheatland Rd, Dallas; Select Specialty Hospital, 800 Kirnwood Dr, DeSoto, 972-780-6500

Libraries: Duncanville Public Library, www.youseemore.com/duncanville, 201 James Collins Blvd, Duncanville, 972-780-5051; DeSoto Public Library, www.desotolibrary. info, 211 E Pleasant Run Rd, DeSoto, 972-230-9656; Zula Bryant Wylie Library, 225 Cedar St, Cedar Hill, 972-291-7323; Lancaster Veterans Memorial Library, www.lancastertxlib.org, 1600 Veterans Memorial Pkwy, Lancaster, 972-227-1080

Adult Education: Cedar Valley College (Dallas Community College), www.dcccd.edu, 3030 N Dallas Ave, Lancaster, 972-860-8201

Public Education: Dallas Independent School District, www.dallasisd.org, 3700 Ross Ave, Dallas, 972-925-3700 (serves small portions of Duncanville); Duncanville Independent School District, www.duncanvilleisd.org, 802 S Main St, Duncanville, 972-708-2000; DeSoto Independent School District, www.desotoisd.org, 200 E Belt Line Rd, DeSoto, 972-223-6666; Cedar Hill School District, www.chisd.com, 270 S Hwy 67, Cedar Hill, 972-291-1581; Lancaster Independent School District, www.

lancasterisd.org, 422 S Centre Ave, Lancaster, 972-218-1400; Wilmer Hutchins Independent School District, http://wilmerhutchins.ednet10.net, 3820 E Illinois Ave, Dallas, 214-376-7311 (serves small northeast portion of Lancaster)

Community Publications: *DeSoto Today, Duncanville Today, Cedar Hill Today, Lancaster Today,* www.todaynewspapers.net; *Focus Daily News,* www.focus-news. com (DeSoto); *Lancaster News*

Community Resources: Duncanville City Hall, 203 E Wheatland, Duncanville, 972-780-5017; Duncanville Chamber of Commerce, www.duncanvillechamber.org, 300 E Wheatland Rd, Duncanville, 972-780-4990; DeSoto City Hall, 211 E Pleasant Run Rd, DeSoto, 972-274-2489; DeSoto Chamber of Commerce, www.desotochamber. org, 205 E Pleasant Run Rd, DeSoto, 972-224-3565; Cedar Hill City Hall, 502 Cedar St, Cedar Hill, 972-291-5100; Cedar Hill Chamber of Commerce, www. cedarhillchamber.org, 300 W Houston, Cedar Hill, 972-291-7817; Lancaster Chamber of Commerce, www.lancastertx.org, 100 N Dallas Ave, Lancaster, 972-227-2579; Lancaster Town Square, www.lancastertownsquare.com, Hwy 342 (Dallas Ave) at Main, Lancaster; Leadership Southwest, www.leadershipsw.com

GLENN HEIGHTS

This incorporated community is located south of DeSoto and surrounded by rural land. It is a residential community of Dallas that is perfect for those seeking a quiet and relaxed pace of life. With half of the town's land undeveloped, new home construction is ongoing in this community. There are plenty of outdoor activities in the surrounding areas, such as hunting, fishing, and camping.

Web Site: www.glennheights.com
Area Codes: 214, 972, 469
Zip Code: 75154
Post Office: Red Oak Station: 104 E Ovilla Rd, Red Oak
Police Department: Glenn Heights Police Department, 1938 S Hampton, Glenn Heights, 972-223-1690 Ext. 207
Emergency Hospitals: Select Specialty Hospital, 800 Kirkwood, DeSoto, 972-780-6500; The Cedars Hospital, 2000 N Old Hickory Trail, De Soto, 972-298-7323
Public Education: DeSoto Independent School District, www.desotoisd.org, 200 E Belt Line Rd, DeSoto, 972-223-6666
Community Resources: Glenn Heights City Hall, 1938 S Hampton, Glenn Heights, 972-223-1690; Glenn Heights Chamber of Commerce, www.inglenheights.com, 139 W Ovilla Rd, Glenn Heights, 972-223-5509
Public Transportation: Dallas Area Rapid Transit, www.dart.org; *Bus:* 206

MID-CITIES

The Mid-Cities refer to the cities and towns between Dallas and Ft. Worth that surround the Dallas/Ft. Worth airport. They include Irving, Grand Prairie, Arlington, Coppell, Hurst, Euless, Bedford, Flower Mound, Grapevine, Colleyville, Dalworthington Gardens, Pantego, and Southlake, which cover the four miles between Dallas and Ft. Worth. Four of the Mid-Cities, Irving, Grand Prairie, Arlington, and Grapevine, are sizable cities and are among the largest in Texas. Grapevine, Colleyville, Flower Mound, Southlake, and Hurst-Euless-Bedford are also Ft. Worth suburbs. The Mid-Cities' central location provides their residents easy access to jobs, entertainment, and other amenities in Dallas and Ft. Worth, as well as the convenience of the nation's second largest airport. Since the construction of the airport and major freeways, all of the Mid-Cities have experienced great growth. People choose the Mid-Cities for the same reasons that other suburbs in the Metroplex are popular: they provide affordable housing, a safe environment to raise a family, and quality school districts.

IRVING

Sandwiched between Dallas and the airport, Irving has it all. Not only is it next door to a major city and the nation's second largest airport, it is also home to a movie studio, an equestrian center, numerous golf courses, several Fortune 500 companies, fine arts, and of course, affordable housing for young families. Irving is not just a mere suburb of Dallas, but a notable Texas city.

North of West Airport Road (Hwy 183) are the affluent communities of Las Colinas and Valley Ranch. Twenty-five years ago, **Las Colinas** was a private ranch dotted by mesquite trees called Hackberry Creek Ranch, also known as El Ranchito de Las Colinas, Spanish for "Ranch of the Hills," from which Las Colinas got its name. The owner, Ben H. Carpenter, developed his ranch with the vision of creating a quality community of homes, businesses, and a town square. Inside Las Colinas is a wealthy corporate community that also serves as Irving's main entertainment and business centers, which are located in the Urban Center. It includes Williams Square Plaza and the famed Mustangs of Las Colinas, the world's largest equestrian sculpture. Capturing the free spirit of life-size mustangs stampeding across a fountain, designed as a running stream on recreated prairie land, the sculpture pays tribute to the area's heritage. Nearby is Mandalay Canal Walk, a cobblestone walkway with shops and restaurants fronting the waterway. Red tile roof and beige buildings provide a European-style village ambience. This relaxing atmosphere is a contrast to the corporate buildings that are located in the Urban Center. The global headquarters of ExxonMobil, Kimberly-Clark, and Fluor, as well as the offices of several other Fortune 500 companies, are here as major employers. Another major, but unconventional, employer is the Las Colinas movie studio. The neighborhoods are surrounded by many nice golf courses, perfect for making those business deals. With its own ballet, symphony orchestra, equestrian center, and polo club, Las Colinas is more like a city or suburb within Irving than a neighborhood.

To the north, past the LBJ Freeway (I-635), is the wealthy community of **Valley Ranch**. It is best known as the headquarters of the Dallas

Cowboys. Below West Airport Road (Hwy 183) is **South Irving**, where the majority of the residential neighborhoods are located.

Web Site: www.ci.irving.tx.us

Area Codes: 972, 214

Zip Codes: 75038, 75039, 75060, 75061, 75062, 75063

Post Offices: Carl Range Station, 2400 W Northgate Dr, Irving; Central Irving Station, 2300 Story Rd W, Irving; Irving Station, 2701 W Irving Blvd, Irving; Las Colinas Station, 3900 Teleport Blvd, Irving; Downtown Irving Station, 125 W 3rd St, Irving

Police Department: Irving Police Department, www.irvingpd.net: South Station, 305 N O'Connor Rd, Irving, 972-721-2518; North Station: 5992 Riverside Blvd, Irving, 972-721-7803

Emergency Hospitals: Baylor Medical Center at Irving, www.baylorhealth.com, 1901 N MacArthur Blvd, Irving, 972-579-8100; Las Colinas Medical Center, www.lascolinasmedical.com, 6800 N MacArthur Blvd, Irving, 972-969-2000

Adult Education: Northlake College (Dallas Community College), www.northlakecollege.edu, 5001 N MacArthur Blvd, Irving, 972-273-3000; University of Dallas (private Catholic University), www.udallas.edu, 1845 E Northgate Dr, Irving, 972-721-5000

Public Education: Irving Independent School District, www.irvingisd.net, 2621 W Airport Fwy, Irving, 972-215-5000; Dallas Independent School District, www.dallasisd.org, 3700 Ross Ave, Dallas, 972-925-3700; Carrollton-Farmers Branch Independent School District, www.cfbisd.edu, 1445 N Perry Rd, Carrollton, 972-968-6100

Community Publication: *Irving News*

Community Resources: Greater Irving Las Colinas Chamber of Commerce, www.irvingchamber.com, 5221 N O'Connor Blvd, Ste 100, Irving, 214-217-8484; Las Colinas Association, www.lascolinasassn.com, 122 W John Carpenter Fwy, Ste 550, Irving, 972-541-2345

Public Transportation: Dallas Area Rapid Transit, www.dart.org, *Bus*: North Irving: 202, 234, 301, 302, 303, 305, 310, 314, 400, 428, 438, 507; South Irving: Trinity Railway Express (TRE), 301, 302, 303, 304, 305, 306, 309, 314, 404, 408, 438, 507; West Irving: Trinity Railway Express (TRE), 305, 311, 314; *Commuter Rail:* Trinity Railway Express, www.trinityrailwayexpress.org, South Irving and West Irving Station

GRAND PRAIRIE

On any given summer day, Grand Prairie residents can see brightly colored sails on the horizon bobbing on Joe Lake Pool, while families picnic nearby. That is just one snapshot of life in this friendly, family-oriented suburb of Ft. Worth. It has a diverse population (47% white, 33% Hispanic; 13.5% African-American) similar to Irving's demographics. Most residents are couples in their early 30s with children. One of the major employers here is Lockheed Martin. Homes here range from $80,000 to $300,000, with the average house costing $130,000. Along with established single-family residences, apartments, and condos, there is also a considerable amount of new home construction in Grand Prairie.

Web Site: www.gptx.org

Area Code: 972

Zip Codes: 75050, 75051, 75052

Post Offices: Grand Prairie Station, 802 S Carrier Pkwy, Grand Prairie; Fountain Station, 505 Fountain Pkwy, Grand Prairie; Westchester Station, 765 W Westchester Pkwy, Grand Prairie

Police Department: Grand Prairie Police Department, www.grandprairiepolice.org, 801 Conover, Grand Prairie, 972-237-8790; Northeast Storefront: 169 Grand Central Shopping Center, Grand Prairie; Southwest Storefront: 617 Royal, Grand Prairie

Emergency Hospital: Kindred Hospital–Tarrant County (Arlington Campus), 1000 N Cooper, Arlington, 817-548-3400

Libraries: Grand Prairie Public Library: Main Branch, 901 Conover, Grand Prairie, 972-237-5700; Betty Warmack Branch, 760 Bardin Rd, Grand Prairie, 972-237-5770

Public Education: Grand Prairie Independent School District, www.gpisd.org, 2602 S Belt Line Rd, Grand Prairie, 972-264-6141

Community Publication: *Grand Prairie Times*, www.grandprairietimes.com

Community Resources: City Hall, 317 College St, Grand Prairie, 972-237-8000; Grand Prairie Chamber of Commerce, www.grandprairiechamber.org, 900 Conover, Grand Prairie, 972-264-1558

Public Transportation: Grand Prairie Transit (curbside service for elderly and disabled only)

TARRANT COUNTY

ARLINGTON

With over 300,000 residents, Arlington is the largest Mid-City. It is located 12 miles east of Ft. Worth and 20 miles west of Dallas. The area was settled by Comanche Indians who named it Marrow Bone Springs because of the large number of prehistoric animal bones found here. Prior to its founding in 1876 as a market town for farmers' produce, the area was farmland that was good for growing fruits and vegetables. It was originally named Johnson Station, but was later named Arlington in honor of General Robert E. Lee's home in Virginia. Arlington offers a variety of housing options, including single-family homes, apartments, condos, townhomes, new construction, lakefront homes, golf course communities, luxury homes, and retirement communities. The city is ideal for young families who are looking for an affordable home under $200,000. Homes generally range from $125,000 to $400,000. However, some can be found for as low as $90,000—and for as high as over a million. Buildings around the University of Texas at Arlington campus are among the city's oldest. The university enrolls 20,000 students and contributes significantly to the city's economy. Tourism is also a major employer and a big industry in Arlington, which markets itself as Fun Central—a place for safe, clean family fun. Attractions include Six Flags over Texas Amusement Park, Hurricane Harbor Water Park, Texas Rangers baseball stadium, a giant skate park, and Lone Star horse racing track. In 2006, the Dallas Cowboys will move from Irving to their new stadium in Arlington. One major drawback for Arlington is that for a city of its size, it has no public transportation.

Web Site: www.ci.arlington.tx.us
Area Code: 817
Zip Codes: 76001, 76002, 76006, 76010, 76011, 76012, 76013, 76014, 76015, 76016, 76017, 76018
Post Offices: Melear Station, 3903 Melear Dr, Arlington; Arlington Station, 300 E South St, Arlington; East Arlington Station, 1828 E Park Row Dr, Ste B, Arlington; Bardin Road Station, 1301 E Bardin Rd, Arlington; Oakwood Station, 1009 Oakwood, Arlington; Tate Springs Station, 4108 SW Green Oaks Blvd, Arlington; Great Southwest Station, 711 106th St, Arlington; Watson Community Station, 1975 Ball Pkwy, Arlington
Police Department: Arlington Police Department, www.arlingtonpd.org: North District, 620 W Division St, Arlington, 817-459-5600; East District, 2001 New York Ave, Arlington, 817-459-5803; West Police District, 2060 W Green Oaks Blvd, Arlington, 817-459-6040
Emergency Hospitals: Arlington Memorial Hospital, www.texashealth.org, 800 W Randol Mill Rd, Arlington, 817-548-6100; Medical Center of Arlington, www.medicalcenterarlington.com, 3301 Matlock, Arlington, 817-422-4850
Libraries: George W. Hawkes Central Library, 101 E Abram St, Arlington, 817-459-6900; East Arlington Branch, 1624 New York Ave, Arlington, 817-275-3321; Lake Arlington Branch, 4000 West Green Oaks Blvd, Arlington, 817-478-3762; Northeast Branch Library, 1905 Brown Blvd, Arlington, 817-277-5573; Southeast Branch Library, 900 SE Green Oaks Blvd, Arlington, 817-459-6395; Woodland West Branch Library, 2837 W Park Row Dr, Arlington, 817-277-5265
Adult Education: University of Texas at Arlington, www.uta.edu, 701 S Nedderman Dr, Arlington, 817-272-2011; Tarrant County College – Southeast Campus, www.tccd.edu, 2100 Southeast Pkwy, Arlington, 817-515-3100; Arlington Baptist College, www.abconline.edu, 3001 W Division, Arlington, 817-461-8741
Public Education: Arlington Independent School District, www.arlington.k12.tx.us, 1203 Pioneer Pkwy, Arlington, 817-460-4611; Kennedale Independent School District, www.kennedale.net, 120 W Kennedale Pkwy, Kennedale, 817-483-3600 (serves small portions of Arlington); Mansfield Independent School District, www.mansfieldisd.org, 605 E Broad St, Mansfield, 817-473-5600 (serves small portions of Arlington)
Community Publication: *Arlington Morning News*
Community Resources: City Hall, 101 W Abram, Arlington, 817-459-6100; Arlington Chamber of Commerce, www.arlingtontx.com, 505 E Border, Arlington, 817-275-2613

DALWORTHINGTON GARDENS AND PANTEGO

Arlington completely surrounds two other independent cities: Dalworthington Gardens and Pantego. **Dalworthington Gardens** was established during the Great Depression as part of a federal government scheme to help families improve their living standard. Located near the major industrial cities of the Metroplex, it was intended to provide residents both part-time industrial employment and a place to grow vegetables and raise animals to supplement their income. The city's name is derived from a combination of the major cities that surrounds it: "Dal" from Dallas, "wor" from Ft. Worth, and "ington" from Arlington. This tiny community covers only 1.8 square miles and has a population of over 2,000. Today, it is an affluent community whose average population is older than Arlington's. The average home value in Dalworthington Gardens is more than in Arlington ($213,900 v. $96,400). Immediately north of Dalworthington is a city similar to it known as **Pantego**. Covering approximately two square miles, it also is an affluent community with similar median house value and average age. Pantego is primarily a residential community and has a history that goes back to the 19th century.

Web Sites: www.cityofdwg.net , www.townofpantego.com
Area Code: 817
Zip Codes: 76013, 76016
Post Offices: Pantego Station, 1114 S Bowen Rd, Pantego; Tate Springs Branch: 4108 SW Green Oaks, Arlington; Melear Station, 3903 Melear, Arlington
Police Departments: Dalworthington Gardens Department of Public Safety, 2600 Roosevelt Dr, Arlington, 817-275-1234; Pantego Police Department, www.pantegopolice.org, 2600 Miller Ln, Pantego, 817-274-2511
Emergency Hospitals: Arlington Memorial Hospital, www.texashealth.org, 800 W Randol Mill Rd, Arlington, 817-548-6100; Medical Center of Arlington, www.medicalcenterarlington.com, 3301 Matlock, Arlington, 817-422-4850
Library: Arlington Public Library System: Woodland West Branch, 2837 W Park Row Dr, Arlington, 817-277-5265
Public Education: Arlington Independent School District, www.arlington.k12.tx.us, 1203 Pioneer Pkwy, Arlington, 817-460-4611
Community Publications: *Arlington Morning News*; *Dallas Morning News*, www.dallasnews.com
Community Resources: Dalworthington Gardens City Hall, 2600 Roosevelt Dr, Arlington, 817-274-7368; Pantego City Hall, 1614 S Bowen Rd, Pantego, 817-274-1381

HURST, EULESS, AND BEDFORD (HEB)

Hurst, Euless, and Bedford are three small towns adjacent to each other that are collectively known as HEB. These are quiet suburbs with a slow pace of life. Compared to the surrounding suburbs, there are few major local attractions here. However, it is only a quick drive to nearby attractions in Irving, Arlington, and Ft. Worth. In addition, Dallas is only a 30-minute train ride away.

Hurst is more of a small town than a suburb of Ft. Worth. It is one of the newer suburbs and consists mostly of new home construction that varies in price and size. Bell Helicopter is the town's major employer, which has attracted residents here and significantly increased Hurst's population. The median home value here is $98,000, which is similar to Euless's median home value of $95,000. In 1999, the city set aside land at Airport Freeway and Precinct Line Road for the Hurst Town Center. The town center is a mixed-use development intended as the city's center. It creates a pedestrian-friendly urban atmosphere that combines office, retail, and residential use.

Euless borders the Dallas/Ft. Worth airport on the east. Part of the airport is within Euless city limits. The airport is a big employer and the main reason why Euless has a significant Tongan population. During the 1970s, many Tongans left their Polynesian island in the South Pacific for well-paying construction jobs at the airport. Others were recruited by airlines such as American Airlines, who offered Tongans cheap or free airfare to Tonga as employment incentives. The locals have embraced and incorporated Tongan culture with a popular small town Texas activity. Before each high school football game, the players perform a traditional Maori dance called a haka. The biggest event in Euless is Arbor Daze, its annual Arbor Day celebration, which is reportedly the largest in the world. Some estimate that it attracts over 100,000 people annually. Thus, Euless has earned the moniker Tree City, USA.

Next door to Euless is the quiet residential community of **Bedford**. The average home here costs about $116,000. Other great values can be found in Bedford, including starter homes in the $80,000 range. Those seeking something more can find beautiful custom built homes from $225,000 to $500,000. Many of the homes here were constructed in the 1990s, though new construction is still continuing. Bedford has a recreational water park (Bedford Splash) for kids and families to enjoy.

Web Sites: www.ci.hurst.tx.us, www.ci.bedford.tx.us, www.ci.euless.tx.us

Area Code: 817

Zip Codes: 76021, 76022, 76039, 76040, 76053, 76054,

Post Offices: Hurst Station, 825 Precinct Ln, Hurst; North Hurst Station, 777 Cannon Dr, Hurst; Euless Station, 216 N Ector Dr, Euless; Central Bedford Station, 2124 Don Dodson Dr, Bedford; Bedford Station, 1300 Harwood Rd, Bedford

Police Departments: Hurst Police Department, 1501 Precinct Ln, Hurst; Euless Police Department, 1102 W Euless Blvd (Hwy 10), Euless, 817-685-1500; Bedford Police Department, 2121 L. Don Dodson Dr, Bedford, 817-952-2400

Emergency Hospitals: Harris Methodist HEB, www.texashealth.org, 1600 Hospital Pkwy, Bedford, 817-685-4000; North Hills Hospital, www.northhillshospital.com, 4401 Booth Calloway Rd, North Richland Hills, 817-255-1000

Libraries: Hurst Public Library, 901 Precinct Line Rd, Hurst, 817-788-7300; Euless Public Library, 201 N Ector Dr, Euless, 817-685-1480; Bedford Public Library, 1805 L. Don Dodson Dr, Bedford, 817-952-2335

Adult Education: Le Tourneau University, 4001 Airport Fwy, Ste 100, Bedford, 817-540-4111

Public Education: Hurst-Euless-Bedford Independent School District, www.hebisd.edu, 1849 Central, Bedford, 817-283-4461

Community Resources: Hurst City Hall, 1505 Precinct Line, Hurst, 817-788-7207; Euless City Hall, 201 N Ector Dr, Euless, 817-685-1420; Simmons Senior Center, 508 Simmons Dr, J.A. Carr Park, Euless, 817-685-1670; Bedford City Hall, 2000 Forest Ridge, Bedford, 817-952-2100; Bedford/Hurst Senior Center, 2819 R.D. Hurt Pkwy, Bedford, 817-952-2325; Hurst-Euless-Bedford (HEB) Chamber of Commerce, www.heb.org, 2109 Martin Dr, Bedford, 817-283-1521

Public Transportation: Trinity Railway Express (commuter rail), www.trinityrailwayexpress.org: Hurst/Bell Station

FLOWER MOUND

When settlers first arrived in the 1840s, flowers covered the 12½ acre mound that rose 50 feet high from the surrounding flat prairie land. The mound may have been a sacred ceremonial site used by Indians. Today, all that remains is a small area protected from private development which has taken over most of the mound. A black gate surrounds the privately owned mound, which is located at the southern part of town next to a grocery store and other commercial development.

Despite its growth, Flower Mound still has a friendly, small town atmosphere, which it strives hard to preserve. To ensure that development does not run amok, the town carefully monitors new construction and development proposals for compliance with zoning regulations. The design of some of the neighborhoods contributes to the small town atmosphere. Many homes are on vast lots and well spaced apart. Most homes have their own individual look—charming Victorians, Georgian, Mediterranean, and contemporary brick-style homes. There are some large fancy homes that would cost millions in Dallas, but cost considerably less here because of the low land prices. Flower Mound offers primarily single-family residential homes, some of which may be within a golf course community or in a luxury home neighborhood. For those who dream of having their own horse in their backyard or going for a ride in the morning, then Flower Mound may be the perfect town. There are plenty of horse farms in the area. Some houses are on a big spread of land, allowing room for a stable to be attached to the property. The average home here is $215,000, while prices range from $130,000 to $1,000,000 plus.

Located between Lake Grapevine and Lake Lewisville, part of Flower Mound is in Denton County. Large parts of the town are still undeveloped and several creeks flow through it. Some parts of town look rural and picturesque with horses grazing behind white fences on farms next to residential neighborhoods. In the western and southern part of Flower Mound, gentle hills and thickly wooded terrain provide the scenic landscape that gives the town its distinctive appeal.

Web Site: www.flower-mound.com
Area Code: 972
Zip Codes: 75022, 75028
Post Office: Flower Mound Station, 2300 Olympia Dr, Flower Mound
Police Department: Flower Mound Police Department, 4150 Kirkpatrick, Flower Mound, 972-539-0525
Emergency Hospitals: Baylor Regional Medical Center at Grapevine, www.baylorhealth.com, 1650 W College, Grapevine, 817-481-1588; Medical Center at Lewisville, lewisvillemedical.com, 500 W Main St, Lewisville, 972-420-1000
Library: Flower Mound Public Library, 3030 Broadmoor Ln, Flower Mound, 972-874-6200
Public Education: Lewisville Independent School District, www.lisd.net, 1800 Timber Creek Rd, Lewisville, 972-539-1551; Denton Independent School District, www.

dentonisd.org, 1359 N Locust, Denton, 940-369-0000 (serves western portions of Flower Mound); Northwest Independent School District, www.northwest.k12.tx.us, 2001 Texan Dr, Justin, 817-215-0000 (serves western portions of Flower Mound)
Community Publication: *Flower Mound Leader*
Community Resources: City Hall, 2121 Cross Timbers, Flower Mound, 972-874-6000; Flower Mound Chamber of Commerce, www.flowermoundchamber.com, 700 Parker Sq, Ste 100, Flower Mound, 972-539-0500

GRAPEVINE

Grapevine is named for the wild Mustang grapes that were abundant when the area was rural and undeveloped. Locals refer to the town and its surrounding area as the GVC (Grapevine-Colleyville). There are many vineyards in Grapevine, most of them established in the early 1990s, which the city heartily promotes with wine festivals, tours, and other celebrations. Located on the southern shores of Lake Grapevine, 21 miles northwest of Dallas and 19 miles northeast of Ft. Worth, it is the oldest settlement in Tarrant County. The city is proud of its heritage and is active in preserving the historic downtown area, which is listed on the National Register of Historic Places. The efforts have created a unique small town atmosphere. Not just a mere Ft. Worth suburb, Grapevine is a town with distinctive character and charm. Traveling to Ft. Worth is not necessary because there are many intown attractions, such as Lake Grapevine, an artificial reservoir created by the Army Corps of Engineers. It offers several parks and many outdoor recreational activities. Since the 1990s, there has been considerable residential development on the lakefront. For those who do desire to go to Ft. Worth, the city has a steam excursion train—the Tarantula Train—that operates between the two cities with stops at Lake Grapevine, the Community Activities Center, the Senior Activities Center, and Dove and Pleasant Glade Swimming Pools. However, like many of the surrounding suburbs, the main reason families move here is because it is a nice, safe place to raise children. Grapevine also has a highly regarded public school system. Like Flower Mound, this is an upper-middle-class community with houses in the same price range.

Web Site: www.ci.grapevine.tx.us
Area Code: 817
Zip Code: 76051
Post Office: Grapevine Station, 1251 William D. Tate Ave, Grapevine
Police Department: Grapevine Regional Police Department, 307 W Dallas Rd, Grapevine, 817-410-8127
Emergency Hospitals: Baylor Regional Medical Center at Grapevine, www.baylorhealth.com, 1650 W College, Grapevine, 817-481-1588
Library: Grapevine Public Library, 1201 Municipal Way, Grapevine, 817-410-3400
Public Education: Grapevine – Colleyville Independent School District, www.gcisd-k12.org, 3051 Ira E. Woods Ave, Grapevine, 817-488-9588
Community Publication: Ft. Worth *Star-Telegram*, www.dfw.com

Community Resources: City Hall, 200 S Main St, Grapevine, 817-410-3000; Grapevine Chamber of Commerce, www.grapevinechamber.org, 200 E Vine, Grapevine, 817-481-1522

Public Transportation: Grapevine Vintage Steam Train, www.tarantulatrain.com, 709 S Main St, Ft. Worth (train to downtown Ft. Worth)

SOUTHLAKE

Immediately west of Grapevine is another lovely and charming suburban town. Like the communities to the east, Southlake places emphasis on keeping the town beautiful. It strives to preserve the town's charm with organizations like Keep Southlake Beautiful. Several homeowner associations, which are listed on the city's web site, are also instrumental in keeping Southlake attractive. Incorporated in 1956, Southlake recognized the impact that the increasing population and residential development would have on the town. In response, it has formulated a plan to deal with construction and mobility issues that may arise in the foreseeable future known as Southlake 2025 Plan. Another step Southlake has taken is to build an amazing town square. The Southlake Town Square contains attractive streetfront stores, pedestrian areas, fountains, and restaurants. Chic brownstones located in the town square are under current construction.

This is a wealthy community with homes ranging from $300,000 to the millions. In general, the homes are large. There are many grand and opulent mansions, even showy, designed to showcase the owners' wealth. There are a variety of styles and locations available including golf course communities, waterfront, lakefront, and canalfront homes, condos, and townhomes. In addition, a million dollar gated retirement community for affluent baby boom retirees is being considered for development. Southlake has a distinguished public school district with several honored by the U.S. Department of Education as National Blue Ribbon schools.

Web Site: www.ci.southlake.tx.us

Area Code: 817

Zip Code: 76092

Post Office: Southlake Station, 300 State St, Southlake

Police Precincts: Southlake Police Services, 817-748-8114: East Station, 667 N Carroll Ave, Southlake; West Station, 2150 West Southlake Blvd, Southlake

Emergency Hospitals: Baylor Regional Medical Center at Grapevine, www.baylorhealth. com, 1650 W College, Grapevine, 817-481-1588; Harris Methodist HEB, www. texashealth.org, 1600 Hospital Pkwy, Bedford, 817-685-4000; North Hills Hospital, www.northhillshospital.com, 4401 Booth Calloway Rd, North Richland Hills, 817-255-1000

Library: Southlake Public Library, 1400 Main St, Ste 130, Southlake, 817-748-8243

Public Education: Carroll Independent School District, www.southlakecarroll.edu, 3051 Dove Rd, Grapevine, 817-949-8282

Community Publication: *Southlake Times*, www.southlaketimes.com

Community Resources: City Hall, 1400 Main St, Southlake, 817-748-8400; Southlake

Chamber of Commerce, www.southlakechamber.com, 1501 Corporate Cir, Ste 100, Southlake, 817-481-4200; Bob Jones Nature Center, www.bjnc.org, 3901 N White Chapel, Southlake, 817-329-4673; Southlake Dog Park, 3500 N White Chapel, Southlake

COLLEYVILLE

Immediately south of Southlake is a wealthy bedroom community of Ft. Worth, named after physician Howard Colley. It is surrounded by beautiful landscape and feels much more like a small town than a suburb. Colleyville homes are generally large brick residences on big plots of land, whose sale prices typically range from $225,000 to $2,000,000. In addition to single-family residences, condos, townhomes, horse property, luxury homes, rentals, and patio homes are also available.

Web Site: www.colleyville.com

Area Code: 817

Zip Code: 76034

Post Office: Colleyville Station, 1501 Hall Johnson Rd, Colleyville

Police Department: Colleyville Police Department, 5201 Riverwalk Dr, Colleyville, 817-503-1200

Emergency Hospitals: Baylor Regional Medical Center at Grapevine, www.baylorhealth.com, 1650 W College, Grapevine, 817-481-1588; Harris Methodist HEB, www.texashealth.org, 1600 Hospital Pkwy, Bedford, 817-685-4000; North Hills Hospital, www.northhillshospital.com, 4401 Booth Calloway Rd, North Richland Hills, 817-255-1000

Library: Colleyville Public Library, 110 Main St, Colleyville, 817-503-1150

Public Education: Grapevine – Colleyville Independent School District, www.gcisd-k12.org, 3051 Ira E. Woods Ave, Grapevine, 817-488-9588

Community Publication: *Colleyville Courier*, www.thenewscourier.com

Community Resources: City Hall, 100 Main St, Colleyville, 817-503-1110; Colleyville Chamber of Commerce, www.colleyvillechamber.org, 6700 Colleyville Blvd, Colleyville, 817-488-8148

NORTH RICHLAND HILLS/RICHLAND HILLS

Southwest of Colleyville are the suburban towns of North Richland Hills and Richland Hills. Developed in the 1950s, **Richland Hills** was one of the first suburbs of Ft. Worth. The town covers only 3.1 square miles and has a population of approximately 8,200. It is a small, quiet suburb whose spacious residential lots provide a country-like setting. The town has implemented a Trails Systems master plan that will preserve this ambience and improve residents' quality of life. The plan calls for the development of a biking and walking trail through several towns, which provides an alternative means of commuting to work. The trail passes through or near some of Richland Hill's more popular subdivisions. For such a small town, Richland Hills offers a good selection of public transportation. Residents can take the train to downtown Dallas or Ft.

Worth, the bus to downtown Ft. Worth, and a different bus service to different parts of Richland Hills and Ft. Worth.

Directly north of Richland Hills is **North Richland Hills**. The area was previously a farm until its owner developed it into a residential community modeled after Richland Hills. The cost of housing here is slightly lower than to the south. Homes begin at about $90,000 for a starter home, $135,000 for an average home, and $225,000 for a custom built home. Like its neighbor to the south, North Richland Hills residents can also take the commuter train to work in downtown Ft. Worth. The town also has a door-to-door transportation service for senior citizens and the disabled.

Web Sites: www.richlandhills.com, www.nrhtx.com

Area Code: 817

Zip Codes: 76180, 76118

Post Offices: North Richland Hills Station, 6051 Davis Blvd, North Richland Hills; Richland Hills Station, 3201 Diana Dr, Richland Hills

Police Departments: Richland Hills Police Department, 6700 Baker Blvd, Richland, 817-299-1880; North Richland Hills Police Department, 7301 NE Loop 820, North Richland Hills, 817-427-7000

Emergency Hospitals: North Hills Hospital, www.northhillshospital.com, 4401 Booth Calloway Rd, North Richland Hills, 817-255-1000

Libraries: Richland Hills Public Library, 6724 Rena Dr, Richland Hills, 817-299-1860; North Richland Hills Public Library, 6720 NE Loop 820, North Richland Hills, 817-427-6800

Public Education: Birdville Independent School District, www.birdville.k12.tx.us, 6125 E Belknap St, Haltom City, 817-547-5700 (serves Richland Hills and parts of North Richland Hills); Hurst-Euless-Bedford Independent School District, www.hebisd.edu, 1849 Central, Bedford, 817-283-4461 (serves part of North Richland Hills); Keller Independent School District, www.kellerisd.net, 350 Keller Pkwy, Keller, 817-744-1000

Community Publication: Ft. Worth Star-Telegram, www.dfw.com

Community Resources: Richland Hills City Hall, 3200 Diana Dr, Richland Hills, 817-299-1800; North Richland Hills City Hall, 7301 NE Loop 820, North Richland Hills, 817-427-6000; Northeast Tarrant County Chamber of Commerce, www.netarrant.org, 5001 Denton Hwy, Haltom City, 817-281-9376

Public Transportation: Ft. Worth Transportation Authority, www.the-t.com; Bus: 40; Trinity Railway Express (commuter rail), www.trinityrailwayexpresss.org, Richland Hills Station

KELLER

Though not as pricey as Southlake to the east nor as developed as North Richland Hills to the south, Keller is developing into a suburban community in its own right. Since the 1980s, Keller has grown from a small town of under 5,000 to a suburban community with over 30,000 residents. It has recreated the small town atmosphere with a new town center. The Keller Town Center is a mixed-use development that combines city government, housing, recreation, work, municipal services, entertainment, retail, and dining all within walking distance of each other. Surrounded by walking trails, lakes, and greenbelts, it features a City Hall, public library, an aquatic center, fitness facilities, and restaurants. The Town Center is linked to the trail system that connects to other Ft. Worth–area towns and communities. Housing here includes lofts, luxury apartments, and individual, free-standing villas. Outside of the Town Center are plenty of other housing options. Homes there usually range from $250,000 to $350,000. However, there are some homes that start at $120,000. On the other extreme, there are also million dollar homes available.

Web Site: www.cityofkeller.com
Area Code: 817
Zip Codes: 76244, 76248
Post Office: Keller Station, 520 E Vine St, Keller
Police Precinct: Keller Police Department, www.kellerpd.com, 330 Rufe Snow Dr, Keller, 817-743-4500
Emergency Hospital: North Hills Hospital, www.northhillshospital.com, 4401 Booth Calloway Rd, North Richland Hills, 817-255-1000
Library: Keller Library, www.kellerlib.org, 640 Johnson Rd, Keller, 817-431-9011
Public Education: Keller Independent School District, www.kellerisd.net, 350 Keller Pkwy, Keller, 817-744-1000
Community Publication: *Keller Citizen*, www.kellercitizen.com
Community Resources: Town Hall, 1100 Bear Creek Pkwy, Keller, 817-743-4050; Keller Senior Center, 660 Johnson Rd, Keller, 817-431-8727; Keller Pointe Public Recreation Center, 405 Rufe Snow Dr, Keller, 817-743-4386; Keller Chamber of Commerce, www.kellerchamber.com, 200 S Main St, Keller, 817-431-2169

WATAUGA/HALTOM CITY

Watauga is a Cherokee word that roughly means village of many springs. This small, quaint town has the charm and friendliness of a small, tight community with the convenience of being near a major city. The average home price is $100,000, though houses range from $70,000 to $200,000, making these homes less expensive than in the surrounding suburbs.

Homes in the same price range as those in Watauga can also be found to the south in **Haltom City**. Nice homes are available for under $200,000, starting at $120,000. Incorporated in 1949, Haltom City grew from a small community and eventually annexed surrounding towns and communities. This suburb of Ft. Worth is still authentically small town, but does not quite have the charm of other small communities in the area. Haltom City attracts middle-income families with its affordable housing and safe environment.

Web Sites: www.ci.watauga.tx.us, www.haltomcitytx.com
Area Code: 817
Zip Codes: 76148, 76117
Post Offices: Watauga Station, 6651 Watauga Rd, Ste 103, Watauga; Haltom City Station, 5709 Broadway Ave, Haltom City

Police Precinct: Watauga Department of Public Safety, 7101 Whitley Rd, Watauga, 817-514-5870; Haltom City Police Department, 5110 Broadway Ave, Haltom City, 817-222-7000

Emergency Hospitals: North Hills Hospital, www.northhillshospital.com, 4401 Booth Calloway Rd, North Richland Hills, 817-255-1000

Libraries: Watauga Public Library, 7109 Whitley Rd, Watauga, 817-514-5855; Haltom City Library, 3201 Friendly Ln, Haltom City, 817-222-7786

Public Education: Birdville Independent School District, www.birdville.k12.tx.us, 6125 E Belknap St, Haltom City, 817-547-5700 (serves Watauga and Haltom City); Keller Independent School District, www.kellerisd.net, 350 Keller Pkwy, Keller, 817-744-1000 (serves part of Watauga)

Community Publication: *Haltom City Citizen*, www.haltomcitycitizen.com

Community Resources: Watauga City Hall, 7101 Whitley Rd, Watauga, 817-514-5800; Haltom City Hall, 5024 Broadway, Haltom City, 817-222-7700; Northeast Tarrant Chamber, www.netarrant.org, 5001 Denton Hwy, Haltom City, 817-281-9376

FORT WORTH

Ft. Worth has often been overshadowed by its bigger and more glitzy neighbor, Dallas. Though only about 30 miles west of Dallas, Ft. Worth avoids the showiness and cosmopolitan flair associated with Dallas. To the contrary, Ft. Worth is a laid-back town with a distinctly Western/Southwestern character. It calls itself the "City where the West begins." This can largely be attributed to the city's Western heritage as a former frontier settlement and a major cattle market.

Named after Mexican War hero Major General William J. Worth, the city was originally established in 1849 as a fort to protect settlers from Indian attacks. Hostile Indians were scarce and the U.S. Army left the fort in 1853. Beginning in the 1860s, the town prospered from the business brought by cowboys driving their cattle through the Chisolm Trail, which passes through the outskirts of Ft. Worth, on their way to the markets and railroads in Kansas. Saloons, blacksmith shops, hotels, brothels, and gambling parlors that catered to cowboys with money to spend emerged in an area of the city known as Hell's Half Acre. A decade later, railroads were expanded into Ft. Worth, allowing cattle to be shipped directly from the city, cementing its place as an important livestock center. At the turn of the century, two major meat packing companies, Swift and Armour, established plants near central Ft. Worth. They would remain a major institution until they closed 60 years later. Because of the city's history with the cattle industry, it earned the nickname Cow Town.

Cattle is no longer the dominant industry in Ft. Worth. The Ft. Worth Stockyards, where cattle was held until shipped north to other markets, is now an entertainment and shopping district. Today, this former rowdy cowboy town is a modern city whose diverse economic base includes technology (Motorola), transportation (American Airlines), manufacturing, retail (Pier 1 Imports), and a heavy emphasis on military defense (Lockheed Martin). In addition, the Barnett Shale, a major natural gas deposit that covers the entire city of Ft. Worth as well as 14 other counties, provides some residents with additional income. The city regulates how drilling is conducted and some neighborhoods prohibit it. Though no homeowner will get rich off of natural gas royalties, those with subsurface rights can receive $100–$200 in extra cash each month. In general, Ft. Worth is a unique town that has incorporated its colorful Western heritage into its contemporary character.

DOWNTOWN

Like other Texas cities, Ft. Worth's Central Business District ("CBD") is also called Downtown. Since its redevelopment in the 1990s, downtown Ft. Worth has been transformed into a trendy residential area. Apartments, lofts, condos, and townhomes have sprung up throughout the district. There is a strong demand for inner city luxury housing and many more downtown residences are being planned and scheduled for construction.

SUNDANCE SQUARE

Boundaries: North: Belknap; East: N Main; South: 6th St; West: Burnett

Named after the Sundance Kid, this area of downtown was at one time known as "Hell's Half Acre," a rowdy red light district where cowboys driving cattle through the Chisolm Trail kicked up their boots. These days, things are more sedate in this pedestrian entertainment district. Set in the backdrop of Ft. Worth's skyscrapers, Sundance Square contains twenty blocks of retail shops, specialty boutiques, restaurants, businesses, fine arts venues (symphony hall, theater, art galleries), movie theaters, offices, hotels, and bars. The square is the site of many big events, including concerts, festivals, and parties. Historic buildings, along with more modern structures, line the leafy district's red brick streets. At night, this popular night spot is lit up with decorative lights. The square is also accented with water fountains and a water garden. The area around Sundance Square contains several new upscale lofts, luxury apartments, and historic buildings that have been converted into elegant residences.

On downtown's West 7th Avenue are several beautiful new condos, townhomes, and apartments in an area known as the **Firestone/Upper West Side.** Currently, there are plans to turn one of the area's twin 20-story towers, known as Tandy Center, into condominiums. The center was a mixed-use facility that housed an indoor shopping mall, office space, and indoor ice skating rink. It was named after the Tandy Corporation, later renamed Radio Shack, which had its headquarters there. A private

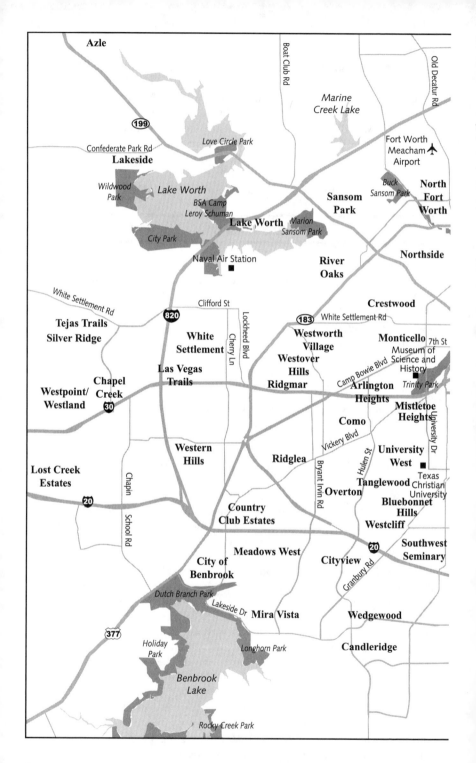

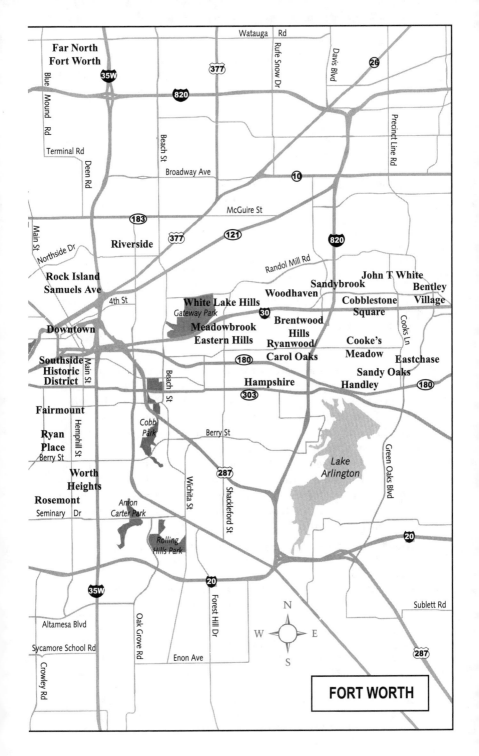

FORT WORTH

subway ran from the office towers to parking lots along the Trinity River. Radio Shack moved to a new office building in north downtown and sold the towers to a development company, which will begin construction of the residential project sometime in 2006. In the southwest corner of downtown is the Cultural District. It is home to Ft. Worth's renowned museums, including the Amon Carter Museum of Art, the National Cowgirl Museum and Hall of Fame, the Cattle Raisers Museum, the Ft. Worth Museum of Science and History, the Modern Art Museum of Ft. Worth, and the Kimbell Art Museum. North of the Cultural District are some nice duplexes, apartments, charming bungalows, and Craftsman homes. Next to the Cultural District is the city's Park District, which contains the Botanical Gardens, Japanese Garden, and Trinity Park. The charming historic Arlington Heights and some nice duplexes and apartments are located just west of the parks.

WEST SEVENTH STREET

Boundaries: North: West 7th St; East: University Dr; South: West 7th St; West: Haskell St

Seventh Street is a six lane artery that connects the city's downtown and Cultural District with the upscale neighborhoods to the west. Recently, the stretch of West Seventh Street that lies just outside of downtown, between the Trinity River and University Drive, has become an up-and-coming urban district with new residential and retail development. Several trendy apartments, townhomes, lofts, and hotels have opened up here and more are planned for the future. Current projects include plans to restore the old Montgomery Ward warehouse for mixed-use development with lofts, shops, office space, and apartments. Currently the Seventh Street strip features a few bars and restaurants, but in a few years it may have many more neighbors.

Web Sites: www.fortworthgov.org, www.sundancesquare.com
Area Code: 817
Zip Code: 76102
Post Offices: Central Ft. Worth Station, 819 Taylor St; Tandy Center Station, 100 Throckmorton St, Ste 151; Downtown Ft. Worth Station, 251 W Lancaster Ave
Police Precinct: Ft. Worth Police Department, www.fortworthpd.com, 350 W Belknap St, 817-355-4222
Emergency Hospitals: Baylor All Saints Medical Center, www.baylorhealth.com, 1400 Eighth Ave, 817-926-2544; John Peter Smith County Hospital, www.jpshealthnet. org, 1500 S Main St, 817-921-3431; JPS Health Center Polytechnic, 1501 Mitchell, 817-920-6600
Library: Ft. Worth Public Library, www.fortworthlibrary.org: Central Branch, 500 W 3rd St, 817-871-7701
Public Education: Ft. Worth Independent School District, www.fortworthisd.org, 100 N University Dr, 817-871-2000

Community Publications: Ft. Worth *Star-Telegram*, www.dfw.com; *Fort Worth Weekly*, www.fwweekly.com

Community Resources: City Hall, 1000 Throckmorton, 817-392-7555; Ft. Worth Chamber of Commerce, www.fortworthcoc.org, 777 Taylor St, Ste 900, 817-336-2491; Downtown Ft. Worth Inc., www.dfwi.org, 777 Taylor St, Ste 100, 817-870-1642

Public Transportation: Ft. Worth Transportation Authority (The T), www.the-t.com, *Bus*: 1, 2, 4, 5, 6, 7, 9, 10, 11, 12, 14, 15, 17, 41, 65E (Express bus); Trinity Railway Express, www.trinityrailwayexpress.org, (Commuter Rail) Downtown Station

---

WEST FORT WORTH

ARLINGTON HEIGHTS/MONTICELLO/ CRESTWOOD AND COMO

ARLINGTON HEIGHTS/MONTICELLO/CRESTWOOD

Boundaries and Contiguous Areas: ARLINGTON HEIGHTS: North: Camp Bowie Blvd; East: Montgomery St; South: I-30; West: Merrick St; MONTICELLO: North: Rivercrest Country Club; East: Monticello Dr; South: Camp Bowie Blvd; West: River Crest Country Club; CRESTWOOD: North: Rockwood Golf Course; East: Greenwood Cemetery; South: White Settlement Dr; West: Rockwood Golf Course

The area that is presently the neighborhood of **Arlington Heights** was once a ranch and then a dairy farm during the 1800s. The unincorporated community outside of Ft. Worth was self-sufficient and even had its own school district. The United States Army took over parts of the area during World War I and established Camp Bowie, a training camp for the Texas-Oklahoma National Guard. In 1922, Ft. Worth annexed Arlington Heights whose school district became part of the Ft. Worth Independent School District.

One of the most charming parts of Ft. Worth, Arlington Heights contains many historical buildings and homes. Residences include one-story wood-frame bungalows, Craftsmans, two-story homes of various architectural styles, large homes on vast lots, duplexes, condos, nice apartments, and newer townhomes. The best homes are located north of Camp Bowie Blvd. However, housing in other parts of this neighborhood is being restored or constructed and provides attractive alternatives. Arlington Heights also encompasses the **North Hi Mount** and **Hillcrest** neighborhoods, where several older homes have been torn down to make room for newer housing developments. Located approximately three miles west of the CBD, Arlington Heights is close to work and nearby recreational activities. Only a few blocks south is the Cultural District, which offers museums, shopping, dining, and entertainment.

Just east of the neighborhood is Camp Bowie, a historic red-brick, tree-lined thoroughfare that contains over 20 blocks of upscale shopping. Architectural styles in this area range from bungalows to Tudors to simple brick and frame cottages. Other neighborhoods commonly included in this area are **Sunset Heights, South Hi Mount, Thomas Place,** and **Hillcrest Addition**.

Immediately north of Arlington Heights, by River Crest Country Club, is the **Monticello** neighborhood. It is named after the Monticello Land Company, which developed it. Most of the homes here are brick, stone, or stucco Spanish-style, Colonial, Tudor, or Mediterranean-style residences built in the late 1920s and 1930s. It contains a mix of large two-story homes and smaller, one-story homes situated amidst tall trees and curving streets. Like Arlington Heights, it is an established, upper-income neighborhood where there is a trend of tearing down the original homes and replacing them with newer structures. The new homes vary in size and style with some complementing the taste and design of the neighborhood, while others are conspicuously out of place. In addition, several new multi-story luxury townhomes have recently been built on the edge of Monticello.

Crestwood is a quiet neighborhood on the West Fork of the Trinity River. Most of the housing was built in the 1940s when the Convair airplane plant (now Lockheed Martin) opened nearby, attracting new residents to the area. In 1949, floods caused the Trinity River to spill over its banks and damage portions of Crestwood. The neighborhood was rebuilt and is currently protected by levees and retaining lakes. That same river has created Crestwood's winding streets, beautiful tall trees, and lush lawns. The residential areas contain mostly quaint one-story bungalows with large porches, wood siding, and wide roofs. The smaller bungalows are located at the north section of the neighborhood, while the southwest part contains grander homes. Several of the bungalows and other modest-sized homes have been torn down to make way for new, larger homes and McMansions. Other recent additions to Crestwood include new townhomes and duplexes.

Como

Boundaries: North: Camp Bowie Blvd; East: Neville St; South: Vickery Blvd to the south; West: Bryant Irvin Rd

Como had its start in the 1890s as a resort on artificial Lake Como, which was named after the Italian resort of the same name. At that time it included a pavilion, a casino, an amusement park, a streetcar, and an inn. An economic downturn in the early 1900s caused the demise of the resort and the sale of the surrounding land at very low prices. As a result, some of the people employed in wealthy Arlington Heights homes to the east were able to afford their own property. Thus, a new community developed in the Lake Como area.

This historically African-American neighborhood is a closely knit community where no one is a stranger. Como is the type of place where the local store owner knows the name of the kid running down the street and where people look after each other. There are many mom and pop stores here, though not as many as there used to be. Once a thriving community, it was besieged by drugs and accompanying high crime during the 1980s and 1990s. The community waged a reasonably successful campaign against the violence. Crime is now lower and not the problem it was in the previous decades. On the contrary, Como is now viewed as hot real estate property by developers who would like to build intown housing. Located five miles west of the CBD, there are already several higher-income developments along Camp Bowie Boulevard in the north and Vickery Boulevard in the south. New brick homes ranging from $80,000 to $200,000 sit alongside wood-framed houses with front porches on small lots, some of which are valued at less than $20,000. Most of the new homebuyers are people who are interested in returning to the neighborhood where they grew up.

Web Site: www.fortworthgov.com

Area Code: 817

Zip Code: 76107

Post Office: Arlington Heights Station, 3301 Darcy St

Police Precinct: Ft. Worth Police Department, www.fortworthpd.com: West Division Unit, 2509 Merrick St, 817-570-2200; Central Division, 350 W Belknap St, 817-335-4222

Emergency Hospitals: Plaza Medical Center, www.plazamedicalcenter.com, 900 Eighth Ave, 817-87-PLAZA; Harris-Methodist Ft. Worth Hospital, www.harrisfw.org, 1301 Pennsylvania Ave, 817-882-2000; JPS Viola Pitts Health Center, www.jpshealthnet.org, 4701 Bryant Irvin Rd N, 817-920-7400

Libraries: Central Branch, 500 W 3rd St, 817-871-7701; Ridglea Branch, 3268 Bernie Anderson, 817-737-6619

Public Education: Ft. Worth Independent School District, www.forthworthisd.org, 100 N University Dr

Community Publications: Ft. Worth *Star-Telegram*, www.dfw.com; *Fort Worth Weekly*, www.fwweekly.com; *Fort Worth Business Press*, www.fortworthbusinesspress.com

Community Resources: City Hall, 1000 Throckmorton St, 817-392-2255; Ft. Worth Chamber of Commerce, www.fortworthcoc.org, 777 Taylor St, Ste 900, 817-336-2491; Thomas Place Community Center, 4237 Lafayette, 817-735-1751; Como Community Center, 4900 Horne St, 817-871-5030

Public Transportation: Ft. Worth Transportation Authority (the T), www.the-t.com, *Bus*: 2, 7, 25, 27, 32, 61E

RIVERCREST/NORTHCREST AND RIDGLEA

RIVERCREST/NORTHCREST

Boundaries: North: White Settlement Rd; East: River Crest Country

Club; South: Camp Bowie Blvd; West: Trinity River and Westover Hills city limits

This exclusive residential neighborhood of historic mansions situated above the West Fork of the Trinity River on 640 acres of hilly and curving tree-shaded streets is the address for many of Ft. Worth's old-money elite. Rivercrest's impressive homes were commissioned during the 1920s and 1930s by those who made their fortunes in oil. Cattle barons, bank presidents, real estate magnates, and wealthy businessmen soon followed and built their own residences. Built around the Rivercrest Country Club and Golf Course, many of the homes have views of the golf course. Houses range from prairie-style, Mediterranean, and Tudor, designed by notable architects, to recently constructed ranch and contemporary-style homes. Most unique are those to the west of Rivercrest, in **Northcrest**, which have been designed to harmonize with the winding and sloping terrain. Though the area is known for its mansions and large homes, there are also some cottages in this neighborhood. In general, Rivercrest is a quiet neighborhood whose tranquility serves as a private enclave for the privileged.

RIDGLEA

Boundaries: North: Camp Bowie Blvd; East: Westridge Ave; South: Vickery Rd; West: Southwest Blvd; COUNTRY CLUB ESTATES: (approximately) North: Vickery Blvd; East: Benbrook City limits; South: Loop 820; West: Benbrook City limits

For a more affordable option than Rivercrest, Arlington Heights, or Monticello, you might consider the Ridglea subdivision, located approximately six miles west of the CBD. This large subdivision is divided into the neighborhoods of Ridglea Hills, Ridglea West, Ridglea North, and Ridglea Country Club Estates. It offers single-family residential homes, apartments, townhomes, and condominiums. **Ridglea Hills** is located between Camp Bowie Blvd and Vickery Blvd/Southwest Blvd, with Westridge Avenue bordering the east and railroad tracks (behind Piedmont) bordering the west. The area was primarily a cattle farm prior to serious development in the 1950s. Though there are a few duplexes and an apartment complex, Ridglea Hills contains mostly brick, single-story, ranch-style, single-family homes. The neighborhood features a hilly, at some points steep landscape covered with trees and winding streets. One of the main attractions of Ridglea Hills is beautiful Luther Lake, located in the heart of the neighborhood. Some residences here have lakeside views.

To the north of Ridglea Hills is **Ridglea North**, bounded by I-30 to the north, Camp Bowie Boulevard on the south, Horne Street to the east, and Lackland Road on the west. The neighborhood contains a mix of large two-story homes and smaller one-story homes built in the 1940s.

Conveniently located nearby on Camp Bowie Blvd are several stores and businesses. Neighborhood attractions and conveniences include the Ridglea Theater, now a special events venue.

Next to Ridglea North is **Ridglea Country Club Estates,** which is named after the country club that surrounds it. This secluded neighborhood can only be reached by one road, Serrano, making it quite a secure and exclusive area. The surrounding landscape of the adjoining golf course, tree-lined streets, and curving roads provide a gentle country atmosphere for the brick, ranch-style homes that sit next to the golf course. One of Ft. Worth's most prestigious neighborhoods, the country club estates also contain some large homes, and some million dollar homes on large lots. There are also some apartments, condos, and garden homes that overlook the golf course. Located approximately 8 miles west of the CBD, it borders the Clear Fork of the Trinity River on the north, Highway 183, railroad tracks, and the western edge of the Ridglea Country Club. This neighborhood was built in the 1970s and 1980s and is one of the more recent neighborhoods in this area. Other neighborhoods in the Ridglea community to consider are **Ridglea Hills Addition, Allen Place, Hampton Place,** and **Ridglea South.**

Web Sites: www.fortworthgov.com, www.ridgleahills.com, www.ridgleahillsaddition. com, www.ridgleanorth.com

Area Code: 817

Zip Code: 76116

Post Office: Ridglea Station, 3020 S Cherry Ln

Police Precinct: Ft. Worth Police Department, www.fortworthpd.com: 3252 Marquita Rd, 817-871-5000

Emergency Hospitals: JPS Viola Pitts Health Center, www.jpshealthnet.org, 4701 Bryant Irvin Rd N, 817-920-7400; Plaza Medical Center, www.plazamedicalcenter. com, 900 Eighth Ave, 817-87-PLAZA; Harris-Methodist Ft. Worth Hospital, www. harrisfw.org, 1301 Pennsylvania Ave, 817-882-2000

Library: Ft. Worth Public Library, www.fortworthlibrary.org: Ridglea Branch, 3628 Bernie Anderson, 817-737-6619

Public Education: Ft. Worth Independent School District, www.forthworthisd.org, 100 N University Dr

Community Publications: Ft. Worth Star-*Telegram*, www.dfw.com; *Fort Worth Weekly*, www.fwweekly.com; *Fort Worth Business Press*, www.fortworthbusinesspress.com

Community Resources: City Hall, 1000 Throckmorton St, 817-392-2255; Ft. Worth Chamber of Commerce, www.fortworthcoc.org, 777 Taylor St, Ste 900, 817-336-2491; R.D. Evans Community Center, 3242 Lackland Rd, 817-731-8789

Public Transportation: Ft. Worth Transportation Authority (the T), www.the-t.com, *Bus*: 2, 27, 61E

CITY OF BENBROOK

Boundaries: North: Chapin Rd, Spur 580, and undeveloped land; East: Ft. Worth city limits; South: Lake Benbrook and Trinity River; West: Loop 820 and undeveloped land

This middle class suburb borders the western city limits of Ft. Worth, including some of its toniest neighborhoods, but still has a country feel to it. Many of the residents work outside of the town in the high tech defense industry or at the adjoining Joint Naval Reserve Base. It attracts people who are looking for a nice, safe, and quiet place to raise their children. Most of the homes and apartments here were built in the late 1970s and 1980s, but there continues to be new home construction. Homes here range from $100,000 to $300,000 with the average home costing around $150,000. Located ten miles from Ft. Worth's CBD, Benbrook is within close driving distance to the attractions and amenities of a major city.

The town was originally called Miranda when it was founded in 1857 by settlers from Tennessee and other southern states. For decades this remained a small sleepy town of under 100 until the completion of the Benbrook Reservoir. Today, it has over 16,000 residents. Residents can enjoy hiking, fishing, hunting, boating, and camping at Lake Benbrook, an artificial lake created by the Army Corps of Engineers to control flooding of the Trinity River. Flooding should not be a problem these days because the lake has dried up due to a severe drought in the region. The drought has also lowered water levels, which has prevented fishing and boating on the lake. Conditions, however, may change.

One notable neighborhood in Benbrook is **Mont Del**, which is often thought of as a Ft. Worth neighborhood rather than part of another city. It is bounded by Legend Road to the north, Bryant Irvin Blvd to the east, Loop I-20 to the south, and the Clear Fork of the Trinity River to the west. The only types of housing here are large single-family residences built in the 1970s with brick or stone in various architectural styles. Mont Del's location among hilly terrain offers wonderful panoramas. Homes that are built on top of the hills have stunning views of the areas around them and many of them have backyard decks to take advantage of this. Because the hilltop visual is one of the neighborhood's greatest assets, developers have taken great care to preserve it. For example, visitors to Mont Del will not see any utility poles because they have been buried underground. Streets here conform to the winding topography of the hills with plenty of trees for shade. The overall design of Mont Del provides a pleasant and tranquil atmosphere reminiscent of the countryside.

At the bottom of the hills of Mont Del is a neighborhood called **Country Day Estates**. This area that lies between Mont Del, the Clear Fork of the Trinity River, and Southwest Blvd was once a dairy farm. The majority of the homes here are custom built. They are more recent than homes in Mont Del with residential development beginning in the late 1970s. New home construction still continues in Country Day Estates.

Web Site: www.ci.benbrook.tx.us
Area Code: 817
Zip Codes: 76126, 76132

Post Offices: Benbrook Station, 9415 Benbrook Blvd, Benbrook; Cityview Station, 7101 Bryant Irvin Rd, Ft. Worth

Police Department: Benbrook Police Department, www.benbrookpd.com, 1080 Mercedes St, Benbrook, 817-249-2752

Emergency Hospitals: JPS Viola Pitts Health Center, www.jpshealthnet.org, 4701 Bryant Irvin Rd N, Ft. Worth, 817-920-7400; Harris Methodist Southwest Hospital, www.harrissw.org, 6100 Harris Pkwy, Ft. Worth, 817-433-5000

Library: Benbrook Public Library, www.benbrooklibrary.org, 1065 Mercedes St, Benbrook, 817-249-6632

Public Education: Ft. Worth Independent School District, www.forthworthisd.org, 100 N University Dr, Ft. Worth

Community Publications: *Benbrook Star; Benbrook News*

Community Resources: City Hall, 911 Winscott Rd, Benbrook, 817-249-3000; Benbrook Chamber of Commerce, www.benbrookchamber.org, 8507 Benbrook Blvd, Benbrook, 817-249-4451; Dutch Branch Park, 1899 Winscott Rd, Ft. Worth

RIDGMAR

North: King's Branch Creek; East: Westover Hills city limit; South: I-30; West: Green Oaks Rd

Just above Ridglea North, **Ridgmar** is probably best known for the very large mall of the same name that is located here. Ridgmar encompasses a very hilly area, which provides some of the homes that sit on the more elevated parts a view of the western area beyond the neighborhood. Located nearby is the Lockheed Martin plant, which was previously owned by General Dynamics and Convair, respectively. Because of Ridgmar's proximity to the Joint Naval Reserve Base, it is not unusual to see people in military fatigues at the local store. The sound of jets can occasionally be heard zooming by, but is not noticeable from indoors.

Ridgmar consists of primarily ranch-style homes that are set back quite a bit on large lots along winding roads. The older homes start on Dakar Rd with the streets named alphabetically thereafter. Though development of the neighborhood began as early as the late-1950s, most of the homes here were built in the 1960s and 1970s. Homes here are more affordable than in the surrounding neighborhoods of Ridglea North and Westover Hills. A four-bedroom home costs under $200,000, but would be more than twice as much in any of the nearby neighborhoods. Ridgmar also has many apartment complexes nearby as well as some nice townhomes on quiet streets off of I-30.

Web Sites: http://ridgmar.org; www.fortworthgov.com

Area Code: 817

Zip Code: 76116

Post Office: Ridglea Station, 3020 S Cherry Ln

Police Precinct: Ft. Worth Police Department, www.fortworthpd.com: West District, 3252 Marquita Rd, 817-871-5000

Emergency Hospitals: JPS Viola Pitts Health Center, www.jpshealthnet.org, 4701

Bryant Irvin Rd N, 817-920-7400; Harris-Methodist Ft. Worth Hospital, www.
harrisfw.org, 1301 Pennsylvania Ave, 817-882-2000

Library: Ft. Worth Public Library, www.fortworthlibrary.org: Ridglea Branch, 3628 Bernie
Anderson, 817-737-6619

Public Education: Ft. Worth Independent School District, www.forthworthisd.org, 100
N University Dr

Community Publications: Ft. Worth *Star-Telegram*, www.dfw.com; *Fort Worth Weekly*,
www.fwweekly.com; *Fort Worth Business Press*, www.fortworthbusinesspress.com

Community Resources: City Hall, 1000 Throckmorton St, 817-392-2255; Ft. Worth
Chamber of Commerce, www.fortworthcoc.org, 777 Taylor St, Ste 900, 817-336-
2491

Public Transportation: Ft. Worth Transportation Authority (the T), www.the-t.com: *Bus*:
2, 26, 27, 61E

WESTOVER HILLS

Boundaries: North: Shady Oaks Country Club and undeveloped areas;
East: Ft. Worth city limits; South: Merrymount and Ft. Worth city
limits; West: Ft. Worth city limits

Drive just a few minutes over the eastern boundaries of Ridgmar and the
neighborhood changes drastically from modest ranch homes to million
dollar mansions. Technically an independent small town, **Westover Hills**
is home to Fort Worth's upper crust. This posh neighborhood contains
some of the city's most magnificent estates that date from the 1940s
to the present. Homes are on considerable lots along winding, tree-
shaded streets. Some of them are situated behind walls or trees and other
landscaping for added privacy. Many of them are custom built, which has
resulted in differing styles throughout the neighborhood. In addition,
several of the streets in this neighborhood are private. The neighborhood's
location on hilly terrain surrounded by the Shady Oaks, Rivercrest, and
Ridglea country clubs, creates a quiet and secluded atmosphere where
residents can enjoy their privacy.

Area Code: 817

Zip Code: 76107

Post Office: Arlington Heights Station, 3301 Darcy St

Police Department: Westover Hills Police Department, 5824 Merrymount Rd, 817-737-
3127

Emergency Hospitals: JPS Viola Pitts Health Center, www.jpshealthnet.org, 4701
Bryant Irvin Rd N, 817-920-7400; Harris-Methodist Ft. Worth Hospital, www.
harrisfw.org, 1301 Pennsylvania Ave, 817-882-2000

Library: Westover Village City Library, 101 Seymour Ave, 817-738-2248

Public Education: Ft. Worth Independent School District, www.forthworthisd.org, 100
N University Dr

Community Publications: Ft. Worth *Star-Telegram*, www.dfw.com; *Fort Worth Weekly*,
www.fwweekly.com; *Fort Worth Business Press*, www.fortworthbusinesspress.com

Community Resources: Town Hall, 5824 Merrymount Rd, 817-737-3127; Ft. Worth
Chamber of Commerce, www.fortworthcoc.org, 777 Taylor St, Ste 900, 817-336-
2491

WESTERN HILLS, LAS VEGAS TRAILS, WESTPOINT/ WESTLAND, LOST CREEK, CHAPEL CREEK, SILVER RIDGE, AND TEJAS TRAILS

Boundaries: WESTERN HILLS: North: U.S. Hwy 80; East: Cork Place/Benbrook city limits; South: Chapin Rd; West: Loop 820; LAS VEGAS TRAILS: North: I-30; East: Texas Hwy 183 (Alta Mere Dr); South: US Hwy 80; West: Loop 820; WESTPOINT/WESTLAND, CHAPEL CREEK, SILVER RIDGE, TEJAS TRAILS: North: Verna Trail N (Ft. Worth city limits); East: Loop 820; South: Mary's Creek and Chapin Rd; West: Ft. Worth city limits; LOST CREEK: North: I-30; East: Diamond Bar Trail (Ft. Worth city limits); South: Ft. Worth city limits: West: Ft. Worth city limits

Western Hills and **Las Vegas Trails** are located below I-30, near US Highway 80 and between the northern city limits of Benbrook and the southern city limits of White Settlement. Western Hills has a name that sounds similar to Westover Hills, but the two could not be more different. This neighborhood features dramatically more modest brick ranch-style homes. There are several low rent apartment complexes near I-30, many of which are deemed undesirable because of ongoing criminal activity. The other neighborhoods are recent suburban developments that push the boundaries of the city westward. Further to the west, past Loop 820, is **Westpoint**, a new residential neighborhood developed in the 1990s. The area was previously a hilly field that is now occupied by approximately 1,200 homes and several commercial structures. Even further west, below I-30, is the **Lost Creek** suburb, which surrounds the Lost Creek Golf Course. It is on the western edge of the city, an island surrounded by countryside and connected only by I-30/US-80. Homes here are no more than 30 years old, with many of them newly constructed. Lost Creek has a variety of houses from starter homes to grand residences on large lots. North of it, above I-30, are the **Chapel Creek**, **Silver Ridge**, and **Tejas Trails** neighborhoods. These suburbs are also situated on the edge of Ft. Worth and surrounded by rural, undeveloped areas. There is substantial new home construction in this area.

Chapel Creek homes are generally one-story brick homes with the garage prominently placed at the front of the house. Homes in this neighborhood are in the mid-$100,000 price range. Silver Ridge is a more expensive neighborhood. There are elegant one story residences surrounded by tall trees on big lots that cost over $300,000. The neighborhood also has some more generally affordable alternatives that cost around $230,000. These homes are typically on smaller lots with little to no trees.

Web Sites: www.fortworthgov.org, http://www.chapelcreekfw.org
Area Code: 817
Zip Codes: 76108, 76116
Post Office: White Settlement Station, 301 N Las Vegas Trl

Police Department: Ft. Worth Police Department, www.fortworthpd.com: West District, 3525 Marquita Dr

Emergency Hospitals: JPS Viola Pitts Health Center, www.jpshealthnet.org, 4701 Bryant Irvin Rd N, 817-920-7400; Harris-Methodist Ft. Worth Hospital, www.harrisfw.org, 1301 Pennsylvania Ave, 817-882-2000

Public Education: Azle Independent School District, www.azle.esc11.net, 300 Roe St, Azle, 817-444-3235; White Settlement Independent School District, www.wsisd.com, 401 S Cherry Ln, Ft. Worth, 817-367-1300

Community Publications: Ft. Worth *Star-Telegram*, www.dfw.com; *Fort Worth Weekly*, www.fwweekly.com; *Fort Worth Business Press*, www.fortworthbusinesspress.com

Community Resources: City Hall, 1000 Throckmorton St, 817-392-2255; Ft. Worth Chamber of Commerce, www.fortworthcoc.org, 777 Taylor St, Ste 900, 817-336-2491

MIRA VISTA/MEADOWS WEST/CITYVIEW

Boundaries: MIRA VISTA: North: Clear Fork Trinity River; East: Bryant Irvin Rd; South: Dirks Rd; West: Lakeside Dr; MEADOWS WEST: North: Loop 820; East: rural undeveloped area; South: Oakmont Blvd; West: Clear Fork Trinity River; CITYVIEW: North: Loop 820; East: edge of development/rural area; South: Oakmont Blvd; West: edge of development/rural area

In **Mira Vista**, residents do not simply live in homes. They live in villas, estates and manors. Of course, it goes without saying that this private, gated country club community will cost any buyer a pretty dime, as most of the homes here are quite grand. Assuming money is no obstacle, it is perfect for people who love golf or simply desire 'round the clock security every day of the week

Many of the homes line the 18-hole championship golf course, which provides a beautiful backdrop of rolling green hills and mature trees. Homes are also elevated on bluffs with a view of the landscape below, while others have waterfront views of the small lakes within Mira Vista's 700 acres. The community is connected by winding roads with trees sprinkled throughout the neighborhood. None of the luxury homes here are identical because they are custom built for the owner. The community has approximately 300 residences, but new ones are continually being built. The development began in the 1980s with a newer development to the north of Mira Vista called **Hawthorne Park Estates** currently under construction.

Meadows West is a residential neighborhood developed by the Meadows West Corporation in 1979 along the Clear Fork of the Trinity River and near I-20. Homes here include lovely large one-story brick traditional-style homes that can cost up to $300,000. The neighborhood is surrounded by beautiful scenery created by the Trinity River on the north and east and undeveloped lands on the western edge. Another neighborhood near here is **Bellaire Park North**, which lies south of Mont Del, along the southern part of the Clear Fork of the Trinity River. These desirable neighborhoods sit on what was once a large 2,500-acre ranch owned by E.G. Rall until it was sold and divided in 1974 for residential development. Bellaire Park North was developed later, in 1985. The trees along the Clear Fork of the Trinity River obscure many of the homes from the view of the river and the interstate. Residents can enjoy the biking and walking trail along the river greenbelt.

Cityview is separated from Meadows West by unspoiled greenery and hills. It contains many relatively new and attractive apartment complexes along Bryant Irvin Road and Overton Ridge Blvd. The apartments here are popular with Texas Christian University college students, who are the predominant residents in most of the rental properties here. Residential property to the west of Bryant Irvin Road has great views of the area's rolling hills and picturesque scenery. Located on the northern boundary are many hotels, businesses, and other commercial developments.

Web Sites: www.fortworthgov.org, www.miravistaclub.com

Area Code: 817

Zip Code: 76132

Post Office: Cityview Station, 7101 Bryant Irvin Rd

Police Department: Ft. Worth Police Department, www.fortworthpd.com: West District, 3525 Marquita Dr

Emergency Hospitals: All Saints Episcopal Hospital at Cityview, 7100 Oakmont Blvd, 817-346-5870; Harris-Methodist Southwest, www.harrissw.org, 6100 Harris Pkwy, 817-433-5000

Public Education: Ft. Worth Independent School District, www.fortworthisd.org, 100 N University Dr, 817-871-2000

Community Publications: Ft. Worth *Star-Telegram*, www.dfw.com; *Fort Worth Weekly*, www.fwweekly.com; *Fort Worth Business Press*, www.fortworthbusinesspress.com

Community Resources: City Hall, 1000 Throckmorton St, 817-392-7555; Ft. Worth Chamber of Commerce, www.fortworthcoc.org, 777 Taylor St, Ste 900, 817-336-2491

WESTWORTH VILLAGE

Boundaries: North: West Fork Trinity River; East: West Fork Trinity River; South: Carb Dr; West: Ft. Worth Naval Base/JRB

This quiet residential suburb of Ft. Worth is located approximately five miles west of the CBD on the banks of the Trinity River and along State Highway 183. Westworth Village owes its development and growth to an air force base that for decades provided thousands of jobs to the area. Starting in 1941, the federal government was granted 1,450 acres for a B-24 bomber plant and a landing field, known as Carswell Force Base, in what is now Westworth Village. That same year Westworth Village incorporated itself. After the end of the Cold War, the federal government decided to close several military bases and schedule others for realignment, including Carswell Air Force Base in Westworth Village. The naval air operations at Dallas Naval Air Station moved to Carswell, which is now the NAS Joint Reserve Base in Ft. Worth. This left the city with 400 acres of federally ceded property and 500 units of military housing. Westworth Village got creative and turned the unused land into a mixed-use development with light industrial and retail businesses. Since the base's closing, the city's population has declined. The new, realigned naval air station currently employs 1,500 civilians and 3,500 military personnel. In addition, approximately 8,000 reservists are on duty at this site.

Westworth Village has the distinction as the only city in Tarrant County that does not have a property tax. This is a nice, laid-back bedroom community with a small town atmosphere. Homes here are generally small one-story brick homes, whose average market value is around $55,000.

Web Site: www.ci.westworth.tx.us

Area Code: 817

Zip Code: 76114

Post Offices: River Oaks Station, 1008 Roberts Cut Off Rd, River Oaks; Naval Air Station/JRB, 1501 Arnold Ave, Naval Air Station/Jrb

Police Department: Westworth Village Police Department, 311 Burton Hill Rd, 817-738-3673 Ext. 2

Emergency Hospital: Harris-Methodist Southwest, www.harrissw.org, 6100 Harris Pkwy, 817-433-5000

Library: Westworth Village Public Library, 101 Seymour, 817-738-2248

Public Education: Ft. Worth Independent School District, www.fortworthisd.org, 100 N University Dr, 817-871-2000

Community Publications: Ft. Worth *Star-Telegram*, www.dfw.com; *Fort Worth Weekly*, www.fwweekly.com; *Fort Worth Business Press*, www.fortworthbusinesspress.com

Community Resources: City Hall, 311 Burton Hill Rd, 817-738-3673; Ft. Worth Chamber of Commerce, ww.fortworthcoc.org, 777 Taylor St, Ste 900, 817-336-2491

RIVER OAKS

Boundaries: North: Ft. Worth city limits; East: Ft. Worth city limits; South: Ft. Worth city limits (Blackstone); West: Ft. Worth city limits (Gillham Rd)

Like Westworth Village to the north, River Oaks also owes its growth and development to the Ft. Worth Naval Air Base directly to its east. Formerly the Carswell Air Force Base, it was a B-24 bomber plant built in the 1940s on land deeded by the Ft. Worth Chamber of Commerce to the federal government. The air base was commonly referred to by local area residents as the "bomber plant." Residents voted to incorporate their community after the construction of the plant. The opening in the area of the General Dynamics Corporation, a defense contractor, further increased River Oaks' population as people were drawn to the town by nearby employment opportunities. The town's population slightly decreased after the post–Cold War decline in federal military spending.

Residents of this solidly working class community are mostly employees at the naval air station and its supporting defense contractors. This sleepy town is primarily a residential community with few entertainment and dining options. Most of the homes are small, single-story residences on quiet streets surrounded by many trees.

Web Site: www.riveroakstx.com
Area Code: 76114
Zip Code: 817
Post Office: River Oaks Station, 1008 Roberts Cut Off Rd, River Oaks; Naval Air Station/JRB, 1501 Arnold Ave, Naval Air Station/Jrb
Police Department: River Oaks Police Department, www.riveroakspd.com, 4900 River Oaks Blvd, River Oaks, 817-626-1991
Emergency Hospital: Harris-Methodist Southwest, www.harrissw.org, 6100 Harris Pkwy, 817-433-5000
Library: River Oaks Library, www.riveroakslibrary.com, 4900 River Oaks Blvd, River Oaks, 817-624-7344
Public Education: Castleberry Independent School District, www.castleberryisd.net, 315 Churchill Rd, 817-252-2000
Community Publications: Ft. Worth *Star-Telegram*, www.dfw.com; *River Oaks News*
Community Resources: City Hall, City of River Oaks, 4900 River Oaks Blvd, River Oaks, 817-626-5421

WHITE SETTLEMENT

Boundaries: North: City Park/Lake Worth; East: Ft. Worth Naval Air Base/JRB; South: I-30; West: Loop 820

White Settlement is a working class community across from the Ft. Worth neighborhood of Ridgmar. The town is named for the white pioneer community that settled this area when it was surrounded by Native American villages. It is one of several small, incorporated communities that are located around the Ft. Worth Naval Air Base/ JRB. The opening of the military base in the 1940s led to the growth of White Settlement and its subsequent incorporation as a city. There are several new, mostly three-bedroom brick homes in the low $100,000 range. White Settlement also has many older homes built in the 1950s that are ideal for an upgrade. These homes typically cost under $90,000. Those looking for less permanent dwellings can choose from the several apartments in White Settlement.

Web Site: www.ci.white-settlement.tx.us
Area Code: 817
Zip Code: 76108
Post Offices: White Settlement Station, 301 N Las Vegas Trail; Ridglea, 3020 S Cherry Ln; Naval Air Station/JRB, 1501 Arnold Ave, Naval Air Station/Jrb
Police Department: White Settlement Police Department, 8900 Clifford St, White Settlement, 817-246-7070
Emergency Hospital: Harris-Methodist Southwest, www.harrissw.org, 6100 Harris Pkwy, Ft. Worth, 817-433-5000

Library: White Settlement Public Library, 8215 White Settlement Rd, White Settlement, 817-367-0166

Public Education: White Settlement Independent School District, www.wsisd.com, 401 S Cherry Ln, White Settlement, 817-367-1300

Community Publications: *White Settlement Bomber News*; Ft. Worth *Star-Telegram*, www.dfw.com

Community Resources: White Settlement Area Chamber of Commerce, www. whitesettlement-tx.com, 601 S Cherry Ln, Ste C, White Settlement, 817-246-1121; City Hall, 214 Meadow Park, White Settlement, 817- 246-4971

SOUTH FORT WORTH

FAIRMOUNT, RYAN PLACE, AND MISTLETOE HEIGHTS/BERKELEY PLACE

FAIRMOUNT AND RYAN PLACE

Boundaries: FAIRMOUNT: North: Magnolia Ave; East: Hemphill St; South: Jessamine St; West: Eighth Ave; RYAN PLACE: North: Jessamine St to the north; East: railroad tracks; South: Berry St; West: 8th Ave

Fairmount and Ryan Place are part of the city's hospital district, where several of Ft. Worth's major hospitals are located. Located two miles south of the CBD, **Fairmount** features Craftsman bungalows, stone and brick houses, wood-frame foursquares, and Victorian-style homes built between 1900 and the late 1930s. Originally designed as a middle-class neighborhood, Fairmount includes some grand homes in its eastern section, on Chase Court. There are also some three-story brick apartment complexes from the 1920s and a few modern duplexes. After the post–World War II flight from the neighborhood to the suburbs, many of the homes were converted into multi-family units and low-income residents started moving into the area. Residents wanting to live closer to work during the gas crisis of the 1970s rediscovered Fairmount, a nice neighborhood with relatively small homes that are spaced close together on large lawns. Restoration and location have increased the value of these historic homes. The neighborhood offers single-family residential homes, duplexes, and some apartment homes, which range from $70,000 to $234,000. Fairmount is very convenient for those working at Baylor All Saints Medical Center, Plaza Medical Center East, and John Peter Smith County Hospital, which surround Fairmount. Also nearby are Cook Children's Medical Center and Harris-Methodist Fort Worth Hospital.

Beyond the white stone and marble pillars that mark the entrance of **Ryan Place** on Elizabeth Street are rows of grand homes in

Mediterranean, Georgian, Period Revival and various other styles along tree-lined streets. This lovely, historic neighborhood's sidewalks are decorated by an occasional ornamental streetlight and shaded by mature trees. The design of Ryan Place promotes an atmosphere that encourages neighbors to interact with each other. Developed by John C. Ryan in the early 1900s for Ft. Worth's wealthy and elite, some of the neighborhood's brick and stone homes feature unique details such as marble columns, ballrooms, fine glasswork, and impressive back porches. Ryan Place contains mostly one-story residences, but the largest and most spectacular homes are located on Elizabeth and neighboring streets. While Fairmount started as a middle-class neighborhood, Ryan Place was designed for wealthier residents during the 1920s. Today, it is one of Ft. Worth's most pleasant neighborhoods with homes valued as high as $600,000, though homes are available for as low as $60,000 depending on the condition and size of the property. However, this was not always the case. After the post–WWII flight to the suburbs, Ryan Place became a neglected neighborhood. During the 1960s, residents got together to save it from proposed street projects. Their efforts restored Ryan Place to its former glory. It is now a Ft. Worth historic district and listed on the National Register of Historic Places.

MISTLETOE HEIGHTS/BERKELEY PLACE

Boundaries: MISTLETOE HEIGHTS: North: Rosedale; East: Granbury Rd; South: Park Pl; West: Mistletoe Dr, Berkeley Pl; Boundaries: BERKELEY PLACE: North: Park Pl; East: railroad track; South: Ward Pkwy; West: Rockridge Terrace

Mistletoe Heights is a small Ft. Worth historic district immediately east of Fairmount and encompassing the Baylor All Saints Medical Center. Named after the Mistletoe Heights Land Company that developed this district, it has a wonderful location on a bluff overlooking the Trinity River. It contains large beautiful homes slightly elevated on manicured lawns. The homes here are generally larger, more stately, and more expensive than in neighboring Fairmount. The average home price here is about $100,000 more than in Fairmount with homes ranging from $60,000 to $600,000. Mistletoe Heights has a mix of Tudor, Spanish/Mediterranean, contemporary, stone mason, and prairie style homes that vary in size from small cottages to large mansions. In addition to the unique historical architecture, its wide, tree-lined streets are decorated with ornamental streetlights. Mistletoe Heights is unique because it is a dry area, which means alcohol may be consumed, but cannot be sold here. Also distinctive are the guest houses in the back of some residences, which once served as servants' quarters.

Located two miles southwest of the Ft. Worth Central Business District, directly south of Mistletoe Heights, **Berkeley Place** is a neighborhood of brick and stucco Tudor-style homes, bungalows, and homes in other architectural styles. Like Mistletoe Heights, some have guest houses in the back that were originally used as housing for servants. Decorative streetlights accentuate the neighborhood's stately charm. Stone gates grace one of the neighborhood's entrances on Forest Park and announce the presence of this historic neighborhood. Home prices are somewhat comparable to Mistletoe Heights, though possibly more expensive.

Web Sites: www.historicfairmount.com, historicryanplace.org, www.fortworthsouth.org, www.mistletoeheights.com, www.berkeleyplace.org, www.fortworthgov.org

Area Code: 817

Zip Codes: 76104, 76110

Post Offices: Eighth Avenue Station, 2600 8th Ave; Berry Street Station, 3110 Townsend

Police Precinct: Ft. Worth Police Department, www.fortworthpd.com, South District: 1000 Magnolia, 817-871-8885

Emergency Hospitals: Baylor All Saints Medical Center, www.baylorhealth.com, 1400 8th Ave, 817-927-6102; John Peter Smith County Hospital, www.jpshealthnet.org, 1500 S Main St, 817-921-3431

Libraries: Ft. Worth Public Library, www.fortworthlibrary.org: Ella Mae Shamblee Branch, 959 E Rosedale, 817-871-6621; Central Branch, 500 W 3rd St, 817-871-7701

Public Education: Ft. Worth Independent School District, www.fortworthisd.org, 100 N University Dr, 817-871-2000

Community Publications: Ft. Worth *Star-Telegram*, www.dfw.com; *Fort Worth Weekly*, www.fwweekly.com

Community Resources: City Hall, 1000 Throckmorton St, 817-392-7555; Ft. Worth Chamber of Commerce, www.fortworthcoc.org, 777 Taylor St, Ste 900, 817-336-2491; Fire Station Community Center, 1601 Lipscomb, 817-924-9976; Southside Community Center, 959 Rosedale, 817-871-6608; Hillside Community Center, 1201 E Maddox Ave, 817-335-0728

Public Transportation: Ft. Worth Transportation Authority (The T), www.the-t.com, *Bus*: 1, 4, 6, 24

TCU AREA AND SURROUNDING NEIGHBORHOODS

The TCU area is immediately east of the campus to Granbury Rd/8th Ave, by the railroad tracks. Texas Christian University ("TCU") is a private four-year institution of higher education that was established in 1869. It was originally located near "Hell's Half Acre," the town's red light district at the time, which was not conducive to its mission of promoting Christian virtue. What really prompted the move to its present location was an offer by the city of 50 acres in south Ft. Worth and $200,000, along with promises of city utility service and a streetcar connection. TCU later sold some of the land it owned, which developed into residential neighborhoods around the campus including **Frisco Heights, Prospect Heights, Forest Park**, and **Park Ridge**. Most of the homes here are small cottages built in the 1920s and 1930s with no sidewalks. Residents of the TCU area are zoned to one of Ft. Worth's best public high schools, Paschal High.

Also located in the shadow of the TCU campus is another private four-year institution of higher education. The College of St. Thomas More is a small liberal arts college located between the TCU campus and Paschal High. Between the high school and St. Thomas More are several apartments and duplexes that are rented by TCU and St. Thomas More students. Recently constructed TCU student housing is located around these apartments and duplexes. The rest of the TCU area contains small, wood-frame homes with siding. The area's most significant focal point is the Gothic Revival St. Stephen's Presbyterian Church, which sits on top of a hill overlooking Forest Park and downtown Ft. Worth.

In south Ft. Worth, below the Trinity River, are a cluster of historic neighborhoods that surround the TCU campus. These areas north, west, and south of the university campus are sometimes referred to as the TCU area. However, they are really independent neighborhoods with their own active neighborhood associations. They are **Bluebonnet Hills, Colonial/Bellaire, University Place, University West, Park Hill, Tanglewood, Westcliff,** and **Overton**. The homes here generally cost more than those in neighboring Fairmount, Ryan Place, Mistletoe Heights, and Berkeley Place.

The TCU area and its surrounding neighborhoods along with Mistletoe, Ryan Place, and Berkeley Place are some of Ft. Worth's most desirable neighborhoods because of their proximity to many attractions. The Trinity River Bike and Jogging Path winds through many of the neighborhoods, providing residents with plenty of outdoor recreational opportunities. In addition, the Colonial Country Club, which hosts an annual PGA golf tournament, is located along the Trinity River. Next door is Forest Park, which encompasses the Ft. Worth Zoo and historic Log Cabin Village. University Drive, which cuts through the TCU area and surrounding neighborhoods, has many restaurants. Hulen Street, which serves as the area's western border, and Berry Street on the southern boundary of the TCU campus, also offer plenty of shopping and dining. In general, these neighborhoods have a reputation as nice, safe places. Their desirability and reputation renders them among the more expensive residential areas of Ft. Worth. However, there has been recent controversy over students living in these neighborhoods. In recent years, parents have been buying homes in these neighborhoods for their children who attend the university because they are an attractive real estate investment that has been made possible by low home mortgage interest rates. This coupled with increasing student enrollment and limited on-campus housing has led several students to live in what was intended for single-family residences. Unfortunately, young college students away from home for the first time do not always make the best neighbors. Though not a major problem, it will remain an issue as long as the university continues to grow.

BLUEBONNET HILLS

Boundaries: North: Berry Dr; Southeast: Granbury Rd; West: University Dr

Bluebonnet Hills, also referred to as Bluebonnet Place, borders the eastern side of TCU. It is a neighborhood of 1930s prairie bungalows and Tudor cottages. Most of the homes are one-story brick and stone residences or wood frames with siding. University Drive divides the neighborhood into eastern and western halves. Homes on the eastern side are slightly older than those on the western side. On University Drive and Berry Drive are some apartments and duplexes that are popular with TCU students.

COLONIAL/BELLAIRE

Boundaries: (roughly) North: Colonial Pkwy/Colonial Country Club; East: University Dr; South: Park Hill/TCU campus; South: TCU campus/Berry; West: Westcliff & Simondale

The **Colonial** neighborhood was a former dairy farm, part of which was turned into the Colonial Country Club in the 1930s. It is sandwiched between the country club and the University West neighborhood. Immediately south of Colonial and west of TCU is **Bellaire**. Colonial and Bellaire homes are typically large, brick or stucco, two-story Colonial, Spanish-inspired, or Tudor-style residences with some ranch-style homes and prairie cottages mixed in. The ranch-style homes are mostly located on the western boundaries of Simondale Drive, where many of the homes are on bluffs overlooking the Trinity River valley and the city's west side. Other homes to the north have views of the golf course, while the southern end contains prairie-style homes. Streets are typically curving, following the natural contours carved by the nearby Trinity River. Homes here can be considerably more costly than in Bluebonnet Hills, which is on the opposite side of the campus.

UNIVERSITY PLACE AND UNIVERSITY WEST

Boundaries: North: Park Hill Dr; East: Merida St; South: Cantey St; West: Walsh Ct

East of Colonial/Bellaire, University Place and University West are adjacent to each other and divided by University Drive. Named for their location along the northern boundaries of the TCU campus, these much sought-after neighborhoods contain a collection of historic homes from the 1920s; the historical and architectural integrity of many of these homes has been preserved. They are attractive places to live because of their location three miles from the CBD, next door to a major university, near a well-regarded golf course, the Ft. Worth Zoo, and a major city park.

University Place is characterized by mature pecan and cedar trees, antique street lamps, and prairie bungalows and Tudor cottages (along with a smattering of other architectural styles) with sharply sloped roofs. Most of them were built in the 1920s by people who made some money during the oil boom at the time. University West has primarily prairie bungalows and Tudor cottages built from the 1920s with ranch-style homes built later in the 1950s and 1960s. Homes here are pricier than in nearby Ryan Place or Berkeley/Mistletoe with the average house valued at around $300,000. The most expensive homes are in University Place. Other housing options here include apartments, townhomes, and duplexes, which are rented mostly by TCU students who also rent the neighborhood's bungalows. Recently, there has been an effort to prevent the construction of new duplexes and to prohibit the renting of property. Some students see this as an attempt to bar them from residing within University Place, while the residents claim that they are merely trying to preserve the value of their property and the ambience of the neighborhood.

Both neighborhoods are served by the University Park Village shopping, dining, and entertainment district. This pedestrian open-air retail center contains shops, unique boutiques, cafes, and restaurants in storefronts that face brick, tree-lined sidewalks.

PARK HILL

Boundaries: North: Winton Terrace Dr; East: Winton Terrace Dr; South: Park Hill Dr; West: Winton Terrace Dr

Tucked against Forest Park and University Place is a collection of historic homes. Bounded by Winton Terrace Drive, which forms a semi-circle around the residential development, it overlooks the park and the city zoo. Homes here are mostly two stories and come in a range of sizes and architectural styles. Though most homes were built in the 1920s, some new construction has taken place here recently. The homes and details seen throughout this neighborhood are a testament to the fact that this place was once the home of prominent Ft. Worth businessmen and community leaders. Park Hill's large trees, antique streetlights, entrance gates, encompassing brick walls, and street names laid in tile on the curb create an old-time elegance. The neighborhood is popular with physicians because of its location near the hospital district.

TANGLEWOOD/WESTCLIFF/STONEGATE

Boundaries: TANGLEWOOD/WESTCLIFF: North: Trinity River; East: TCU campus; South: Bellaire Dr; West: Hulen Dr; STONEGATE: North: Clear Fork of Trinity River; East: Tanglewood; South: Tanglewood neighborhood; West: Hulen St

These three neighborhoods, along with the Overton neighborhood, were once part of Edwards Ranch. They are characterized by tall trees, large lots, and upscale ranch-style homes. The Tanglewood, Westcliff, and Stonegate neighborhoods are within minutes of the CBD, fine restaurants, the university, shopping districts, a noted country club and golf course, private schools, and good public schools.

Tanglewood is an affluent neighborhood between the TCU campus and Hulen Drive, with Bellaire Drive to the south, and the Trinity River to the north. Known as a safe neighborhood with a picturesque landscape, it is set among towering trees and winding roads created by the Trinity River to the north. This neighborhood has an enjoyable and relaxing atmosphere. A biking and walking trail—well shaded by Tanglewood's tall trees—winds through the neighborhood. Great portions of Tanglewood, especially the northern part closest to the river, are low-lying, fertile valley. Located on the site of a former ranch, it is quite fitting that most of the homes here are single-story ranch-style residences made from brick or stone.

Westcliff/Westcliff West contains trees that tower over the mostly one-story cottages built in the 1940s and 1950s. Townhomes are located on the southwest side near Willow Lake while further south are ranch-style homes built in the late 1950s to mid-1960s.

Stonegate is a fairly new neighborhood. This former private ranch was sold to various development companies and private owners in the 1980s. However, residential and commercial development did not seriously begin until the mid-1990s. Most of the residential areas are master-planned, gated communities. The private streets, common areas, and landscaping inside the gated communities are maintained through homeowner's association fees. In this posh neighborhood of grand two-story brick homes, a three-bedroom home can cost around $450,000. On the northern part of Stonegate there are several apartment complexes, some of which are right along the Trinity River. An upscale shopping center is planned for the western part of the neighborhood.

OVERTON

Boundaries: North: Bellaire Dr and Trinity River; East: Overton Park and Foster Park; South: Loop 820/I-20; West: unincorporated areas

Overton, which includes Overton Park, Overton West and Overton Woods, is located five miles from the CBD along the Trinity River. Just south of Tanglewood, it shares many of the same geographic features as Tanglewood such as tall trees, especially in Overton Woods with its heavily forested neighborhoods. Also like Tanglewood, most of the homes are brick or stone ranch-style residences, though other styles such as French manor, Colonial, and traditional can be seen scattered throughout Overton Park. Homes here are usually single story, but quite large. Overton Park is on a higher plane, and many of its homes have views of the city. Prior to its development in the 1950s and 1960s, Overton Park was part of the same cattle ranch that is now the Tanglewood neighborhood. Additional homes were later developed to the west in what is now Overton West and Overton Woods (during the late 1960s and 1980s, respectively). Overton shares the same bike and walk trail as Tanglewood. In addition, the neighborhood has beautiful Willow Lake on the southwest side and is near Hulen Mall with its shopping and dining attractions. Several upscale townhomes are located along Willow Lake.

Web Sites: www.fortworthgov.com, www.uwna.org
Area Code: 817
Zip Codes: 76109, 76110, 76129
Post Offices: TCU, 2800 S University Dr; Trinity River Branch, 4450 Ln; Eighth Avenue Station, 2600 8th Ave
Police Precinct: Ft. Worth Police, www.fortworthpd.com, South District: 3128 W Bolt, 817-922-3461; 1000 Magnolia, 817-871-8885
Emergency Hospital: Baylor All Saints Medical Center, www.baylorhealth.com, 1400 8th Ave, 817-927-6102; John Peter Smith County Hospital, www.jpshealthnet.org, 1500 S Main St, 817-921-3431
Library: Ft. Worth Public Library, www.fortworthlibrary.org: Southwest Regional Branch, 4001 Library Ln, 817-782-9853
Adult Education: Texas Christian University, www.tcu.edu, 2800 S University Dr, 817-257-7000; College of St. Thomas More, www.cstm.edu, 3020 Lubbock Ave, 817-923-8459
Public Education: Ft. Worth Independent School District, www.fortworthisd.org, 100 N University Dr, 817-871-2000
Community Publications: Ft. Worth *Star-Telegram*, www.dfw.com; *Fort Worth Weekly*, www.fwweekly.com; *Converging News*, www.convergingnews.tcu.edu; *Neighborhood News*, www.neighborhoodnews.tcu.edu
Community Resources: City Hall, 1000 Throckmorton, 817-392-7555; Ft. Worth Chamber of Commerce, www.fortworthcoc.org, 777 Taylor St, Ste 900, 817-336-2491
Public Transportation: Ft. Worth Transportation Authority (The T), www.the-t.com, *Bus*: 7, 24, 25, 29

SOUTHWEST SEMINARY/WEDGEWOOD/CANDLERIDGE

SOUTHWEST SEMINARY

Boundaries: (approximately) North: Berry; East: US 35W; South: Loop 820; West: Granbury

Worth Heights, Rosemont, and Seminary
These three neighborhoods surround the Southwestern Baptist Theological Seminary. Amenities include nearby Echo Lake, Town Center Mall, and easy access to I-35W.

The Ft. Worth Town Center is now La Gran Plaza de Ft. Worth. The change is in response to the neighborhood's shift to a largely Hispanic population.

Across from Overton on the other side of the railroad tracks is **South**

Hills. Because of its location next to the Southwestern Baptist Theological Seminary, the homes in this neighborhood are popular with students attending the seminary. This large neighborhood contains mostly small frame houses built in the 1960s.

WEDGEWOOD

Boundaries: North: Loop 820; East: Granbury Rd; South: Altamesa; West: Westcreek Dr

The area that is now Wedgewood was for decades a cattle ranch. The owners sold it to the Wedgewood Development Company and it was developed in 1955 as a residential community. Development continued as late as 1983 in southern Wedgewood, where home prices are higher. The homes in Wedgewood are primarily one-story brick ranch-style residences on streets whose names begin with "W." Unlike nearby neighborhoods, there are no sidewalks here. Eight miles southwest of the Central Business District, it is near Hulen Mall. Wedgwood has several parks, including those that offer youth programs and recreational activities such as tennis, soccer, and basketball.

CANDLERIDGE

Boundaries: (approximately) North: Altamesa; East: McCart; South: Sycamore; West: Granbury

Candleridge is a master-planned community with a very suburban atmosphere. It is located near major freeways I-10 and I-35, and convenient shopping. Designed and built by national home-building companies, homes here are among the most affordable in South Ft. Worth, with a three-bedroom house starting as low as $100,000. Candleridge is ideal for young families. The neighborhood offers many recreational activities, including water sports at Benbrook Reservoir, golfing, and a 110-acre park for jogging and biking. Developed in the late 1970s and 1980s, Candleridge is one of the youngest neighborhoods in South Ft. Worth. Still, new neighborhoods and other master-planned communities are continually springing up near it. New communities in the vicinity include Hulen Meadows, Meadow Creek, Southgate, Southpark, and Summer Creek.

Web Site: www.fortworthgov.org

Area Code: 817

Zip Codes: 76110, 76115, 76133

Post Office: Wedgewood, 3701 Altamesa

Police Precincts: Ft. Worth Police Department, www.fortworthpd.com, South District: 3128 W Bolt, 817-922-3400; West District, 5043 Granbury Rd, 817-871-5480

Emergency Hospitals: Baylor All Saints Medical Center, www.baylorhealth.com, 1400 8th Ave, 817-927-2544; Baylor All Saints Episcopal at Cityview, 7100 Oakmont Blvd; Harris Methodist Southwest, www.harrissw.org, 6100 Harris Pkwy, 817-433-5000

Libraries: Ft. Worth Public Library, www.fortworthlibrary.org, Wedgwood Branch: 3816
   Kimberly Ln, 817-292-3368; Seminary Branch, 501 E Bolt, 817-926-0215
Adult Education: Southwestern Baptist Theological Seminary, www.swbts.edu, 2001
   W Seminary, 817-923-1921
Public Education: Ft. Worth Independent School District, www.fortworthisd.org, 100 N
   University Dr, 817-871-2000
Community Publications: Ft. Worth *Star-Telegram*, www.dfw.com; *Fort Worth Weekly*,
   www.fwweekly.com
Community Resources: City Hall, 1000 Throckmorton, 817-392-7555; Ft. Worth
   Chamber of Commerce, www.fortworthcoc.org, 777 Taylor St, Ste 900, 817-336-
   2491; Worth Heights Community Center, 3551 New York Ave, 817-871-8722
Public Transportation: Ft. Worth Transportation Authority (The T), www.the-t.com,
   Bus: 6, 25, 32, 66E, 72

EAST FORT WORTH

This part of Ft. Worth provides a variety of affordable housing options.
Its location near several major highways gives residents here convenient
access to many of the city's amenities. The easternmost part of the area
was once inhabited by Comanche Indians. It was the site of many battles
between Indians and the U.S. military, who were sent to protect settlers.
A battle took place in the 1840s between an expedition led by General
Ed H. Tarrant and Colonel William Cooke and the Indians. Tarrant and
Cooke were the victors, which strengthened their influence and expanded
territory for settlement.

MEADOWBROOK/EASTERN HILLS, HAMPSHIRE, RYANWOOD/CAROL OAKS, AND HANDLEY

HAMPSHIRE AND MEADOWBROOK/EASTERN HILLS

Boundaries: MEADOWBROOK/EASTERN HILLS: North: I-30; East:
Loop 820; South: E Lancaster Ave; West: Riverside Dr; Boundaries:
HAMPSHIRE: North: Lancaster Ave; East: Loop 820; South: Union
Pacific Railroad; West: Beach St

Meadowbrook is separated from Hampshire by Texas State Highway 180,
also known as Lancaster Avenue. This large neighborhood is a few minutes
from the CBD on the western end and six to seven miles from central Ft.
Worth at the eastern end. It is an established neighborhood with several
types and styles of housing. Residences here include expensive mansions,
fanciful homes that look like European castles, Southern plantations,
prairie bungalows, and gingerbread cottages. There are also some newer,
more affordable homes and apartments, with newer brick homes near the
Meadowbrook Country Club. As an older neighborhood, large trees are
common here. The neighborhood has many parks and a golf course for

residents to enjoy. One of the largest parks is Tandy Hills Park, which has rough, hilly terrain that is ideal for hiking. Located within Meadowbrook along its northeastern corner is the neighborhood of **Eastern Hills**, which is sometimes called Meadowbrook Hills. It is next to the Meadowbrook Golf Course and bounded by I-30 to the north, Oak Hill Rd on the east, Meadowbrook Dr to the south, and Weiler Blvd on the west. Eastern Hills was established in the 1950s by the Eastern Hills Development Company. It contains primarily large ranch-style homes on spacious parcels of land. There are some new townhomes here that were built in the early 1980s. The neighborhood has even more trees than Meadowbrook and is really a wooded area with an undulating landscape.

Located across from the Union Pacific Railroad tracks, immediately above Polytechnic Heights, the **Hampshire** neighborhood is sometimes referred to as South Meadowbrook, after the neighborhood to its north. It is conveniently located three miles east of the Ft. Worth CBD. The typical Hampshire home is a small two-bedroom wood-frame house on a sizable lot with mature trees.

RYANWOOD/CAROL OAKS

Boundaries: North: I-30; East: Morrison Rd; South: Meadowbrook Dr; West: Loop 820

Located south of the western portion of the John T. White neighborhood, Ryanwood was initially developed in the 1940s around the now defunct town of Ederville. Ederville's original buildings have been demolished and replaced by a mix of homes, including several one-story ranch-style homes. Adjacent to Ryanwood's western boundary is the neighborhood of Carol Oaks. Development of the southern section of Carol Oaks began in 1968, while the northern portion followed in 1972. This quiet neighborhood contains traditional brick homes in various architectural styles. There are also apartments on Ederville Road to the north, along I-30.

HANDLEY

Boundaries: North: Meadowbrook Dr; East: Hitson Ln; South: Lancaster Ave; West: Loop 820

Handley was originally a small town named after Confederate Major James Madison Handley, who first settled the area. It was established in 1876 as a railroad town that served the Texas and Pacific Railroad, which is on the southern border of Handley. Across from the railroad tracks further south is Lake Arlington. In the early 1900s, another lake, Lake Erie, existed here. It was a popular recreational spot with a resort built along the lake. A power plant operated there to provide electricity to the inter-urban electric railroad. However, it was eventually swallowed up by Lake Arlington and no longer exists today. By 1946, Ft. Worth had expanded beyond its original borders and annexed Handley.

Handley is an older, historic neighborhood surrounded by large, mature trees. It is a primarily residential area with one- and two-story wood frame homes and a few apartments and commercial areas along Handley Drive. The heart of historic Handley is Lancaster Avenue on the southern border of the community, where several commercial areas are located. Lancaster Avenue passes through the Sandy Oaks neighborhood and extends to the City of Arlington. It once served as a trail connecting the settlement of Ft. Worth to Arlington, which was then called Johnson's Station. Lake Arlington is easily accessible via Loop 820 or Spur 303 (Rosedale Street) for residents who want to go boating, sailing, or picnicking.

Web Site: www.fortworthgov.org
Area Code: 817
Zip Code: 76112
Post Office: Handley Station, 1475 Handley Dr
Police Precinct: Ft. Worth Police Department, www.fortworthpd.com, East Division: 5924 Boca Raton, 817-451-2332; 5650 E Lancaster Ave, 817-871-5200
Emergency Hospitals: Harris Methodist Ft. Worth, www.harrisfw.org, 1301 Pennsylvania Ave, 817-882-2000; John Peter Smith County Hospital, www.jpshealthnet.org, 1500 S Main St, 817-921-3431; JPS Community Health Partnership Ft. Worth, 1855 E Lancaster Ave, 817-852-2838; JPS Health Center Arlington, 601 Sanford, Arlington, 817-920-6300
Library: Meadowbrook Branch: 2800 Stark St, 817-451-0916
Public Education: Ft. Worth Independent School District, www.fortworthisd.org, 100 N University Dr, 817-871-2000
Community Publications: Ft. Worth *Star-Telegram*, www.dfw.com; *Fort Worth Weekly*, www.fwweekly.com
Community Resources: City Hall, 1000 Throckmorton, 817-392-7555; Ft. Worth Chamber of Commerce, www.fortworthcoc.org, 777 Taylor St, Ste 900, 817-336-2491; Handley/Meadowbrook Community Center, 6201 Beaty St, 817-451-0222
Public Transportation: Ft. Worth Transportation (The T), www.the-t.com, *Bus*: 2, 21, 22, 25

WHITE LAKE HILLS, WOODHAVEN, AND BRENTWOOD HILLS

WHITE LAKE HILLS

Boundaries: North: Randol Mill Rd; East: Woodhaven; South: I-30; West: Oakland Blvd

Immediately north of Meadowbrook is the quiet neighborhood of **White Lake Hills**. This hilly area has some amazing views of the untouched landscape to its west, which includes White Lake and Gateway Park. Gateway Park, located along Randol Mill Rd, which turns into 1st Street, is a major Ft. Worth recreational space that includes a top quality dog park named Fort Woof.

The White Lake dairy farm was located near here until residential development began in the 1960s. In 1967, a private development company bought the land from the Carter Foundation, owned by Amon G. Carter, the founder of the Ft. Worth *Star-Telegram* newspaper and creator of the Amon Carter Museum, and began development of the area. White Lake Hills is secluded, with few roads leading into the neighborhood. It is surrounded by undeveloped land, except to the south where it borders the Meadowbrook neighborhood. The two neighborhoods are separated by I-30, which provides Meadowbrook residents easy access to the CBD. White Lake Hills contains mostly one-story brick traditional homes. An apartment complex is located along Willow Lake on the eastern edge of the neighborhood, which looks out into the open spaces beyond and one of the two White Lakes that are located on opposite ends of the neighborhood.

WOODHAVEN

Boundaries: North: Randol Mill Rd; East: Loop 820; South: I-30; West: Woodhaven Dr

Located along two major freeways, I-30 and Loop 820, Woodhaven has convenient access to the Mid-Cities, the CBD, which is about six miles to the west, and other parts of Ft. Worth. The neighborhood is named after the Woodhaven Development Company, which began residential construction in 1969. Large attractive homes surround the private Woodhaven Country Club in the northwestern corner of Woodhaven, which covers a big portion of the neighborhood. There are also several townhomes, apartments, and golf course communities near the country club. Like adjacent White Lake Hills, Woodhaven has a hilly terrain resulting in winding streets. The gated community of **Riverbend Estates** is to the north of Woodhaven, between Randol Mill Road and the West Fork of the Trinity River. The country club and Riverbend Estate residents have leased their subsurface rights to oil and natural gas companies for natural gas drilling. However, golfers and residents have not been inconvenienced as the drilling is several hundred feet underground and from a remote site using a horizontal line.

BRENTWOOD HILLS

Boundaries: (approximately) North: I-30; East: Loop 820; South: Meadowbrook Dr; West: Sandy Ln

The neighborhood's name accurately describes its heavily wooded and hilly landscape. Most of the homes here are brick or stone masonry ranch-style homes with low roofs. The southern part of Brentwood Hills is largely undeveloped, privately owned property.

This small neighborhood is located six miles east of the Ft. Worth Central Business District.

Web Site: www.fortworthgov.org
Area Code: 817

Zip Codes: 76103, 76112, 76120

Post Office: Handley Station, 1475 Handley Dr

Police Precinct: Ft. Worth Police Department, www.fortworthpd.com: 5924 Boca Raton, 817-451-2332; 5650 E Lancaster Ave, 817-871-5200

Emergency Hospitals: Arlington Memorial Hospital, www.texashealth.org, 800 W Randol Mill Rd, Arlington, 817-548-6100; Harris Methodist Ft. Worth, www.harrisfw.org, 1301 Pennsylvania Ave, 817-882-2000; John Peter Smith County Hospital, www.jpshealthnet.org, 1500 S Main St, 817-921-3431

Library: Ft. Worth Public Library, www.fortworthlibrary.org; East Regional Branch, 6301 Bridge St, 817-871-6436

Public Education: Ft. Worth Independent School District, www.fortworthisd.org, 100 N University Dr, 817-871-2000

Community Publications: Ft. Worth *Star-Telegram*, www.dfw.com; *Fort Worth Weekly*, www.fwweekly.com

Community Resources: City Hall, 1000 Throckmorton, 817-392-7555; Ft. Worth Chamber of Commerce, www.fortworthcoc.org, 777 Taylor St, Ste 900, 817-336-2491; Fort Woof Dog Park, www.fortworthdogpark.org, 1701 N Beach St, 817-838-9765

Public Transportation: Ft. Worth Transportation Authority (The T), www.the-t.com, *Bus*: 2, 21, 40

JOHN T. WHITE/SANDYBROOK/COBBLESTONE SQUARE, COOKE'S MEADOW, SANDY OAKS, AND BENTLEY VILLAGE

JOHN T. WHITE/SANDYBROOK/ COBBLESTONE SQUARE

Boundaries: North: Randol Mill Rd; East: Randol Mill Rd; South: I-30; West: Loop 820

John T. White served as former superintendent of the Ft. Worth Independent School District in 1929. The neighborhood that is named after him contains a mix of old frame houses and newer ranch-style homes. It is a large, diverse community with many large lots and empty fields. **John T. White** includes the **Sandybrook** area, which features tract homes, mass-produced houses constructed by one builder. Sandybrook homes date back to 1979 and are primarily constructed of stone masonry with low roofs.

The John T. White neighborhood surrounds **Cobblestone Square**, a small neighborhood that covers only a few blocks. It borders John T. White Rd to the north, Cooke Rd to the east, I-30 on the south, and Morrison Dr on the west. This area was privately held land for many decades until the Ray Rothwell Development Corporation began residential construction in 1969. Most of the residences here are traditional ranch-style homes built of brick. Located eight to ten miles east of central Ft. Worth on the edge of the city, Cobblestone Square, along with John T. White, is surrounded by undeveloped land.

COOKE'S MEADOW AND SANDY OAKS

Boundaries: COOKE'S MEADOW: North: I-30; East: Cooke's Ln; South: Meadowbrook Dr; West: Morrison Dr; SANDY OAKS: North: Meadowbrook Dr; East: Cooke's Ln; South: Lancaster Ave; West: Hitson Ln

Cooke's Meadow is named after Colonel William Cooke, who along with General Edward Tarrant and their troops, fought with Comanche Indians to protect settlers from harassment by Indians trying to protect their land from the settlers. One of the easternmost neighborhoods in Ft. Worth, Cooke's Meadow is closer to the City of Arlington than to central Ft. Worth. It covers a small area full of towering trees and mainly brick ranch-style homes with low-pitched roofs. There are also a few duplexes in this neighborhood, but not apartments.

Adjacent to Handley is another primarily residential community known as **Sandy Oaks**. Most of the homes here are traditional brick ranch-style houses with low roofs built in the 1970s. As an older neighborhood, it has many tall trees. At the southern edge of Sandy Oaks are some recently built larger custom homes. Though it is nine miles from the Central Business District, the older homes are very affordable, with a three-bedroom home available on the market for $110,000. There are also some apartments here.

BENTLEY VILLAGE

Boundaries: North: West Fork of the Trinity River; East: Village Creek; South: I-30; West: Eastchase Pkwy

Located approximately 10 miles from the CBD, this is a neighborhood of master-planned communities. Construction of major roads into the area has resulted in better access and serious residential development. Bentley Village contains large custom and luxury homes that typically measure over 2,000 square feet. There are a mix of one- and two-story homes in a variety of architectural styles, which provides each residence a unique identity. Most of the homes have a stone or mason work exterior with garages located out of sight to the rear of the house. This quiet, suburban-like community also has several new residential developments near Cottonwood Creek and Waterchase Golf Course. Its design and layout is reminiscent of a suburban community, which it pretty much is given its distance from central Ft. Worth. It is the farthest of the east Ft. Worth neighborhoods and sits on the edge of town around largely undeveloped land. In fact, Bentley Village is closer to the City of Arlington than to Ft. Worth.

EASTCHASE

Boundaries: North: Meadowbrook and Eastchase Pkwy; East: Arlington city limits; South: Arlington city limits; West: Cooke's Ln

This is a relatively new neighborhood on the eastern edge of Ft. Worth near undeveloped land. It is actually closer to Arlington city limits than to central Ft. Worth, which is approximately 10 miles to the west. Development of Eastchase began in the early 1970s and consists mostly of apartments and townhomes. An exclusive single-family residential community was developed in this area in the late 1980s and early 1990s at the southern end of the neighborhood. The homes here are on large lots in a heavily wooded area.

Web Site: www.fortworthgov.org
Area Code: 817
Zip Codes: 76103, 76112, 76120
Post Offices: Riverbend Station, 2414 Gravel Dr; Handley Station, 1475 Handley Dr
Police Precinct: Ft. Worth Police Department, www.fortworthpd.com: 5924 Boca Raton, 817-451-2332; 5650 E Lancaster Ave, 817-871-5200
Emergency Hospital: Arlington Memorial Hospital, www.texashealth.org, 800 W Randol Mill Rd, Arlington, 817-548-6100
Library: Ft. Worth Library, www.fortworthlibrary.org, East Regional Branch, 6301 Bridge St, 817-871-6436
Public Education: Ft. Worth Independent School District, www.fortworthisd.org, 100 N University Dr, 817-871-2000
Community Publications: Ft. Worth *Star-Telegram*, www.dfw.com; *Fort Worth Weekly*, www.fwweekly.com
Community Resources: City Hall, 1000 Throckmorton, 817-392-7555; Ft. Worth Chamber of Commerce, www.fortworthcoc.org, 777 Taylor St, Ste 900, 817-336-2491
Public Transportation: Ft. Worth Transportation Authority (The T), www.the-t.com, *Bus*: 2, 21, 22, 40

NORTH FORT WORTH

Boundaries: (approximately) North: Long Ave; East: TX 199; South: Northside Dr; West: US 287/81/35W

NORTHSIDE

The Northside of Ft. Worth is a predominantly Hispanic neighborhood where most of the residents are immigrants from Latin America or the first-generation children of these immigrants. There are Spanish-language signs, and Spanish is heard more often than English here. It is one of the city's poorest areas, with a significant number of residents below the poverty level. Most of its residents work entry-level or menial low-wage jobs.

There has, however, been new home construction in recent years due to the growing interest in living near the CBD. Three-bedroom brick, single-family residences for young families have popped up, and the Northside is fast becoming one of the city's most affordable and popular neighborhoods. It is located around the Stockyards historical entertainment district and the retail shops on Main Street. Neighborhoods include the Diamond Hill Area and the Stockyards.

Near downtown, the Stockyards are a historic reminder of the city's past as a cattle and livestock town. When the railroads arrived in Ft. Worth in 1876, beef was shipped directly from the city to Chicago and other points up north. The opening of the Swift and Armour meat packing plants located north of the CBD, around this area, ensured the continuation of the city's traditional industry until they closed in the 1960s. The Stockyards, once a holding area for meat waiting to be shipped via rail, is now a museum that celebrates Ft. Worth's cattle industry. The area also features bars, nightclubs, rodeo, restaurants with a Western theme, and murals of the Old West.

Web Sites: www.fortworthgov.org, www.fortworthstockyards.org, www.stockyardstation. com

Area Code: 817

Zip Codes: 76106, 76161

Post Offices: Stockyard Station, 2120 Ellis Ave; Jack D. Watson Finance Station, 4600 Mark IV Pkwy

Police Precinct: Ft. Worth Police Department, www.fortworthpd.com: North District, 3457 Decatur, 817-740-2100

Emergency Hospitals: John Peter Smith County Hospital, www.jpshealthnet.org, 1500 S Main St, 817-921-3431; Twin Oaks Medical Center, 2919 Markum Dr, Haltom City

Libraries: Ft. Worth Public Library, www.fortworthlibrary.org: Northside Branch, 601 Park St, 817-626-8241; Diamond Hill/Jarvis Branch, 1300 NE 35th St, 817-624-7331

Public Education: Ft. Worth Independent School District, www.fortworthisd.org, 100 N University Dr, 817-871-2000

Community Publications: Ft. Worth *Star-Telegram*, www.dfw.com; *Fort Worth Weekly*, www.fwweekly.com

Community Resources: City Hall, 1000 Throckmorton, 817-392-7555; Ft. Worth Chamber of Commerce, www.fortworthcoc.org, 777 Taylor St, Ste 900, 817-336-2491; Ft. Worth Northside Community Health Center, www.tachc.org, 2100 N Main, Ste 214, 817-378-0855; Ft. Worth Boys and Girls Club, www.fortworthkids.org: North Ft. Worth, 2000 Ellis Ave, 817-624-8406; Safe Haven Diamond Hill, 3201 Refugio, 817-624-3591; Northside Community Center, 1901 Harrington, 817-871-5820; North Tri-Ethnic Community Center, 2950 Roosevelt Ave, 817-871-5850

Public Transportation: Ft. Worth Transportation Authority (The T), www.the-t.com, *Bus*: 1, 1c, 1d, 14, 15, 17

RIVERSIDE

Boundaries: North: Long Ave; East: Beach St; South: I-30; West: I-35

Riverside is a neighborhood east of Northside, on the other side of I-35, and is noted for its racial diversity. Its current reputation belies its history as the site of past racial tension. In 1956, an African-American family moved into the then predominantly white neighborhood, sparking protests, verbal attacks, and death threats. Today, residents of Asian, white, black, and Hispanic backgrounds all live together in this mainly working class neighborhood. Riverside has a quiet suburban atmosphere with well-maintained pre–World War II homes. It is next to the suburb of Haltom City and near major interstates I-30 and I-35, which provide access to the other communities in the Metroplex.

Web Site: www.fortworthgov.org
Area Code: 817
Zip Code: 76111
Post Office: Riverside Station, 400 N Retta St
Police Precinct: Ft. Worth Police Department, www.fortworthpd.com, 3457 Decatur, 817-740-2100
Emergency Hospitals: John Peter Smith County Hospital, www.jpshealthnet.org, 1500 S Main St, 817-921-3431; Twin Oaks Medical Center, 2919 Markum Dr, Haltom City
Libraries: Ft. Worth Public Library, www.fortworthlibrary.org: Northside Branch: 601 Park St, 817-626-8241; Diamond Hill/Jarvis Branch: 1300 NE 35th St, 817-624-7331
Public Education: Ft. Worth Independent School District, www.fortworthisd.org, 100 N University Dr, 817-871-2000
Community Publications: Ft. Worth *Star-Telegram*, www.dfw.com; *Fort Worth Weekly*, www.fwweekly.com
Community Resources: City Hall, 1000 Throckmorton, 817-392-7555; Ft. Worth Chamber of Commerce, www.fortworthcoc.org, 777 Taylor St, Ste 900, 817-336-2491; Riverside Community Center, 3700 E Belknap, 817-871-7670
Public Transportation: Ft. Worth Transportation Authority (The T), www.the-t.com, *Bus*: 12

ROCK ISLAND/SAMUELS AVENUE

Boundaries: North: Northside Dr; East: Wilderman St; South: E Bluff St; West: Samuels/Bennett

Rock Island is a historic neighborhood northeast of downtown near the county court house. Tucked against the Trinity River and hidden behind trees, it was forgotten by time until recently. Once inhabited by Ft. Worth's wealthy, it has long been neglected. The decline started when the Swift and Armour meat packing plants opened across the Trinity River, sending offending odors into the area. However, residents stayed on until the late 1960s. Afterwards, Rock Island mostly became a neglected area. Today, most of the homes are boarded up or deteriorating. The neighborhood's empty lots have become illegal dumping grounds and homeless hangout areas. Down by the river, illegal dumping has polluted the Trinity and scarred the scenery. Nevertheless, its location along the Trinity on the top of a bluff has attracted a developer, who has visions of turning Rock Island into an intown community known as Trinity Bluff. Plans include a residential area on top of the bluff that will provide views of north Ft. Worth, the river, and downtown Ft. Worth. Apartments, condos, townhomes, retail shops, and hiking/biking trails are planned along the riverfront. Development plans are to have buildings in architectural styles of the 1880s to the 1920s, the height of the neighborhood's glory. There are still remnants of the Victorian era and Gothic-style homes that were built by wealthy citizens. Grand and stately homes are located on top of the bluffs that slope down onto **Samuels Avenue**, while smaller bungalows and cottages were later built at the bottom of the bluffs.

Below the Rock Island/Samuels Avenue neighborhood and the Trinity River, near downtown, are several duplexes that are available to renters with moderate incomes and a few Section 8 renters. The area is attractive to downtown workers because of its convenient location.

Web Site: www.fortworthgov.org

Area Code: 817

Zip Code: 76102

Post Offices: Central Ft. Worth Station, 819 Taylor St; Tandy Center Station, 100 Throckmorton St, Ste 151; Downtown Ft. Worth Station, 251 W Lancaster Ave

Police Precinct: Ft. Worth Police Department, www.fortworthpd.com: North District, 500 E 1st St, 817-871-6400

Emergency Hospitals: John Peter Smith County Hospital, www.jpshealthnet.org, 1500 S Main St, 817-921-3431; Baylor All Saints Medical Center, www.baylorhealth.com, 1400 Eighth Ave, 817-926-2544

Library: Ft. Worth Public Library, www.fortworthlibrary.org, Central Branch: 500 W 3rd St, 817-871-7701

Public Education: Ft. Worth Independent School District, www.fortworthisd.org, 100 N University Dr, 817-871-2000

Community Publications: Ft. Worth *Star-Telegram*, www.dfw.com; *Fort Worth Weekly*, www.fwweekly.com

Community Resources: City Hall, 1000 Throckmorton, 817-392-7555; Ft. Worth Chamber of Commerce, www.fortworthcoc.org, 777 Taylor St, Ste 900, 817-336-2491

Public Transportation: Ft. Worth Transportation Authority (The T), www.the-t.com, *Bus*: 12

FAR NORTH FORT WORTH

Boundaries: North: Keller-Hicks Rd; East: Union-Pacific Railroad; South: Loop 820; West: I-35W

In the past ten years, this area of Ft. Worth has grown tremendously. Several new master-planned communities have now replaced the previously undeveloped area next to the suburbs of Keller, Watauga, and Haltom City. Fairly new neighborhoods such as **Park Glen, Summerfields, Arcadia Park**, and **Fossil Creek** offer affordable, quality housing that has attracted many young families. Homes here range from the mid $100,000s to over $250,000, depending on the neighborhood and the builder. New homes are still being constructed in this part of the city. Amenities in the area include Fossil Creek Golf Club, a trail park, and several other green spaces. In addition, retailers and other businesses have opened alongside the new neighborhoods.

Web Sites: www.fortworthgov.org, http://parkglen.org; www.arcadiapark.net
Area Code: 817
Zip Codes: 76137, 76248
Post Offices: Watauga Station, 6651 Watauga Rd, Ste 103, Watauga; Keller Station, 520 E Vine St, Keller
Police Precinct: Ft. Worth Police Department, www.fortworthpd.com: North District, 7451 N Beach, 817-212-2875
Emergency Hospitals: Twin Oaks Medical Center, 2919 Markum Dr, Haltom City; North Hills Hospital, www.northhillshospital.com, 4401 Booth Calloway Rd, North Richland Hills, 817-255-1000
Library: Ft. Worth Public Library, www.fortworthlibrary.org: Summerglen Branch, 4205 Basswood Blvd, 817-232-0478
Public Education: Keller Independent School District, www.kellerisd.net, 350 Keller Pkwy, Keller, 817-744-1000
Community Publications: Ft. Worth *Star-Telegram*, www.dfw.com; *Fort Worth Weekly*, www.fwweekly.com
Community Resources: City Hall, 1000 Throckmorton, 817-392-7555; Ft. Worth Chamber of Commerce, www.fortworthcoc.org, 777 Taylor St, Ste 900, 817-336-2491
Public Transportation: Ft. Worth Transportation Authority (The T), www.the-t.com, *Bus*: 62E (express route)

NORTHWEST FORT WORTH

SANSOM PARK/LAKE WORTH

Boundaries: SANSOM PARK: North: Azle Ave; East: Ft. Worth city limits; South: Ft. Worth city limits; West: Roberts Cut Off and Lake Worth Blvd; LAKE WORTH: North: Ft. Worth city limits; East: Lake Worth; South: Lake Worth Ave and Navajo Trail; West: Ft. Worth city limits

Sansom Park is one of several small independent communities that surround Lake Worth in northwest Ft. Worth. This is a low-income community with a significant Hispanic population. The median house value here is $39,000. North of Sansom Park is **Lake Worth**, originally a popular residential and recreational town called Indian Oaks. The community started in the late 1920s and early 1930s and featured a casino, dance hall, boardwalk, and nightclub. After being known as Indian Oaks for decades, it was incorporated in the 1950s as Lake Worth Village. This residential community right outside of northwest Forth Worth is named after the nearby lake. Like Sansom Park Village, Lake Worth has a significant Hispanic population and is comprised of mostly lower middle income residents.

Web Sites: www.ci.sansom-park.tx.us, www.lakeworthtx.org
Area Code: 817
Zip Codes: 76114, 76135

Post Offices: Oaks Station, 1008 Roberts Cut Off Rd, River Oaks; Naval Air Station/ JRB, 1501 Arnold Ave, Naval Air Station/Jrb; Lake Worth Station, 3930 Telephone Rd

Police Departments: Sansom Park Police Department, 5500 Buchanan St, 817-626-1921; Lake Worth Police Department, 3805 Adam Grubb Dr, Lake Worth, 817-237-1224

Emergency Hospitals: Baylor All Saints Medical Center, www.baylorhealth.com, 1400 8th Ave, 817-927-2544; Baylor All Saints Episcopal at Cityview, 7100 Oakmont Blvd; Harris Methodist Southwest, www.harrissw.org, 6100 Harris Pkwy, 817-433-5000

Library: Mary Lou Reddick Public Library (Lake Worth), 3801 Adam Grubb Dr, Lake Worth, 817-237-9681

Adult Education: Tarrant County Community College, Northwest Campus, 4801 Marine Creek Pkwy, 817-515-7100

Public Education: Lake Worth Independent School District, www.lake-worth.k12. tx.us, 6800 Telephone Rd, Lake Worth, 817-306-4200; Castleberry Independent School District, 315 Churchill Rd, 817-252-2000 (most of Sansom Park); Ft. Worth Independent School District, www.fortworthisd.org, 100 N University Dr, 817-871-2000 (part of Sansom Park)

Community Publications: *Northwest Tarrant County Times Records*, www. timesrecordonline.com

Community Resources: Sansom Park City Hall, 5500 Buchanan St, 817-626-3791; Lake Worth City Hall, 3805 Adam Grubb, Lake Worth, 817-237-1211; Northwest Tarrant County Chamber of Commerce, www.nwtcc.org, 3900 Merrett Dr, Ste A, Lake Worth, 817-237-0060

AZLE/PELICAN BAY/LAKESIDE

Boundaries: AZLE: North: Sandy Beach Rd; East: Eagle Mountain Lake; South: Jacksboro Ave; West/Southwest: unincorporated areas; PELICAN BAY: North: unincorporated areas; East: unincorporated areas; South: Liberty School Rd; West: Liberty School Rd; LAKESIDE: North: unincorporated areas; East: Rankin Rd and Lake Worth Blvd; South: Camp Joy Park and Wildwood Park; West: Silver Creek Rd and Timberwolfe Ln

Azle is a small town located 16 miles northwest of Ft. Worth on the western banks of Eagle Mountain Lake. It is quite removed from Ft. Worth in the far northwest corner of Tarrant County. Part of it extends into Parker County. Despite its distance from the city, Ft. Worth can easily be reached by Texas State Highway 199, which runs through Azle.

This once agricultural community has been the site of major housing development in the past few decades. Azle recently annexed the area surrounding the Cross Timbers Golf Course in the western edge of the city. The town has been transformed into a suburban master-planned community with a relaxed rural quality of life. However, there are still pastures with roaming cattle and horses. Starter homes are available for as low as $80,000, while more elaborate homes can cost up to $500,000. People are attracted by the availability of affordable new homes, a safe and friendly environment, the country atmosphere, child-friendly community, its lakeside location, and convenient access to Ft. Worth. Just east of Azle, **Pelican Bay** is a small community that covers only .7 square miles. This young resort community developed along Eagle Mountain Lake in the 1970s and was incorporated in 1981. It currently has a population under 2,000. Pelican Bay is approximately 17 miles from Ft. Worth and relatively isolated, with the nearest access to Ft. Worth in the neighboring town of Azle. A substantial portion of the housing here consists of vacation homes and cottages, and weekend rentals.

Lakeside is named for its location along the banks of Lake Worth. It is a nature lover's dream. The town lies between the Ft. Worth Nature Center and Refuge on the north and Camp Joy Park, Wildwood Park, and Lake Worth to the south. This is a small town of a little over 1,000, with a standard of living that is higher than some of the other lakeside communities.

Web Site: www.azle.govoffice.com

Area Code: 817

Zip Codes: 76020, 76108

Post Office: Azle Station, 409 Commerce St, Azle; White Settlement Station, 301 N Las Vegas Trl, Ft. Worth

Police Departments: Azle Police and Civil Defense, 613 SE Pkwy, Azle, 817-444-3221; Lakeside Police Department, 9830 Confederate Park Rd, Ft. Worth, 817-626-1921; Pelican Bay Police, 1300 Pelican Circle, Azle, 817-444-1234

Emergency Hospital: Harris Methodist Northwest Hospital, www.texashealth.org, 108 Denver Trl, Azle, 817-444-8600

Library: Azle Public Library, 609 Southeast Pkwy, Azle, 817-444-7114

Public Education: Azle Independent School District, www.azle.esc11.net, 300 Roe St, Azle, 817-444-3235 (serves Azle, Pelican Bay, and Lakeside); Little Elm Independent School District, 500 Lobo Ln, Little Elm, 972-292-1847 (serves portions of Lakeside)

Community Publications: *Azle News*, www.azlenews.net, *Lakeside Times*, www.lakesidetimes.com

Community Resources: Azle City Hall, 613 Southeast Pkwy, Azle, 817-444-2541; Azle Chamber of Commerce, 252 W Main, Ste A, Azle, 817-444-1112; Lakeside Town Hall, 9830 Confederate Park Rd, Lakeside, 817-237-1234; Northwest Tarrant County Chamber of Commerce, www.nwtcc.org, 3900 Merrett Dr, Ste A, Lake Worth, 817-237-0060

SOUTH SUBURBS

CROWLEY

Crowley is a rural suburban community 15 miles south of downtown Ft. Worth. Settled in 1848, it was supported by dairy farming, railroad-related activities, and ranching. Until the end of World War II, Crowley was a small town with a few hundred residents. By the end of the 1970s, it the original buildings, which are still standing. New brick buildings that blend in with the area's design and a parking garage in the rear have been added to the district. Rice Village is known for the unique boutiques and independently owned shops like the five and dime store that has been operating here for decades. Among the over 300 shops in the Village are also several national clothing chains and retailers in the newer sections.

Visitors looking for someplace to eat have an array of options, including Thai, Japanese, Turkish, Greek, American, Chinese, Spanish, Mexican, and Italian restaurants. On the weekends, the casual bars, pubs, and trendy upscale lounges that mingle side by side are packed with patrons. Parking on the weekends can be a hassle and difficult, especially along Morningside and University. Evidently, though, many people believe it is worth it, as witnessed by the crowds here. Across from the Village, on the other side of Kirby Drive, are several townhomes, some of them recently constructed. There are also many rental properties in the West Village that are usually occupied either by university students or medical residents from the Medical Center.

Tucked into West University is an L-shaped area known as **Southside Place**. This very affluent community covers only nine streets, which are in alphabetical order. This secluded neighborhood dates back to the 1920s, when it was a small community. It has the same small town, family-friendly atmosphere as West University and Bellaire. Sometimes it is difficult to tell the difference between West University and Southside Place. Almost all of the commercial businesses are located along Bellaire Boulevard/ Holcombe, which also runs through West University and Bellaire.

The **Old Braeswood** neighborhood dates back to the 1930s and is located across from West University on the other side of Holcombe Blvd. Previously called Braeswood, it was renamed Old Braeswood in the 1980s to distinguish itself from the other neighborhoods, commonly referred to as Braeswood, that were developing along Brays Bayou. Though not one of the most recognizable neighborhoods by name, it rivals Houston's most prestigious residential areas. Homes here have steadily increased in value over the years and many are now worth about $400,000 or more. Old Braeswood is characterized by large trees and historic homes. The architectural design, street layout, and ambience are similar to West University Place. However, some of the old homes are slowly being replaced by large multi-story townhomes that seem conspicuously out of place in a quiet residential neighborhood.

Web Sites: www.ci.bellaire.tx.us, www.westu.org, www.ci.southside-place.tx.us, www. oldbraeswood.com

Area Code: 713

Zip Codes: 77401, 77005, 77025

Post Offices: Bellaire Station, 5350 Bellaire Blvd, Bellaire; William Rice Station, 5201 Wakeforest St, Houston; Astrodome Station, 8205 Braeswood Dr, Houston; Medical Center Station, 7205 Almeda Rd, Houston

Police Departments: Bellaire Police Department, 5110 Jessamine, Bellaire, 713-668-0487; West University Police Department, 3814 University Blvd, West University Pl,

had over 2,000 residents. This quiet and peaceful residential community has quite a few ranches still in existence. With most of the land still undeveloped, homebuilders are continually constructing new homes, neighborhoods, and subdivisions. Crowley has a good selection of old and new homes in varying price ranges. Homes start at $80,000 and can go as high as over $250,000 for a new custom home. The typical home here costs about $135,000 to $160,000, which is considerably cheaper than in some of the neighborhoods near central Ft. Worth. I-35 is the major route into Ft. Worth and Arlington.

Web Site: www.ci.crowley.tx.us

Area Code: 817

Zip Code: 76036

Post Office: 200 S Crowley Rd, Crowley

Police Department: Crowley Police Department, 201 S Texas St, Crowley, 817-297-2276

Emergency Hospital: Huguley Memorial Medical Center, www.huguley.org, 11801 South Fwy (I-35), Burleson, 817-293-9110

Library: Crowley Public Library, www.crowleylibrary.org, 409 Oak St, Crowley, 817-297-6706

Public Education: Crowley Independent School District, www.crowley.k12.tx.us, 512 Peach St, Crowley, 817-297-5800

Community Publication: *Crowley Star-Review*

Community Resources: City Hall, 201 E Main St, Crowley, 817-297-2201; Crowley Area Chamber of Commerce, www.crowleyareachamber.org, 200 E Main St, Ste D, Crowley, 817-297-4211; Crowley Youth Association, www.cyasports.org; Dionne Bagsby All Sports Complex, 1501 Longhorn Trl, Ft. Worth, 817-297-2588

JOHNSON COUNTY

BURLESON

Burleson is perhaps best known as the hometown of American Idol winner Kelly Clarkson. This small, quiet town is ideal for young families. Most of the people who move here are young couples looking for a nice, affordable place to raise small children. The atmosphere is more country than suburban, but it has all the conveniences of a suburb or city. There are two golf courses in the area, Hidden Creek and Mountain Valley, and the entertainment attractions of Ft. Worth and the Mid-Cities are within short driving distance.

Burleson offers a variety of housing options that include new and old single-family homes, apartments, lots for new home construction, golf course communities, luxury residences, farms, and waterfront property. Homes here cater to a range of income levels and vary from $85,000 to over $500,000. The town has grown along with the population of Ft. Worth. It continues to attract new residents with its quality public school system, small town friendliness, and rural atmosphere.

Web Site: www.burlesontx.com

Area Code: 817
Zip Code: 96028
Post Office: Burleson Station, 232 SW Johnson, Burleson
Police Department: Burleson Police Department, 225 W Renfro, Burleson, 817-447-5300
Emergency Hospital: Huguley Memorial Medical Center, www.huguley.org, 11801 South Fwy (I-35), Burleson, 817-293-9110
Library: Burleson Public Library, www.burlesonlibrary.com, 248 SW Johnson Ave, Burleson, 817-295-6131
Public Education: Burleson Independent School District, www.burlesonisd.net, 1160 SW Wilshire, Burleson, 817-447-5730
Community Publications: *Burleson Star, Joshua Tribune, Burleson Star-Review*
Community Resources: City Hall, 141 W Renfro St, Burleson, 817-447-5440; Burleson Chamber of Commerce, www.burleson.org, 1044 SW Wilshire, Burleson, 817-295-6121; Bartlett Park Sports Complex, 550 Summercrest, Burleson, 817-447-2255

SOUTHEAST SUBURBS

FOREST HILL AND EVERMAN

Forest Hill is an old residential suburb approximately 8 miles southeast of Ft. Worth. Established in 1896, it had few residents until the late 1940s, when population increased steadily each year forward. Its growth mimicked that of Ft. Worth's. Forest Hill is at the intersection of Interstate Highway 20/820 and State Highway 496, eight miles southeast of Ft. Worth in south central Tarrant County. It is a lower-middle to low-income community with a diverse population (57% African-American, 33% white, 18% Hispanic).

Among the most distinctive sights in **Everman** are the huge bird-nests built on the city's telephone lines by the wild Quaker parakeet colonies. The origin of these green birds is a mystery, but they have been in the town for years. The city has been settled since the 1800s and was known as Oak Grove. The arrival of the International-Great Northern Railroad in 1902 led to the development of a more stable town. In 1917, the establishment of a flight training school for the Canadian Royal Flying Corps and the Aviation Section of the United States Signal Corps at Barron Field, just outside the city, expanded the economy of Everman and its population. The population has steadily grown since then. In response, the city has recently built a new police station and library and completed repairs on critical infrastructures. Everman is located on the southern edge of Ft. Worth near U.S. Highway 820 in southeastern Tarrant County. Like Forest Hill, this suburban residential community has a racially diverse population of mostly lower-middle to middle-class income residents.

Web Sites: www.ci.foresthill.tx.us; www.evermantx.net
Area Code: 817
Zip Codes: 76119, 76140

Post Offices: Glencrest Station, 5125 Wichita St, Ft. Worth; Southeast Station, 500 S
  Forest Hill Dr, Ft. Worth
Police Departments: Forest Hill Police Department, 3336 Horton Rd, Forest Hill, 817-
  531-5250; Everman Police Department, 404 West Enon, Everman, 817-293-2923
Emergency Hospital: Huguley Memorial Medical Center, www.huguley.org, 11801
  South Fwy (1-35W), Burleson, 817-293-9110
Library: Everman Public Library, 100 N Race St, Everman, 817-551-0726
Public Education: Everman Independent School District, www.eisd.org, 608 Townley
  Dr, Everman, 817-568-3500
Community Publication: Ft. Worth *Star-Telegram*, www.dfw.com
Community Resources: Forest Hill City Hall, 6800 Forest Hill Dr, Forest Hill, 817-568-
  3000; Everman City Hall, 212 N Race St, Everman, 817-293-0525; South Tarrant
  County Chamber of Commerce, 6800 Forest Hill Dr, Arlington, 817-568-2685

MANSFIELD

Mansfield is a suburb located approximately 16 miles south of Ft.
Worth. The community is partly rural with a downtown that looks like
stereotypical small town Main Street America. For many decades, it was a
small agricultural community. Growth really took off in the 1990s and it
now serves as a bedroom community. Homes can start as low as $90,000
although they can also cost as much as $1 million. There are single-
family homes, apartments, new construction, golf course communities,
and luxury homes alongside farmland and horse property. The premier
residential areas in Mansfield are located along Walnut Creek. Other
small towns near Mansfield to consider are **Bisbee** and **Kennedale.**

Web Site: www.mansfield-tx.gov
Area Code: 817
Zip Code: 76063
Post Office: Mansfield Station, 752 N Main St, Mansfield
Police Department: Mansfield Police Department, www.mansfieldpolice.com, 1200 E
  Broad St, Mansfield, 817-276-4700
Emergency Hospital: Medical Center of Arlington, www.medicalcenterarlington.com,
  3301 Matlock Rd, Arlington, 817-472-4850
Library: Mansfield Public Library, 104 S Wisteria, Mansfield, 817-473-4391
Public Education: Mansfield Independent School District, www.mansfieldisd.org, 605 E
  Broad St, Mansfield, 817-473-5600
Community Publication: *Mansfield News Mirror*
Community Resources: City Hall, 1200 E Broad St, Mansfield, 817-276-4200;
  Mansfield Area Chamber of Commerce, www.mansfieldchamber.org, 116 N Main
  St, Mansfield, 817-473-0507

NORTH SUBURBS

HASLET

Haslet is a small town with a little over 1,000 residents in far north

Tarrant County that serves as a bedroom community for Ft. Worth. Located approximately 16 miles from central Ft. Worth, it has a quiet, country atmosphere. Homes here average about $200,000, with a four-bedroom, two-bath home usually costing $300,000. Like most suburbs, housing here is a bargain compared to the central Ft. Worth area. Buyers can get more space for the same amount they would pay in desirable Ft. Worth neighborhoods such as the TCU area.

Haslet was settled as early as the 1880s, with only a few hundred residents up until the 1940s. Since then it has slowly attracted new residents as new housing construction has increased over the years. Though it is not as established of a suburb as Grapevine or other northwestern suburbs, it is steadily growing.

Web Site: www.cityofhaslet-dfw.net
Area Code: 817
Zip Code: 76052
Post Office: Haslet Station, 1097 Schoolhouse Rd, Haslet
Police Department: Haslet Police Department, 817-884-1212
Emergency Hospital: North Hills Hospital, www.northhillshospital.com, 4401 Booth Calloway Rd, North Richland Hills, 817-255-1000
Library: Haslet Library, 817-439-4278
Public Education: Northwest Independent School District, www.northwest.k12.tx.us, 2001 Texan Dr, Justin, 817-215-0000
Community Publication: *Haslet Harbinger*
Community Resources: City Hall, 105 Main St, Haslet, 817-439-5931; Northwest Metroport Chamber of Commerce, www.nwmetroportchamber.org, 99 Trophy Club Dr, Trophy Club, 817-491-1222

HOUSTON

"Houston, we have a problem." Since that memorable phrase was first uttered by Apollo 13 astronaut James Lovell, the city has often been associated with NASA and entered the nation's consciousness as Space City, one of the city's nicknames. However, Houston has been more popularly known—and some will argue still is more popularly known—as the Bayou City because of the many bayous (slow moving waterways along low lying or swampy land) that cross through it. It was founded in 1836 by brothers Augustus and John Allen on the banks of Buffalo Bayou; the two enterprising businessmen had dreams of turning their plot of real estate along the navigable bayous into a successful commercial town. They named the town in honor of General Sam Houston, the hero of the Battle of San Jacinto during the fight for Texas' independence from Mexico and the Republic's first president. Since those early beginnings as a small commerce and frontier town, Houston has transformed itself into a cosmopolitan city that has grown into the nation's fourth largest city.

Unlike most major U.S. cities, Houston has no zoning laws. This has resulted in several urban districts instead of a single city center. The unofficial districts in Houston are Medical Center, Theater District, NASA area, Galleria/Uptown, Memorial/River Oaks, Museum District, Downtown, Midtown, Southwest, Northside/airport, Northwest/Cypress, and Eastside. The decentralized layout of the city has contributed to the city's sprawl. Drive an hour in any direction and you will likely still be in Houston. Freeways and the personal vehicle play a major role in Houstonians' lives. Traffic can be difficult at times, especially with the endless road construction and expansion, but residents handle these challenges with patience and grace. It is customary for one driver to let another into traffic, which is appreciated with a hand wave. However, one sure way to identify yourself as a nonresident is to honk your horn during a traffic jam.

Though the space, medical, and other industries play a major role in the city's economy, none comes close to the impact that the energy industry, primarily oil and gas, has on the city. While New York has the financial district, Los Angeles the motion picture industry, and Detroit the automobile, Houston is known worldwide as a key oil, gas, and energy center. Since the famed Spindletop derrick gushed forth oil 90 miles away in Beaumont in 1901, Houston has been at the forefront of oil-related technology, refining, and distribution. The Port of Houston is a factor in the city's position as a major energy market. The city is home to more than 3600 energy-related companies, including the headquarters of 17 Fortune 500 companies and 600 exploration and production firms.

Many of these companies are foreign firms representing countries from every continent. This has contributed to sizable expatriate communities in addition to the several immigrant communities in Houston. Significant communities include the Vietnamese, Chinese, South Asian, Nigerian/ African, South American, Mexican, Central American, British, Middle Eastern, and a smaller group of European expatriates composed primarily of French, Germans, Dutch, and Belgians.

Houston is a city of immigrants and migrants with an optimistic attitude. From the oil boom of the 1970s, when approximately 1300 people a week, mostly from the Rust Belt states, were moving into the city, to as recently as 2005, when over 200,000 New Orleanians fleeing Hurricane Katrina relocated to Houston, the city has always attracted people seeking to make a fortune or a fresh start. The cost of living here is relatively low, housing is still affordable, and temperatures are mild to hot, just a few of the reasons why each year thousands of new residents call Houston their home.

INNER LOOP

The inner loop is the area inside Interstate 610, one of the several major freeways that traverse Houston. Revitalization initiatives have made it a much sought-after residential area. Almost all of Houston's major attractions are inside the loop, including Downtown, the Theater District, Main Street bars and restaurants, the Toyota Center for basketball and hockey, Minute Maid (Baseball) Park, the Museum District, the zoo, Hermann Park, and the George R. Brown Convention Center. No wonder so many are now clamoring to live "inside the loop." Communities inside Loop 610 include Montrose, River Oaks, Bellaire, West University/ Southside Place, Upper Kirby, Museum District, Rice Military/Camp Logan/Crestwood, Downtown, Midtown, the Heights, the historic wards, and the Rice University area.

DOWNTOWN, MIDTOWN, AND THE WARDS

DOWNTOWN

Boundaries: North: I-10 (Katy Freeway); East: Chartres; South: US-59; West: Bagby

Downtown is Houston's Central Business District, which is located in the center of the city. It has undergone an amazing transformation in the last 10 years. A decade ago, the area was strictly a business and commercial area with imposing steel, glass, and concrete structures. Forget about living downtown—people did not even stay after work. Nobody ventured here

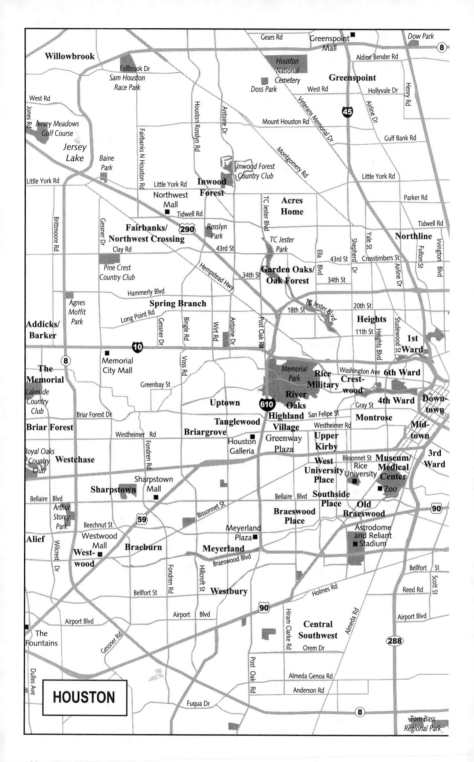

HOUSTON

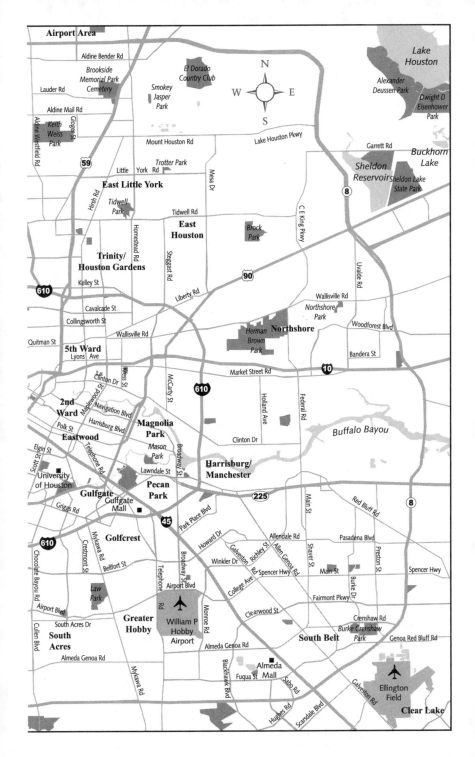

unless they worked here. With the exception of the **Theater District**, where the symphony, ballet, music, theater, and opera venues are located, there were few reasons for residents to come downtown since most of the entertainment and sports venues were located in other parts of town.

These days, there are plenty of reasons to come and stay in Downtown. Redevelopment of the area has erased many of the eyesores that had plagued it, replacing them with new shops, restaurants, hotels, and bars. Smart tile and glass artwork decorates the light rail platforms; sidewalks have been planted with trees, and several blocks spiffed up with streetfront shops and restaurants. Main Street has undergone an extensive makeover, resulting in a pedestrian-friendly cosmopolitan atmosphere. Parts of it have been blocked off from traffic to create a pedestrian-only district. To add a little style, designers have included a dancing fountain which shoots water over the light rail line that runs through Main Street. All of this is part of the urban revitalization effort that started in the 1990s to attract people to visit and live in Downtown.

The oil bust in the 1980s caused many businesses to declare bankruptcy and quite a few office buildings remained unoccupied, creating ghost towns in parts of Downtown. Since then, the steadily improving economy has allowed investment and speculation in Downtown real estate and development. Empty lots and vacant buildings have been replaced by the Minute Maid Park, which hosted the 2004 MLB All-Star Game, and the Toyota Center, which hosted the 2006 NBA All-Star Game. Several boutique hotels in the area have opened for business. One of the biggest developments is Bayou Place, located in the Theater District. This entertainment complex features restaurants, an art cinema, concert venue, and lofts currently under construction. Jones Plaza, a public outdoor square across the street, hosts concerts, socials, and outdoor viewing parties during the World Series playoffs and other major sporting events. In addition, Bayou Place is located across the street from the Theater District, which has seen some upgrades as well. A new performance hall, the Hobby Center, has been added to the numerous venues already in the area. Houston has one of the largest and best fine arts and theater districts in the U.S. Many famous performers such as the up-and-coming soprano Ana Maria Martinez and famed mezzo-soprano Cecilia Bartoli made their U.S. debuts at the Houston Grand Opera before moving on to such bigger venues as New York's Metropolitan Opera. In addition, it has been a center for new productions such as the play *Angels in America* and the opera *The Little Prince*. All around Downtown, lofts and condominiums are being constructed or renovated from old buildings as fast as developers can build them. One of the most ambitious projects is the current construction of a terraced riverwalk that extends down to the banks of Buffalo Bayou.

A few historic structures remain in Downtown surrounded by new gleaming towers: The Italianate Esperson Building, Art Deco City Hall, turn-of-the-century brick Julia Ideson branch of the Houston Public

Library, and the former Rice Hotel where JFK slept before that fateful afternoon in Dallas.

For further intown living, look to **Allen Parkway**. New apartments, luxury condos, and townhomes in all varieties of architectural design and color line winding Allen Parkway, which leads straight into Downtown. No matter how hot or humid the weather, joggers can be seen daily along the Buffalo Bayou greenbelt that is situated next to the neighborhood.

MIDTOWN

Boundaries: North: I-45; East: SH 288; South: U.S. 59; West: Bagby

A few years ago, what is now Midtown was mainly a blighted area occupied largely by drug users and the homeless. Empty boarded-up buildings and vacant lots outnumbered the handful of businesses and single-family residences. Once a prosperous residential community known as Southside Place, the area fell into decline during the oil bust of the 1980s, which affected the city's housing market. The community of Victorian-style homes that dated back to the turn-of-the-century and flourished in the post–World War II decades was nearly abandoned by the 1990s. A hot housing market and the demand for housing inside the city led to the development and revitalization of this area in the late 1990s. Apartments, townhomes, and lofts have replaced almost all of the aging wooden homes. Only a handful of these homes remain, appearing out of place amongst the new, trendy mid-rise developments. When the first residential development was completed here, it was conspicuous among the empty concrete lots. The first urban pioneers to settle here were primarily interested in living near downtown or the Medical Center. With the exception of a few businesses run by Vietnamese immigrants, there were no retail stores or amenities nearby.

Midtown is home to Houston's original and second Vietnamese communities, with Vietnamese street signs posted around several midtown blocks denoting the presence of this ethnic commercial district. Since the revitalization of the area, additional Vietnamese businesses have opened here and the community is thriving more than ever. Also located here is Brennan's restaurant, the Houston location of the famed New Orleans eatery, considered by some to be the finest restaurant in town. This established culinary institution has been at the same French Quarter–inspired building for several decades.

Since the first residential development, the rest have fallen into place like dominoes. New mixed-use communities with brick sidewalks, outdoor patios, shops on the ground floors of lofts, and restaurants have opened up. Many new townhomes occupy the area now. With the opening of grocery stores, drugstores, restaurants, strip shopping centers, and other amenities across from residential complexes, Midtown is slowly turning into a viable residential community, currently the "it" place. Located next to Loop 228, which is a quick drive into the Medical Center, and at the edge of downtown Houston, the area has attracted young urban professionals who work in the vicinity. With wonderful views of the downtown skyline at night, Midtown lounges, bars, and clubs are among the most popular nightspots in Houston. On the weekends, the streets are lined with cars, whose owners are hoping or waiting to get into one of the new lounges and bars.

Redevelopment of this area has not been without controversy though. Many in the nearby Fourth Ward neighborhood fear that current and proposed development will change or displace their community. Others worry that low-income residents who have been priced out of the area will have a difficult time finding affordable housing.

THE WARDS

A historic designation of six communities that straddle or are part of various neighborhoods, including Downtown (3rd Ward), Midtown (4th Ward), and East Houston

In the shadow of Downtown's skyscrapers lies a cluster of historic communities with origins in old political subdivisions known as wards. Though political wards were abolished in the early 1900s, the neighborhoods here continue to be known as the first, second, third, fourth, fifth, and sixth wards. The wards have a reputation as low-income minority neighborhoods. Though this is true to some degree, not all the property values here are depressed nor are they all undesirable areas to live. Some of the wards and areas around them are experiencing heavy investment and revitalization that have people clamoring to move there. Other wards have lovely established neighborhoods unknown to most Houstonians that feature above-average property prices.

The **First Ward** is located north of Congress Avenue and west of Main Street, immediately northwest of Downtown, next to the Theater District. Currently an ethnically diverse neighborhood composed of Hispanic, African-American, and white residents, it was historically a working class community inhabited mainly by African-Americans and Italian immigrants. Also here is the landmark Old Jeff Davis hospital, which originally served as the city's first public hospital and was later used for a variety of purposes including a sanitarium and warehouse. Abandoned for many years, this historic neoclassical building was restored and has been converted into affordable loft apartments for artists.

The **Second Ward** is roughly bounded by Buffalo Bayou to the north, Lockwood Avenue to the east, railroad tracks to the south, and Congress Street to the west. Originally an upper-class suburb at the beginning of the 20th century, it still features many of its original large homes standing next to smaller, more recently constructed homes. Most of the buildings here were built in the 1920s and feature the art deco style. The area experienced white flight after World War II, and today it is a predominantly Hispanic neighborhood. There are many industrial buildings here, especially on the northern end along Buffalo Bayou. New development has begun in the past few years, with loft apartments constructed on the western boundary. Some of the buildings on the west side near Minute Maid Park have been converted into lofts.

The historic African-American neighborhood of **Third Ward** was settled by freed slaves at the end of the Civil War. Project Row House, a public art project featuring 22 restored shotgun houses (narrow, rectangular, one-story dwellings with no halls), is located here. Another notable site in Third Ward is Emancipation Park, built in the late 1800s. Texas Southern University, a historically black college, and the University of Houston are both located in Third Ward. For information on residential areas surrounding the universities, refer to the **East Houston** section.

Fourth Ward is known as Freedman's Town because it was founded by freed slaves. This historic community is becoming an endangered community because of the gentrification of neighboring Midtown and Downtown. Many of the shotgun-style houses that line the brick paved streets are in poor condition. This is an unfortunate period in the history of a community that at the height of its glory was considered this city's Harlem, with jazz clubs and restaurants.

Fifth Ward is north of Buffalo Bayou and east of Little Oak Bayou. Founded after the Civil War by freed slaves, Fifth Ward is one of the city's oldest black neighborhoods. During the 1920s, many blacks from Louisiana migrated here and opened up businesses. Their influence can be seen in some of the architecture in this neighborhood. At one time, Fifth Ward was a major industrial and transportation center.

Sixth Ward is below First Ward and bounded by Washington, Houston, and Capitol streets and the Glenwood Cemetery. It is listed on the National Register of Historic Places for the large collection of intact wood-frame Victorian homes. Though many of these homes are in shabby condition, preservation efforts have begun and are continuing. The two major streets here are Washington Avenue and Memorial Drive.

Web Sites: www.houstonmidtown.com, www.downtownhouston.org, www.houstontheaterdistrict.org, www.houstontx.gov

Area Code: 713

Zip Codes: 77002, 77010

Post Offices: Sam Houston Finance Station, 701 San Jacinto St, Ste 149; Civic Center Station, 700 Smith St; Sam Houston Carrier Station, 1500 Hadley St; Houston Station, 401 Franklin St

Police Precincts: Houston Police Department: Central Division, 61 Riesner, 713-247-4400; Downtown Patrol, 1415 Fannin, Ste 200, 713-308-8000

Emergency Hospitals: Christus St. Joseph, www.christusstjoseph.com, 1401 St. Joseph Pkwy, 713-757-1000; Texas Medical Center, www.tmc.edu: Hermann Hospital, www.memorialhermann.org, 6411 Fannin, 713-704-4000; Ben Taub, www.hchdonline.com, Ben Taub General Hospital, 1504 Taub Loop, 713-873-2000; Methodist Hospital, www.methodisthealth.com, 6565 Fannin St, 713-790-3311;

VA Hospital, www.houston.med.va.gov, 2002 Holcombe Blvd, 800-553-2278; St. Luke's, www.sleh.com, 6720 Bertner Ave, 832-355-1000; Texas Children's Hospital, www.texaschildrenshospital.org, 6621 Fannin St, 832-824-1000

Adult Education: Houston Community College–Central Campus, http://ccollege.hccs. edu, 1300 Holman, 713-718-6000; University of Houston Downtown, www.uhd.edu, One Main St, 713-221-8000; South Texas College of Law, www.stcl.edu, 1303 San Jacinto St, 77002, 713-659-8040

Public Education: Houston Independent School District, www.houstonisd.org, 4400 W 18th, 713-556-6005

Community Publications: *Houston Chronicle*, www.chron.com; *Houston Press*, www. houstonpress.com

Community Resources: City Hall, 900 Bagby, 713-837-0311; YMCA Downtown, www. ymcahouston.org, 1600 Louisiana, 713-659-8501

Public Transportation: Metropolitan Transit Authority of Harris County, www.ridemetro. org: Metro Light Rail; *Bus:* Midtown: 1, 8, 11, 60, 65, 132, 163, 261, 262, 265, 274, 283, 292, 297; Downtown: 1, 5, 8, 15, 25, 52, 78, 44, 56, 79, 20, 102, 108, 201, 202, 204, 212, 283, 131, 214, 216, 221, 228, 48, 50, 37, 40, 77, 30, 6, 3, 70, 36, 40, 60, 30, 80, 77, 88, 11, 15, 35, 52, 60, 163, 261, 262, 265, 274, 35, 53, 82, 283, 9

HEIGHTS

Boundaries: North: Loop 610; East: Yale and Oxford; South: I-10; West: Dian and Blare

Although Houston has been particularly bad about preserving its historic buildings, the historic Heights neighborhood is an exception. This charming neighborhood is best known for the well-preserved and restored Victorian homes and mansions. It is really a small town community located within the heart of the city. The Heights even has its own opera company and newspaper. Many neighborhood businesses are well-known, established shops that have been operated by the same family for generations. The best time to shop in the Heights is the first Saturday of each month, when retailers offer specials and in-store activities. Another Heights tip for potential homebuyers and visitors is that parts of the community are dry, which means there are no alcohol sales, though consumption of alcohol is permitted.

Established in 1896 as a small town outside of Houston, the community was named for its location on high land (62 feet above sea level) above White Oak Bayou. In fact, it is the highest point in the city. At the time of its annexation by the City of Houston in 1918, it had a population of approximately 9000. The neighborhood began to decline during the 1950s, but was revitalized in the 1970s by residents interested in preserving the history and architecture of the Heights. Today, several of the buildings here are listed on the National Register of Historic Places and the neighborhood is noted by a Texas Historical Commission marker. Though the Heights is currently a livable and desirable neighborhood, approximately 20 years ago it was a high-crime area. There are still some shady areas bordering this community, but as redevelopment continues to expand throughout the Heights and neighboring areas, the criminal elements and disreputable character of some areas may slowly disappear as they have with past redevelopment projects.

The Heights area includes the **Woodland Heights** neighborhood and **Sunset Heights**, whose small bungalows are under siege from townhouse builders. It features mostly historic bungalows with wide verandas and overhanging eaves, and a few cottages, four-squares, and Victorian homes. Nearby neighborhoods with historic homes in similar architectural designs are **Norhill** to the east and **Timbergrove West** to the west.

Web Sites: www.houstonheights.org, www.woodland-heights.org, www.houstontx.gov

Area Code: 713

Zip Code: 77008

Post Offices: TW House Station, 1300 W 19th St; Heights Station, 1050 Yale St; Anson Jones Station, 634 W Cavalcade St

Police Precincts: Houston Police Department: Heights Storefront, 910 N Durham, # D, 713-803-1151; Central Division, 61 Riesner, 713-247-4400

Emergency Hospital: St. Joseph's Hospital, www.christusstjoseph, 1401 St. Joseph Pkwy, 713-757-1000

Library: Houston Public Library, www.hpl.lib.tx.us: Heights Branch, 1302 Heights Blvd, 832-393-1810

Public Education: Houston Independent School District, www.houstonisd.org, 4400 W 18th St, 713-556-6005

Community Publications: *Houston Tribune*, www.houstontribune.com; *Heights Pages*, www.heightspages.com; *Houston Chronicle*, www.chron.com; *Houston Press*, www.houstonpress.com

Community Resources: Greater Heights Chamber of Commerce, www.heightschamber. com, 545 W 19th St, 713-861-6735; HITS Unicorn Theater, www.hitstheatre.org, 311 W 18th St, 713-861-7408; www.houstonheightsonline.com

Public Transportation: Harris County Metropolitan Transit Authority, www.ridemetro. org: *Bus*: 8, 9, 26, 27, 34, 40, 50

EAST HOUSTON

Boundaries: North: I-10; East: 610; South: I-45; West: US-59

Houston's origin and past lie in the East End, with many of the city's early settlements and industries located there. The city's factories and industrial plants, including the Oak Farms Dairy plant, oil refineries, Maxwell Coffeehouse, Sara Lee Coffee and Tea Service, and Anheuser-Busch brewery, are concentrated in east Houston. However, the biggest economic engine here is the Port of Houston, the nation's number one port for foreign cargo. The East End is blue collar while the western half of Houston is more white collar.

In the early part of the 20th century, East Houston was a melting pot of German, Italian, and Latino families. Most of the families have since moved out of here. Today it contains two of Houston's oldest Hispanic neighborhoods, Magnolia Park and Second Ward. The murals, artwork, Catholic churches, and neighborhood institutions attest to the area's cultural identity. Established neighborhood stores, restaurants, and mercados create a unique atmosphere and proud ethnic character in these working-class Hispanic communities. Most people think of East End Houston as a predominantly Hispanic part of town. While it is true that the east end of Houston is a center of Latino culture, this section of Houston has a diverse population where other cultures likewise exist. It is home to two major universities, the University of Houston and Texas Southern University, and Houston Community College. The Orange Show, a folk art center, is also located here. In recent decades, this low-income area has attracted the interests of developers, which may change the character of the community. Many new townhomes and retail centers have been constructed just east of U.S. 59.

East Houston has somewhat of a negative reputation because of parts of the area's heavy industrialization and accompanying pollution, largely low-income population, and supposed crime rate. That is an overgeneralization though. Parts of it can be an eyesore and it lacks some of the amenities, luxuries, and glamour of other parts of Houston, but it is a relatively safe and diverse community. There are several charming neighborhoods with historic homes and nice lawns. However, East Houston is essentially the inner city. Though there are many local mom-and-pop shops and independently owned businesses, do not expect to find any big box stores, chain restaurants, or malls in the area. In some areas, supermarkets tend to be smaller, if they exist, and in some cases the nearest food store is a small neighborhood grocery shop. Neighborhoods in the east side of Houston include the following:

Lindale Park, north of I-10, east of the Heights, contains bungalows from the 1950s set among large trees. This is one of those lovely established neighborhoods with character and charm.

Idylwood is bounded by Lawndale on the north, Brays Bayou on the east, Sylvan on the south, and Wayside on the west. Cottage-style bungalows here are reminiscent of the style and architecture of highly desirable neighborhoods such as the Heights or West University, but much more affordable. This charming and beautiful neighborhood sits on a small hill that slopes down into Buffalo Bayou while tall pines and oaks line the winding streets. On the west, a large, wooded area surrounding the Villa de Matel Catholic convent borders the neighborhood. Nearby are other hidden East Houston finds such as **Mason Park**, **Pecan Park**, and **Glen Brook**.

Though people generally do not consider the area surrounding the **University of Houston/Texas Southern University** as a place to live because of its perceived crime rate and lack of nearby amenities, there are many neighborhoods hidden behind the campuses that are as lovely and charming as those in more desirable areas such as West University or the Heights. They feature grand historic homes, smaller graceful residences, and lovely lawns. These neighborhoods have character and charm that are often lacking in the newer, suburban developments. They include **Washington Terrace** to the west of Texas Southern University and bounded by Almeda to the west, Alabama to the north, and Blodgett to the south. This has historically been and still is a neighborhood where the city's affluent African-American citizens reside. South of the University of Houston is **University Oaks**. Farther south from Blodgett, between North and South MacGregor is **Riverside Terrace**.

One of the oldest communities in Houston has recently experienced revitalization as more people seek to live inside the loop. During its heyday, **Eastwood** was a master-planned community where notable Houstonians such as billionaire Howard Hughes grew up. Later characterized by graffiti, abandoned buildings, and blight, it is now, once again, a lovely neighborhood that is aesthetically on a par with some of Houston's most esteemed residential areas. Single professionals, couples, and young families have restored many of the historic Craftsman and Prairie-style homes. The charm and architecture of this neighborhood is reminiscent of the Heights, but more affordable. In fact, it is a good option for those desiring to live in a close-knit neighborhood with the grace, history, and character of the Heights, but without the price tag. People who are priced out of the Montrose or Heights neighborhoods often opt for Eastwood. Located near downtown Houston and Minute Maid Park, residents have the advantage of being near the city's major sports venues, fine arts district, and nightlife.

The status of the **Gulfgate** neighborhood is best reflected in the fortunes of Gulfgate Mall, the city's first indoor regional shopping mall. Once an upscale shopping destination, it fell into decline as other malls opened alongside new residential development in the suburbs during the late 1960s and early 1970s. It was a time of suburban flight and the average household income dropped significantly. Since then, the average income here has remained at around the same level. Today, Gulfgate is a predominantly Hispanic community where many recent immigrants reside. However, its location along the intersection of Loop 610 and I-45 attracts a diverse population to the businesses by the freeways.

An initiative by the city and private developers that is intended to revive the community's economy recently culminated in the million-dollar redevelopment of Gulfgate Mall and shopping center. Nevertheless, it is unlikely that Gulfgate will return to the middle-class neighborhood of yesteryear. The community is not targeted for urban gentrification, which would bring higher income residents into the area. In addition, the Hispanic new immigrant community has established deep roots and strong connections that have cemented their presence and influence in Gulfgate.

Other nearby neighborhoods include **Harrisburg, Manchester, Golfcrest,** and **Magnolia Park.**

Web Sites: www.houstontx.gov, www.greatereastend.com, www.idylwood-houston.org, www.lindalepark.org

Area Code: 713

Zip Codes: 77003, 77004, 77011, 77020, 77087

Post Offices: Franklin Station, 401 Franklin St; Sam Houston Finance Station, 701 San Jacinto St, Ste 149; Sam Houston Carrier Station, 1500 Hadley St; Southmore Station, 4110 Almeda Rd; Jensen Drive Station, 3520 Jensen Dr; Broadway Station, 4020 Broadway St

Police Precincts: Houston Police Department: Central Patrol, 61 Riesner, 713-247-4400; East Patrol (Magnolia), 7425 Sherman, 713-928-4600; Lyons Avenue Storefront, 6702 Lyons #3, 713-672-5809; Market Street (5th Ward) Storefront, 4300 Lyons, 713-672-5890; Southmore Storefront, 3711 Southmore, 713-526-1255

Emergency Hospital: St. Joseph's Hospital, www.christusstjoseph, 1401 St. Joseph Pkwy, 713-757-1000

Libraries: Houston Public Library, www.hpl.lib.tx.us: Flores Branch, 110 N Milby, 832-393-1780 (under renovation); Fifth Ward Branch, 4014 Market, 832-393-1770; Mancuso Branch, 6767 Bellfort, 832-393-1920

Adult Education: Texas Southern University, www.tsu.edu, 3100 Cleburne St, 713-313-7011; University of Houston, www.uh.edu, 4800 Calhoun Rd, 713-743-2255

Public Education: Houston Independent School District, www.houstonisd.org, 4400 W 18th, 713-556-6005

Community Publications: *Houston Defender; Houston Chronicle*, www.chron.com; *Houston Press*, www.houstonpress.com

Community Resources: Ninos de la Comunidad, 2805 Garrow St; Third Ward Multi-Service Center, 3611 Ennis, 713-527-4002; East End Chamber of Commerce, www.eecoc.org, 550 Gulfgate Center, 713-926-3305; Talento Bilingue de Houston, www.tbhcenter.com, 333 S Jensen Dr, 713-222-1213; Our Lady of Guadalupe Church, www.olghouston.org, 2405 Navigation Blvd, 713-222-0203

Public Transportation: Harris County Metropolitan Transit Authority, www.ridemetro.org: *Bus*: 11, 20, 26, 27, 29, 30, 36, 37, 40, 42, 48, 50, 68, 77, 88, 244, 246, 247

MONTROSE

Boundaries: North: Allen Pkwy; East: Bagby; South: US-59; West: Shepherd

To many Houstonians, Montrose is synonymous with the gay community. However, this funky, alternative neighborhood is home not only to many of the city's gay and lesbian inhabitants, but also to an eclectic mix of college students, artists, young urban professionals, intellectuals, bohemian types, tattoo and piercing enthusiasts, families, and couples.

Montrose's diverse population is a result of its proximity to the Museum District, several small art museums such as the de Menil museum, St. Thomas University (a private Catholic four-year institution of higher learning), tony River Oaks, the Chinese consulate, Midtown and its nightlife, urban lofts, and other single-family residential areas. With Montrose's location near so many attractions, there are always plenty of activities and events in the neighborhood. In fact, Montrose is the site of the annual Greek festival, Art Car parade, and gay pride parade.

Montrose's narrow pedestrian-friendly streets (by Houston standards), unique shops, and open-minded attitude give the area its own character and strong sense of community. You will not see any Starbucks in the center of Montrose, along Montrose Boulevard and Westheimer. Several independently owned coffee houses line these streets, offering coffee from all over the world at prices more affordable than the Seattle chain. Like many of the other colorful local shops in this neighborhood, they espouse an anti-corporate, pro-neighborhood ethos.

Though this neighborhood attracts progressive, open-minded types, as well as gay and lesbian teen runaways, the recent revitalization of downtown and the housing boom of the late 1990s has transformed parts of this neighborhood and increased the price of housing. Towards the eastern part of Montrose, near Midtown, new condos and apartments have been constructed, replacing the artists and hippies with urban professionals.

Located between downtown and the Texas Medical Center, **Neartown** is a charming neighborhood of predominantly two-story homes of various designs. Independently owned shops line Richmond and major thoroughfares, which tend to be narrow. Neartown is sometimes lumped together with Montrose and is also composed of a unique array of residents, including politicians, businessmen, and medical doctors. Past local luminaries include pioneering heart surgeon Denton Cooley, Howard Hughes, Lyndon B. Johnson, and Walter Cronkite.

The Neartown association was established in the 1960s to preserve some of the city's oldest and most historic homes. Other neighborhoods in the area such as **Courtlandt Place**, **Winlow Place**, **Hyde Park**, and **Cherryhurst** are also old Houston neighborhoods. Newer subdivisions include **Audubon**, **Avondale**, **Lancaster Place**, **Castle Court**, and **Roseland Estates**.

Web Site: www.cityofhouston.net

Area Code: 713

Zip Code: 77006

Post Offices: University of Houston Station, 1319 Richmond; River Oaks Station, 1900 W Gray

Police Precinct: Houston Police Department: Neartown Storefront, 802 Westheimer, 713-284-8604

Emergency Hospitals: Christus St. Joseph, www.christusstjoseph.com, 1401 St. Joseph Pkwy, 713-757-1000; Texas Medical Center, www.tmc.edu: Hermann Hospital, www.memorialhermann.org, 6411 Fannin, 713-704-4000; Ben Taub, www.hchdonline.com, Ben Taub General Hospital, 1504 Taub Loop, 713-873-2000; Methodist Hospital, www.methodisthealth.com, 6565 Fannin St, 713-790-3311; VA Hospital, www.houston.med.va.gov, 2002 Holcombe Blvd, 1-800-553-2278; St. Luke's, www.sleh.com, 6720 Bertner Ave, 832-355-1000; Texas Children's Hospital, www.texaschildrenshospital.org, 6621 Fannin St, 832-824-1000

Library: Houston Public Library, www.hpl.lib.tx.us: Freed-Montrose Branch, 4100 Montrose Blvd, 832-393-1800

Public Education: Houston Independent School District, www.houstonisd.org, 4400 W 18th, 713-556-6005

Community Publications: *Houston Chronicle*, www.chron.com; *Houston Press*, www. houstonpress.com

Community Resources: Houston City Hall, 900 Bagby; Cherryhurst Community Center, 1700 Missouri St, 713-284-1992

Public Transportation: Harris County Metropolitan Authority, www.ridemetro.org: *Bus:* 3, 25, 26, 27, 34, 35, 42, 78, 82, 170, 291, 292, 298

BELLAIRE, WEST UNIVERSITY PLACE, SOUTHSIDE PLACE, AND OLD BRAESWOOD

Boundaries: BELLAIRE: North: US-59; East: Southern Pacific Railroad track; South: Beechnut/N Braeswood; West: Renwick; WEST UNIVERSITY PLACE: North: University Blvd; East: Virginia; South: Gramercy; West: Auden; SOUTHSIDE PLACE: North: University; East: Edloe; South: Gramercy; West: Bellaire and Auden; OLD BRAESWOOD: North: Holcombe Blvd; East: Main; South: Brays Bayou; West: Kirby

Bellaire, West University Place, and Southside Place are a collection of wealthy, independently governed communities with a significant population of medical professionals who work at the nearby Medical Center and professors employed at Rice University. Residents here are zoned to two of the top public high schools in Houston: Bellaire and Lamar. They are the only public high schools within the city of Houston and two of three in the metropolitan area that offer the rigorous and prestigious International Baccalaureate Program. Though there are some reasonably priced residences here, property taxes can be quite high.

The **City of Bellaire** is an affluent bedroom community in southwest Houston that is actually a city within a city. Established in 1908, Bellaire was connected by a trolley to Houston, which was then several miles away. The trolley was discontinued in 1927 and today sits on Bellaire Boulevard as a historical exhibit. However, Houston continued to grow and sprawled westward, eventually surrounding Bellaire. Houston never annexed Bellaire, which is still an independent municipality with its own mayor, city council, police department, fire department, and library. Its schools, however, are part of the Houston Independent School District.

Despite being surrounded by a big city, Bellaire has managed to retain a quiet, small town ambience that is family-friendly. Children can often be seen riding their bikes in the street, alongside young couples pushing baby strollers. Each year, residents eagerly support their Little League baseball team, which won the 2000 Little League World Series, and their high school baseball team, which has won numerous state championships. Education and children are major focus points of this community.

Bellaire is known as the "City of Homes" because it is primarily a residential area with a combination of '50s-style bungalows, spacious ranch houses, two-story homes, multi-million-dollar mansions that have replaced smaller one-story homes, and a few recently constructed townhomes. There is a current trend of new homebuyers tearing down the smaller existing homes and building larger residences, or McMansions, on the site. The city has several independently owned shops, businesses, and offices, but few attractions. However, the city makes up for its lack of attractions with its close proximity to Houston's downtown sports and theater district, the Medical Center, Rice University, the Galleria shopping district, the Museum district, the zoo, Hermann Park, and Reliant football stadium.

Bellaire is also conveniently located by US-59 and Loop 610, which connects the city to Houston and beyond. Add excellent public schools to the city's geographic location and atmosphere and one can quickly see why Bellaire is one of the Houston area's most desirable places to live.

When the first homes in **West University Place** were sold in 1917, its founder, Tennessee Governor Ben W. Hooper, and developer, the Houston West End Realty Company, could not have envisioned the success that West University Place would become in the following decades. When development first began, the area was swampy, muddy, and had difficulty attaining utilities. Hardly the type of place that one would have imagined would one day become one of Houston's most desirable neighborhoods. Its future was uncertain at the time and Hooper had to use his own money to develop critical infrastructure and utilities after the City of Houston refused to take such a risk. Nevertheless, the residents persisted and voted to incorporate as a city in 1924. By the 1940s, it was a thriving community that was a far cry from the once-rural backwater community.

West University Place, also commonly referred to as West University or West U., is named for its location west of Rice University. Like Bellaire, this very wealthy bedroom community located next to it, is an independent city surrounded by Houston. One of the most charming communities in Houston, it is characterized by beautiful lawns and elegant homes, which include small Tudor cottages, large brick mansions, Colonials, modern designs, and various other architectural styles. Strict deed restrictions have helped preserve the community's aesthetic appeal. Regardless of the street, each home in West University is unique. The neighborhood streets here are narrow, reflecting an era before cities were built around automobiles and before large vehicles played a prominent role in the daily lives of Americans. The layout and design of the neighborhoods promote children playing in the streets and residents stopping and chatting with each other. When people talk about smart urban or community design that is child-friendly and socially oriented, they are probably thinking about someplace like West University.

One of the most popular places in this neighborhood is **Rice Village**, a pedestrian shopping district that spans several blocks. It is a favorite place not only of Rice University students and locals but also of residents from all over Houston. One of Houston's premier shopping districts, Rice Village dates back to the 1930s. Since then, it has expanded beyond

713-668-0330; Southside Place Police Department, 6309 Edloe Ave, Houston, 713-668-2341; Houston Police Department, South Central Patrol, 2202 St. Emanuel, Houston, 713-651-8100

Emergency Hospitals: Texas Medical Center, www.tmc.edu: Hermann Hospital, www.memorialhermann.org, 6411 Fannin, 713-704-4000; Ben Taub, www.hchdonline.com, Ben Taub General Hospital, 1504 Taub Loop, 713-873-2000; Methodist Hospital, www.methodisthealth.com, 6565 Fannin St, 713-790-3311; VA Hospital, www.houston.med.va.gov, 2002 Holcombe Blvd, 1-800-553-2278; St. Luke's, www.sleh.com, 6720 Bertner Ave, 832-355-1000; Texas Children's Hospital, www.texaschildrenshospital.org, 6621 Fannin St, 832-824-1000

Libraries: Bellaire City Library, 5111 Jessamine, Bellaire, 713-662-8166; Harris County Public Library, www.hcpl.net, 6108 Auden, Houston, 713-668-8273

Public Education: Houston Independent School District, www.houstonisd.org, 4400 W 18th, Houston, 713-556-6005

Community Publications: *Bellaire Examiner* and *West University Examiner*, www.westuexaminer.com

Community Resources: Bellaire City Hall, 7008 S Rice Ave, Bellaire, 713-662-8222; West University Place City Hall, 3800 University Blvd, West University Place, 713-668-4441; Southside Place City Hall, 6309 Edloe Ave, Houston, 713-668-2341; Southwest Chamber of Commerce www.gswhcc.org. PO Box 788, Bellaire, 713-666-1521

Public Transportation: Metropolitan Transit Authority of Harris County, www.ridemetro.org: *Bus:* 2, 49, 33, 65

MUSEUM/MEDICAL CENTER

RICE UNIVERSITY AREA/MUSEUM DISTRICT/TEXAS MEDICAL CENTER

Boundaries: North: US-59; East: Hwy 288; South: Old Spanish Trail and Braeswood; West: Greenbriar

One of the loveliest parts of Houston, the area surrounding Rice University is popular with joggers and visitors, who enjoy its shaded trees and beautiful landscape. The Rice University Area's most distinctive characteristic is the canopy of oak trees that line South Main Street and other parts of the community. The area is beautiful year 'round, but the most gorgeous time of the year is during spring, when the azaleas and other flowers come into full bloom. The spectacular Mecom Fountain display sits in the center of South Main, forming the city's only major circle drive. One fork of this road takes drivers directly to the Museum District, while the other fork heads towards Montrose. Within walking distance of each other are the Museum of Fine Arts, Contemporary Arts Museum, and the Museum of Natural Science. Also nearby are the Rothko Chapel, de Menil Museum, Holocaust Museum, the Children's Museum of Houston, and other art galleries. Right across from the university is the Houston Zoo, Hermann Park, the Botanical Gardens, and the Museum of Natural Science. Hermann Park, a natural oasis amid the traffic and noise of the city, is one of the city's most tranquil and well-maintained parks, due in large part to the nonprofit Hermann Park Conservancy. A small number of high-rise condominiums are located across from this area overlooking the park, and the Museum District as a whole contains many luxury condominiums. The light rail system stops in front of the park and heads downtown.

Modern contemporary, traditional, antebellum, Colonial, bungalow, Tudor, Mediterranean, Italianate, and other uniquely designed homes are hidden in the streets off South Main. The individuality of the houses contributes character and appeal to this safe and peaceful community. It also doesn't hurt that some of the stately homes are just plain lovely, while others are more exclusive and hidden among shady oak trees behind lightly ivy-covered walls. The university has constructed several apartments and dorms for international students, graduate students, and families in the neighborhoods in recent years. The neighborhoods in this area include:

- **Southampton:** Developed in 1922, most of the older homes here are large bungalows and Georgian style residences with some new construction of million-dollar homes.
- **Southgate:** This neighborhood is bordered by West Holcombe on the south, Greenbriar on the west, University on the north, and Travis on the west. Most of the homes here were built in the 1930s and 1940s.
- **Boulevard Oaks:** Bounded by the Southwest Freeway (US-59) on the north, Morningside on the west, Bissonet on the south, and Graustark/Parkway on the east, this neighborhood is surrounded by beautiful landscape. Developed in the 1920s and 1930s, its diverse architectural styles include bungalows, ranch-style homes, and mansions.

Medical Center and South Loop Area (Astrodome/Reliant Center)

The area surrounding the Medical Center contains many apartments and townhomes, most of which are located along Braeswood. The rentals here are fairly recent and are usually large multi-building complexes that cater to medical students, interns, and residents. Many of the Medical Center employees and medical students also live around the Astrodome area, located further down South Main and Fannin. This was a run-down area until the development of the light rail and the building of the new Reliant football stadium initiated the area's revitalization. The area immediately next to Reliant Stadium is currently composed of affordable, low-rise apartments, while on the other side of the stadium several new apartments and townhomes have sprung up over the past few years as developers saw an opportunity with the increased demand for intown housing and the completion of the light rail. Though there are still pockets of eyesore, the area has steadily improved and more development is expected in the future. The AstroWorld amusement park recently closed and is being torn down for a mixed-use residential/commercial development.

Braeswood Place

Boundaries: North: Southside and West University Pl; East: Southern Pacific Railroad; South: Brays Bayou; West: Old Braeswood neighborhood

Primarily a single-family residential neighborhood developed in the 1950s, Braeswood Place is one of several neighborhoods and subdivisions that line Brays Bayou. The others are located outside of the 610 Loop. Because of its location next to the bayou, flooding can be a problem for residents. During Tropical Storm Allison in 2001, many of the small ranch-style homes that predominated before the storm were flooded out and had to be torn down. Larger two-story homes built on higher foundations have replaced the ranch houses. Generally a middle-class neighborhood before the flood, more upper-middle-income families have moved into the newer homes constructed after Allison. Subdivisions here include **Ayrshire, Braes Heights, Braes Manor, Braes Oaks, Braes Terrace,** and **Southern Oaks**.

Stella Link/Linkwood

Just inside the loop, the Linkwood neighborhood features one-story ranch-style homes with low-slung roofs. Homes here have large front and back yards.

Web Sites: www.houstontx.gov, www.braeswoodplace.org, www.houstonsouthgate.org

Area Code: 713

Zip Codes: 77005, 77030, 77054, 77025, 77098

Post Offices: William Rice Station, 5201 Wakeforest St; Medical Center Station, 7205 Almeda Rd; Greenbriar Station, 3740 Greenbriar St

Police Departments: Houston Police Department: South Central Division, 2202 St. Emanuel, 713-651-8100; Central Division, 61 Riesner, 713-247-4400; Rice University Police Department MS-551, 6100 Main St, 713-348-6000; University of Texas Medical Center Police, 1515 Holcombe Blvd, 713-792-2890

Emergency Hospitals: Texas Medical Center, www.tmc.edu: Hermann Hospital, www.memorialhermann.org, 6411 Fannin, 713-704-4000; Ben Taub, www.hchdonline.com, Ben Taub General Hospital, 1504 Taub Loop, 713-873-2000; Methodist Hospital, www.methodisthealth.com, 6565 Fannin St, 713-790-3311; VA Hospital, www.houston.med.va.gov, 2002 Holcombe Blvd, 1-800-553-2278; St. Luke's, www.sleh.com, 6720 Bertner Ave, 832-355-1000; Texas Children's Hospital, www.texaschildrenshospital.org, 6621 Fannin St, 832-824-1000

Libraries: Houston Public Library: McGovern–Stella Link Branch, 7405 Stella Link, 832-393-2630; Clayton Library Center for Genealogical Research, 5300 Caroline, 832-393-2600; Parent Resource Library in the Children's Museum, 1500 Binz, 713-522-1138 ext. 264; Rice University Fondren Library, 6100 Main, 713-348-5113; Houston Academy of Medicine–Texas Medical Center Library, 1133 John Freeman Blvd, 713-795-4200

Adult Education: Rice University, www.rice.edu, 6100 Main, 713-348-7423

Public Education: Houston Independent School District, www.houstonisd.org, 4400 W 18th, 713-556-6005

Community Publications: *Houston Chronicle*, www.chron.com; *Houston Press*, www. houstonpress.com; *Rice Thresher*, ricethresher.org

Community Resources: City Hall, 900 Bagby, 713-837-0311; Greater Houston YMCA, www.ymcahouston.org: Texas Medical Center Childcare, 5614 H Mark Croswell Jr., 713-747-2173; MD Anderson YMCA, 705 Cavalcade, 713-697-0648; Weekley Family YMCA, 7101 Stella Link Blvd, 713-664-9622; Hermann Park, 6001 Fannin; Miller Outdoor Theater, www.milleroutdoortheater.org, 100 Concert Dr, 713-284-8354; Museum District, www.houstonmuseumdistrict.org

Public Transportation: Metropolitan Authority of Harris County, www.ridemetro.org: Light Rail; *Bus*: 292, 298, 8, 34, 87, 326, 321, 322, 320, 73, 27, 26, 65, 132, 163, 292, 297, 1, 65, 60, 68, 170, 4, 10, 14, 73, 2; *Rice University Shuttle*

RIVER OAKS/UPPER KIRBY/GREENWAY PLAZA

Boundaries: RIVER OAKS: North: Buffalo Bayou; East: Shepherd; South: US-59; West: Loop 610; UPPER KIRBY: North: Westheimer; East: Shepherd; South: Westpark; West: Buffalo Speedway; GREENWAY PLAZA: North: Richmond; East: Shepherd; South: US-59; West: Loop 610

RIVER OAKS

River Oaks has a reputation as Houston's poshest neighborhood—the location that the city's crème de la crème call home. Many of the residences here are lavishly elegant and all of them have beautiful front and back yards. This neighborhood contains a combination of stately mansions, single-family residential homes, luxury condominiums, and recently constructed townhomes. Some of the million-dollar estates are hidden from view behind gates or large estates. The neighborhood shows off its homes and gardens each year during the annual Azalea Trail. This springtime event showcases the beautiful flowers in all shades of pink that grace the select residences on this tour.

Highland Village Area

Around the upscale Highland Village shopping center on Westheimer are several affluent neighborhoods. Many of them are located behind high brick walls that shield residents from the busy traffic on Westheimer. Neighborhoods here include **Afton Oaks, Oak Estates, Avalon Place,** and **Royden Oaks.** Homes vary from newly constructed two-story red brick homes to older elegant residences. Regardless of the age or size, the homes here are all lovely and very expensive. Behind Highland Village are more splendid homes with lavish yards, including Mediterranean inspired designs and other large homes that are almost mansions. Because of its location inside the loop and right next to Westheimer, one of the city's major thoroughfares, and Loop 610, homes here are very much coveted. Residents have the advantage of being within walking distance of one of the city's best shopping centers—Highland Village—where the stores and restaurants are closely packed together, facilitating a pedestrian shopping experience.

Upper Kirby

Upper Kirby is hard to pin down. It is trendy, upscale, a bit unconventional, and refined all at once. The red British telephone booths that are scattered throughout the neighborhood are an easy give-away that you are in Upper Kirby. It is in line with the British theme that the neighborhood has adopted to go with Upper Kirby's initials, U.K. Another indication that you are in Upper Kirby is the red street signs, rather than the usual green ones. Upper Kirby is a popular entertainment area full of pubs, bars, and a wide selection of restaurants and trendy hangout spots, which can make parking difficult on the weekends. This cosmopolitan area mixes its commercial district with residential neighborhoods that include elegant homes, apartments, and townhomes.

Greenway Plaza Area

Greenway Plaza is the name of a cluster of tall office buildings located off of U.S. 59 (Southwest Freeway). Until the past decade, the area around it consisted mainly of business buildings with plots of green grass surrounding them. The undeveloped land has been swallowed up in the past few years by residential development and there are no more open patches of grass. Most of the construction here has been luxury apartments, corporate rentals, townhomes, a few lofts, and condominiums. Strip centers, shops, and other businesses have opened up alongside the new residences. No longer a commercial wasteland, Greenway Plaza is slowly evolving into a viable residential area with all the amenities located within close proximity. Sushi restaurants, banks, dry cleaners, and take-out joints are all nearby. Travel farther down Buffalo Speedway, under the Southwest Freeway, into the edge of West University and there is a large upscale shopping center with a flagship grocery store, coffee shops, numerous restaurants, cell phone stores, and many other businesses. In addition, residents who live around Greenway Plaza are located near the shopping, dining, and entertainment of West University and Upper Kirby. The location next to the freeway also provides easy access to other parts of Houston.

Web Sites: www.upperkirby.org, www.houstontx.gov
Area Code: 713
Zip Codes: 77098, 77019, 77046

Post Offices: River Oaks Station, 1900 W Gray St; Greenbriar Station, 3740 Greenbriar St; Greenway Plaza Station, 3 E Greenway Plaza; Julius Melcher Station, 2802 Timmons Ln; Neartown (Montrose) Storefront, 802 Westheimer

Police Precinct: Houston Police Department: Central Division, 61 Riesner, 713-247-4400

Emergency Hospitals: Texas Medical Center, www.tmc.edu: Hermann Hospital, www.memorialhermann.org, 6411 Fannin, 713-704-4000; Ben Taub, www.hchdonline.com, Ben Taub General Hospital, 1504 Taub Loop, 713-873-2000; Methodist Hospital, www.methodisthealth.com, 6565 Fannin St, 713-790-3311; VA Hospital, www.houston.med.va.gov, 2002 Holcombe Blvd, 1-800-553-2278; St. Luke's, www.sleh.com, 6720 Bertner Ave, 832-355-1000; Texas Children's Hospital, www.texaschildrenshospital.org, 6621 Fannin St, 832-824-1000

Libraries: Houston Public Library, www.hpl.lib.tx.us: Looscan Branch, 2510 Willowick (closed for renovation until Fall 2007); Freed-Montrose Branch, 4100 Montrose, 832-393-1800

Public Education: Houston Independent School District, www.houstonisd.org, 4400 W 18th, 713-556-6005

Community Publications: *Houston Chronicle*, www.chron.com; *Houston Press*, www.houstonpress.com

Community Resources: City Hall, 900 Bagby, 713-837-0311; River Oaks Community Center, 3600 Locke Ln, 713-622-5998

Public Transportation: Metropolitan Transit Authority of Harris County, www.ridemetro.org: *Bus*: 65, 132, 163, 25, 78, 82, 35, 18, 35, 3, 6, 70, 48, 34, 42, 9, 27

RICE MILITARY/CAMP LOGAN/CRESTWOOD

Located along the winding streets next to scenic Memorial Park and across from the Memorial neighborhood, Rice Military and Camp Logan are currently two popular residential neighborhoods. Although the area had once been largely forgotten and somewhat neglected, people are rediscovering the beauty and tranquility of the Rice Military and Camp Logan subdivisions. Much of the appeal lies in their location inside 610 Loop, near downtown, the Medical Center, and the Galleria area. This has not gone unnoticed by developers, who have descended into the area in the past few years building new homes, including many townhomes. This upper-middle-class neighborhood is now one of the hottest residential markets in Houston.

There are many neighborhoods and communities located near the city center and its amenities, but few have **Rice Military**'s advantage of immediately bordering **Memorial Park**. This scenic oasis, Houston's answer to Central Park, is one of the city's most cherished public areas. It was named Memorial Park in commemoration of the lives lost during World War I. During World War I, it was the site of a U.S. Army training camp known as Camp Logan, the namesake of the present-day neighborhood. One of the most notable chapters in Houston and U.S. history occurred in 1917, when soldiers from the camp were involved in a racially charged riot that resulted in a citywide curfew and the court martial of over a hundred men. The park land was donated in 1924 by

William C. Hogg, a wealthy influential turn-of-the-century city leader. Covering 1466 square miles, it has one of the best urban biking, hiking, and jogging trails. In addition, it features a soccer field, a highly rated municipal golf course, horse rentals, and other amenities. Like the area in general, towering pine trees and large leafy trees cover the park, creating a forest in the heart of the city. It attracts not only nearby residents but citizens from all over the city who are attracted by the excellent running and walking trails and golf course. The trails are open 24 hours and lighted at night. This popular park is often crowded and it is often difficult to get a spot on the golf course.

Rice Military contains a mix of single-story and two-story homes of unique designs that range from $300,000 to over $750,000. In addition, many new three- and four-story high-end townhomes have recently been constructed in **Camp Logan**, replacing the tiny bungalows in Rice Military. Like the park next to it, these subdivisions are surrounded by tall trees and lush, lavishly landscaped lawns. The origins of Rice Military's name are unclear. However, it appears to have been named after the family of Rice University founder William Marsh Rice, whose relatives owned most of the area at one time. This subdivision predates Camp Logan, so "military" was most likely added when Rice Institute, now Rice University, was converted to a military school–like environment during World War I.

Crestwood, just east of Memorial Park, features new custom homes that range from half a million to over two million dollars.

Web Sites: www.houstontx.gov, www.ricemilitary.org

Area Code: 713

Zip Code: 77007

Post Offices: Heights Station, 1050 Yale St; River Oaks Station, 1900 W Gray St

Police Precinct: Houston Police Department: Central Division, 61 Riesner, 713-247-4400

Emergency Hospitals: Memorial Hermann Hospital–Memorial City, www.memorialhermann.org, 921 Gessner Rd; Texas Medical Center, www.tmc.edu: Hermann Hospital, www.memorialhermann.org, 6411 Fannin, 713-704-4000; Ben Taub, www.hchdonline.com, Ben Taub General Hospital, 1504 Taub Loop, 713-873-2000; Methodist Hospital, www.methodisthealth.com, 6565 Fannin St, 713-790-3311; VA Hospital, www.houston.med.va.gov, 2002 Holcombe Blvd, 1-800-553-2278; St. Luke's, www.sleh.com, 6720 Bertner Ave, 832-355-1000; Texas Children's Hospital, www.texaschildrenshospital.org, 6621 Fannin St, 832-824-1000

Library: Houston Public Library, Looscan Branch, 2510 Willowick (closed for renovation until Fall 2007)

Public Education: Houston Independent School District, www.houstonisd.org, 4400 W 18th, 713-556-6005

Community Publications: *Houston Chronicle*, www.chron.com; *Houston Press*, www.houstonpress.com

Community Resources: City Hall, 900 Bagby, 713-837-0311; Memorial Park, 6501 Memorial Dr, 713-845-1000

Public Transportation: Metropolitan Transit Authority of Harris County, www.ridemetro.org: *Bus*: 6, 20, 36, 70, 85

OUTER LOOP

Also referred to as "outside the loop," the Outer Loop area refers to any place outside of Loop 610. Residents often ask whether one lives "inside the loop" or "outside the loop" to gauge whether someone is centrally located. The Outer Loop consists primarily of residential neighborhoods and suburban areas. Though lacking in the cultural attractions and entertainment of the Inner Loop, the areas beyond Loop 610 offer many unique and excellent dining options.

UPTOWN

Uptown, also commonly known as the Galleria area, is an upscale district surrounded by high-end designer fashion stores and hotels and business towers. It is centered around Houston's premier shopping center—the Galleria. This shoppers' mecca and the other shopping centers nearby feature couture shops and designer brands, as well as more generic, recognizable national clothing retailers. Its location next to tony River Oaks probably explains the proliferation of designer goods and fancy retailers. Uptown has always been an upscale area, but in recent years it has become even more image-conscious. Though Houston is generally a down-to-earth town and eschews pretentiousness, this is one part of the city where you'll find well-dressed yuppies and the high maintenance crowd.

Uptown, primarily the Galleria, is a big tourist destination, especially for those coming from Mexico and South America, where American and European designer fashions are rare to nonexistent. Even if they are available in their home countries, import taxes make them prohibitively expensive to purchase as compared with the U.S. There is a huge selection of restaurants here that includes Japanese, Italian, American, Tex-Mex, Chinese, Thai, Middle Eastern, Mediterranean, and Indian cuisines, which range in price and ambience from casual to upscale. During major events that Houston has hosted, such as the Super Bowl and NBA All Star event, the Galleria has been the place most visited by tourists and partygoers. Because Houston has no zoning laws, there is no city center. Thus, with so much to offer, the Galleria has become the city's de facto hot spot. One of the most popular events here is the Uptown lighting ceremony during Christmas.

When the Galleria was constructed approximately thirty years ago, this area was a mostly undeveloped suburban area. The 1970s oil boom increased the city's population and soon spurred residential development here. Many Houstonians' bank accounts increased, providing them with enough money to spend on luxury goods at the Galleria. The Uptown area has been experiencing a second residential development boom. Much of it started in the 1990s, when the economy was on an upswing, and continued because of low mortgage interest rates and an increased demand for housing near the city's center. Empty grass lots behind the Galleria have been completely filled in by the malls' expansion and construction of new townhomes and shopping strips. More recently, there has been a flurry of construction of high-rise condominiums, lofts, townhomes, and a few luxury apartments.

With its steel and glass buildings, sleek new metallic street signs, contemporary-style bus stops, and busy street and pedestrian traffic, Uptown has the feel of a sophisticated cosmopolitan environment. The most notable building here and in all of Houston is the Williams Tower, formerly the Transco Tower. Designed by famed architect Phillip Johnson, it features a water tower in the backdrop and a park at the front. This 64-story landmark skyscraper, constructed of blue glass, stands out in an area where buildings are typically mid- or low-rise. Because of its height, it serves as a reference point in a city with a very flat landscape. The nearer the tower appears, the closer you are to the Galleria area.

The strip down Westheimer and Richmond until Westchase is often referred to as the Galleria area even though it is not immediately near the Galleria. The main thoroughfares are blocks of strip shopping centers and popular restaurants. Step off Westheimer and Richmond and you'll find many quiet residential neighborhoods nestled amid leafy trees. These neighborhoods include luxury townhomes and large one-story ranch-style homes with big yards.

Tanglewood/Briargrove

Tanglewood is a close-in affluent neighborhood like Memorial and River Oaks. Though technically outside Loop 610, this wealthy enclave located near the Uptown/Galleria area is conveniently near Loop 610, Memorial/Woodway, and other major thoroughfares that lead to the city's business centers and amenities—so much so that it is like living intown. At the same time, it has a tranquil country setting atmosphere that is not infringed upon by its proximity to the hustle and bustle of the city. Large arching oak trees line the neighborhood's streets, and tall trees shade many of the properties here. The elegant luxury homes are uniquely designed and include Georgian, contemporary, and chateau-inspired homes. They range from large estates to low-maintenance garden homes. Several years ago, developers began tearing down many of the one-story residences on large, heavily treed lots and began building magnificent residences in their place. These include large homes in traditional, Georgian, and Mediterranean styles. Home to the Houston Country Club, this is one of Houston's most exclusive addresses. Its most famous resident is former U.S. President George H. W. Bush. However, other residents have more mundane backgrounds, mostly families of business executives and other professionals. Home prices and property taxes here are at the high end of the Houston housing market. Tanglewood was developed in the 1940s from prairie land into a beautiful and heavily treed neighborhood. Over the years, high-end retailers and restaurants have moved nearby.

Briargrove enjoys many of the same amenities but offers more modestly priced housing.

Web Sites: www.houstontx.gov, www.uptown-houston.com

Area Code: 713

Zip Codes: 77056, 77057

Post Offices: Galleria Station, 5015 Westheimer Rd, Ste 1200; CPU Tanglewood Pharmacy Station, 5750 Woodway Dr, Ste 156

Police Precinct: Houston Police Department: Central Division, 61 Riesner, 713-247-4400

Emergency Hospitals: Texas Medical Center, www.tmc.edu: Hermann Hospital, www.memorialhermann.org, 6411 Fannin, 713-704-4000; Ben Taub, www.hchdonline.com, Ben Taub General Hospital, 1504 Taub Loop, 713-873-2000; Methodist Hospital, www.methodisthealth.com, 6565 Fannin St, 713-790-3311; VA Hospital, www.houston.med.va.gov, 2002 Holcombe Blvd, 1-800-553-2278; St. Luke's, www.sleh.com, 6720 Bertner Ave, 832-355-1000; Texas Children's Hospital, www.texaschildrenshospital.org, 6621 Fannin St, 832-824-1000

Library: Houston Public Library, Jungman Branch, 5830 Westheimer, 832-393-1860

Public Education: Houston Independent School District, www.houstonisd.org, 4400 W 18th, 713-556-6005

Community Publications: *Houston Chronicle*, www.chron.com; *Houston Press*, www.houstonpress.com

Community Resources: City Hall, 900 Bagby, 713-837-0311

Public Transportation: Metropolitan Transit Authority of Harris County, www.ridemetro.org: *Bus:* 6, 25, 33, 35, 49, 53, 70, 73

WESTCHASE

The **Westchase District** is primarily a commercial district located along Westheimer and Beltway 8. Gleaming glass office towers and strip centers line parts of Beltway 8, which is the feeder road for the Sam Houston Tollway. The tollway provides quick access to I-10, US 290, U.S. 59, and other parts of the Houston metropolitan area. Traffic can be very bad around here during rush hour because both the Beltway and Westheimer are major thoroughfares. Parts of Beltway 8 are quite unattractive and resemble nothing more than massive stretches of concrete. There are several apartments and townhomes in the area, mostly on Westheimer, west of the Beltway. Off of Westheimer are several secluded single-family residential neighborhoods such as **Rivercrest, Briar Grove Park,** and **Briar Court** east of the Beltway, and **Lakeside Country Club, Walnut Bend, Lakeside Estates, Village West,** and **Royal Palms** to the west of Beltway 8. Homes here are located among lush vegetation and quiet scenic settings. Residents can choose from several chain restaurants and outstanding dining establishments located here that include international cuisine from Malaysia/Indonesia, Japan, France, South America, and Britain.

Web Sites: www.houstontx.gov, www.westchasedistrict.com, www.briargrovepark.org, www.lakesidecc.com, www.rivercrestestates.com, www.royaloakscc.com, www.walnutbend.org, http://myroyalpalms.com

Area Codes: 713, 281

Zip Codes: 77042, 77063

Post Offices: Debora Sue Schatz Station, 2909 Rogerdale Rd; Westchase Station, 3836 S Gessner Rd

Police Precincts: Houston Police Department: Clarkcrest Storefront, 8940 Clarkcrest St, 713-952-0182; Southwest Patrol, 4503 Beechnut, 713-314-3900

Emergency Hospital: West Houston Medical Center, www.westhoustonmedical.com, 12141 Richmond Ave, 281-558-3444

Library: Houston Public Library, www.hpl.lib.tx.us: Robinson-Westchase Branch, 3223 Wilcrest, 832-393-2011

Public Education: Houston Independent School District, www.houstonisd.org, 4400 W 18th, 713-556-6005 (north of Westheimer); Alief Independent School District, alief. isd.tenet.edu, 12302 High Star, 281-498-8110 (south of Westheimer)

Community Publication: *Houston Chronicle*, www.chron.com

Community Resource: West Houston Association, www.westhouston.org, 820 Gessner, Ste 190, 713-461-9378

Public Transportation: Harris County Metropolitan Transit Authority, www.metro.org: *Bus*: 2, 25, 46, 82, 132, 274

THE MEMORIAL AREA

Memorial is one of Houston's most prestigious communities. This wealthy community is distinguished by the towering pine trees, tall moss-covered oaks, and lush vegetation that create a forest-like ambience. Fed by the waters of Buffalo Bayou, the trees in this area are mature and grander than in any part of Houston. Memorial is highly sought-after for its beauty, location, and quality of life. In addition, Memorial is known for good public schools at the elementary and secondary level. Many have been rated exemplary, the highest state rating, and several are nationally recognized.

An established community that dates back to the 1930s, residences here once sat on large expanses with horse stables in the rear. Memorial was where the wealthy kept country estates. At that time, it was a popular area for horseback riding, and riders could often be seen jaunting through the forested acres. Over the years the large estates have been sold and divided for residential development. One of the last private stables in the area, along South Gessner, was sold in the early 1990s and turned into a gated upscale residential development. The area is more densely populated now, but it has still managed to retain its arboreal environment. Many of the streets follow the contours of the bayou and feel like winding country lanes. The homes here vary in size and style from bungalows to fairytale cottages to brick Georgian residences. Memorial is not the type of place where you will find cookie cutter neighborhoods with tract housing. Here, houses of individual designs sit next to each other. There are also many gated communities, condominiums, and townhomes.

The jewel of the Memorial area is Memorial Park. It is just inside the loop, immediately east of Memorial and next to the inner loop neighborhood of Rice Military (see Rice Military/Camp Logan/Crestwood, above, for more about Memorial Park).

Memorial is comprised of several neighborhoods and subdivisions such as **Woodlake/Woodlake Square** located along Gessner. It features gated townhome communities. Further down Gessner, it is difficult to miss the huge brick structure that marks the **Teal Wood** neighborhood, a portion of which is in Bunker Hill Village. Just east of Gessner and south of Memorial Drive, **Whispering Oaks** and **Warrenton** are two lovely neighborhoods established in the late 1950s and early 1960s. Some of the homes here are perched at the edge of a bluff and have dramatic backyard views of the bayou below. Warrenton and a portion of Whispering Oaks are located in Bunker Hill. Another lovely neighborhood located nearby is **Sandlewood.** This beautiful lakeside neighborhood features large, old shade trees. Hidden among towering trees between Buffalo Bayou and Memorial Drive, this private neighborhood features three manmade lakes that date as far back as a hundred years. The banks of the bayou, lake, and the woods provide wonderful places for residents to walk or jog.

The Villages

Within Memorial are several tiny incorporated self-governing municipalities that refer to themselves as villages. Some of the villages, with their small geographic coverage, small population, close community, and wooded environment, definitely have a country village or small town atmosphere. The Memorial Villages are one of the most affluent parts of Houston and contain a large concentration of wealth packed into just a few square miles. This is one of the nicest residential areas with some of the most spectacular homes in Houston. They are surrounded by beautiful natural scenery of the woods and bayou, excellent public schools, and are in proximity to Houston's business centers, major freeways, and local attractions. Bunker Hill Village, Hedwig Village, Piney Point, and Hunters Creek are located south of I-10, and Hillshire Village and Spring Valley are located north of I-10.

A charmingly quaint incorporated village, **Bunker Hill Village** is a highly sought-after residential neighborhood. Protected from the worries of the outside world by a forest of towering trees, life here seems almost idyllic. Concerns about annexation by Houston and possible loss of its quiet country-style atmosphere led residents to incorporate the area in the 1950s. A little over 1000 families live in huge homes that cover these few square miles bounded by Taylorcrest Lane to the north, Blalock to the east, Memorial Drive to the south, and the City of Houston to the west.

Hedwig Village is named after Hedwig Jankowski Shroeder, a German immigrant who was the original owner of part of the land that is the present site of the village. Ms. Shroeder came to the U.S. in 1906 and purchased the land, which she later donated to the county for a right of way. The area was incorporated in 1954 and is the smallest of the Memorial Villages. It is located immediately north of Bunker Hill Village and Piney Point Village, south of I-10, west of Hunters Creek Village, and east of the City of Houston. Unlike most of the other villages, which contain only residences, Hedwig Village has its own commercial zone featuring banks, groceries, and other amenities. Nearby Katy Freeway (I-10) and the Sam Houston Tollway provide easy access to the city's business centers and local attractions.

The area that is now incorporated as **Hunters Creek** was originally settled by German farmers, who later established a sawmill. Some of the homes here were built by the people who worked at the sawmill, which no longer exists. In the past few years, several new residential developments have been constructed here. Many of the homes built in the 1960s have been torn down and replaced with magnificent custom built homes. Bounded by I-10 to the north, the City of Houston to the east, Buffalo Bayou to the south, and Piney Point Village to the west, Hunters Creek is one of the larger villages.

Piney Point covers 2.5 square miles of heavily forested area devoted solely to single-family residential homes. Businesses are restricted from operating within this village. In the early 1930s, it was still considered the far west of Houston, where many people from the city had weekend country homes. After Memorial Drive developed into a major thoroughfare in the 1950s, Houston began growing westward. Fearing annexation by the city, Piney Point residents incorporated their community in 1954. Its boundaries are the City of Hunters Creek to the north and east; Buffalo Bayou and Piney Point Gully to the south; and Blalock to the west.

The smallest of the incorporated villages, **Hillshire Village** is bounded by Westview to the north, Wirt Road to the east, I-10 to the south, and Spring Branch Bayou/city limits of Spring Valley to the west.

Spring Valley

Spring Valley residents incorporated their community in 1955, primarily to have zoning, which the City of Houston does not have. It is solely a single-family residential community. It is west of Hillshire Village, north of I-10, east of the City of Houston, and south of Spring Branch bayou.

Briar Forest

This neighborhood is definitely forest-like. At one time it served as a Boy Scout camp, but today, large residences and mansions are tucked behind heavily wooded areas and lush green vegetation. Though many of the homes date back to the 1970s, when development in the area began, there has also been recent construction on once undeveloped wooded acres near Briar Forest Road. Many of the newer homes are extravagant estates in the Mediterranean style with red tile roofs, tennis courts, and swimming pools. Older residences are quite large as well and beautifully elegant. Roads here are narrow and resemble quiet country lanes. A quiet community set among towering pines, it is like living in the country, but surprisingly close to major arteries such as Beltway 8, and along a major thoroughfare, Briar Forest Road.

Memorial West

Beyond Beltway 8 is Memorial West, which consists of newer residential developments. The farther west you travel, the newer the communities. Carved out of Memorial's pristine forests, it has much of the lush vegetation and ancient towering trees that provide a great deal of the ambience and character of Memorial. Memorial West includes the Energy Corridor, the area along I-10 between Beltway 8 and Grand Parkway where many energy companies including British Petroleum, Shell Exploration, ExxonMobil Chemical, and Conoco Phillips have offices. It is near the Addicks/Barker, Bear Creek, and Mission Bend communities. Homes here are similar to those in Memorial.

Spring Branch

Just northwest of Memorial is the **Spring Branch** community, originally established as a religious community settled by German farmers in the 1830s. Like Memorial, it has a similar natural environment of lush flora and tall shady trees. However, Spring Branch is less upscale and more diverse. Its large Hispanic population has replaced many of the white residents, who have moved elsewhere. In addition, the Korean community has opened up many commercial businesses here.

Web Sites: www.houstontx.gov, www.springvalleytx.com, www.cityofhunterscreek.com, www.cityofpineypoint.com, www.thecityofhedwigvillage.com, www.bunkerhill.net

Area Codes: 713, 281

Zip Codes: 77055, 77063, 77024

Post Offices: Long Point Station, 8000 Long Point Rd; John Dunlop Station, 8728 Beverlyhill St; Memorial Park Station, 10505 Town and Country Way; Rich Hill Station, 2950 Unity Dr; James Griffith Station, 9320 Emnora Ln

Police Precincts: Houston Police Department: Spring Branch Storefront, 8400 Long Point #A, 713-464-6901; Gessner Storefront, 1331 Gessner, 713-772-7691; Memorial Villages Police Department, www.mvpdtx.org, 11981 Memorial Dr, 713-365-3700; Hedwig Village Police Department, 6000 Gaylord; Spring Valley Police Department, 1025 Campbell Rd, 713-465-8323

Emergency Hospitals: Memorial City Hospital, www.memorialhermann.org, 921 Gessner Rd, 713-242-3000; Spring Branch Medical Center, www.springbranchmedical.com, 8850 Long Point, 713-467-6555

Libraries: Harris County Public Library, www.hcpl.net: Spring Branch Branch, 930 Corbindale, 713-464-1633; Houston Public Library, www.hpl.lib.tx.us: Ring Branch, 8835 Long Point, 832-393-2000

Adult Education: Houston Community College, www.hccs.cc.tx.us, Town and Country Center Campus, 1010 W Sam Houston Pkwy N, 713-718-5700

Public Education: Spring Branch Independent School District, www.springbranchisd.com, 955 Campbell Rd, 713-464-1511; Houston Independent School District, www.houstonisd.org, 4400 W 18th, 713-556-6005 (small parts of Briar Forest subdivision)

Community Publications: *Memorial–Spring Branch Sun*; *Memorial Examiner*, http://examinernews.com/memorial; *Houston Chronicle*, www.chron.com; *Houston Press*, www.houstonpress.com

Community Resources: Memorial Park, 6501 Memorial Dr, 713-845-1000

Public Transportation: Harris County Metropolitan Transit Authority, www.metro.org:
Bus: 6, 46, 70, 131

KATY

Old Town Katy, as the **City of Katy** is commonly known, is a small agricultural town and former rail town 25 miles west of downtown Houston. It has a small town atmosphere with the convenience of a major city nearby. Originally called Cane Island, Old Town Katy is located north of I-10 and was settled in the 1830s when the Missouri-Kansas-Texas railroad passed through the area. The main agricultural crop here was and still is rice. In honor of its primary cash crop, the city holds an annual Rice Harvest Festival. Oil was discovered here in 1934 and the Humble (now Exxon) Oil Company built a plant out here. Old Town Katy is often confused with the Katy area, a series of suburban developments to the east that are not all within the City of Katy's boundaries. Main attractions here are the Katy Mills Mall and the Forbidden Gardens, a miniature replica of China that covers the country's culture and history.

The **Katy Area**, where most of the new development is taking place, is located east of the City of Katy along I-10 and U.S. Highway 90, in parts of Harris, Waller, and Fort Bend counties. The Katy area has grown tremendously in the last 20 years into a major suburb. Many of the older Katy neighborhoods still exist, featuring mostly very affordable single-story homes. However, it is the new master-planned residential developments that are attracting families here. These include new developments such as **Cinco Ranch** and **Grand Lakes** and older ones from the 1970s and 1980s, such as **Memorial Parkway** and **Nottingham Country**. Cinco Ranch is a large affluent master-planned community that includes the most up-to-date amenities. Within the community is an artificial beach surrounding a large, shallow community swimming pool and a well-maintained golf course. Grand Lakes is a similar but smaller master-planned development with central parks, recreation centers, pools, spray parks, tennis courts, playgrounds, and putting greens. New residences are mostly dark brick homes that vary in size, but are almost identical in style. Many of the neighborhoods feature large subdivisions of tract houses. With plenty of open space, homes are relatively affordable and there is still plenty of new construction in the Katy area.

Most of the development is the result of the expansion of the Energy Corridor along I-10 West. Residents who live near here have two of the largest urban parks, George Bush and Cullen/Bear Creek, for jogging, rollerblading, and cycling. They also feature soccer fields, picnic sites, nature trails, dog parks, a velodrome, and skeet and clay pigeon shooting facilities. The proximity to nature, quiet residential streets, and good public schools are primary reasons residents choose the Katy area despite the traffic on I-10, which some will argue has the worst gridlock in the metropolitan area. However, it is precisely the rapid and continuing development of the area that has contributed to the congestion. The freeway is currently being expanded to deal with the increasing population, but until its completion the construction itself may create additional headaches for commuters.

One of the other main distinctions between the City of Katy and the Katy Area is that the Katy Area lies within an unincorporated district that is controlled by the City of Houston, which has the ability to annex it.

Web Sites: www.cincoranch.com, www.energycorridor.org, www.westfieldkaty.org, www.ci.katy.tx.us

Area Codes: 281, 832

Zip Codes: 77449, 77450, 77493, 77494

Post Offices: Katy Station, 20180 Park Row Dr; Katy Annex Station, 1331 Pin Oak Rd; Katy Finance Station, 5701 4th St

Emergency Hospital: Memorial Hermann Katy Hospital, www.memorialhermann.org, 5602 Medical Center Dr, 281-392-1111

Libraries: Harris County Public Library, www.hcpl.net: Katy Branch, 5414 Franz Rd, 281-391-3509; Maud Smith Marks Branch, 1815 Westgreen Blvd; Fort Bend County Public Library, Cinco Ranch Branch, www.fortbend.lib.tx.us, 2620 Commercial Center Blvd, 281-395-1311

Adult Education: University of Houston at Cinco Ranch, www.cincoranch.uh.edu, 4242 South Mason Rd, 832-842-2800; Houston Community College, Katy Mills, 25403 Kingsland Blvd, 281-644-6080; Houston Community College, Cinco Ranch, 4242 South Mason Rd, 713-718-5757

Public Education: Katy Independent School District, www.katyisd.org, 6301 S Stadium Ln, 281-396-6000

Community Publications: *Katy Times*, www.katytimes.com; *Katy Sun*

Community Resource: Katy Area Chamber of Commerce, www.katychamber.com, 2501 S Mason Rd, Ste 230, 281-828-1100

Public Transportation: Harris County Metropolitan Transit Authority, www.metro.org, *Bus*: 131, 221, 298 (Park and Ride)

ADDICKS/BARKER

Farther west on I-10 between the Barker Reservoir and Addicks Reservoir are several recent residential neighborhoods known collectively as the Addicks/Barker area. It encompasses the **Bear Creek** subdivisions and **Bear Creek Park**. The homes here are designed in various styles and sizes, but almost all are constructed of the same red brick, which tends to dilute the differences in the design of the homes and make them look nearly identical. The Addicks/Barker area was largely rural and densely forested before new home construction, still going on, began. Its location far away from the city or major commercial areas has resulted in quiet neighborhoods and affordable homes. Two major features of this community are the large reservoirs, Barker and Addicks, which border the neighborhoods. They were built when this part of Houston was a rural area far removed from the city.

Though Addicks is considered a suburb of Houston, it was actually a small unincorporated town before it was swallowed up by sprawl. Its history goes back to the 1850s, when the area was settled by German immigrants. Destroyed during the 1900 Galveston hurricane, the town rebuilt. The town was relocated in the mid 1940s when the Addicks Dam Reservoir was constructed to protect Houston from floods.

Web Site: www.co.harris.tx.us

Area Codes: 281, 832

Zip Codes: 77079, 77084

Post Offices: Ashford West Station, 12655 Whittington Dr; Fleetwood Station, 315 Addicks Howell Rd; Bear Creek Station, 16015 Cairnway Dr; Addicks Barker Station, 16830 Barker Springs Rd, Ste 401

Emergency Hospital: West Houston Medical Center, www.westhoustonmedical.com, 12141 Richmond Ave, 281-558-3444

Library: Harris County Public Library, www.hcpl.net: Katherine Tyra @ Bear Creek Branch, 16719 Clay Rd, 281-550-0885

Public Education: Katy Independent School District, www.katyisd.org, 6301 S Stadium Ln, Katy, 281-396-6000

Community Publication: *Houston Chronicle*, www.chron.com

Community Resource: Katy Area Chamber of Commerce, www.katychamber.com, 2501 S Mason Rd, Ste 230, Katy, 281-828-1100

Public Transportation: Harris County Metropolitan Transit Authority, www.metro.org: *Bus:* 131, 221, 228, 298 (Park and Ride)

SOUTHWEST HOUSTON

Southwest Houston is perhaps the most diverse part of the city. It contains a variety of ethnic communities, religions, and socioeconomic levels. In addition to long-time residents, the southwest area is home to many immigrants from Asia, Africa, Latin America, and the former Soviet Union. You are unlikely to find such a mix of people of different races and varying backgrounds in any other part of the city. Practitioners of different religions should not have difficulty finding a place of worship here because the area contains many churches, some catering to a specific ethnic community or language, several synagogues, Buddhist temples, and at least one mosque.

Southwest Houston features development from all decades, with the older neighborhoods dating back to the late 1950s and early 1960s, and newer residential development continuing to the present. The area's large geographical coverage makes for varying landscapes and neighborhoods of differing characteristics. Almost any type of housing from blocks of cheap, low-rise apartment complexes to modest single-family residential homes, large elegant residences, townhomes, and mansions can be found here.

MEYERLAND

Meyerland was established in the 1950s by George Meyer, whose family owned the area just south of Bellaire, along Brays Bayou. It quickly became associated with Houston's post–World War II Jewish community. Several institutions, such as the Jewish Community Center, Congregation Beth Israel, Congregation Beth Yeshurun, and a few smaller synagogues are located here. The greenbelt along Brays Bayou, a major bayou, is a popular place for residents to go jogging, walking, or biking. Graced by moss-covered oaks, its scenic route meanders through the neighborhood.

Homes here include older one-story bungalows, ranch houses, and more recent brick structures. They range from $150,000 to over $500,000, but are generally more affordable than those inside the 610 loop. In addition, most of the residents are zoned to Bellaire High School, but do not have to pay Bellaire property tax rates or home prices. Meyerland is next to the inner loop neighborhood of Stella Link/Linkwood and the City of Bellaire. Because of its location along the bayou, flooding has been a problem at times. Brays Bayou is deep and takes quite a bit of rain for it to overflow. However, the growth of the city and recent severe weather has made flooding a bigger issue. The last great flood was during Tropical Storm Allison, when almost the entire city was under water. Another factor contributing to the flooding is the fact that the area that is now Meyerland was once a rice field and is in a low lying area.

Web Sites: www.houstontx.gov, www.meyerlandonline.com

Area Code: 713

Zip Code: 77096

Post Office: South Post Oak Station, 5505 Belrose Dr, Bldg A, Houston

Police Precincts: Houston Police Department: Fondren Patrol, 11168 Fondren, 713-773-7900; Southwest Patrol, 4503 Beechnut, 713-314-3900

Emergency Hospitals: Twelve Oaks Hospital, 4200 Portsmouth St, 713-623-2500; Texas Medical Center, www.tmc.edu: Hermann Hospital, www.memorialhermann.org, 6411 Fannin, 713-704-4000; Ben Taub, www.hchdonline.com, Ben Taub General Hospital, 1504 Taub Loop, 713-873-2000; Methodist Hospital, www.methodisthealth.com, 6565 Fannin St, 713-790-3311; VA Hospital, www.houston.med.va.gov, 2002 Holcombe Blvd, 1-800-553-2278; St. Luke's, www.sleh.com, 6720 Bertner Ave, 832-355-1000; Texas Children's Hospital, www.texaschildrenshospital.org, 6621 Fannin St, 832-824-1000

Libraries: Houston Public Library, www.hpl.lib.tx.us: Meyer Branch, 5005 W Bellfort, 832-393-1840; McGovern–Stella Link Branch, 7405 Stella Link, 832-393-2630

Adult Education: Houston Community College, West Loop Center, 5601 West Loop, 713-718-7868

Public Education: Houston Independent School District, www.houstonisd.org, 4400 W 18th, Houston, 713-556-6005

Community Publications: Houston Chronicle, www.chron.com; Houston Press, www.houstonpress.com

Community Resources: City Hall, 900 Bagby, Houston, 713-837-0311; Jewish Community Center, www.jcchouston.org, 5601 S Braeswood, Houston, 713-729-3200; YMCA Weekley Family Branch, www.ymcahouston.org, 7101 Stella Blvd, Houston, 713-664-9622; Southwest Houston Chamber of Commerce, www.gswhcc.org, 6900 South Rice Ave, Bellaire, 713-666-1521

Public Transportation: Harris County Metropolitan Authority, www.ridemetro.org: *Bus*: 10, 33, 47, 49, 65, 68, 261

WESTBURY

Located just outside Loop 610, Westbury is conveniently near the Medical Center, the Galleria/Uptown area, and Reliant football stadium, and maintains easy access to downtown Houston. In addition, many of the sprawling ranch-style homes are relatively affordable at around $120,000 to $200,000. As housing prices have increased inside the Loop, many are looking to Westbury as an alternative market. The closer you are to Loop 610, the nicer the residential areas. As you step away from Loop 610, towards South Gessner, the quality of the neighborhood starts to decline.

Westbury was developed in the 1950s and 1960s as a suburban community. Eventually annexed by Houston as the city grew, it is no longer considered part of the suburbs. When the real estate market crashed in the 1980s, many businesses in the area closed. Homes here are typically sprawling one-story ranch-style homes with low-slung roofs and large front and back yards on quiet residential streets. There are also many low-rise apartment complexes, mainly around the Westbury Square shopping center.

Greater Fondren Southwest Area

This area bounded by Braeswood on the north, Fondren on the east, West Airport on the south, and Gessner on the west, was largely undeveloped until the 1970s, when developers built large fancy homes on the pristine land here. Fondren Southwest homes were highly sought by prospective buyers. Secluded behind a brick wall, Fondren Southwest had the feel of a special neighborhood. These days, the neighborhood is less special. A maze of apartment complexes was built in the empty lots around it in the 1970s and 1980s. After the housing slump in the 1980s, the area deteriorated. Struggling to find people to occupy the complexes, landlords decreased rent prices and rented to anyone regardless of criminal background history or character. Though the Fondren Southwest homes behind the brick barrier are generally safe and isolated from the surrounding apartments, the apartment complexes around them have very high crime rates.

Glenshire

Farther down south of Fondren Southwest, behind West Bellfort, is the hidden neighborhood of Glenshire. The main entrance is lined by tall trees that form a canopy of leaves over the entrance. This well-kept secret contains affordable homes of varying sizes and styles. The variety of designs is a departure from the uniform-looking brick homes that populate most of the new residential neighborhoods. There are Old English style Tudor homes, traditional, Tidewater-style, and other designs. East Glenshire homes are larger and feature lovely landscaped lawns and yards. West Glenshire homes are smaller and feature some townhomes. Outside of East Glenshire is a recently constructed neighborhood named Villages of Glenshire, featuring smaller one- and two-story brick homes with minimal lots.

Web Site: www.houstontx.gov
Area Code: 713
Zip Codes: 77031, 77071, 77035, 77096
Post Offices: South Post Oak Station, 5505 Belrose Dr, Bldg A; Westbury Station, 11805 Chimney Rock Rd; Westbrae Station, 10910 S Gessner Dr
Police Precincts: Houston Police Department: Fondren Patrol, 11168 Fondren; Southwest Patrol, 4503 Beechnut, 713-314-3900; Westbury Storefront, 5550 Gasmer, 713-728-2424
Emergency Hospitals: Memorial Hermann Southwest Hospital, www.memorialhermann. org, 7600 Beechnut; Texas Medical Center, www.tmc.edu: Hermann Hospital, www. memorialhermann.org, 6411 Fannin, 713-704-4000; Ben Taub, www.hchdonline. com, Ben Taub General Hospital, 1504 Taub Loop, 713-873-2000; Methodist Hospital, www.methodisthealth.com, 6565 Fannin St, 713-790-3311; VA Hospital, www.houston.med.va.gov, 2002 Holcombe Blvd, 800-553-2278; St. Luke's, www. sleh.com, 6720 Bertner Ave, 832-355-1000; Texas Children's Hospital, www. texaschildrenshospital.org, 6621 Fannin St, 832-824-1000
Libraries: Houston Public Library, www.hpl.lib.tx.us: Meyer Branch, 5005 W Bellfort, 832-393-1840; Morris Frank Branch, 6440 W Bellfort, 832-393-2410
Adult Education: Houston Community College, West Loop Center, 5601 West Loop, 713-718-7868
Public Education: Houston Independent School District, www.houstonisd.org, 4400 W 18th, 713-556-6005
Community Publications: *Houston Chronicle*, www.chron.com; *Houston Press*, www. houstonpress.com
Community Resources: City Hall, 900 Bagby, Houston, 713-837-0311, Southwest Houston Chamber of Commerce, www.gswhcc.org, 6900 S Rice Ave, Bellaire, 713-666-1521; Westbury Civic Club, www.westburycrier.com, 713-723-5437; Marian Community Center, 11101 S Gessner, Houston, 713-773-7015
Public Transportation: Harris County Metropolitan Authority, www.ridemetro.org: *Bus*: 8, 10, 46, 47, 65, 68, 163, 262, 265, 292

WESTWOOD/HARWIN, SHARPSTOWN, AND ALIEF

Westwood/Harwin

Westwood is a working-class, lower-income neighborhood, primarily consisting of low-rise apartments and commercial areas. There are a few townhomes and small homes here, but low-rent apartments predominate in this neighborhood. The Harwin area is named after a street that is known throughout Houston as the place to buy counterfeit goods. Nearby on Hillcroft are several Persian, Indian, and Pakistani restaurants, grocery stores, and clothing stores. This is the city's South Asian commercial center, and many recent immigrants from South Asian countries live in the apartments off of Bellaire Boulevard, on the other side of U.S. 59 across from Sharpstown Mall. A large white mosque stands out in this quiet residential area surrounded by a few commercial businesses. However, most of the city's South Asian and Middle Eastern residents do not reside here, but are instead spread throughout Houston.

Braeburn

Those interested in the Sharpstown or Fondren Southwest area may also want to consider the small neighborhood of Braeburn. Bounded by Bissonnet on the north, Hillcroft on the east, Brays Bayou on the south, and U.S. 59 on the west, Braeburn is located between Sharpstown and Fondren Southwest. It features mostly single-story residential homes on tidy but lush, well-maintained lawns on quiet residential streets.

Sharpstown

Sharpstown was a groundbreaking community at the time of its development in the late 1950s and early 1960s. It was the largest suburban community in Texas with the first indoor air-conditioned mall. Young families flocked to this new, promising community with tidy homes on neatly divided lots, wide streets, convenient shopping, and new schools. From the 1960s to early 1970s, this was Houston's premier suburb. The success of communities like Sharpstown jump-started the development of similar future communities. Sharpstown's sprawling suburban model was adopted many times over and continues to be used in new residential developments. However, Sharpstown started to steadily decline in the 1980s, when oil prices fell and many workers were laid off, causing the banks to foreclose on their homes. The decline was also due in part to white flight and the attraction of newer suburbs. Though Sharpstown has never recovered its former glory, there is no shortage of buyers interested in the homes here. It has an excellent location near U.S. 59 and major arteries like Bellaire Boulevard. The community lies between the inner loop and the suburbs.

Recent immigrants from Asia and Latin America have taken the place of former residents, making Sharpstown one of the most diverse neighborhoods in Houston. All along Bellaire Boulevard between U.S. 59 and Beltway 8, drivers can see shop signs in English, Spanish, Chinese, and Vietnamese. Stores that cater to the Hispanic population's tastes have replaced many of the stores that closed and relocated to other areas. The Safeway is now a Fiesta grocery store and instead of Winchell's Donuts, there are taco stands and Mexican bakeries. On some streets like Beechnut, neighborhood Hispanic mercados fill the gap for residents who need daily necessities and have no transportation.

The city's Chinatown and Vietnamese commercial centers are located here and have replaced open land. Houston actually has two Chinatowns. The original one is downtown, but most are familiar only with the one located in Sharpstown. It is more a commercial district with shops, grocery stores, restaurants, banks, and other businesses than a residential area. Chinatown starts in Sharpstown on Bellaire Blvd and extends past

Beltway 8 into the Alief community. Visitors will find some of the city's best Chinese restaurants and bakeries and plenty of bubble tea here. Most of the signs are in Chinese and you really get the feeling that you have stepped into another zone, even possibly a foreign land. However, over the years it has slowly developed into a residential community as well. Many new immigrants live in the apartments behind Bellaire Blvd, which allows them to be within walking distance of all the necessities and amenities. In addition, senior citizen apartments are being constructed in the middle of an area of several shops, creating a pedestrian village. On the other side of Bellaire Boulevard, hidden behind the busy thoroughfare, is a single-family residential neighborhood. Homes vary in size and style and are relatively affordable.

Because Sharpstown covers such a large area, the housing here is diverse and varies from neighborhood to neighborhood. Sharpstown's only high-rise condominium—the Conquistador—is located across from Sharpstown Mall. The area around Houston Baptist University, along the feeder of U.S. 59 at Fondren, is a series of strip shopping centers, university dorms, and single-family residential homes off the street. One of the biggest employers in the area, Hermann Memorial Hospital Southwest, is located by the university and many of the employees live in Sharpstown and its surrounding areas. Beechnut Street contains many low-rise apartment complexes and duplexes, mostly rented by Mexican and Latin American immigrants. The single-family residential homes hidden behind this street are similar in style and price to those behind Bellaire Boulevard. Behind Sharpstown High School are homes on large lots secluded behind trees.

Sharpstown further declined in the 1990s as residents and businesses began moving further out to newer suburbs. Some of the boarded-up buildings in strip shopping centers along Gessner and Beechnut make the area look like a deserted ghost town. The many car dealerships along Bellaire Boulevard have all moved further down U.S. 59 near the new suburbs in Sugar Land, leaving empty deserted lots or open land. However, do not let the appearance of the major thoroughfares fool you. Once you deviate from the main roads onto the residential streets, you will find nice residential neighborhoods with homes that have large lawns.

Sharpstown has a bad reputation as a shady part of town, and indeed parts of it are considered a high-crime area. The crimes are mostly concentrated in the area's numerous low-rise apartments. The community itself is too large to fit into this general stereotype though. The 1950s-style ranch homes and bungalows still attract many buyers to this diverse community with a balanced mix of African-Americans, whites, Hispanics, and Asians.

Alief

Like Sharpstown, Alief has seen better days. The difference between the two is that parts of Alief, mainly the western portions, have bounced back from the housing slump of the 1980s. During the 1970s and 1980s Alief was a popular residential suburb. It was one of the newest developments of the time, attracting many families with its affordable housing and latest amenities. Many people were also drawn to this community by its high-quality schools. The local high school was one of the largest in the state and eventually had to be divided into two.

The downturn in the real estate market following the oil bust in the 1980s changed Alief. Many homeowners faced foreclosure. New home construction stopped, but picked up again during the 1990s' economic boom. Most of the new residential construction is further west, near the Fort Bend County line. However, new homes mix with older homes in some of the old neighborhoods. The area closer to Sharpstown is glum, with row after row of strip shopping centers lining the major thoroughfares. There are also many auto repair shops and light industries in the eastern part of Alief near the Beltway 8. Further down the street, past the Beltway 8 into Alief, is a continuation of Chinatown though the businesses here are primarily Vietnamese. Just 15 years ago, this area was largely flat open land. KBR (Halliburton) was one of the few businesses here and the Beltway had just been completed a few years earlier.

The homes here include townhomes and small one-story homes dating from the 1970s. Further west towards the newly constructed Westpark Tollway are a mix of new and established residential developments. Homes here are surrounded by lush vegetation and other lovely flowers planted by the owners. The neighborhoods here are quieter than in eastern Alief and more compatible with the description of a residential community because of the absence of commercial businesses, such as the light industries in east Alief.

Alief is now considered by many as a part of Houston, but is also a community with a separate and independent identity. Its history dates back to 1861, when the first settlers moved in. Back then the town was known as Dairy or Dairy Station, but was changed to Alief in 1895 in honor of the town's first postmistress, Alief Ozella Magee. This rural community grew primarily corn, cotton, and rice, and raised cattle. By the 1970s, most of Alief was annexed by Houston. The population grew tremendously between 1970 and 1985 as it became a primarily urban area. The opening of the Westpark Tollway provides a quick and direct route for commuters in the outer Alief neighborhoods to inside the loop and downtown.

The outlying master-planned community of **Mission Bend**, which straddles Harris and Fort Bend counties, is located at the outermost edge of Alief. The community consists of seemingly identical brick single-family residential homes and strip malls.

Web Site: www.houstontx.gov
Area Code: 713
Zip Codes: 77036, 77074, 77072, 77081, 77083, 77082, 77099
Post Offices: De Moss Branch, 6500 De Moss Dr; Beechnut Station, 11703 Beechnut

St; Alief Station, 11936 Bellaire Blvd, Alief; Rich Hill Station, 2950 Unity Dr; Ashford West Station, 12655 Whittington Dr

Police Precincts: Houston Police Department: Southwest Patrol, 4503 Beechnut, 713-314-3900; Ranchester Storefront, 9146 Bellaire, 713-272-3673; Westwood Storefront, 9700 Bissonnet, Ste #1740-W, 713-773-7000

Emergency Hospital: Memorial Hermann Southwest Hospital, www.memorialhermann. org, 7600 Beechnut, 713-456-5000

Libraries: Houston Public Library, www.hpl.lib.tx.us: Walter Branch Library, 7660 Clarewood, 832-393-2500; Henington-Alief Branch, 7979 South Kirkwood, 832-393-1820

Adult Education: Houston Baptist University, www.hbu.edu, 7502 Fondren Rd, 281-649-3000; Houston Community College, Alief Center, 13803 Bissonnet, 713-718-6870

Public Education: Houston Independent School District, www.houstonisd.org, 4400 W 18th, Houston, 713-556-6005; Alief Independent School District, www.alief.isd. tenet.edu, 12302 High Star, Houston, 281-498-8110

Community Publications: *Houston Chronicle*, www.chron.com; *Houston Press*, www. houstonpress.com

Community Resources: City Hall, 900 Bagby, 713-837-0311; Southwest Houston Chamber of Commerce, www.gswhcc.org, 6900 S Rice Ave, Bellaire, 713-666-1521; Burnett Bayland Park Community Center, 6200 Chimney Rock, 713-668-4516; Sharpstown Community Center, 6600 Harbor Town, 713-988-5328; Lansdale Community Center, 8201 Roos, 713-272-3687; Houston Chinese Community Center, www.ccchouston.org, 9800 Town Park Dr, 713-271-6100; Alief Community Center, 11903 Bellaire, 281-564-8130

Public Transportation: Harris County Metropolitan Transit Authority, www.ridemetro. org: *Bus:* 2, 4, 19, 25, 46, 47, 65, 67, 68, 82, 132, 163, 262, 265, 274, 292

SOUTHWEST SUBURBS

FORT BEND COUNTY

Fort Bend County is one of the fastest growing counties in Texas. It has one of the region's most diverse populations: 57% white, 20% African-American, 11% Asian, and 12% Hispanic. In the past 15–20 years, this once agricultural county has experienced explosive growth due to the development of new residential communities, though in the northeastern part of the county, where most of the population and businesses are concentrated—Sugar Land, Missouri City, Stafford, and the Meadows— new housing development has stretched as far out as Richmond, the county seat.

MEADOWS PLACE AND STAFFORD

Meadows Place
Traveling from U.S. 59 north, Meadows Place will be the first incorporated city you approach in Fort Bend County. Residents who commute from

here to Houston avoid coming home to the rush hour traffic gridlock further south on U.S. 59 past Highway 6. Meadows Place is a tiny area that consists mostly of a few blocks of homes. It is primarily a residential community with a small number of commercial businesses within the city limits. A few restaurants, fast food joints, a bank, Walgreen's drugstore, car dealerships, and a Sam's Wholesale Club are located along U.S. 59 within Meadows Place. The limited number of shops is hardly an inconvenience for residents as several major shopping centers and restaurants are next door in Stafford or within quick driving distance. In fact, it is difficult to tell which establishments are in Meadows and which are in adjoining Stafford since the two cities flow into each other. Homes date from the 1970s and vary in size and variety, including one-story traditional homes and two-story Tidewater style homes. Because of its small geographic area, there is a small community feel and residents can easily become acquainted with each other.

Stafford

The small town of Stafford has in the past few decades promoted itself as a business-friendly community. As a result, many stores have opened up along U.S. 59 and several companies, such as Texas Instruments and UPS, have major offices here. Its lower than average sales tax rate and location between Houston and Sugar Land are main reasons for its success in attracting revenue-generating businesses. As a result, Stafford's financial position is strong enough that in 1995 it abolished municipal property taxes. Stafford is also unique in that it runs its own school district, the only municipal school district in Texas.

The northern boundaries of the city limits are primarily a commercial area. Many businesses have opened up along U.S. 59, the artery into Sugar Land and many other communities south of Houston, making it a booming commercial district. The glowing signs of restaurants and a few motels border both sides of the freeway until it hits Highway 90. At the intersection of U.S. 59 and Highway 90 are several business parks. In addition, several light industries are located further inside the city near the railroad tracks.

The town was settled in the 1820s by William Stafford, the namesake of this town. His was one of the original 300 families that took up Spain's offer of land grants to settle the Texas territory. During the war for Texas's independence from Mexico, Mexican General Santa Anna's troops stopped in the area and survived on the area's food. Farming was the main industry of this town until the 1950s, when light industry and other businesses began moving into the area. All that remains of historic Stafford are a few old buildings of a small farming town that are reminiscent of old Main Street, USA.

It is estimated that more people work in or visit Stafford than actually live here. However, there are a few new single-family residential developments here. There are also some older bungalow homes with wood siding that date back to the 1950s located further inside the city.

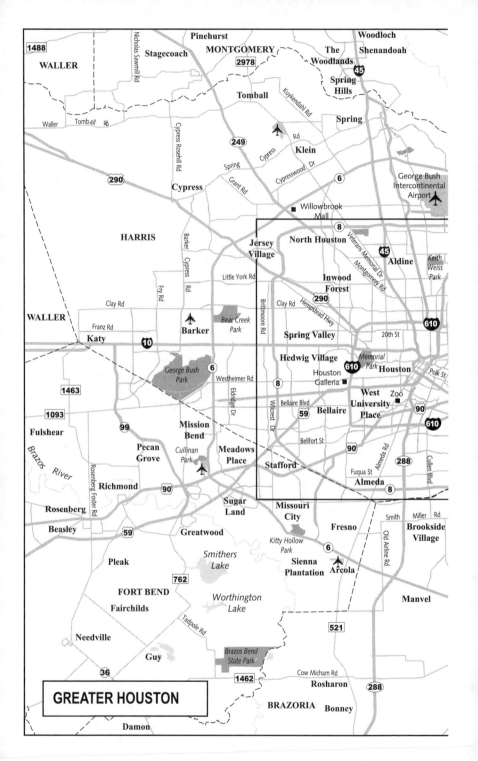

GREATER HOUSTON

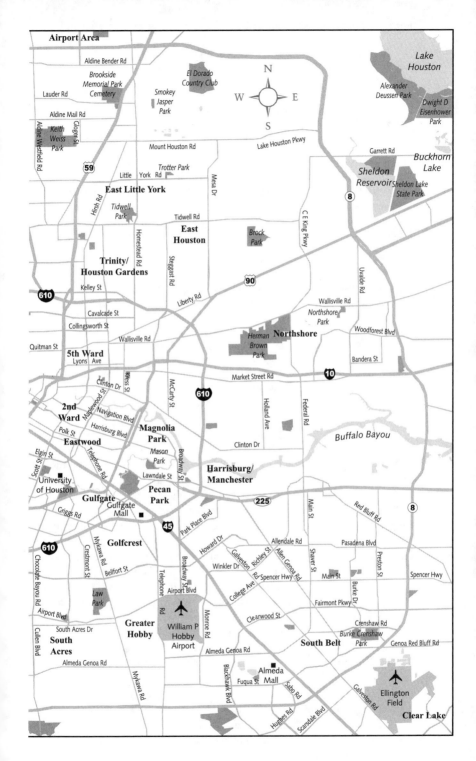

Web Sites: www.cityofmeadowsplace.org, www.cityofstafford.com
Area Code: 281
Zip Code: 77477
Post Office: Stafford Station, 4110 Bluebonnet Dr, Stafford
Police Departments: Meadows Police Department, One Troyan Dr, Meadows Place, 281-983-2900; Stafford Police Department, www.staffordpd.com, 2702 S Main St, Stafford, 281-261-3950
Emergency Hospitals: Fort Bend Medical Center, www.memorialhermann.org, 3803 FM 1092, Missouri City, 281-499-4800; Methodist Hospital–Sugar Land, www.methodisthealth.com, 16655 Southwest Fwy, Sugar Land, 281-274-7000; Memorial Hermann Southwest Hospital, www.memorialhermann.org, 7600 Beechnut, Houston, 713-456-5000
Library: Fort Bend County Library, www.fortbend.lib.tx.us: Mamie George Branch, 320 Dulles Ave, Stafford, 281-491-8086
Adult Education: Houston Community College–Stafford, http://swc2.hccs.edu, 9910 Cash Rd, Stafford, 713-718-7800
Public Education: Fort Bend Independent School District (Meadows Place), www.fortbend.k12.tx.us, 16431 Lexington Blvd, Sugar Land, 281-634-1000; Stafford Municipal School District, www.stafford.msd.esc4.net, 1625 Staffordshire Rd, Stafford, 281-261-9200
Community Publication: *Fort Bend Southwest Star*, www.fortbendstar.com; *Fort Bend Southwest Sun*, www.fortbendsouthwestsun.com
Community Resources: Meadows Place City Hall, One Troyan Dr, Meadows Place, 281-983-2950; Stafford City Hall, 2610 S Main St, Stafford, 281-261-3900; Stafford Centre, www.staffordcentre.com, 10505 Cash Rd, Stafford, 281-208-6900

SUGAR LAND

The City of Sugar Land is named after what was once its main economic export: sugar. The area was at one time a sugar plantation. At the turn of the twentieth century, the Imperial Sugar Company headquarters and refinery built Sugar Land, a self-contained company town with its own housing, schools, and hospital. For decades, the Imperial Sugar Company was the economic base and major employer of this town. However, in the past 25 years, Sugar Land has evolved from a blue-collar refinery town and agriculturally based economy to a booming, affluent suburb of Houston.

This quintessential suburb of master-planned communities, some with their own country clubs, golf courses, and lakes, attracts families from ethnically diverse backgrounds. The city is over 60% white, almost one-quarter Asian, 8% Hispanic, and 5% African-American. These statistics also reflect the many immigrants from India, China, Taiwan, Russia, and Latin America who have settled in Sugar Land. Like many others who choose Sugar Land, they too are drawn by the relatively lower property taxes, the wide selection of single-family residential housing at prices ranging from the relatively affordable to millions of dollars, and the well-regarded public school system. Therefore, it comes as no surprise to many that this popular suburb was named by *Money* magazine as one of its top 100 places to live in 2005.

Being mostly a series of master-planned communities, the city has an almost uniform look of elegant dark brick buildings and evenly spaced trees. In 2003, the city opened a newly constructed town square that includes apartments, condos, the new city hall, shops, hotel, and restaurants all within walking distance of each other. This smartly designed mixed-use area provides the city with a center and sense of community, as well as reflecting its shift from an agricultural area to an urban/suburban community.

Though the sugar refinery closed in 2003, its impact on the local economy was minimal. The city has attracted major companies such as Schlumberger, Fluor Daniel, and Unocal that provide employment to residents.

Sugar Land consists of several large subdivisions and communities. The most recognizable of them is **First Colony**. The city's City Hall, shopping, entertainment, and dining establishments are located here at Town Center. First Colony contains a mix of single-family residential homes, apartments, lofts, and townhomes. Other subdivisions in Sugar Land include **Sugar Creek, Settlers Way/Settlers Park/Settlers Grove, New Territory, Greatwood**, and **Avalon**. Some of these subdivisions are self-contained communities featuring amenities such as manmade lakes, waterfalls, fountains, and streams, as well as sailing, canoeing, and a recreation center.

Web Site: www.ci.sugar-land.tx.us

Area Code: 281

Zip Codes: 77478, 77479, 77477

Post Offices: Sugar Land Station, 225 Matlage Way; First Colony Station, 3130 Grants Lake Blvd

Police Department: Sugar Land Police Department, 1200 Hwy 6 S, 281-275-2500

Emergency Hospital: Methodist Hospital–Sugar Land, www.methodisthealth.com, 16655 Southwest Fwy, 281-274-7000

Libraries: Fort Bend County Library, www.fortbend.lib.tx.us: Sugar Land Branch, 550 Eldridge Rd, 281-277-8934; First Colony Branch, 2121 Austin Pkwy, 281-265-4444

Adult Education: University of Houston–Sugar Land Branch, www.uhsa.uh.edu, 14000 University Blvd, 281-275-3300

Public Education: Fort Bend Independent School District, www.fortbend.k12.tx.us, 16431 Lexington Blvd, 281-634-1000

Community Publications: *Fort Bend Southwest Star*, www.fortbendstar.com; *Fort Bend Southwest Sun*, www.fortbendsouthwestsun.com; *Fort Bend Herald*; *Texas Coaster*

Community Resources: City Hall, 2700 Town Center North, 281-275-2700; Fort Bend Chamber of Commerce, www.fortbendchamber.org, 445 Commerce Green Blvd, 281-491-0800

MISSOURI CITY

In the 1890s, two Houston real estate investors advertised land for sale in northeast Fort Bend/Southwest Harris County, Texas. To attract St. Louis buyers, they called the area in northeast Fort Bend County, Missouri City. Enough residents moved here for the area to develop into a farming and ranching community. It remained an agricultural area until the period between the 1970s and 1980s when its population went from under 5000 to over 20,000. Unlike the surrounding Fort Bend County communities, Missouri City does not have any significant industry or economic base to support it. Most of the residents commute to Houston for work. This bedroom community has one of the area's most diverse populations: 38% white, 38% African-American, and 11% Hispanic. Missouri City's significant African-American middle-class population began settling here in the 1970s. Homes here are available in various price ranges, including one-story brick homes, million-dollar mansions, and gated estates. Apartments and condominiums, however, are rare to nonexistent because of zoning ordinances.

A small portion of Missouri City lies within Harris County. The homes closer to the Harris County line are usually older and more affordable. Farther out past Highway 6 are several master-planned communities with homes in various price ranges.

The suburbs of Houston are full of master-planned communities far from the center of the City. In many instances they are not suburbs, but isolated communities designed by developers to take advantage of the low land values and scenic natural surroundings. They often attract people who are concerned about crime in the city or public schools and are lured by the idea of being in an area surrounded by nature. Communities such as these include the following:

Oyster Creek
Named for a nearby creek of the same name, Oyster Creek is distinguished by pecan groves, lakes, and golf courses. Nearby is **Quail Valley**, which is located among pecan groves along Oyster Creek.

Lake Olympia
Lake Olympia features waterfront homes, gated communities, and single-family residential homes from $150,000 into the millions. Residents can enjoy the use of two Olympic-sized pools, tennis courts, a private marina, boating and fishing piers, and four parks.

Sienna Plantation
Sienna Plantation is on the site of a former sugar cane plantation owned by Jonathan Waters, a planter from South Carolina. Known at the time as the Waters Plantation, it became a prosperous estate with sugar cane, cotton, and other crops. The estate also includes an impressive mansion overlooking a pecan grove with a sugar mill and sawmill. After the Civil War, the plantation was sold and changed hands several times before Lillian and Stella Scanlan inherited the property upon the death of their father, former Houston Mayor T.H. Scanlan. The two single sisters

renamed it Sienna Plantation and converted it to a working ranch. From 1955 to 1967, it was used as a retreat for Catholic nuns. The mansion was restored by developers when work began on this residential community. The opening of the Fort Bend Toll Road has provided residents who work at the Medical Center a quicker route to work.

Sienna Plantation contains a variety of homes that range from $130,000 to over $2 million. It is located in a scenic and rural area that overlooks the Brazos River. The community's isolation and distance from nearby development provides the kind of quiet, safe atmosphere that makes people willing to put up with a long commute. To compensate, developers have created a resort-style recreation complex known as Club Sienna, with a golf course, private stables, outdoor amphitheater, and outdoor sports park. Club Sienna gives residents the feeling that they are in a park or resort rather than a residential neighborhood.

Web Sites: www.ci.mocity.tx.us, www.siennaplantation.com, www.lakeolympia.org
Area Code: 281
Zip Codes: 77459, 77479, 77489
Post Offices: Missouri City Annex Station, 3701 Glenn Lakes Ln, Missouri City; Missouri City Station, 1902 Texas Pkwy, Missouri City
Police Departments: Missouri City Public Safety Headquarters, 3849 Cartwright Rd, Missouri City, 281-261-4200; Fort Bend Sheriff's Office, 1410 Ransom Rd, Richmond, 281-341-4700
Emergency Hospital: Memorial Hermann Fort Bend Medical Center, www.memorialhermann.org, 3803 FM 1092, Missouri City, 281-499-4800
Library: Fort Bend County Public Library, www.fortbend.lib.tx.us: Missouri City Branch, 1530 Texas Pkwy, Missouri City, 281-499-4100
Public Education: Fort Bend Independent School District, www.fortbend.k12.tx.us, 16431 Lexington Blvd, Sugar Land, 281-634-1000; Houston Independent School District, www.houstonisd.org, 4400 W 18th St, Houston, 713-556-6005 (some portions of Missouri City)
Community Publications: *Fort Bend Southwest Star*, www.fortbendstar.com; *Fort Bend Southwest Sun*, www.fortbendsouthwestsun.com; *Fort Bend Herald*; *Texas Coaster*
Community Resources: City Hall, 1522 Texas Pkwy, Missouri City, 281-261-4260; Fort Bend Chamber of Commerce, www.fortbendchamber.org, 445 Commerce Green Blvd, Sugar Land, 281-491-0800

RICHMOND AND ROSENBERG

Located in the heart of Fort Bend County, along the Brazos River, **Richmond** is steeped in history. It was the first settlement in the county and the first incorporated city of the Republic of Texas. Early residents included prominent figures such as Jane Long, Mirabeau B. Lamar, and Deaf Smith, all of whom helped found the Republic and were instrumental in its early years. Until recently, most of the development in Fort Bend County has been confined to Sugar Land, Missouri City, and the areas near Houston. As growth increases, development is expanding out into Richmond as well.

One of the biggest planned communities out here is **Pecan Grove Plantation**. This affluent residential community is located approximately four miles northeast of Richmond. Most of the residents commute to work in Houston 26 miles away. It is farther than most of the Fort Bend neighborhoods, but its location is part of the attraction. Developed in the 1970s, Pecan Grove Plantation is built around the private Pecan Grove Country Club and golf course. The community is situated among stately pecan trees, huge oak trees, and wooded areas.

Next to Richmond is the city of **Rosenberg**. It developed in 1880 around the Gulf, Colorado, and Santa Fe railroad three miles west of the city of Richmond after the railroad was denied access through Richmond. Rosenberg is still primarily an agricultural town. However, the population has changed from the original Czech, Polish, and German settlers to a majority Hispanic population today.

There are many more planned communities in Fort Bend County with new home construction continuing in almost all of them. These developments are scattered and spread out around Fort Bend County. For a complete list of Fort Bend's planned communities, check out the following link: www.fortbendcounty.org/plan.pdf.

Web Sites: www.ci.richmond.tx.us, www.ci.rosenberg.tx.us, www.pecangrove.org
Area Code: 281
Zip Codes: 77471, 77469
Post Offices: Rosenberg Station, 2103 Ave G, Rosenberg; Richmond Station, 5560 FM 1640 Rd, Richmond
Police Departments: Richmond Police Department, www.richmondtxpolice.com, 600 Preston St, Richmond, 281-342-2849; Rosenberg Police Department, 2120 4th St, Rosenberg, 832-595-3700; Fort Bend Sheriff's Office, 1410 Ransom Rd, Richmond, 281-341-4700
Emergency Hospital: OakBend Medical Center, www.oakbendmedialcenter.org, 1705 Jackson St, Richmond, 281-341-3000
Libraries: Fort Bend County Public Library, www.fortbend.lib.tx.us: George Memorial Library, 1001 Golfview Dr, Richmond, 281-342-4455; Fort Bend County Law Library, Richmond, 401 Jackson, Rm 302, Richmond, 281-341-3718
Public Education: Lamar Consolidated School District, www.lcisd.org, 3911 Ave I, Rosenberg, 281-341-3100
Community Publications: *Fort Bend Southwest Sun*, www.fortbendsouthwestsun.com; *Herald-Coaster* (Rosenberg), www.herald-coaster.com; *Fort Bend Now*, www.fortbendnow.com
Community Resources: Richmond City Hall, 402 Morton, Richmond, 281-342-5456; Rosenberg City Hall, 2110 Fourth St, Rosenberg, 832-595-3400; Fort Bend Chamber of Commerce, www.fortbendchamber.org, 445 Commerce Green Blvd, Sugar Land, 281-491-0800; George Ranch Historical Park, www.georgeranch.org, 10215 FM 762, Richmond, 281-343-0218; Brazos Bend State Park, 21901 FM 762, Needville, 979-553-5101

NORTHWEST HOUSTON

This part of Houston continues to grow due to constant construction of new residential developments that attract buyers with affordable options, quiet lifestyle, and beautiful natural surroundings. Northwest Houston is a heavily treed area surrounded by lush vegetation. Until the 1950s, it was primarily a rural area composed of old German farming communities that date back to the mid-1800s. Serious development of the northwest countryside first started in the 1960s when it was announced that an international airport would be constructed north of the city. Though residential communities have been in the northwest area, development really took off in the late 1980s and early 1990s when the Sam Houston Tollway and improvements to other highways that run through the area (Highway 6, FM 1960, and Highway 290) made the area more easily accessible to prospective homeowners.

Many major companies are located here, which has also led to the growth of the communities. The biggest employers are Hewlett Packard, Baker Hughes, Continental Airlines, Cooper Industries, and Dresser Industries. In addition, many retail stores and services, most of which are along the heavily traveled FM 1960, provide additional jobs. The opening of major malls in the 1980s and 1990s has also created further employment in the area.

INWOOD FOREST, CANDLELIGHT, GARDEN OAKS, AND OAK FOREST

Inwood Forest
As one of the first neighborhoods in northwest Houston, Inwood Forest dates back to the late 1960s and early 1970s; consequently you may be able to find some affordable homes in the low $100,000s. Houses vary in size from small ranch-style designs to large upscale residences. The major feature of this neighborhood is the recently renovated private Inwood Forest Golf Club. Inwood Forest has a diverse ethnic population of young families, retiree communities, and a few professionals. The neighborhood has lost the luster that was once associated with Inwood Forest since the construction of low-income apartment complexes. However, those who are simply looking for a nice house near major freeways on the northwest side of town will find a good bargain here.

Candlelight
Quietly secluded among winding roads and a forest of towering trees, Candlelight is one of those hidden finds. It was developed in the 1970s and remained in an out-of-the-way location until West Tidwell was extended through the neighborhood in the late 1980s. The greenbelts along Cole Creek and White Oak Bayou provide recreational space for walking, biking, and other outdoor activities. Candlelight is divided into the **Candlelight Estates, Candlelight Oaks, Candlelight Forest, Candlelight Place, Candlelight Plaza,** and **Candlelight Woods**

subdivisions. The homes here vary in size and design and cost more than those in surrounding neighborhoods.

Garden Oaks and Oak Forest

The name **Garden Oaks** is appropriate for an area surrounded by lovely gardens, tall pine trees, magnolias, and other vegetation. Development of this neighborhood initially began in 1937 with several sections added up until the 1950s. For many decades its population was predominantly Catholic working-class families of mostly Polish and Italian backgrounds. The homes here are generally one-story bungalows and ranch-style homes with cedar siding and large well-landscaped lawns that were built for returning World War II vets. Other sections of the neighborhood have larger plantation, ranch, and traditional homes. Because of its location near downtown, Loop 610, and Highway 290, the secret is out on this neighborhood. It is increasingly becoming a much-sought-after place to live and the site of a great deal of revitalization and redevelopment. Garden Oaks has attracted many young couples looking for an affordable home near the city center that they can fix up or add onto. Nearby neighborhoods include **Shepherd Park**, which is bounded by West Tidwell Road on the north, North Shepherd Drive on the east, West 43rd on the south, and Ella Boulevard on the west.

Located south of the Candlelight neighborhood and west of Garden Oaks, **Oak Forest** is another neighborhood with similar natural surroundings. Development began in 1946 in a rural area surrounded by tall pine trees, and Oak Forest was annexed by the City of Houston in 1949. It was the largest suburban neighborhood at the time. Most of the original bungalows were built for returning GIs. Many commercial businesses are located on West 43rd Street and Ella Boulevard. Buyers who have been pushed out of the Garden Oaks housing market because of rising prices due to increasing demand often find Oak Forest a more affordable option. It has the same convenient location near Loop 610 and the city center as Garden Oaks.

Web Sites: www.houstontx.gov, www.candlelightoaks.org, www.gardenoaks.org, www. ofha.org

Area Code: 713

Zip Codes: 77018, 77091, 77092

Post Offices: Garden Oaks Station, 3816 N Shepherd Dr; Oak Forest Station, 2499 Judiway St; Irvington Station, 7825 Fulton St

Police Precincts: Houston Police Department: Northwest Patrol, 6000 Teague, 713-744-0900; Near North Storefront, 1335 W 43rd St, 713-956-3140

Emergency Hospitals: Memorial Hospital Northwest, 1635 North Loop W, 713-867-2000; LBJ Hospital, 5656 Kelley, 713-636-5000

Libraries: Houston Public Library, www.hpl.lib.tx.us: Oak Forest Branch, 1349 W 43rd St, 832-393-1960; Collier Regional Branch Library, 6200 Pinemont, 832-393-1740

Public Education: Houston Independent School District, www.houstonisd.org, 4400 W 18th, 713-556-6005

Community Publications: *Houston Chronicle*, www.chron.com, *Houston Press*, www. houstonpress.com

Community Resources: Antoine Health Center, 5668 W Little York, 281-447-2800; Northside Clinic, 8523 Arkansas, 713-696-5900; Northwest Health Center, 1100 W 34th, 713-861-3939; Candlelight Community Center Parks, 1520 Candlelight, 713-682-3587
Public Transportation: Harris County Metropolitan Authority, www.ridemetro.org, *Bus*: 8, 9, 23, 40, 44, 45, 50, 64, 79

CYPRESS AREA

Cypress

Cypress was settled in the 1840s by German immigrants who joined the few ranchers and farmers that were already in the area. It remained an agricultural community, primarily rice and dairy farming, until the 1950s when suburban development began to encroach on this community. By the 1980s, the surrounding area was a major Houston suburb that included many subdivisions and neighborhoods. Cypress had an estimated population of over 18,000 in 2000; however, the actual community of Cypress was never incorporated. One notable building, Tin Hall, built in the 1880s still stands. It is reportedly Texas's oldest reception hall and is still in operation.

Located 20 miles from downtown Houston along U.S. Highway 290, the neighborhoods in Cypress are surrounded by large trees. Unlike its cosmopolitan neighbor, Houston, the Cypress area is more country western in character. A rural area not too long ago, the continual construction of new homes here is taking over the countryside. Many people are attracted by the relatively affordable homes, safe family-oriented neighborhoods, and public schools.

Jersey Village

Within the Cypress area is the incorporated city of Jersey Village. It is located in far northwest Houston on the former F&M dairy ranch. The F&M dairy was not only a working farm, but also an agricultural entertainment enterprise that allowed the public to watch cows being milked, buy ice cream made from the milk, ride ponies, and enjoy musical entertainment. In 1954, the farm's owner, Clark W. Henry, sold it for residential development. The new community was named for the Jersey dairy cattle that once populated the area. It was incorporated in 1956 and remains an independently governed community.

Jersey Village is no longer the countryside. Suburban sprawl has filled in many of the surrounding areas between Jersey Village and Houston. Most of the commercial development is concentrated along U.S. Highway 290. Despite the suburbanization of this area, it still has a quiet, rural atmosphere. The area is very green, filled with many mature trees and other flora. This community primarily attracts families looking for a quiet neighborhood to raise their kids and quality schools. Jersey Village has a mix of single-family residential homes that start in the $100,000 range, as well as townhomes and patio homes. Though single-family residential homes predominate, lofts have recently been added to the housing options.

Klein

This unincorporated community halfway between Tomball and Spring has a strong German influence. Evidence of the area's German heritage is noticeable in local family surnames such as Wunderlich, Hassler, Doerre, and Schindewolf. It is named in honor of Adam Klein, who established the area's first post office station, which the U.S. Government named after him. He and his wife Friederika, natives of Stuttgart, Germany, along with several other German immigrant families, settled the area by Cypress Creek in the 1840s. They established an agricultural community, which they called Big Cypress. It included a Lutheran church, post office, and drugstore. Many of the settler's early descendants still reside here. Country singer Lyle Lovett, who grew up here, is a direct descendant of Adam Klein.

This former, quiet, agricultural community is now a growing Houston suburb. Yet, it still has a country atmosphere and rural landscape that attract many homebuyers. Tall pine trees, wooded lots, and green spaces are characteristic of neighborhoods here. Klein's high-quality public schools are a further draw.

Champion Forest

Living in Champion Forest is like having your own country estate. Grand homes sit on large wooded lots with towering leafy trees. These magnificent residences are unique in design and are a departure from the uniform brick style homes that characterize most new suburban neighborhoods. Though Champion Forest is known for its magnificent mansions and residences, there are also more modest patio homes. Located 23 miles from downtown Houston, this neighborhood has a secluded country atmosphere. Daily conveniences and amenities are only a quick drive outside of Champion Forest. Additionally, Highway U.S. 290, I-45, and the Sam Houston and Hardy Tollways are nearby and offer easy access to other parts of Houston. Nearby attractions include adjacent Raveneaux Country Club. Residents are likely to see many migratory birds as the area has been designated an official bird sanctuary. Initial development began in the 1970s on farmland. Nearby are the **Woodlands** community, Willowbrook Mall, Greenspoint Mall, several golf courses and country clubs, Sam Houston Race Park, and the Aerodrome Ice Skating Complex.

Those fortunate enough to live in Champion Forest are part of one of Houston's most prestigious neighborhoods. Splendid homes and beautiful natural surroundings are the primary appeal of this neighborhood.

Gleannloch Farms

Developed in the 1950s as a horse farm, Gleannloch Farms was renowned for decades as the premier place for Egyptian Arabian horses. Today it is better known as a master-planned community featuring homes from $160,000 to $1,000,000. This very suburban development contains walking and running paths, swimming pools, ponds, recreational lakes, a recreation center, and a 27-hole golf course. Of course, there is an equestrian center as well. Shopping is only minutes away along FM 1960 and nearby Willowbrook Mall.

Gleannloch Farms is divided into neighborhoods by price range. The most expensive homes, ranging from $400,000 to $1,000,000, are located in the Estates subdivision. Homes here are located on large lots in wooded areas. Residents of the estates have first rights to the stables and horse boarding at the equestrian center.

Copperfield
Copperfield's streets reflect careful consideration of the neighborhood's design and layout. Commercial areas are characterized by uniform-looking buildings and well-maintained streets that are actively enforced by deed restrictions and regulations. Most of the commercial businesses are located on Highway 6.

This master-planned community, developed by the Friendswood Development Corporation, is located just north of the Bear Creek area and approximately 22 miles from downtown Houston. Copperfield is divided into seven subdivisions that it calls "villages," each with their own recreational facilities. These "villages" have their own amenities, including parks, pools, tennis courts, greenbelts, neighborhood markets, and specialty stores. Residents can also use the community park's picnic facilities, playgrounds, baseball fields, an exercise/running track, a covered pavilion, and a community center. Perhaps one of the most impressive recreational facilities here is the Copperfield Racquet & Health Club, a private club established in 1980 that is open to Copperfield residents. Outside of the villages are numerous churches, shopping centers, shops, restaurants, and recreational amenities.

Like many of the master-planned communities in the northwest corridor, Copperfield is near a rural part of the county. It is the type of place that tends to attract families who prefer a quiet place away from the troubles of the city. Although it was initially developed in 1977, homebuilders continued to construct new, affordably priced homes, custom homes, and townhomes up until 2003. Homes are priced from the $80,000s to the $400,000s, with the newer developments located on the east side of Highway 6.

Fairfield
Fairfield is located far away from "civilization" in a semi-rural area along U.S. Highway 290. Though it is quite removed from the city, the Hardy Toll Road provides direct access to downtown Houston. In addition, residents can take U.S. Highway 290 into town, though it is a slower drive. It is a self-contained community with its own shops, schools, restaurants, entertainment, and other amenities. The community has an athletic club

that includes a full-sized basketball court, swimming pools, tennis courts, and 20-acre sports park, soccer field, and baseball diamond. In addition, there are plenty of parks, neighborhood pools, and greenbelts.

Developed by the Friendswood Development Company, Fairfield continues to grow as it enters its final phase of development. This large master-planned community has enough room for all types of homes, including those on large lots, wooded lots, private culs-de-sac, and lakeside property. Home prices vary greatly depending on size and location.

Web Sites: www.houstontx.gov, www.visitfairfield.com, www.jersey-village.info, www.gleannlochfarms.com, www.copperfield.org

Area Code: 713

Zip Codes: 77040, 77095, 77410, 77429, 77433, 77379, 77069

Post Offices: Cypress Station, 16635 Spring Cypress Rd, Cypress; Fairbanks Station, 7050 Brookhollow W Dr, Houston; Willow Place Station, 12955 Willow Place Dr W, Houston; Cornerstone Station, 14403 Walters Rd, Houston; Klein Station, 7717 Louetta Rd, Spring

Police Precincts: Houston Police Department: Willowbrook Storefront, 12932 Willow Chase, Houston, 281-807-9054, Jersey Village Police Department, 16401 Lakeview Dr, Houston, 713-466-5824; Harris County Sheriff's Office, Northwest Command Station, 23828 FM 249, Tomball, 281-290-2100

Emergency Hospitals: Cypress Fairbanks Medical Center, www.cyfairhospital.com, 10655 Steepletop Dr, Houston, 281-890-4285; Memorial Hospital Northwest, 1635 North Loop West, Houston, 713-867-2000

Libraries: Harris County Public Library, www.hcpl.net: Cy-Fair College Branch, 9191 Barker-Cypress Rd, Cypress, 281-290-3210; Northwest Branch, 11355 Regency Green Dr, Cypress, 281-890-2665; Barbara Bush @ Cypress Creek Branch, 6817 Cypresswood Dr, Spring, 281-376-4610

Adult Education: Cy-Fair College, www.cy-faircollege.com, 9191 Barker Cypress Rd, Cypress, 281-290-3200

Public Education: Cy-Fair Independent School District, www.cfisd.net, 10300 Jones Rd, Houston, 281-897-4000 (serves Cypress, Fairfield, and Copperfield); Klein Independent School District, www.kleinisd.net, 7200 Spring Cypress Rd, Klein, 832-484-7899 (serves Klein, Champion Forest, and Gleannloch Farms)

Community Publication: *Houston Chronicle*, www.chron.com

Community Resources: Bear Creek Park, 3535 War Memorial Dr, Houston, 281-496-2177; Cy-Fair Chamber of Commerce, www.cyfairchamber.org, 11050 FM 1960 W, Ste 100, Houston, 281-955-1100

Public Transportation: Harris County Metropolitan Authority, www.ridemetro.org, *Bus*: 86, 214 (Park and Ride)

TOMBALL

Located partially in far northwest Harris County and partially in Montgomery County, Tomball is a town with a decidedly country twist. Unlike its more cosmopolitan neighbor to the south, the town prides itself on its small town country character. Though it is only approximately 30 miles northwest of downtown Houston, it is easy for people to mistake Tomball for a city in another corner of the state when they hear the residents' noticeable twang. The area features tall pine trees, creeks, new developments, and historic buildings. Residents usually do not wander out of the area because everything they need, including commercial businesses, shopping, restaurants, and entertainment, is located either in Tomball or nearby surrounding communities.

The town was settled in the early 1800s by German and other European settlers and soon developed into a small farming community called Peck. In 1907, the town was renamed Tomball in honor of Senator Thomas Ball for his work in routing railroads through the town. The trains were instrumental in transporting agricultural produce from here and contributing to Tomball's prosperity. It remained an agricultural and ranching community for the next few decades. The discovery of oil in 1933 allowed the Humble Oil Company to negotiate a deal with the city where residents would receive free gas and water for the next 90 years in exchange for drilling rights within the city.

Individuals considering moving this far out might also want to consider the nearby town of **Magnolia**, located minutes away in Montgomery County.

Web Site: www.ci.tomball.tx.us

Area Codes: 281, 832

Zip Code: 77375

Post Office: Tomball Station, 122 N Holderrieth Blvd, 77375-9998

Police Precinct: Tomball Police Department, 400 Fannin St, 281-255-3908

Emergency Hospital: Tomball Regional Hospital, www.tomballhospital.org, 605 Holderrieth, 281-401-7500

Library: Harris County Public Library: www.hcpl.net, Tomball Branch, 30555 Tomball Pkwy, 832-559-4200

Adult Education: Tomball College, wwwtc.nhmccd.edu, 30555 Tomball Pkwy, 281-351-3300

Public Education: Tomball Independent School District, www.tomballisd.net, 221 W Main, Tomball, 281-357-3100

Community Publication: *Tomball Magnolia Tribune News*, www.tribunenews.com

Community Resource: Tomball Area Chamber of Commerce, www.tomballchamber. org, 14011 Park Dr, Ste 111

NORTH HOUSTON AND SURROUNDING COMMUNITIES

NORTHLINE AND GREENSPOINT

Northline

The Northline is a lower-middle to low-income neighborhood immediately north of downtown. It contains a mix of residential areas, light industries, and strip retail centers. The residences here are mostly small wood frame homes and low-rise apartment complexes. When development began in the 1960s and 1970s, Northline was an undeveloped area covered by open land and trees. Much has changed since then and it is now a densely populated area with a diverse population. As with any neighborhood near Loop 610 or downtown, there is talk of redeveloping and revitalizing this area.

Greenspoint

Greenspoint's tall glass office buildings and towers stand out conspicuously among the surrounding flat landscape and low-lying structures. It looks more like the downtown central business district, but is actually one of several business districts in the metropolitan area. In fact, this is north Houston's major commercial center. The area contains a concentration of retailers, hotels, office space, and other businesses, as well as light industry. Many of the businesses here are related to or cater to those generated by the nearby international airport. Named for its location along Greens Bayou, Greenspoint is 14 miles from downtown Houston and near the airport and communities north of Houston. It is ideally situated in the center of major commercial activity. The swift increase in job and population growth in the 1970s led to rapid development of new communities in north Houston. I-45, U.S. 59, and the construction of the Hardy Tollway/Sam Houston Parkway provide easy access into and out of the area and have contributed to its commercial and residential growth.

Before the 1960s, the area that is now Greenspoint was a mere travel stop located along a major travel route. It originally consisted of undeveloped land with some agricultural activity and a few businesses off the major freeways that serviced people passing through the area. The opening of the Bush Intercontinental Airport during the 1960s created a new local economy that today provides many of the area's jobs. New residential development alongside existing ones such as Champions and Imperial Valley offers many additional subdivisions and apartment complexes. Housing here is very affordable when compared to the inner loop and even the northwestern suburbs. It has a reputation as a moderate to low-income area and some parts are considered undesirable. Nevertheless, the Greenspoint area has the distinction of being home to the Shell Houston Open golf tournament, which draws big-name stars like Vijay Singh and Tiger Woods. In addition, private investors have made recent efforts to revive run-down sections of Greenspoint and convert them into attractive, new residential developments. One of these projects is City View, a large upscale apartment community with two parks.

Web Sites: www.greenspoint.org, www.houstontx.gov
Area Code: 713
Zip Codes: 77038, 77060, 77066, 77067
Post Offices: Greens North Station, 1530 Greensmark Dr; Cornerstone Station, 14403 Walters Rd
Police Precinct: Houston Police Department: Greenspoint Storefront, 105 Greenspoint Mall, 281-875-6155

Emergency Hospital: York Plaza Hospital and Medical Center, 2807 Little York Rd, 713-697-7777

Adult Education: North Harris Community College, Parkway Center campus, www. nhmccd.edu, 2700 W.W. Thorne Dr, 281-618-5400

Public Education: Aldine Independent School District, www.aldine.k12.tx.us, 14910 Aldine Westfield Rd; Spring Independent School District, www.springisd.org, 16717 Ella Blvd, 281-586-1100

Community Publication: *Houston Chronicle*, www.chron.com

Community Resources: City Hall, 900 Bagby, 713-837-0311; North Greenspoint Chamber of Commerce, www.nhgcc.org, 15600 JFK Blvd, Ste 150, 281-442-8701

Public Transportation: Metropolitan Transit Authority of Harris County, www.ridemetro. org, *Bus*: 56, 86, 102

ALDINE AND SPRING

Aldine

Aldine is one of those small towns that is both beneficiary and victim of proximity to a major city's suburban sprawl. Once an independent community, a small portion is now part of the City of Houston, while the rest remains an unincorporated area that is within Houston's extraterritorial jurisdiction. In other words, Houston has the right to annex the rest of Aldine. Originally established along the International–Great Northern Railroad as a stop along the train, its population peaked in 1925 at 100. It was not until the 1970s, when north Houston started developing, that this community grew. Today its population is over 10,000.

Aldine is primarily a lower-middle-income community. Though it is racially diverse, the population is mostly Hispanic. Several new residential developments in the area around it offer affordable housing under $200,000. There are also many apartment complexes here. Its location near the Sam Houston Tollway (Beltway) and I-45 north offers residents easy access to downtown Houston and employment centers in north Houston.

Spring

Spring is a small town with a history that goes back to the 1840s, when German immigrants began farming here. The town grew considerably after the Houston and Great Northern Railroad began running through here in 1871. The next great growth was the construction of new suburban communities in the 1970s. Spring is one of the fastest growing communities in the Houston area, and residential neighborhoods are continually being constructed.

Spring has a unique historical district known as **Old Town Spring**. Many of the town's oldest buildings are located here and serve as shops. The unique and independently owned retail businesses here include several antique shops, restaurants, and museums. It is now a tourist attraction where city dwellers and suburbanites come to shop on the weekends.

The town is surrounded by densely wooded forest, which is part of its allure. Spring is a scenic area with neighborhoods surrounded by natural beauty. Homes here vary in price, size, and design. There are also townhomes and apartments here. The variety of housing options, natural beauty, and good public schools contribute to the area's popularity and growth. Residents here work in downtown Houston, The Woodlands, Intercontinental Airport, and the northwest corridor. Residents who work in downtown Houston can get there by getting on I-45. A much quicker route is the Sam Houston Tollway, but it costs $1 per toll booth each way. The Woodlands shopping districts and Mitchell concert pavilion are only minutes away.

Web Sites: www.houstontx.gov, www.oldtownspringtx.com

Area Codes: 713, 281

Zip Codes: 77315, 77039, 77379, 77389, 77391, 77373, 77380, 77381, 77382, 77386, 77388, 77389

Post Offices: North Houston Station, 4600 Aldine Bender Rd, Rm 224, North Houston; Spring Station, 1411 Wunsche Loop, Spring; Panther Creek Station, 10800 Gosling Rd, Spring; The Woodlands Station, 9450 Pinecroft Dr, Spring

Police Precincts: Houston Police Department: North Patrol, 9455 W Montgomery, Houston, 281-405-5300; Aldine Community Storefront, 10966 North Fwy, Houston, 281-272-4784; Harris County Sheriff's Office, Substation I–Northwest, 6831 Cypresswood Dr, Spring, 281-376-2997; Harris County Constable Pct 4: 6831 Cypresswood Dr, Spring, 281-376-3472, http://www.co.harris.tx.us/pct4; Harris County Sheriff's Office: Cypresswood Substation, 6831 Cypresswood Dr, Spring, 281-376-2997; 249 Storefront, 7614 Fallbroook Dr, Houston, 281-537-9492, http://www.hcso.hctx.net/index.asp

Emergency Hospital: Memorial Hermann The Woodlands Hospital, www.memorialhermann.org, 9250 Pinecroft, The Woodlands, 281-364-2300

Adult Education: Houston Community College, North Harris College, www.nhmccd.edu, 2700 W.W. Thorne Dr, Houston, 281-618-5400

Public Education: Aldine Independent School District, www.aldine.k12.tx.us, 14910 Aldine Westfield Rd, Houston; Klein Independent School District, www.kleinisd.net, 7200 Spring-Cypress Rd, Klein, 832-249-4000; Spring Independent School District, www.springisd.org, 16717 Ella Blvd, Houston, 281-586-1100

Community Publication: *Houston Chronicle*, www.chron.com

Community Resources: City Hall, 900 Bagby, Houston, 713-837-0311; Spring City Hall, Montgomery County, www.co.montgomery.tx.us

Public Transportation: Metropolitan Transit Authority of Harris County, www.ridemetro.org: *Bus*: 86, 204 Aldine: 83, 205, 206, 257

MONTGOMERY COUNTY

Woodlands

The name of this master-planned community is a perfect description. Set among heavily wooded piney forests, it feels like living on a country lane that is straight out of a storybook. Conceived as a residential development isolated far from the city, the Woodlands has proven a popular community for those seeking a serene place to retreat after work. Many communities in the north/northwest area have a similar concept of incorporating the surrounding natural environment with the community. However, none has come as close as the Woodlands in achieving such a high level of aesthetic beauty and environmental design.

When it was first developed in 1974, the Woodlands was considered extremely far and quite removed from Houston. In fact, it is approximately a one-hour drive from here to downtown Houston, making it the ideal place for people who work in the city and enjoy its conveniences, but prefer a less urban environment. As recently as a few years ago, residents had to drive to Spring or other communities half an hour away for dining, entertainment, shopping, and groceries. The only exception was the Cynthia Mitchell Woodlands Pavilion, an outdoor concert venue that hosts performances by big-name acts. Now, residents do not even have to leave the Woodlands to enjoy themselves. The recently constructed pedestrian-oriented Woodlands Town Center offers dining and shopping within its brick-paved streets. Across the street, water taxis ferry people from the town center to the Mitchell concert pavilion along the artificially constructed Woodlands Waterway. In some instances, it is not even necessary to commute to Houston for work. With the development of north and northwest Harris County, many companies and businesses have moved into the Woodlands area, including Anadarko Petroleum Company, Hewitt and Associates, Hughes Christensen, Maersk Sealand, and Chevron Phillips Chemical Company. In addition, Research Forest houses many biomedical and research companies. The Woodlands has achieved its dream of becoming a self-sustaining community within a forest and is fast becoming a major city.

With the current development of north/northwest Harris County, civilization seems to be encroaching on the Woodlands. Though the community is still pretty much surrounded by undeveloped woods, the woods along U.S. 59 between the Woodlands and the nearest community are being taken up for commercial development at an increasingly rapid rate.

Homes in this predominantly wealthy community come in a wide price range and most are on wooded lots. Some of the metropolitan area's most magnificent residences are located here. The Woodlands contains six championship golf courses in its country club, miles of hiking and biking trails, and neighborhood parks.

Shenandoah

Just north of the Woodlands, this upscale community is located approximately 35 miles north of Houston along I-45 in the piney forest. It is in a semi-rural community that includes new subdivisions and country homes on spacious lots or several acres. Development originally began in the 1960s as a suburban development, leading to incorporation as a city in 1974. The growth of the Woodlands and the northern Harris

County/Montgomery County area has resulted in increasing commercial development and a growing population here.

Web Sites: www.houstontx.gov, www.thewoodlands.com, www.ci.shenandoah.tx.us
Area Codes: 281, 936
Zip Codes: 77381, 77380
Post Office: The Woodlands Station, 9450 Pinecroft Dr, Spring
Police Precinct: Montgomery County Sheriff's Office, www.mocosheriff.com, South Montgomery County Office, 281-297-6500
Emergency Hospital: Memorial Hermann The Woodlands Hospital, www.memorialhermann.org, 9250 Pinecroft, The Woodlands, 281-364-2300
Adult Education: The University Center, www.tuc.edu, 3232 College Park Dr, The Woodlands, 936-273-7500
Public Education: Conroe Independent School District, www.conroeisd.net, 3205 W Davis, Conroe, 936-709-7751
Community Publication: Houston Chronicle, www.chron.com; www.woodlandsonline.com
Community Resources: Montgomery County, 301 N Thompson, Ste 210, Conroe, 936-756-0571; South Montgomery County Woodlands Chamber of Commerce, www.smcwcc.org, 1400 Woodloch Forest Dr, Ste 300, The Woodlands, 281-367-5777
Public Transportation: Brazos Transit District: The Woodlands Express Park and Ride, Sawdust Road facility, 701 West Ridge, Spring, 281-363-0882; Research Forest facility, 3900 Marisico Pl, The Woodlands, 936-273-6100

NORTHEAST HOUSTON

Humble

Pronounced "umble," with a silent "h," this town was established in the 1840s as an agricultural community and lumber town. The discovery of an oilfield in 1904 transformed it into a boomtown overnight. The Humble Oil Company moved its headquarters to Houston in 1912 and is known today as Exxon. Humble's population began to decline as quickly as it had expanded because of decreasing production from the field. Subsequent boom and bust cycles related to the oil industry would continue until after World War II. The town never grew to over 3000 and remained a small, quiet community until the opening of the George Bush Intercontinental Airport. The Humble area currently encompasses the area surrounding the airport, which is one of the major employers here. Furthermore, the completion of U.S. 59 from Humble to Houston attracted new development and more residents.

For decades, Humble had an image as a blue-collar town centered around the oil industry, transportation, and agriculture. Today, it is a thriving community outside of Houston with over 12,000 residents. The town has a down-to-earth, country feel. Many of the residents work in downtown Houston 20 miles away or in industries related to the airport. Old Humble, the historic section of town, contains many antique shops and artists' studios.

Kingwood

This master-planned community was developed in the 1970s as a place where residents could live among the heavily wooded areas of north Houston. The Friendswood Development Company, which built Kingwood, attempted to preserve the tall pines, oaks, and other species of trees that cover the 14,000 acres on the shores of Lake Houston. Neighborhoods were built into or around the wooded area, where local wildlife abounds. In hindsight, this was a wise move because the natural beauty and quiet serenity of the area are two of the reasons people are attracted to Kingwood. Retailers moved here over the decades, creating a self-contained community where everything residents needed was inside Kingwood. In addition, miles of greenbelts and hiking/biking trails, parks, swimming pools, private boat launch, and equestrian center provide residents with plenty of outdoor recreational activities.

The community is divided into villages—26 at last count—each of which has its own distinct architecture. Homes here range from the low $100,000s to million-dollar residences. They include patio homes, townhomes, golf course communities, and lakeside estates. Kingwood was named after King Ranch, which once owned the land here. In 1995, Houston annexed Kingwood, despite fierce opposition from some residents.

Though 22 miles from the city, residents can easily get to downtown Houston via U.S. 59—the only major freeway that runs through here. The county's public transportation operates a park and ride where residents park their cars at the bus depot for an easy commute to major employment centers in downtown Houston, Greenway Plaza, and Greenspoint. In addition, the international airport is nearby.

Atascocita

Atascocita is named after the Atascosito Road, which was the precursor to the present day FM 1960. Atascocita is Spanish for obstruction and is thought to have once been the site of a garrison used by the Spanish to defend themselves from the French.

This wealthy community located on FM 1960 is approximately six miles east of Humble and 18 miles from downtown Houston. It has continued to grow since development began in the 1970s. This unincorporated community is located in a rural part of the county by Lake Houston. It is known as the site of Tour 18, a golf course that recreates some of the most celebrated golf holes in the U.S. Within this same community containing swanky neighborhoods and country clubs is a state jail and residential probation program.

Web Sites: www.houstontx.gov, www.cityofhumble.net, Kingwoodonline.com
Area Code: 281
Zip Codes: 77325, 77346, 77338, 77339, 77345, 77346, 77396
Post Offices: Kingwood Station, 4025 Feather Lakes Way, Kingwood; Humble Station, 1202 1st St E, Humble; Houston Airport Mail Facility, 19175 Lee Rd, Ste 100, Humble

Police Precincts: Houston Police Department: Kingwood Patrol and Storefront, 3915 Rustic Woods, Kingwood, 281-913-4500; Humble Police Department, www. humblepolice.com, 310 Bender, Humble, 281-446-7127

Emergency Hospitals: Kingwood Medical Center, www.kingwoodmedical.com, 22999 U.S. 59, Kingwood, 281-348-8000; Northeast Medical Center, www.nemch.org, 18951 Memorial North, Humble, 281-540-7700

Adult Education: Kingwood College, www.kingwoodcollege.com, 20000 Kingwood, Kingwood, 800-883-7939

Public Education: Humble Independent School District, www.humble.k12.tx.us, 20200 Eastway Village Dr, Humble, 281-641-1000; New Caney Independent School District, www.newcaneyisd.org, 21580 Loop 494, New Caney, 281-577-8600 (serves small parts of Kingwood)

Community Publications: *Kingwood Observer*, www.kingwoodobserver.com; *Houston Chronicle*, www.chron.com

Community Resources: City Hall, 900 Bagby, Houston, 713-837-0311; Humble Area Chamber of Commerce, www.humbleareachamber.org, 110 W Main St, Humble, 281-446-2128; Kingwood Chamber of Commerce, www.kwcommerce.org, 2825 W Town Center Circle, Kingwood, 281-360-4321

Public Transportation: Metropolitan Transit Authority of Harris County, www.ridemetro. org: Kingwood Park and Ride, 3210 Lake Houston Pkwy, *Bus*: 205; Eastex Park and Ride, 14400 Old Humble Rd, east of Eastex, *Bus*: 83, 205, 206, 257

EAST OF HOUSTON

Communities here may be prone to flooding in the event of a hurricane because this is a lower-lying area than other parts of Houston. As a result, the towns and cities here are part of the hurricane evacuation zone. The Greater Houston Transportation and Emergency Center's web site, www.houstontranstar.org/weather/hurricane_routes.aspx, provides an evacuation map with evacuation routes. Further information on hurricane preparedness can be found at the appropriate municipality's web site. In addition, the Texas Governor's Office of Emergency Management has established a 211 hotline where those with special healthcare needs and individuals with no transportation can register *in advance* for transportation.

PASADENA, DEER PARK, AND BAYTOWN

Pasadena

Pasadena is the heart of the metropolitan area's petrochemical refining and shipping industries. Its location east of Houston near the Ship Channel and Port of Houston provides companies here with the logistics and transportation necessary to import materials and export products worldwide. This truly is a gritty, blue collar town. Think *Urban Cowboy* with John Travolta, which was actually partly filmed in Pasadena at the famous Gilley's, which burned down in 1989. This is the type of place where you will find the oil field workers, construction workers, longshoremen, and other individuals employed in heavy industry. Most people's first introduction to Pasadena is the unpleasant smell coming from the oil refineries and factories. The residents do not seem to mind, though, but they are probably used to it. Pasadena was not always an industrial town. Before the 1930s the lush, fertile land irrigated by the bayous and Gulf waters produced strawberries, cucumbers, flowers, and numerous other fruits. The town still holds a strawberry festival every year in celebration of its past as a major strawberry producing center.

Pasadena has an ethnically diverse population, approximately half of which is Hispanic. Its residents are primarily in the middle-lower-income bracket. There are a variety of housing options here that range in price from below $100,000 to over a million. They include apartments, townhomes, modest one-story homes, two-story residences in new residential developments, and million dollar homes. Housing in Pasadena has traditionally been apartments and small one-story homes, reflective of the lower to middle income salary of its residents. Only in recent years has there been development of new suburban neighborhoods with large brick homes and million-dollar mansions.

Deer Park

Next door to Pasadena and the Houston ship channel, Deer Park is home to many major refineries and light industries. It was established in 1893 on the site of a former park dedicated to deer. This is predominantly a single-family residential community that offers homes in a range of styles and sizes from small one-story bungalows to two-story brick homes. Home prices here are relatively affordable with most of them below $200,000. Like the rest of the metropolitan area, several new and affordable residential developments have been constructed here in recent years. Some larger and more extravagant homes or large residential properties are also available in Deer Park.

Baytown

Baytown is one of the cities in the Houston–Sugar Land–Baytown metropolitan area, a U.S. Census–designated metropolitan area. This highly industrialized city is a major center of oil refining, rubber, chemical, and carbon black plants. The Humble Oil and Refining Company (now Exxon Corporation) was the first to establish an oil refinery here in and 1917 and was the largest at the time. The town was built around the Humble refinery. The company built employee housing, paved the roads, and established utility service and schools. Baytown was finally incorporated in 1947 when it consolidated with two other neighboring towns, Pelly and Goose Creek.

It is located thirty miles east of downtown Houston in southeastern Harris and western Chambers County. As its name indicates, this town is located on Galveston Bay. The Lynchberg Ferry crosses the San Jacinto River and provides free transportation around Baytown. Major attractions include boating spots and the Houston Raceway Park, a stadium that hosts drag racing events. The city has a variety of housing options that include apartments, single-family residential homes, several new subdivisions with affordable homes, mansions, and large custom-built homes. Some of the region's most spectacular homes are located in Baytown.

Web Sites: www.ci.deer-park.tx.us, www.baytown.org, ci.pasadena.tx.us

Area Codes: 281, 409

Zip Codes: 77502, 77503, 77504, 77505, 77506, 77507, 77520, 77521, 77536, 77590, 77591

Post Offices: Pasadena Station, 1199 Pasadena Blvd, Pasadena; John Foster Station, 1520 Richey St, Pasadena; Bob Harris Station, 102 N Munger St, Pasadena; Delbert Atkinson Station, 6100 Spencer Hwy, Pasadena; Baytown Station, 601 W Baker Rd, Baytown; Station A Baytown, 3508 Market St, Baytown; Deer Park Station, 200 E San Augustine St, Deer Park

Police Departments: Baytown Police Department: Main Station, 3200 N Main, Baytown, 281-422-8371; Community Services Bureau, 220 W Defee, Baytown; McLemore Substation, 3530 Market St, Baytown; Pasadena Police Department, 1114 Jeff Ginn Memorial Dr, Pasadena, 713-477-1221; Deer Park Police Department, 1410 Center St, Deer Park, 281-478-2000

Emergency Hospitals: San Jacinto Methodist Center, www.methodisthealth.com/sanjacinto, 4401 Garth Rd, Baytown, 281-420-8600; Bayshore Medical Center, www.bayshoremedical.com, 4000 Spencer Hwy, Pasadena, 713-359-2000; Harris County Hospital District, 925 Shaw Ave, Pasadena, 713-740-8180

Libraries: Pasadena Public Library, 1201 Jeff Ginn Memorial Dr, Pasadena, 77506, 713-477-0276; Harris County Public Library, South Houston Branch, www.hcpl.net, 607 Ave A, South Houston, 713-941-2385; Sterling Municipal Library (Baytown), www.sml.lib.tx.us, Mary Elizabeth Wilbanks Ave, Baytown, 281-427-7331; Deer Park Public Library, 3009 Center St, Deer Park, 281-478-7208

Adult Education: San Jacinto College, www.sjcd.cc.tx.us: District Campus, 4624 Fairmont Pkwy, Pasadena, 281-998-6150; Central Campus, 8060 Spencer Hwy, Pasadena, 281-476-1501; Texas Chiropractic College, www.txchiro.edu, 5912 Spencer Hwy, Pasadena, 281-487-1170; Lee College (Baytown), www.lee.edu, main campus at Lee Dr and Gulf St, Baytown, 281-427-5611

Public Education: Pasadena Independent School District, www.pasadenaisd.org, 1515 Cherrybrook, Pasadena, 713-740-0000; Deer Park Independent School District, www.dpisd.org, 203 Ivy, Deer Park (also serves eastern portions of Pasadena); La Porte Independent School District, www.laporte.isd.esc4.net, 1002 San Jacinto St, La Porte (serves parts of southern Pasadena); Clear Creek Independent School District, www.ccisd.net, 2425 E Main St, League City, 281-284-0000 (serves parts of southern Pasadena); Goose Creek Independent Consolidated School District, www.gccisd.net, 4544 Interstate 10 E, Baytown, 281-420-4800 (serves Baytown)

Community Publications: *Pasadena Citizen*, www.thepasadenacitizen.com; *Baytown Sun*, www.baytownsun.com; *Deer Park Progress*, www.deerparkprogress.com

Community Resources: Pasadena Chamber of Commerce, www.pasadenachamber.org, 4334 Fairmont Pkwy, Pasadena, 281-487-7871; Baytown Chamber of Commerce, www.baytownchamber.com, Amegy Bank Bldg, 1300 Rollingbrook, Ste 400, Baytown, 281-422-8359; Deer Park Chamber of Commerce, www.deerpark.org, 110 Center St, Deer Park, 281-479-1559

Public Transportation: Lynchburg Ferry, 1001 S Lynchburg Rd, Baytown, 281-424-3521

NORTH HOUSTON SHIP CHANNEL AREA

The North Houston Ship Channel Area encompasses Channelview, North Shore, Galena Park, Jacinto City, and unincorporated parts of Sheldon. This is a heavily industrial area mixed with some suburban communities. **Channelview**—an oil refinery town—is home to many of the refinery and factory workers that work at the local plants. Housing options here include mobile home communities, newly constructed and older single family residential homes in a range of styles and sizes (two-story, new brick homes in typical suburban neighborhoods, large acreage in the country, and older small one-story homes with wood siding), and apartments.

North Shore is the newest community in the North Channel area. Most of the new home construction in the North Channel area is concentrated here. Smaller neighborhoods include Cloverleaf, Hidden Forest, Home Owned Estates, New Forest, Pine Trails, River Grove, Riviera East, and Woodforest. The references to woods and forests are a tribute to this quiet community's location among the tall pine trees of east Harris County.

Galena Park began as a farming and ranching community called Clinton. After the opening of the Port of Houston, the town's character slowly evolved into today's heavily industrial city. At the turn of the 20th century its location along the Houston Ship Channel attracted oil companies which needed the warm shallow waters of the Gulf to transport their oil to other destinations. The town's name was later changed to Galena, after the oil company that built the first refinery here. Today, Galena Park is considered a part of east Houston. Many of the homes here are small, plain, one-story homes with wood siding and range from $70,000 to $100,000. Other residents live in apartments spread throughout the area.

Jacinto City is named for its location near the San Jacinto battleground. It started in 1941 as a small subdivision built by Houston developer Frank Sharp. The initial residents were shipyard workers and employees from the local steel and war plants. Today, most of the residents work at local petrochemical refineries. Jacinto City is a solidly Hispanic working to lower class community. The housing here is similar to nearby Galena Park: small one-story homes and apartments.

Web Sites: www.ci.jacinto-city.tx.us, www.galenaparktexas.com, www.houstontx.gov
Area Codes: 713, 281, 832
Zip Codes: 77530, 77547, 77029
Post Offices: Channelview Station, 531 Sheldon Rd, Channelview; Galena Park Station, 1805 Clinton Dr, Galena Park
Police Departments: Houston Police Department: East Freeway Storefront, 12001 E

Fwy, Houston, 713-637-2120; Galena Park Police Department, 2207 Clinton Dr, Galena Park, 713-675-3471; Jacinto City Police Department, 10429 Market St, Jacinto City, 713-672-2455

Emergency Hospitals: Triumph Hospital East Houston, www.triumph-healthcare.com, 15101 E Fwy, Channelview, 832-200-5500; East Houston Regional Medical Center, www.easthoustonrmc.com, 13111 E Fwy, Houston, 713-393-2000

Libraries: Harris County Public Library, www.hcpl.net: Jacinto City Branch, 921 Akron St, 713-673-3237; Galena Park Branch, 1500 Keene St, Galena Park, 713-450-0982; North Channel Branch, 15741 Wallisville Rd, Houston, 281-457-1631

Adult Education: San Jacinto College, www.sjcd.cc.tx.us: Galena Park High School Extension Center, 1000 Keene St, Galena Park, 281-459-7103; Galena Park Community Resource/Training Center, 1721 16th St, Galena Park, 713-672-4606

Public Education: Channelview Independent School District, www.channelview.isd. esc4.net, 1403 Sheldon Rd, Channelview, 281-452-8002; Galena Park Independent School District, www.galenaparkisd.com, 14705 Woodforest Blvd, Houston, 832-386-1000 (Galena Park neighborhoods south of Market St, North Shore, and Jacinto City); Houston Independent School District, www.houstonisd.org, 4400 W 18th St, Houston, 713-556-6005 (Galena Park neighborhoods north of Market St)

Community Publications: *North Channel Sentinel* (Channelview), www. northchannelsentinel.com; *Houston Chronicle*, www.chron.com

Community Resource: North Channel Chamber of Commerce, www.northchannelarea. com, I-10 East, Ste 100, Houston, 713-450-3600

Public Transportation: Harris County Metropolitan Transit Authority, www.ridemetro. org: Maxey Park and Ride, *Bus:* 137, 236

LA PORTE/BAYSHORE

As far back as the 1920s and 1930s, La Porte was well-known as a seaside resort and recreational community. Popular big bands of the day such as the Benny Goodman Orchestra performed for visitors and summer residents at the Sylvan Beach Amusement Park in the nearby city of Shoreacres. After World War II, the growing petrochemical industry along the ship channel attracted new residents to the city. Though many of its residents still consider La Porte a small vacation village, it is also a residential community for employees of nearby refineries and industries along the ship channel. Nonetheless, many still visit for a nice weekend getaway. The town's main street features many unique shops and antique stores. More famously, it is home to the San Jacinto Monument, which commemorates Texas's independence, and the Battleship Texas, which served in World War I and II. Many Houstonians have boats or vacation homes in the La Porte/Bayshore area, including the nearby towns of Morgan's Point and Shoreacres. La Porte/Bayshore has apartments, townhomes, condominiums, and single-family residential homes that range from the relatively affordable to the very expensive. One-story homes located in neighborhoods or new planned communities occupy the more affordable end of the market. At the opposite end are million dollar waterfront properties on large parcels of land. Of course, La Porte/Bayshore also offers everything else in between.

The **City of Morgan's Point**, a charming resort city, is historically significant as the origin of the Yellow Rose of Texas which, legend has it, refers to a mulatto slave girl who warned the town of the approaching Mexican Army during the battle for Texas's independence. The founder, Colonel James Morgan, owner of the Morgan Plantation, did own a slave girl named Emily, who is reputed to be the basis for the Yellow Rose of Texas. This small town contains expensive waterfront property, large two-story brick homes, and older one-story homes with wood siding.

The **City of Shoreacres** is home to the Houston Yacht Club and a bird sanctuary. This small bayside town is partly in Chambers and partly in Harris County. Some of the neighborhoods here tend to be heavily covered by trees, while others have no curbs or sidewalks. In addition to homes set in a typical neighborhood, there are also homes with waterfront views and on large acres surrounded by trees.

Web Sites: www.ci.la-porte.tx.us, www.cityofshoreacres.us, www.morganspoint-tx.com
Area Codes: 281, 409
Zip Code: 77571
Post Office: LaPorte Station, 801 W Fairmont Pkwy, La Porte
Police Departments: La Porte Police Department, 915 S 8th St, La Porte, 281-471-3811; Morgan's Point Police Department, 1415 E Main St, La Porte, 281-471-2171; Shoreacres Police Department, 601 Shore Acres Blvd, La Porte, 281-471-3340
Library: Harris County Public Library, www.hcpl.net: La Porte Branch, 600 S Broadway, La Porte, 281-471-4022
Emergency Hospitals: Mainland Medical Center, www.mainlandmedical.com, 6801 Emmet F. Lowry Expy, Texas City, 409-938-5000; University of Texas Medical Branch Galveston, www.utmb.edu, 301 University Blvd, Galveston, 409-772-2618; San Jacinto Methodist Center, www.methodisthealth.com/sanjacinto, 4401 Garth Rd, Baytown, 281-420-8600; Bayshore Medical Center, www.bayshoremedical.com, 4000 Spencer Hwy, Pasadena, 713-359-2000
Public Education: La Porte Independent School District, www.laporte.isd.esc4.net, 1002 San Jacinto St, La Porte, 281-604-7000
Community Publication: Galveston County Daily News, www.galvestondailynews.com
Community Resources: Shoreacres City Hall, 601 Shoreacres Blvd, Shoreacres, 281-471-2244; Morgan's Point City Hall, 1415 E Main St, Morgan's Point; La Porte–Bayshore Chamber of Commerce, www.laportechamber.org, 712 W Fairmont Pkwy, La Porte, 281-471-1123
Public Transportation: none

BAY AREA

The Bay Area is the area between Houston and Galveston and covers parts of Harris County, Chambers County, Brazoria County, and Galveston County. Originally centered around the fishing and agricultural industries, its economy has diversified since the 1930s to include the petrochemical, tourism, and aerospace industries. Oil was discovered in many of the communities here in the 1930s, which contributed to the temporary increase in the populations of many Bay Area communities. The population increased permanently and dramatically after 1961, when it was announced that NASA, which originally had offices in Houston, would be building its Mission Control (Johnson Space Center) here. Today, NASA and aerospace-related companies are the major employers here. It is probably more accurate to say that Houston is the Bayou City and the Bay Area is Space City. In addition, the region's temperate climate draws visitors here year round. The water in this part of the Gulf of Mexico is mostly brown, which is its natural color. Heavy sediment and shallow waters produce a muddy colored surface that resembles the waters of the Mississippi River. Though some people enjoy swimming in the warm Gulf waters, boating and fishing are by far the most popular activities here. Neighborhoods and communities in Bay Area Houston include Clear Lake, Clear Lake Shores, El Lago, League City, Kemah, Nassau Bay, Seabrook, South Shore Harbour, Taylor Lake Village, Victory Lakes, and Webster.

Because of its proximity to the Gulf of Mexico, the communities in this area are vulnerable to hurricanes and strong tropical storms. Though a hurricane has not struck this region in over 20 years, residents choosing to live in the Bay area should be prepared for mandatory and voluntary evacuations. The Greater Houston Transportation and Emergency Center's web site, www.houstontranstar.org/weather/hurricane_routes. aspx, provides an evacuation map with evacuation routes. Evacuation orders are given by each city's mayor and by the county judge if in an unincorporated area. Further information on hurricane preparedness can be found at the appropriate municipality's web site. In addition, the Texas Governor's Office of Emergency Management has established a 211 hotline where those with special healthcare needs and individuals with no transportation can register *in advance* for transportation.

CLEAR LAKE

Even though Clear Lake is part of Houston, it certainly does not feel like it. Whereas the rest of Houston is an active urban environment with lush green vegetation and large concrete freeways snaking through it, Clear Lake is a laid-back seaside town. Instead of freeways or greenery, marinas with boats and yachts dot the landscape. You get the feeling that Clear Lake is a separate town. In fact, it once was. Unlike Houston, Clear Lake did not experience the same downturn in the housing market in the 1980s because it was largely unaffected by the oil bust. Its economic base is different and largely independent from Houston's. Clear Lake relies on the tourism and aerospace industries. NASA originally had offices in Houston, but when it decided to build a mission control center in 1961, it chose this area. As a result, owners of the nearby property decided to develop it for residential use. It is interesting to note that though NASA is often associated with Houston, it actually is located in Clear Lake City.

Apparently Houston took notice of this also and decided that NASA, and thus Clear Lake, should be within Houston. Despite much protest from the residents, Clear Lake was annexed in 1977.

Clear Lake is named after the large lake next to it. The area is low lying and there is a noticeable difference in the elevation between here and downtown Houston. This is generally an upper-middle-income area. Homes here include vacation homes, apartments, mansions, and single-family residential homes. The population here is diverse and highly educated. Many of them are engineers, most of whom work in the aerospace industry.

The Clear Lake area communities are:

- Spanish for "the lake," **El Lago** is located on Taylor Lake, Clear Lake, and NASA Parkway (also called NASA Road 1 and Farm Road 528). Pirate Jean Lafitte and his gang once hid out in what is now El Lago. The area is home to many aerospace employees and is very proud of the numerous astronauts who reside or previously resided here. Residents mostly live in apartments and single-family residential homes. There are also several condo complexes in El Lago, though some of them are owned as weekend vacation getaways. There is a diverse selection of single-family homes, including million-dollar homes and large two-story brick homes.

- **Nassau Bay** homes are more affordable than in Clear Lake and include a variety of options. Prospective residents can choose from lakeside estates, apartments, townhomes, single-family residential homes, and condominiums. It attracts many individuals employed in the aerospace and petrochemical industries. Nassau Bay is located on Nassau Lake across from FM 528.

- **Taylor Lake Village** is located on Taylor Lake, west of Seabrook. It is strictly a residential community and no commercial businesses are allowed to establish here. This semi-exclusive community has some of the area's priciest homes that average in the $200,000 to $600,000 range. Some of the more expensive homes have waterfront views, boat houses, large yards, acreage, and other luxurious amenities.

- **Seabrook** is right on Galveston Bay and Clear Lake, next to the town of Kemah. It is a prime place to dock your boat or have a vacation home. Most of Seabrook is along the waterfront. The town is known for its fresh seafood markets, coastal bird sanctuary, antique stores, and shops featuring local artists. It has one of the largest populations in the Bay Area. Seabrook offers housing options for a range of income levels. There are apartments, townhomes, condominiums, and single-family residential homes. Many of the residences here have beautiful views of the waterfront. Homes here range from middle-class suburban, two-story brick homes to older, smaller one-story homes. On the extreme end are million-dollar homes and mansions.

- **Webster** is on State Hwy 3 and the Galveston, Houston, and Henderson railroad twenty miles south of Houston and three miles west of the Lyndon B. Johnson Space Center. It was settled in 1879 as Gardentown by James Webster, leader of a group of English settlers. In 1904, 70 Japanese farmers settled here to grow rice and oranges. In addition to single-family residences, there are also several established low-rise condominium complexes and townhomes here. Homes range from affordable single-story residences to two-story brick suburban-style homes, waterfront property, and homes on several acres.

Web Sites: www.houstontx.gov, www.nassaubay.com, www.ellago-tx.com, www.cityofwebster.com

Area Code: 281

Zip Codes: 77062, 77058, 77586, 77598

Post Offices: Albert Thomas Station, 14917 El Camino Real, Houston; Nassau Bay Station, 18214 Upper Bay Rd, Houston; Seabrook Station, 1600 2nd St, Seabrook; Webster Station, 17077 Texas Ave, Webster

Police Precincts and Departments: Houston Police Department: Clear Lake Substation, 2855 Bay Area Blvd, Houston, 281-218-3800; Nassau Bay Police Department, 1800 NASA Pkwy, Nassau Bay, 281-333-4200; El Lago Police Department, 98 Lakeshore Dr, Seabrook, 281-326-1098; Lakeview Police Department, 500 Kirby Rd, Seabrook, 281-326-5900 (Taylor Lake Village); Webster Police Department, www.websterpd.com, 217 Pennsylvania Ave, Webster, 281-332-2426

Emergency Hospitals: Clear Lake Regional Medical Center, www.clearlakermc.com, 500 Medical Center Blvd, Webster, 281-332-2511; Christus St. John Hospital, www.christusstjohn.org, 18300 St. John Dr, Nassau Bay, 281-333-5503

Libraries: Harris County Public Library, www.hcpl.net: Clear Lake City-County Freeman Branch, 16616 Diana Ln, Houston, 281-488-1906; Evelyn Meador Branch, 2400 Meyer Rd, Seabrook, 281-474-9142

Adult Education: University of Houston Clear Lake, www.uhcl.edu, 2700 Bay Area Blvd, Houston, 281-283-7600

Public Education: Clear Creek Independent School District, www.ccisd.net, 2425 E Main St, League City, 281-284-0000

Community Publications: *Houston Chronicle*, www.chron.com; *Clear Lake Citizen Online*, www.thecitizen-online.com; *Bay Area Citizen*

Community Resources: City of Houston—Clear Lake, 2855 Bay Area Blvd, Houston, 281-218-3800; Taylor Lake Village City Hall, 500 Kirby Rd, Seabrook, 281-326-2843; Nassau Bay City Hall, 1800 NASA Pkwy, Houston, 281-333-2677; El Lago City Hall, 98 Lakeshore Dr, El Lago, 281-326-1951; Seabrook City Hall, 1700 1st St, Seabrook, 281-291-5600; Webster City Hall, 101 Pennsylvania St, Webster, 281-332-1826; Clear Lake Area Chamber of Commerce, www.clearlakearea.com, 1201 E NASA Pkwy, Houston, 281-488-7676

GALVESTON COUNTY

Galveston County has many small-sized cities and towns that are popular tourist destinations and weekend getaways. The continually growing cruise industry in Galveston has brought more and more visitors to the city and surrounding areas. Some like it so much that they have purchased vacation or permanent homes on the isle. Living in this county has its rewards, but like Bay Area residents, those in Galveston County must be prepared to evacuate during hurricane season. The communities in this county are even more vulnerable to hurricanes than the Bay Area because little to nothing separates it from the Gulf of Mexico. City web sites provide good hurricane preparation and evacuation tips. Many of them have local numbers to contact if special assistance is needed during evacuation. In addition, the Texas Governor's Office of Emergency Management has established a 211 hotline where those with special healthcare needs and individuals with no transportation can register *in advance* for transportation. Other resources include the local media and the Greater Houston Transportation and Emergency Center's web site, www.houstontranstar.org/weather/hurricane_routes.aspx, which provides an evacuation map with evacuation routes.

KEMAH

This charming seaside town, just minutes from Clear Lake, is a favorite weekend getaway for Houstonians and residents of neighboring communities. Streets are lined with colorfully painted, quaint, one-story wood frame cottages that house local shops. Kemah's buildings are built close together, making it convenient to walk from place to place. Before the Kemah Boardwalk was built in the 1990s by well-known Houston restauranteur Tillman Fertitta, Kemah was a lovely and quiet place for a day trip. It still is, but more crowded and ostentatious. The Boardwalk was constructed to feature the dozen or so restaurants that are owned by Fertitta's Landry Corporation. Designed as a family-friendly entertainment/food complex, it has become a popular draw. The wooden boardwalk wraps around the waterfront, providing diners with a view of the Gulf of Mexico and an opportunity to soak in the breeze coming off the water. A giant ferris wheel and other carnival rides and games are located on the boardwalk. The boardwalk offers a free way to have fun as it costs nothing to sit along it and enjoy the view. The other big draw here is boating. The marina is packed with rows and rows of sailboats, motorboats, and yachts. Originally a shrimping village, you can still see the shrimp boats coming in from the day's catch at dusk. In addition to the older quaint homes, newer and more ostentatious homes have recently been built in Kemah. Several of these are multi-million-dollar homes or mansions.

Clear Lake Shores, a small island community with approximately

1200 residents, is also a vacation destination. Surrounded by water on three sides and a mile from Galveston Bay, most of the homes here are on stilts. It is located on the southeastern side of Clear Lake at the entrance to Jarboe Bayou, where a water bird sanctuary and animal habitat are under development. The town has four major marinas and is home to several yacht clubs. Clear Lake Shores has a peaceful and quiet small town atmosphere while being near the conveniences of Clear Lake City.

Web Site: www.kemah.net
Area Code: 281
Zip Code: 77565
Post Office: Kemah Station, 1129 Hwy 146, Kemah
Police Departments: Kemah Police Department, 1401 Hwy 146, Kemah, 281-334-5414; Clear Lake Shores Police Department, 1006 S Shore Dr, Kemah, 281-334-1034
Emergency Hospitals: Clear Lake Regional Medical Center, www.clearlakermc.com, 500 Medical Center Blvd, Webster, 281-332-2511; Christus St. John Hospital, www.christusstjohn.org, 18300 St. John Dr, Nassau Bay, 281-333-5503
Public Education: Clear Creek Independent School District, www.ccisd.net, 2425 E Main St, League City, 281-284-0000
Community Publications: *Bay Area Citizen; Galveston County Daily News*, www.galvestondailynews.com
Community Resources: Kemah City Hall, 603 Bradford Ave, Kemah, 281-334-3181; Clear Lake Shores City Hall, 1006 South Shore Dr, Clear Lake Shores, 281-334-2799; Clear Lake Area Chamber of Commerce, www.clearlakearea.com, 1201 E NASA Pkwy, Houston, 281-488-7676; Kemah Boardwalk, www.kemahboardwalk.com, Bradford and 2nd St, Kemah

LEAGUE CITY

League City is much like Clear Lake—a waterfront community whose residents largely work in the aerospace industry, tourism industry, or nearby petrochemical refineries. Boating is a popular recreational activity here as well. Pockets of the town contain charming tree-lined commercial districts. League City has many waterfront homes, homes with views of the lake or bay, golf course communities, historic turn-of-the-century homes, and single-family residential neighborhoods. The location, character, and vacation town feel of this place lend to it a nice quality of life. There are several water-side resorts that are visited mostly by Houstonians. It is located on the south shore of Clear Lake and along I-45 which goes directly to Houston, 20 miles away.

One of the most notable communities here is **South Shore Harbour**. This master-planned community is located along Clear Lake. Developers have attempted to recreate a resort-style atmosphere with palm trees and waterways. This community is ideal for those who like to live near the water. Many of the subdivisions, or villages as they are called here, have homes on the water where owners can dock their boats.

Another community to consider is **Victory Lakes**. This master-planned community features seven lakes, walking trails, a golf course, and a recreational center. It is located directly on I-45 South at Highway 646.

Web Sites: www.ci.league-city.tx.us, southshoreharbour.com

Area Code: 281

Zip Code: 77573

Post Office: League City Station, 240 W Galveston St, League City

Police Department: League City Police Department, www.lcpd.com, 500 W Walker St, League City, 281-332-2566

Library: League City Helen Hall Library, www.leaguecitylibrary.org, 100 W Walker, League City, 281-554-1111

Emergency Hospitals: Clear Lake Regional Medical Center, www.clearlakermc.com, 500 Medical Center Blvd, Webster, 281-332-2511; Christus St. John Hospital, www. christusstjohn.org, 18300 St. John Dr, Nassau Bay, 281-333-5503

Public Education: Clear Creek Independent School District, www.ccisd.net, 2425 E Main St, League City, 281-284-0000

Community Publication: *Galveston County Daily News*, www.galvestondailynews. com

Community Resources: League City City Hall, 300 W Walker, League City, 281-554-1000; Clear Lake Area Chamber of Commerce, www.clearlakearea.com, 1201 E NASA Pkwy, Houston, 281-488-7676

Public Transportation: Harris County Metropolitan Authority, www.ridemetro.org: Bay Area Park and Ride, *Bus*: 246

GALVESTON

This barrier island was the scene of the worst hurricane in U.S. history. The unnamed hurricane of 1900 completely flattened what was at the time Texas's wealthiest town and changed the city forever. At the turn of the century, Galveston was a bustling commercial center with the largest cotton port in the nation. In fact, it was referred to as the Wall Street of the South. The city displayed its wealth through its elegant and ornate buildings. Many of the historic Victorian buildings and mansions managed to survive the hurricane and now serve as tourist attractions. Today Galveston is protected by a seven-foot high seawall. However, the island never returned to its former glory after the devastating hurricane. It played a secondary role to the emerging city of Houston, 50 miles away. These days, Galveston is best known as a weekend getaway. It relies heavily on the tourism industry. However, Galveston is currently experiencing a resurgence in its popularity. A cruise ship industry has developed around the Port of Galveston and continues to grow as more and more cruise lines dock here. Moody Gardens, Schlitterbahn Water Park, and other attractions have all done their part to lure visitors onto the island. Most noticeable is the recent residential building boom on this island. The risk of hurricanes has not deterred homebuyers, who are lured by oceanfront views and seaside living. Homes closer to the water are built on stilts while further inland homes are what one would normally find in any residential neighborhood in Houston. However, it is the restored Victorian residences that are Galveston's showcase homes. Much of the new construction has primarily been high-rise condominiums near the coastline. Incorporated areas on or near Galveston include the **Village of Tiki Island** (www.villageoftikiisland.com), **Jamaica Beach, High Island**, and **Crystal Beach**.

Web Site: www.cityofgalveston.org
Area Code: 409
Zip Codes: 77550, 77551, 77553, 77554
Post Offices: Galveston Station, 601 25th St, Galveston; Bob Lyons Station, 5826 Broadway St, Galveston
Police Department: Galveston Police Department, www.galvestonpd.com, 2517 Ball St, Galveston, 409-797-3702
Emergency Hospital: University of Texas Medical Branch Galveston, www.utmb.edu, 301 University Blvd, Galveston, 409-772-2618
Library: Galveston County Public Library System: Rosenberg Library, www.rosenberg library.com, 2310 Sealy Ave, Galveston, 409-763-8854
Adult Education: University of Texas Medical Branch, www.utmb.edu, 301 University Blvd, Galveston, 409-772-2618; Texas A&M Galveston, www.tamug.edu, 200 Seawolf Pkwy, Galveston
Public Education: Galveston Independent School District, www.gisd.org, 3904 Ave T, Galveston, 409-766-5100
Community Publication: *Galveston County Daily News*, www.galvestondailynews. com
Community Resources: Galveston Convention and Entertainment, www.galveston. com; Galveston Chamber of Commerce, www.galvestonchamber.org, 519 25th St, Galveston, 409-763-5326
Public Transportation: Island Transit, www.islandtransit.com

TEXAS CITY AND LA MARQUE

Texas City

This is largely an oil refinery town. Some of the nation's largest refineries are located here. It made headlines in the region when an explosion at the British Petroleum plant in 2005 killed over a dozen people and injured several others. Residents who live in the shadows of the neighboring petrochemical plants, usually in small one-story wood frame homes, may occasionally be told to stay indoors or even evacuated when there is a chemical leak, fire, or explosion. Further away from the plants, residential neighborhoods tend to be bigger and newer. Anything from apartments to modest brick, one-story homes and large grand homes are available.

La Marque

La Marque was historically known as Highlands, a small farming community until the industrialization of the area. Its population grew as employees from the refineries and factories in nearby Texas City moved in. Several new subdivisions with affordable homes have been constructed in this primarily residential community. Many people come to La Marque to visit its bird sanctuary, the Gulf Greyhound Park, and outlet shopping. Other smaller towns in the area are **Dickinson** (www.ci.dickinson. tx.us) and **Bacliff.**

Web Sites: www.texas-city-tx.org, www.ci.la-marque.tx.us

Area Code: 409

Zip Codes: 77590, 77591, 77568

Post Offices: Texas City Station, 2002 11th Ave N, Texas City; La Marque Station, 509 Laurel St, La Marque

Police Departments: Texas City Police Department, 1004 9th Ave N, Texas City, 409-643-5760; La Marque Police Department, 409-938-9269

Emergency Hospital: Mainland Medical Center, www.mainlandmedical.com, 6801 Emmet F. Lowry Expy, Texas City, 409-938-5000

Libraries: Moore Memorial Library (Texas City), 1701 9th Ave N, Texas City, 409-643-5979; La Marque Public Library, 1011 Bayou Rd, La Marque, 409-938-9270

Public Education: Texas City Independent School District, www.texascity.isd.tenet. edu, 1041 Ninth Ave N, Texas City, 409-942-2713; La Marque Independent School District, http://198.216.228.10/education/district/district.php?sectionid=1, 1727 Bayou Rd, La Marque, 409-938-4251

Community Publication: *Galveston County Daily News*, www.galvnews.com

Community Resource: Texas City–LaMarque Chamber of Commerce, www. texascitychamber.com, 8419 Emmett F Lowry Expy, Texas City, 409-935-1408

SOUTH OF HOUSTON

BRAZORIA COUNTY

Pearland

Pearland's history goes back to the 1880s, when it was centered around the agriculture industry. Named for the abundance of pear trees in the area, residents mostly grew fruit and figs as a cash crop. The devastating hurricane of 1900 destroyed most of the crops, but the community replanted and continued to produce fruit. As late as the 1960s, Pearland was a small agricultural community with fewer than 1500 residents. Pearland has grown tremendously in the last decade. Largely a rural community, it has become one of the hottest suburban communities in Houston. The selection of affordable housing and quiet atmosphere has attracted many homebuyers. Located partially within Harris, Brazoria, and Fort Bend counties, Pearland is directly south of downtown Houston. It is popular with medical professionals who work in the Texas Medical Center because State Highway 288 provides direct access from Pearland to the medical center. It is also popular with those who work in downtown Houston, which is not far from the medical center.

Two of the most notable master-planned communities here are

Silverlake and Shadow Creek Ranch. **Shadow Creek Ranch** is a lake-themed community with homes from the $140,000s to over $1 million. **Silverlake** also has a lake theme and homes in varying price ranges. Though the construction of new subdivisions and ensuing commercial development is gradually transforming Pearland into a more suburban/urban environment, the older neighborhoods are still rural in character. The older neighborhoods are generally on narrow roads that lack a curb and are densely covered by big trees and other plants. Farm property and country lots are available in Pearland.

Friendswood
Founded by the Society of Friends, also known as Quakers, this town was originally a Quaker community established in a wooded area. Thus, it was named Friendswood. From its founding in the late 1880s to the 1930s, it remained largely an agricultural Quaker community. When the Johnson Space Center was constructed 10 miles away in the 1960s, more people began moving here either to work at the space center or to commute to Houston. Since then, it has remained one of the area's major bedroom communities. Today, Friendswood is no longer a Quaker stronghold as people of varying faiths have made their homes there. A notable aspect of Friendswood is that it has been a dry community since 1963, which means no alcohol is sold in the town.

Web Sites: ci.pearland.tx.us, www.ci.friendswood.tx.us, silverlaketexas.com, shadowcreekranch.net
Area Codes: 281, 832
Zip Codes: 77581, 77584, 77546
Post Offices: Pearland Station, 3519 E Walnut St, Pearland; Friendswood Station, 310 Morningside Dr, Friendswood
Police Departments: Pearland Police Department, 2703 Veterans Dr, Pearland, 281-652-1100; Friendswood Police Department, 109 E Willowick Ave, Friendswood, 281-996-3318
Emergency Hospitals: Memorial Hermann Southeast Hospital, www.memorialhermann.org, 11800 Astoria, Houston, 281-929-6100; Christus St. John Hospital, www.christusstjohn.org, 18300 St. John Dr, Houston, 281-333-5503; Clear Lake Regional Medical Center, www.clearlakermc.com, 500 Medical Center Blvd, Webster, 281-332-2511
Libraries: Brazoria County Public Library System, www.bcls.lib.tx.us, 3522 Liberty Dr, 281-485-4876; Friendswood Public Library, www.friendswood.lib.tx.us, 416 S Friendswood Dr, Friendswood, 281-482-7135
Adult Education: Alvin Community College—Pearland College Center, ww2.alvincollege.edu, 2319 N Grand Blvd, Pearland, 281-756-3900
Public Education: Pearland Independent School District, www.pearlandisd.org, 2337 N Galveston, Pearland, 281-485-3203; Alvin Independent School District, www.alvinisd.net, 301 E House St, Alvin, 281-388-1130 (portions of Pearland, including Shadow Creek Ranch subdivision); Friendswood Independent School District, www.friendswood.isd.tenet.edu, 108 E Shadowbend Ave, Friendswood, 281-482-1198
Community Publications: *Pearland Journal*, www.pearlandjournal.com; *Friendswood Journal*, www.friendswoodjournal.com

Community Resources: Pearland Chamber of Commerce, www.pearlandchamber.com, 3501 Liberty Dr, Pearland, 281-485-3634; Friendswood Chamber of Commerce, www.friendswood-chamber.com, 1100 S Friendswood Dr, Friendswood, 281-482-3329

AUSTIN

Twenty years ago, Austin was just a small, sleepy, university town with an unconventional character. Since the dot-com boom of the 1990s, it has grown tremendously. Small town no more, its metropolitan area now boasts approximately 1.5 million residents. New residential development is popping up everywhere, especially in the hills that overlook the city. The rapid growth and building in some of Austin's most environmentally sensitive and pristine areas has caused concern among environmentalists. It has also created congestion in some areas and new roads continually have to be built or expanded to meet the growing population. Despite the increased traffic, getting around town should be pretty easy. Capital Metro, the city's public transportation system, operates one of the most used and efficient bus systems in a major Texas city. The city is geographically small enough to provide efficient service. Unlike most major Texas cities where public transportation is used mainly by lower-income and minority residents, many Austinites use it to get around and do daily chores. This can largely be attributed to the fact that Austin has a large college student population, primarily from the University of Texas, but also from St. Edwards University and Austin Community College. Capital Metro also operates the university campus shuttles, which are noted by their burnt orange trim and longhorn decal. Parking near the campuses and downtown can be extremely difficult. In some instances, residents just simply do not own a car and get around by bike and the bus.

Some old timers still lament the days when Austin was a smaller city with few to no big-box stores, when local businesses were the major retailers in town, there were no traffic jams, and no young millionaires carving up the hills to build their estates. Yet, the city still retains many of the unique characteristics that make Austin *Austin*. In this city, transvestites run for city council, nudists bathe in the lake, and anything alternative is celebrated. To outsiders the town may have many oddities, but Austin revels in its weirdness. There is even a movement to keep it that way. There are T-shirts, bumper stickers, and other items proudly proclaiming "Keep Austin Weird." This city stands out in Texas as a liberal town that is on the same wavelength as the hippie, vegetarian, all-natural, eco-friendly crowd. Perhaps what is most unique about this city, though, is not its offbeat characters, but the beautiful natural surroundings of the area that are conducive to a relaxed lifestyle, strong local support for homegrown, independent businesses, and a city design that is pedestrian- and bike-friendly. Austin is located in the Texas Hill Country, an area characterized by undulating green hills, abundant wildlife, numerous lakes, natural springs, rivers, and limestone formations. The hills around

Austin make it a favorite training ground for bicyclists, the most notable of whom is Lance Armstrong.

Austin goes by several monikers, which may leave the impression that the city has a bit of an identity crisis. There are several businesses around town with the name Waterloo, which is the city's previous name. It also calls itself "Bat City" for the large colony of bats that reside underneath the Congress St. Bridge and the "Live Music Capital of the World" for its prominent live music scene.

A large percentage of the population in Austin is university and college students as well as politicians, lobbyists, and state government employees; during the summer, when the legislature is out of session and the college semester has ended, you'll enjoy a considerably less crowded town. Until recently, it has been primarily a renters' town, largely related to these transient populations. It also is not unusual, though, to find someone who has been renting for decades. New home construction, however, has really taken off in recent years. Now, there are just as many homeowners as there are renters in the city.

CENTRAL AUSTIN

Central Austin is generally designated as the area bounded by Anderson Lane (US-183) on the north, I-35 on the east, Town Lake on the south, and MoPac on the west. It is characterized by unique shops, coffeehouses, historic homes, and live entertainment. Here, the funky, elegant, alternative, and charming are side by side. This is the heart of the city that bustles not only during the day with business, but also at night with entertainment and fun. Central Austin's independent, quirky, and laid-back character best defines this city. It has the most diverse housing options in the city, including single-family residential homes, plenty of apartments, condos, co-ops, lofts, townhomes, and duplexes.

DOWNTOWN

Boundaries: North: Martin Luther King Blvd; East: I-35; South: Town Lake; West: Lamar Blvd

Unlike the downtowns in other major Texas cities, downtown Austin has always been a thriving area that is not just for business. Famous Sixth Street, with its bars, clubs, and restaurants, is always a main attraction, especially for college-age visitors. During the weekends, streets are often closed off to allow for pedestrian-only traffic. It gets even more hectic when the city hosts major events such as the South by Southwest Music Festival. A few blocks away in the Warehouse District on 3rd and 4th streets is a newer entertainment district with restaurants and bars that cater to a more mature, non-college crowd. Right next door to all the

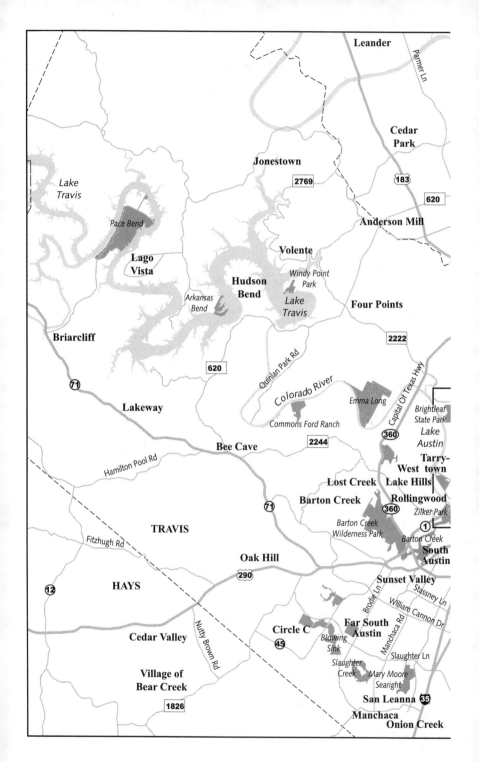

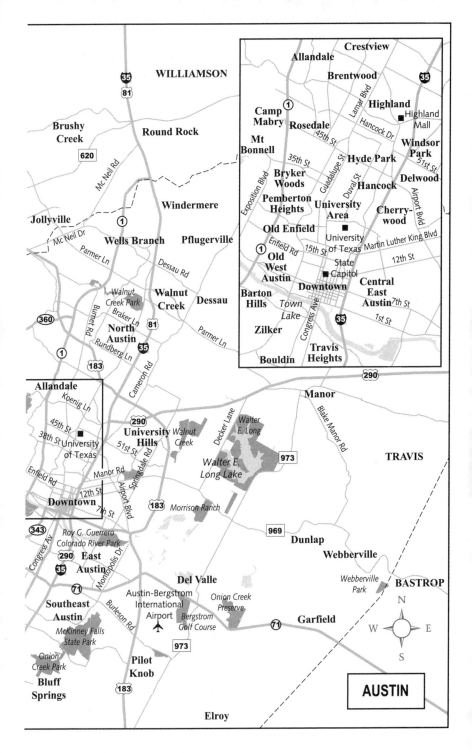

AUSTIN

drinking and partying is the stately and serious Texas State Capitol complex, a granite and limestone structure designed in the Renaissance Revival style. In the past, few people, except maybe some politicians and lobbyists, lived downtown. However, many new apartments, lofts, condos, and townhomes have been built here in recent years. Some argue that the area is becoming increasingly gentrified and less "Austin." Those looking for a reasonably priced accommodation might want to consider another part of town because the residences here tend to be towards the higher end of the market.

Web Sites: www.downtownaustin.org, www.ci.austin.tx.us
Area Code: 512
Zip Codes: 78701, 78702
Post Offices: Downtown Austin Station, 510 Guadalupe; Capitol Station, 111 E 17th St
Police Precinct: Austin Police Department, Downtown Area Command, 512-974-5253
Emergency Hospital: Brackenridge Hospital, www.seton.net, 601 E 15th St, 512-324-7000
Library: Austin Public Library, Faulk Central Library, 800 Guadalupe, 512-974-7400
Adult Education: Austin Community College – Rio Grande Campus, www.austincc.edu, 1212 Rio Grande, 512-223-3137; University of Texas, www.utexas.edu, 925 San Jacinto Blvd, 512-475-7348
Public Education: Austin Independent School District, www.austin.isd.tenet.edu, 1111 W 6th St, 512-414-1700
Community Publications: *Austin American-Statesman*, www.statesman.com; *Austin Chronicle*, www.austinchronicle.com; *Austin Business Journal*, www.bizjournals.com/austin
Community Resources: Texas State Capitol, 1100 Congress Ave, 512-305-8400; City Hall, 500 E Cesar Chavez St, 512-482-9407; Waterloo Park, 403 E 15th St; Duncan Park, 900 W 9th St; Austin Farmers Market I (Republic Square Park), 422 Guadalupe, 512-236-0074
Public Transportation: Capital Metro, www.capmetro.org; *Bus:* 1L/1M, 2, 3, 4, 5, 6, 7, 9, 14, 15, 17, 18, 19, 20, 21, 22, 29, 37, 101, 100, 103, 127, 137, 142, 171, 174, 410, 411, 412, 470, 481, 484, 485, 486, 490, 935, 982, 983, 984, 986, 987; *University of Texas Shuttle:* ER, LA, BD, PL, WL, ER, NR, LA, LS

UNIVERSITY AREA AND HANCOCK

University Area

Boundaries: North: 38th St; East: I-35; South: Martin Luther King, Jr. Blvd; West: Shoal Creek; WEST CAMPUS: North: 29th St; East: Guadalupe Blvd; South: Martin Luther King Jr. Blvd; West: Lamar Blvd

A few blocks north of downtown is the University of Texas ("UT") campus, the flagship campus of the University of Texas system. The campus, with its signature red tile roof and white brick/limestone walls, is spread out over 300 acres of hilly terrain. Still, Austinites often refer to the campus as the 40 acres, which is the original amount of land granted to the university by the state. A frenzy of activity during the weekdays, the area is deserted on the weekends, when the overfed pigeons outnumber people. However, it is during this time that most families and individuals stop by for a Sunday walk through the tree-shaded grounds that are peppered with Spanish/Mediterranean-influenced buildings. Bass Concert Hall, the LBJ Presidential Library, the Texas Memorial Museum of Science and History, and the Erwin Special Events Center are all located on campus. In addition, the university also has one of the rare copies of the Gutenberg Bible, housed on campus at the Harry Ransom Center.

The main thoroughfare here is Guadalupe Boulevard, also referred to as the Drag by college students. This pedestrian strip features coffee shops, bookstores, a few churches, vintage clothing shops, Thai restaurants, record shops, tattoo parlors, and hair salons. Behind Guadalupe, off of one of the side streets, is **West Campus**. This is the main residential area for UT college students. It is a mix of fraternity houses, sorority houses, new and old apartments, condos, and historic Victorian homes. The majority of the residences here are rental property, including several of the homes. Many of them are old and worn apartments, with some really needing an upgrade. Nevertheless, there is constantly a high demand for housing here because of its location next to campus. In response to the demand, some new residential towers have been built on Guadalupe towards the northern end of campus, and many townhomes and apartments have been built inside West Campus. Numerous neighborhood shops, bars, and hangout spots dot West Campus. It is a very urban, high population and residential density area. Almost everything is within walking distance. If the destination is too far, residents simply bike or take advantage of the several buses that run through the neighborhood.

More housing options are available on the opposite end of the campus along Red River Street, where there are several apartment complexes. A steady demand for student housing keeps the rental prices in this area pretty high. If you want more room at an affordable price, head farther out away from campus. Just about any complex or neighborhood with a bus stop that goes towards campus is a good bet. For a more traditional residential area, check out the **North University** neighborhood immediately north of West Campus's northern boundaries.

HANCOCK

Boundaries: North: 45th St; East: I-35; South: 32nd St; West: Duval St

Further down Red River is the Hancock neighborhood. It is conveniently located near the UT campus, downtown, and amenities in the area such as Hancock Public Golf Course, the Hancock Shopping Center, and the Hancock Recreational Center, all of which are accessible by bus. Near the Hancock Shopping Center there are several apartments which are more affordable than the rental units near campus. This middle-class community features mainly one-story brick residences.

Web Sites: www.ci.austin.tx.us, www.main.org/hna, www.main.org/nuna
Area Code: 512
Zip Codes: 78705, 78712, 78751
Post Offices: University Austin Station, 2201 Guadalupe; North Austin Station, 4300 Speedway; Central Park Station, 3507 N Lamar Blvd
Police Precincts: Austin Police Department, North Central Area Command, 512-974-5500; University of Texas Campus Police, www.utexas.edu/police, 2201 Robert Dedman Dr, 512-471-4441
Emergency Hospitals: St. David's Medical Center, www.stdavidsmedicalcenter.com, 919 E 32nd St, 512-476-7111; Brackenridge Hospital, www.seton.net, 601 E 15th St, 512-324-7000
Libraries: Austin Public Library, Faulk Central Library, 800 Guadalupe, 512-974-7400; Austin History Center, 810 Guadalupe, 512-974-7480; Perry-Castaneda Library (university campus), Speedway & 21st St, 512-495-4250
Adult Education: University of Texas, www.utexas.edu, 925 San Jacinto Blvd, 512-475-7348; Concordia Lutheran College,www.concordia.edu, 3400 IH 35 N, 512-486-2001
Public Education: Austin Independent School District, www.austin.isd.tenet.edu, 1111 W 6th St, 512-414-1700
Community Publications: *Austin American-Statesman*, www.statesman.com; *Austin Chronicle*, www.austinchronicle.com; *Austin Business Journal*, www.bizjournals. com/austin; *Daily Texan* (university), www.dailytexanonline.com
Community Resources: Harry Ransom Center, 21st and Guadalupe, 512-471-8944; Texas Memorial Museum of Science and Natural History, 2400 Trinity St, 512-471-1604; LBJ Library and Museum, 2313 Red River St, 512-721-0200; Hancock Golf Course, 811 E 41st St, 512-453-0276; Hancock Recreation Center, 811 E 41st St, 512-453-7765
Public Transportation: Capital Metro, www.capmetro.org; *Bus*: 1, 5/26, 7/27, 10, 15, 16, 18/4, 19, 20, 21, 22, 29, 100, 101, 103, 110, 127, 142, 171, 174, 410, 450, 455, 456, 462, 470, 481, 935, 982, 983, 984, 986, 987, 990; *University of Texas Shuttle*: BD, CP, CR, DF, ER, FA, FW, IF, LA, LS, NR, PL, PRC, RR, WC, WL

HYDE PARK

Boundaries: North: 48th and 46th; East: Duval; South: E 38th; West: Guadalupe

Hyde Park is a cozy neighborhood with convenience stores, laundromats, coffee shops, and eateries located inside the neighborhood and within walking distance of most of the residences. This neighborhood covers a small area that packs a lot of character and amenities into it. Because everything is located within walking distance, residents are likely to recognize many of the people on the street.

Hyde Park is surrounded by tall trees and dense foliage. As one of Austin's first planned suburbs developed in 1891, it features many historic Victorian-style residences and other styles that vary in size. Its location, pleasant neighborhood atmosphere, and good public schools have pushed homes here to about $250,000 or more. Just north of the university with bus routes that run along Duval to campus, the apartments, townhomes, and other rental property here are popular with college students. The university's Intramural Fields are located in this neighborhood and the area surrounding it is sometimes referred to as the IM fields. Next to the IM fields are old, single-family residential homes with wood siding and large front porches.

Web Sites: www.austinhydepark.org, www.ci.austin.tx.us

Area Code: 512

Zip Code: 78751

Post Offices: North Austin Station, 4300 Speedway; Central Park Station, 3507 N Lamar Blvd

Police Precinct: Austin Police Department, North Central Area Command, 512-974-5500

Emergency Hospital: Seton Medical Center, www.seton.net, 1201 W 38th St, 512-324-1000

Libraries: Austin Public Library, Faulk Central Library, 800 Guadalupe, 512-974-7400; Austin History Center, 810 Guadalupe, 512-974-7480

Public Education: Austin Independent School District, www.austin.isd.tenet.edu, 1111 W 6th St, 512-414-1700

Community Publications: *Austin American-Statesman*, www.statesman.com; *Austin Chronicle*, www.austinchronicle.com; *Austin Business Journal*, www.bizjournals. com/austin

Community Resources: City Hall, 500 E Cesar Chavez St, 512-482-9407; Hyde Park Senior Activity Center, 304 E 44th St, 512-458-2255

Public Transportation: Capital Metro, www.capmetro.org; *Bus*: 1L/1M, 5, 7, 101, 481; *University of Texas Shuttle*: IF

HISTORIC WEST AUSTIN

The historic West Austin district comprises Old Enfield, Pemberton Heights, Bryker Woods, and Old West Austin. These are established wealthy enclaves developed in the early 1920s. Homes here are unique in style and vary in size. Their location in central Austin, near downtown, the university campus, and cultural and entertainment centers, elevates their appeal, but also creates high home values.

OLD ENFIELD

Boundaries: North: West 24th St; East: Lamar Blvd; West: MoPac; South: Enfield Rd

Old Enfield is centrally located a few minutes from downtown with several major thoroughfares bordering the neighborhood. Majestic oak trees form a canopy around this neighborhood's hilly landscape. This is a desirable and wealthy residential area with homes of varying styles, including antebellum mansions, brick and mason residences, small bungalows, Colonials, and Tudors, that sell for $250,000 into the millions. Old Enfield has many historic homes and some of the oldest colonial style homes are located here. Though the homes here are old, that does not mean they are run down. On the contrary, excellent construction and materials have ensured that most of the homes have been well preserved. While most of the properties here are owner-occupied, single-family residences, there are also apartments and duplexes along Enfield Road, where there are University of Texas and Capital Metro bus stops.

PEMBERTON HEIGHTS

Boundaries: North: Westover Rd; East: Lamar Blvd; South: 24th St; West: MoPac

One of the most beautiful and sought-after neighborhoods, Pemberton Heights contains a mix of housing styles. There are elegant mansions, brick Tudors, Colonials, traditional, and other lovely styles that line its oak-shaded streets. Inside this neighborhood is a distinctive residence built in 1926 and designed as a medieval-style castle, known as Pemberton Castle. Like its neighbors, Pemberton Heights has lush lawns and beautiful landscaping. Homes here are similar to those in Enfield, but some areas can be pricey, with many properties selling for between $500,000 and over $1,000,000.

OLD WEST AUSTIN/CLARKSVILLE

Boundaries: OLD WEST AUSTIN: North: Enfield Rd; East: Lamar Blvd; South: Town Lake; West: Mopac Expressway; CLARKSVILLE: North: Waterston Ave; East: West Lynn St; South: 9th St; West: MoPac Blvd

Old West Austin is separated from downtown by Shoal Creek. As one of the oldest neighborhoods in Austin, it is rich in history and character. There are several historical buildings that serve as schools, offices, and residences. Of note is the former Texas Military Institute building built in 1869 on West 11th Street known as the Castle because of its appearance. One of the most significant landmarks here is not a building, but a 600-year-old oak tree known as the Treaty Oak where the city's namesake, Stephen F. Austin, is rumored to have signed a treaty with local Indians.

Old West Austin encompasses the **Clarksville** neighborhood, which is recognized as a National Register Historic District. The historic Clarksville neighborhood was founded by Charles Clark, a freed slave, as a community for emancipated blacks in 1871. At one time it was a thriving African-American community on the west side of town. Its location near downtown increased property values in the area over the years and by 1970, property values became too high for many of the original residents, who have since moved to more affordable neighborhoods. Today it is inhabited mainly by artists, urban professionals, and some college students. There are plenty of rental properties in the area, including apartments, homes, garage apartments, condos, and duplexes. It is one of the hottest neighborhoods in Austin, so rent and housing prices can be relatively costly. Most homes are small, three-bedroom, single-story wood frame structures built between 1920 and 1930. Many of the residences do not have garages, though there are driveways for vehicles. Clarksville has some of the hippie, artistic elements that are associated with Austin. Whole Foods, an organic grocery store currently located on Lamar Avenue, started in this area as the Clarksville Natural Grocery, in 1979. On other streets such as West 6th, there are many art galleries alongside some bakeries, restaurants, and other independently owned shops.

BRYKER WOODS

Boundaries: North: 35th St; East: Shoal Creek; South: Westover; West: MoPac Blvd

Further north of Old Enfield, Bryker Woods is covered by many mature trees, beautiful lawns, and lovely homes. The neighborhood was developed between the 1930s and 1950s. Quite a few of the original bungalows are still there, but there are also numerous newer and larger homes. Several of the residents work at nearby Seton Hospital and its surrounding facilities. Though very close to downtown, this quiet, family-oriented neighborhood feels quite removed. It is separated from downtown and the University of Texas campus by Shoal Creek. However, there are concerns that the pass-through traffic from MoPac freeway and the intrusion of commercial businesses on the northeast corner of Bryker Woods could impact the quality of life here.

Web Sites: www.owahd.org, www.owana.org, www.brykerwoods.org, www.ci.austin.tx.us
Area Code: 512
Zip Code: 78703
Post Office: West Austin Station, 2418 Spring Ln
Police Precinct: Austin Police Department, Central West Area Command, 512-974-5088
Emergency Hospital: Seton Medical Center, www.seton.net, 1201 W 38th St, 512-324-1000
Libraries: Austin Public Library: Faulk Central Library, 800 Guadalupe, 512-974-7400; Austin History Center, 810 Guadalupe, 512-974-7480; Howson Branch, 2500 Exposition, 512-472-3584; UT Campus: Perry-Castaneda Library, Speedway & 21st St, 512-495-4250
Public Education: Austin Independent School District, www.austin.isd.tenet.edu, 1111 W 6th St, 512-414-1700
Community Publications: *Austin American-Statesman*, www.statesman.com; *Austin Chronicle*, www.austinchronicle.com; *Austin Business Journal*, www.bizjournals.com/austin
Community Resources: City Hall, 500 E Cesar Chavez St, 512-482-9407; West Enfield

Park, 2008 Enfield; Pease District Park, 1100 Kingsbury St; Caswell Tennis Center, 2312 Shoal Creek Blvd, 512-478-6268; Bryker Woods, Seider Springs Park, and Shoal Creek Trail, 2600-2799 Lamar Blvd; Bailey Park, 1101 W 33rd St
Public Transportation: Capital Metro, www.capmetro.org; *Bus*: 3, 9, 19, 21, 22, 151, 171, 338, 982, 983, 987; *University of Texas Shuttle*: LA, ER, FW, PRC

TARRYTOWN

Boundaries: North: W 35th St; East: MoPac Blvd; South: Enfield Rd; West: Lake Austin

Tarrytown is a charming community west of downtown. It is located near scenic Lake Austin with the hills in the background. This is one of the most sought-after neighborhoods in Austin because of its location, nearby amenities, beauty, and excellent public schools. Homes here can range from $300,000 to $3 million. They vary in size from small cottages built in the 1920s to Southern-style mansions. However, many of the smaller cottages are being torn down and replaced by larger homes. The most magnificent homes are located along Lake Austin. Most of the residents in Tarrytown are families, with a few college students occupying rental properties, mostly along Enfield Road.

Tarrytown is a friendly neighborhood with a strong sense of community. It almost feels like a small town within Austin. It even has its own privately funded recreational association similar to the YMCA. Tarrytown also has the advantage of having amenities like Deep Eddy Pool, the Laguna Gloria Art Museum, Mayfield Park, Reed Park, Triangle Park, and the Lions Municipal Golf Course located in the neighborhood. Deep Eddy Pool is Austin's oldest swimming center that dates back to 1936. During the hot Texas summer nights, families can watch movies while cooling off in the pool. The Laguna Gloria Art Museum is a 1916 Italianate building that houses the Austin Museum of Art's collection. The most well-known and visited local attraction is Lake Austin. The lakefront has an outdoor deck area with benches where visitors can enjoy the view, which is especially beautiful at sunset. Local musicians often come here to perform for the public, which provides a relaxing outdoor atmosphere while the breeze blows in from the lake. Though the main reason many people come here is to dine at the restaurants and cafes that surround the deck, it is also a popular place for socializing and boating.

Web Sites: www.ci.austin.tx.us, www.historicclarksville.org
Area Code: 512
Zip Code: 78703
Post Office: West Austin Station: 2418 Spring Ln
Police Precinct: Austin Police Department, Central West Area Command, 512-974-5088
Emergency Hospitals: Seton Medical Center, www.seton.net, 1201 W 38th St, 512-324-1000
Library: Austin Public Library, Howson Branch, 2500 Exposition Blvd, 512-472-3584

Public Education: Austin Independent School District, www.austin.isd.tenet.edu, 1111 W 6th St, 512-414-1700

Community Publications: *Tarrytown News*, www.tarrytownnews.com; *Austin American-Statesman*, www.statesman.com; *Austin Chronicle*, www.austinchronicle.com; *Austin Business Journal*, www.bizjournals.com/austin

Community Resources: Deep Eddy Pool, 401 Deep Eddy Ave, 512-472-8546; Austin Museum of Art – Laguna Gloria, www.amoa.org, 3809 W 35th St, 512-458-8191; West Austin Youth Association, http://waya.org, 1314 Exposition Blvd, 512-473-2528

Public Transportation: Capital Metro, www.capmetro.org; *Bus*: 9, 21, 22, 828; *University of Texas Shuttle*: ER

WEST CENTRAL AUSTIN

CAMP MABRY AREA/MT. BONNELL AND ROSEDALE

CAMP MABRY AREA AND MT. BONNELL

Boundaries: North: FM 2222; East: MoPac; South: 35th St; West: Lake Austin

Camp Mabry is the Texas National Guard's training camp. When the camp was first established, it was still considered a rural area outside of Austin. Since then, the city has grown around the base, surrounding it with residential and some commercial development. Prior to September 11, that area was pretty much open, with citizens enjoying free access to the grounds for outdoor activities such as jogging. It is now fenced off from the public.

Mt. Bonnell refers to the natural limestone formation that stands 200 feet above the surrounding Austin area. It looks down past the surrounding trees, wildflowers, and grass, and onto a spectacular view of the Colorado River and Lake Austin. This beautiful and scenic area is a nice place to go hiking, picnicking, or just to enjoy the outdoors. It is the perfect place to relax with a cold drink and view the surrounding panorama. Best of all it is free. The residential area that surrounds it is set along sharply winding paths and steep hills that lead to Mt. Bonnell. The homes in this affluent neighborhood were largely developed in the mid-1980s. They offer wonderful hilltop views of the valley below and are surrounded by dense foliage.

ROSEDALE

Boundaries: North: North Loop/Hancock Dr; East: Lamar Blvd; South: 38th St; West: Shoal Creek

Rosedale is a charming old Austin neighborhood located near downtown, major thoroughfares, and many amenities. There are a mix of old homes and newer residences here in this very lovely and sought-after area. Many of the homes are small two-bedroom, one-bathroom bungalows or cottages, some of which, dating back to the 1930s and '40s, resemble storybook houses. Its location near downtown, the UT campus, and other area attractions are a major factor in its high property values. What also really makes this neighborhood attractive is the feeling that residents are living in a small town within the city. This pedestrian community has many shops within walking distance—especially on Lamar. There are many old-time residents who have lived here for decades. The heart of Rosedale is Ramsey Park, a neighborhood park that offers a swimming pool, tennis courts, playgrounds, a basketball court, a baseball diamond, and picnic areas. The average home starts at the upper $200,000s with the median home value at $300,000. The neighborhood also offers some townhomes and a few rental properties.

Web Sites: www.rosedale-na.org, www.main.org/hpwbana, www.ci.austin.tx.us
Area Code: 512
Zip Codes: 78756, 78731
Post Office: Central Park Station, 3507 N Lamar Blvd
Police Precinct: Austin Police Department, North Central Area Command, 512-974-5500
Library: Yarborough Branch, 2200 Hancock Dr, 512-454-7208
Public Education: Austin Independent School District, www.austin.isd.tenet.edu, 1111 W 6th St, 512-414-1700
Emergency Hospital: Seton Hospital, www.seton.net, 1201 W 38th St, 512-324-1000
Community Publications: *Austin American-Statesman*, www.statesman.com; *Austin Chronicle*, www.austinchronicle.com; *Austin Business Journal*, www.bizjournals.com/austin
Community Resources: City Hall, 500 E Cesar Chavez St, 512-482-9407; Ramsey Park, 4301 N Rosedale Ave; Shoal Creek Greenbelt, 2600-2799 Lamar Blvd
Public Transportation: Capital Metro, www.metro.org; *Bus*: 3, 5, 9, 338, 21, 151, 982, 983, 987; *UT Shuttle*: FW, PRC

ALLANDALE/CRESTVIEW/BRENTWOOD

Boundaries: ALLANDALE: North: Anderson Ln; East: Burnet Rd; South: Hancock Dr; West: MoPac; CRESTVIEW: North: Anderson Ln; East: N Lamar Blvd; South: Justin Ln; West: Burnet Rd; BRENTWOOD: North: Justin Ln; East: North Lamar Blvd; South: North Loop Rd; West: Burnet Rd

Allandale and Crestview are located north of the Enfield and Bryker Woods neighborhoods. These are middle-class neighborhoods with a mix of old residents who have lived here for 50 years, young families, and young professionals. Both neighborhoods were developed around the 1950s and 1960s. They are friendly, quiet areas with plenty of trees, numerous churches, and local businesses.

Allandale is a family-oriented community with quality neighborhood schools, hike and bike trails, swimming pools, and ball parks. Just west of Allandale, past Burnet Road, is the **Crestview** neighborhood. Once considered the far northwest part of Austin, these communities are now part of central Austin, as more neighborhoods have sprung up further north. As Austin grows, the property value of intown residential neighborhoods is increasing. Properties in Allandale and Crestview can easily cost $200,000 to $300,000, what with the congenial environments and child-friendly atmospheres offered by their communities. Homes here are mostly one-story, ranch-style houses with two to three bedrooms. There are also condominiums and apartments near the two neighborhoods. Another neighborhood in the north central area worth taking a look at is **Brentwood**; located immediately south of Crestview, it features similar styles of housing at around the same prices as Allandale and Crestview.

Highland

Bounded by Highway 183 on the north, Interstate 35 on the east, Denson on the south, and Lamar on the west, the Highland neighborhood is located by Highland Mall. This middle class neighborhood offers homes on large yards, but does not quite have the charm or historic appeal of any of the above-mentioned neighborhoods.

Web Sites: www.main.org/brentwood, www.main.org/highlandna/

Area Code: 512

Zip Codes: 78757, 78756, 78752

Post Offices: Northcross Station, 7700 Northcross Dr; Northeast Austin Station, 900 Blackson Ave

Police Precinct: Austin Police Department, North Central Area Command, 512-974-5500

Emergency Hospital: Seton Medical Center, www.seton.net, 1201 West 38th St, 512-324-1000

Libraries: Austin Public Library, Yarborough Branch, 2200 Hancock Dr, 512-454-7208; North Village Branch, 2139 W Anderson Ln, 512-458-2239

Adult Education: Austin Community College–Highland Business Center, 5930 Middle Fiskville Rd, 512-454-3774

Public Education: Austin Independent School District, www.austin.isd.tenet.edu, 1111 W 6th St, 512-414-1700

Community Publications: *Austin American-Statesman*, www.statesman.com; *Austin Chronicle*, www.austinchronicle.com; *Austin Business Journal*, www.bizjournals.com/austin

Community Resources: City Hall, 500 E Cesar Chavez St, 512-482-9407; Northwest Recreation Center, 2913 Northland Dr, 512-458-4107; Beverly Sheffield Park, 7000 Ardath St; Brentwood Park, 6710 Arroyo Seco; Travis County Farmers Market, 6701 Burnet Rd, 512-454-1002; North Loop Activity Center, 2300 North Loop, 512-458-9052

Public Transportation: Capital Metro, www.metro.org; *Bus*: 3, 19, 151, 338, 982, 983, 987; *UT Shuttle*: FW, ER, PRC

WEST AUSTIN

West Austin is home to many of the city's wealthiest residents. Some of the newest and most upscale neighborhoods are located here. It is situated across from the Colorado River and Lake Austin, whose natural boundary buffers West Austin from the rest of the city. The area's mansions and luxury homes are designed to take advantage of the gorgeous hilly landscape and lakeside views. Highly rated golf courses, primarily located within neighborhoods, abound here. Like Northwest Austin, it also has steep hills, canyons, and exposed limestone cliffs. In fact, the hills in West Austin are probably higher and steeper than in Northwest Austin.

TRAVIS COUNTRY, BARTON CREEK, AND RIVERPLACE

TRAVIS COUNTRY

Boundaries: North: Barton Creek Greenbelt; East: MoPac; South: Southwest Pkwy; West: undeveloped land

Located north of Southwest Parkway and west of MoPac, this master-planned community is an example of the old and the new coming together. Initially developed in the 1970s, construction leveled off during the real estate bust of the 1980s, but picked up again during the tech boom of the late 1990s. There are single-family residential homes, condos, and garden homes. This suburban community is far enough away from the city to enjoy the beauty of the natural landscape in the aquifer zone, but is actually very close to central Austin.

BARTON CREEK

Boundaries: (roughly) North: Barton Creek; East: Barton Creek and Travis Country neighborhood; South: Southwest Pkwy; West: undeveloped land

The Barton Creek area is an environmentally important zone that contains some of Austin's most important natural resources. It is located within the Edwards Aquifer Zone, whose underground bedrock acts as nature's filtration system for rain water and runoff water. Underground water from the Edwards Aquifer Zone provides water for large parts of central Texas. The preserve also contains many species of plants and animals that are endangered, such as the Golden Cheeked Warbler, the Barton Springs Salamander, and the Black Capped Verio. Development here has always been a contentious issue between environmentalists and developers. Nevertheless, both parties recognize the significance of preserving Barton Creek's sensitive landscape. Buyers love the gorgeous vistas of the tree-covered hills that stretch out into the horizon. Beautiful views like these are hard to beat and boost property prices. As a result, the neighborhoods and subdivisions nestled in the trees and hills of the region have been built so that the beauty of the landscape is preserved. Private land has been donated for the Barton Creek Nature Preserve. Driving along Highway 290, the major freeway into the area, you can see limestone cliffs exposed along parts of the highway.

Barton Creek is one of Austin's most prestigious residential areas and the wealthiest area in the city. Many luxury homes and golf courses are located here. Three championship golf courses designed by PGA pros Tom Fazio, Arnold Palmer, and Ben Crenshaw are located within Barton Creek Country Club. In addition, a lavish spa and resort is located inside Barton Creek.

Barton Creek contains the following neighborhoods and subdivisions:
- **Barton View** was developed in the late 1950s in the beautiful natural surroundings next to the pristine Barton Creek Wilderness Park, along Highway 290.
- **Barton Creek Bluffs** has an estimated 34 homes between Southwest Parkway, FM 2244, and Highway 71.
- **Barton Creek Estates** is a haven for the wealthy. This neighborhood features million dollar homes. One of its most prestigious subdivisions is Escala, which is adjacent to the Fazio Canyons Golf Course. Escala homes are perched on the hilltop that offers vistas of Austin, the surrounding Hill Country, and Barton Creek Preserve.
- **Barton Creek North** is a collection of 11 gated communities located next to the Barton Creek Country Club.
- **Barton Creek West**; developed in the 1980s, this upscale community features homes in the $400,000 to million dollar range.

River Place

Boundaries: North: FM 2222; East: Westminster Glen; South: Lake Austin; West: Balcones Canyonland Preserve

River Place is luxury-living on the waterfront in a quiet, tranquil and isolated area. This beautiful master-planned, waterfront/country club community is one of the few residential neighborhoods in Austin with lots that have direct access to Lake Austin. Some portions of the neighborhood have private boat slips. In addition, half of the land in River Place has been set aside for a nature preserve. Developed in the 1990s, River Place is located across from the 3M facility and built into the hills. Homes are perched high on the hills, providing residents spectacular and amazing views of the surrounding landscape, including Lake Austin.

Several other recently constructed neighborhoods similar in concept to River Place are located nearby. Residential communities like **City Place**, **Grandview**, and **Jester**, located near River Place along FM 2222, are options to look into for those who like the layout or surrounding landscape of River Place.

Web Sites: www.ci.austin.tx.us, www.bartoncreekliving.com, www.bartoncreeknorth. com, www.traviscountrywest.org, www.traviscountry.com

Area Code: 512

Zip Codes: 78735, 78730

Post Office: Oak Hill Station, 6104 Old Fredericksburg Rd; Chimney Corners Station, 3575 Far West Blvd

Police Department: Travis County Sheriff, www.tcsheriff.org, 512-974-0845

Emergency Hospital: South Austin Hospital, www.southaustinhospital.com, 901 W Ben White Blvd, 512-447-221

Public Education: Austin Independent School District, www.austin.isd.tenet.edu, 1111 W 6th St, 512-414-1700; Eanes Independent School District, www.eanes.k12.tx.us, 601 Camp Craft Rd, 512-732-9000

Community Publications: *Austin American-Statesman*, www.statesman.com; *Austin Chronicle*, www.austinchronicle.com; *Austin Business Journal*, www.bizjournals. com/austin

Community Resources: Barton Creek Wilderness Park, 2631 S Capitol of Texas Hwy; Lost Creek MUD Office, http://lostcreekmud.org, 1305 Quaker Ridge, 512-327-6243

VILLAGE OF BEE CAVE

Boundaries: North: Lake Austin; East: Loop 360; South: Barton Creek Tributary/Barton Creek Blvd/Lost Creek Blvd; West: Village of Bee Cave

Bee Cave was named by early settlers for a large cave of wild bees that was discovered in the area. This community approximately 20 miles west of Austin, along Texas Highway 71, has become increasingly popular over the years. One of the reasons is its location along RM 620, Texas Highway 71, and FM 2244 (Bee Cave Road), which provide convenient access to major tech and other employers in northwest Austin. In addition, Lake Travis is located nearby for those who want to enjoy the lakefront or recreational water sports. Perhaps the biggest draw is its secluded country charm and lovely tranquil surroundings.

Bee Cave contains a mix of new and established residential neighborhoods and subdivisions, including older neighborhoods and subdivisions such as Lost Creek, luxurious Rob Roy, Cuernavaca, Austin Lake Hills, and Barton Creek West, and newer ones such as The Uplands, Lake Pointe, and The Homestead. In general, it is a high-income community, though plenty of non-wealthy individuals have lived here long before it became a popular residential community.

One of the more well known neighborhoods in Bee Cave is Spanish Oaks. Located next to a beautiful nature preserve, this master-planned community was designed to blend in with the surrounding landscape, which includes terraced limestone hills that in certain sections reveal natural spring water seeping through the rocky crevices into the canyon. At the heart of this private, gated golf course community is the Spanish Oaks Golf Club. Luxury homes on large lots surround the golf course. The idea was to build an upscale lifestyle while providing the security and atmosphere of a small town community, but still near the conveniences of the city. This unique community attracts various individuals and families.

Web Sites: www.ci.bee-cave.tx.us, www.spanish-oaks.com

Area Code: 512

Zip Codes: 78736, 78738

Post Office: Lake Travis Station, 2110 Ranch Rd 620 S, Lakeway

Police Department: Bee Cave Police Department, 13333-A Hwy 71 W, Bee Cave, 512-767-6650

Emergency Hospitals: South Austin Hospital, www.southaustinhospital.com, 901 W Ben White Blvd, 512-447-2211; St. Davids Pavilion, www.stdavidspavilion.com, 1025 E 32nd St, 512-867-5800

Library: Bee Cave Public Library, 13333-A Hwy 71 W, Bee Cave, 512-767-6620

Public Education: Eanes Independent School District, www.eanes.k12.tx.us, 601 Camp Craft Rd, 512-732-9000; Lake Travis Independent School District, www.laketravis.txed.net, 3322 Ranch Rd 620 S, 512- 533-6000

Community Publication: *Austin American-Statesman*, www.statesman.com

Community Resource: Lake Travis Chamber of Commerce, www.laketravischamber.com, 1415 RR 620 S, Lakeway, 512-263-5833

WESTLAKE HILLS AND ROLLINGWOOD

Boundaries: WESTLAKE HILLS: North: Bee Creek; East: Colorado River and Bee Creek; South: Rollingwood city limits; West: Capital of Texas Hwy (Loop 360); ROLLINGWOOD: North: Austin city limits; East: Austin city limits and Zilker Park; South: Austin city limits; West: Austin and Westlake Hills city limits

Westlake Hills, often referred to as just Westlake, is one of Austin's most prestigious and wealthy communities. Located on Farm Road 2244, six miles west of downtown Austin, this fairly new community was founded and incorporated in the 1950s. This bedroom community is situated in one of the most scenic landscapes of the Austin area. Residents know what a natural treasure they have and are committed to preserving the rural environment. Though many other Austin neighborhoods are also passionate about guarding the surrounding natural environment, Westlake is probably the most successful neighborhood in that regard. A drive through the community and it seems as if you have left the Austin area and are out in the country. Undulating green hills stretch out across the winding roads, some parts of which are bordered by limestone cliffs. Leafy trees and green vegetation surround the neighborhoods. Each home here is unique, varying in style and size, and is usually tucked away behind trees or set back from the street. Most of the residents here are families, who choose Westlake mainly for its public schools but also because of its beautiful and highly desirable location.

Next door to Westlake, **Rollingwood** is another wealthy West Austin community, though not as well known as Westlake. It was incorporated in the 1960s and also contains homes with differing architectural styles.

Web Sites: www.westlakehills.org, www.cityofrollingwood.com

Zip Code: 78746

Post Office: Westlake Station, 3201 Bee Cave Rd, Suite 120

Police Department: Westlake Hills Police Department, 911 Westlake Dr, 512-327-1195

Emergency Hospitals: St. David's Pavilion, www.stdavidspavilion.com, 1025 E 32nd St, 512-867-5800; South Austin Hospital, www.southaustinhospital.com, 901 W Ben White Blvd, 512-447-2211; Seton Medical Center, www.seton.net, 1201 W 38th St, 512-324-1000; Brackenridge Hospital, www.seton.net, 601 E 15th St, 512-324-7000

Library: Westbank Community Library, www.westbank.lib.tx.us, 1309 Westbank Dr, 512-327-3045

Public Education: Eanes Independent School District, www.eanes.k12.tx.us, 601 Camp Craft Rd, 512-732-9000

Community Publication: *Westlake Picayune*

Community Resources: Westlake City Hall, 911 Westlake Dr, 512-327-3628; Rollingwood City Hall, 403 Nixon Dr, 512-327-1838; Westlake Chamber of Commerce, www.westlakechamber.com, P.O. Box 160216, Austin, 78716, 512-306-0023; Wild Basin Wilderness Preserve, 805 N Capital of Texas Hwy, 512-327-7622

SOUTHWEST AUSTIN

Southwest Austin is roughly the area bounded by US Highway 290 on the north, I-35 on the east, Slaughter Lane on the south, and MoPac on the east. The neighborhoods here are generally suburban in character. They are quiet family-oriented places where parents can raise their children. What distinguishes the neighborhoods here is the pristine wilderness that surrounds them. Deer, limestone cliffs, trees, birds, and other wildlife are abundant in this once rural area. It is also located in the sensitive Edwards Aquifer Zone, which provides water for large populations in Central Texas. Residents are vocal, even passionate, in their protection of the area's natural treasures and quality of life.

Southwest Austin contains numerous single-family residential neighborhoods and subdivisions that offer homes in varying price ranges. These are typically new large-scale developments constructed by major corporate homebuilders. Neighborhoods are usually divided into subdivisions based on price range. A community pool, playground, or park is usually designed into the residential area. Many of the neighborhoods in Southwest Austin were built in the last 10 years and are fairly new. In some areas there is still new home construction. The homes here are more affordable than in South Austin and some make great starter homes.

The following are some of the most well-known communities and neighborhoods in Southwest Austin:

OAK HILL

Boundaries: North: Southwest Pkwy; East: Brodie Ln; South: Travis County line; West: US 290/Circle Dr

Originally a small town outside Austin on U.S. Highway 290 and Williamson Creek, Oak Hill is now an Austin suburb. It was settled as early as the 1860s and called Live Oak Springs and then Shiloh, which is now the name of another southwest Austin neighborhood. The community is composed of many neighborhoods, most of them fairly new. Many of the residents work at the nearby Motorola plant. Housing here is affordable and near many outdoor recreational spots such as the Barton Creek greenbelt. In addition, the community is located just minutes from rural areas.

Oak Hill neighborhoods and subdivisions include:

- **Western Oaks**, a small village west of MoPac and off Davis Ln before it was annexed in 1997 by Austin. A significant area in this subdivision is the Karst Preserve, a tract of land that has been protected because of its sinkholes and caves that are a vital part of the aquifer system.
- **Southland Oaks**, located at Brodie Ln and Frate Barker Rd.
- **Southview Estates**, off US Highway 290.
- **Lewis Mountain Ranch**; described as country-in-the-city-living, this wealthy neighborhood includes estates and mansions valued over $500,000.
- **Granada**, along US Hwy 290 on the edge of town, includes the Granada Hills, Granada Estates, and Granada Oaks subdivisions.
- **Geneva Estates** features approximately 72 homes in the Hwy 290 Circle Dr area.
- **Shady Hollow**; located between El Dorado Trail on the south, Doe Run on the east, Squirrel Hollow on the north, and Lost Oasis Hollow on the west, this is an older neighborhood that was built in the early 1980s. Some like this neighborhood because of its good public high schools, large yards, and shady trees.
- **Blue Hills Estates**; approximately 28 homes off Thomas Springs Rd.
- **Scenic Brook**; located off of Circle Dr.
- **Ridge at Thomas Springs**; between Hwy 71 West and Circle Dr.

- **Bee Caves Road**; bounded by Cobblestone Dr to the east and Sunset Ridge to the west.
- **West Park**; located on FM 1826 at US Hwy 290 West, in a wooded area adjacent to ACC between Scenic Brook and Hwy 290.
- **West Creek**; North: US Hwy 290 West; South: William Cannon Dr; East: Westcreek Dr/White Elm Dr/Yellow Rose Trail; West: Steer Trail/Fair Valley Trail
- **Arroyo Doble**; Bear Creek Park, Hillcrest, Legend Oaks, Legends Park, Onion Creek Meadows, The Hielschers
- **Oak Plantation**; north of Davis and west of Brodie Ln

Deer Park at Maple Run

A small, quiet master-planned community in Southwest Austin at the corner of MoPac and Slaughter Lane, this is the typical suburban, kid-friendly neighborhood. The homes are large with well-tended common areas, built primarily in the 1990s by national homebuilders Kaufman and Broad (K&B).

Sendera

East of Mopac and Slaughter Lane, Sendera contains the subdivisions of Sendera Oaks, Sendera Glen, and Sendera Place. Developed between 1997 and 2003, it contains a community pool and playground for children.

Circle C

Boundaries: North: Davis Ln; East: Brodie Ln; South: just past Hwy 45; West: FM 1826

Circle C is perhaps the most well known master-planned community because it was also the first one in Austin. The suburban neighborhood was controversial when it was first proposed in the 1980s. It pitted environmentalists against developers because of its location in the sensitive aquifer zone. To their credit, the developers have preserved the hundred-year-old oak trees and incorporated much of the area's green terrain. Circle C contains large, two-story brick homes, some with pretentiously grand facades that are typical of the new houses being built by major homebuilders. There are also smaller garden homes with no yards, and condos. Circle C is pretty much a self-contained community with its own soccer complex, tennis courts, golf course, and Olympic-sized swimming pool.

Web Sites: www.lewismountainranch.com, www.ohan.org, www.granadahoa.org, www. deerparkhoa.org, www.ci.austin.tx.us
Area Code: 512
Zip Codes: 78735, 78748, 78749, 78739
Post Office: Oak Hill Station, 6104 Old Fredericksburg Rd

Police Precinct: Austin Police Department, Southwest Area Command, 512-974-8100
Emergency Hospital: Seton Southwest Medical Center, www.seton.net, 7900 FM
     1826, 512-324-9000
Library: Hampton Branch at Oak Hill, 5125 Convict Hill Rd, 512-892-6680
Adult Education: Austin Community College, Pinnacle Campus, www.austincc.edu,
     7748 Hwy 290 W, 512-223-8001
Public Education: Austin Independent School District, www.austin.isd.tenet.edu, 1111
     W 6th St, 512-414-1700
Community Publications: *Austin American-Statesman,* www.statesman.com; *Austin
     Chronicle,* www.austinchronicle.com; *Austin Business Journal,* www.bizjournals.
     com/austin
Community Resources: Karst Preserve and Blowing Sink Park, www.bseacd.org/
     western_oaks.htm, 3900 Deer Ln; Slaughter Creek Veloway and Slaughter Creek
     Metropolitan Park and Southwest Soccer Complex, 6401 W Slaughter Ln; Dick
     Nichols District Park, 8011 Beckett Rd; Oak Hill Community Health Center (West
     Rural), 8656-A Hwy 71 W, Suite C, 512-854-2170
Public Transportation: Capital Metro, www.capmetro.org; *Bus:* 171, 333

OUTLYING COMMUNITIES

Two small bedroom communities right outside of Austin provide country
living for those looking for the peace, charm, and safety of a small town.

Village of San Leanna
The tiny village of San Leanna covers only .4 square miles. It is home to
fewer than 400 mostly upper-middle-income families. It originally began
in the 1950s as a suburb 10 miles south of Austin, but incorporated itself
in the 1970s. San Leanna's charming single-family residences create a
small village atmosphere. The village is located along the southernmost
edge of Austin and surrounded by countryside on its three other borders.
FM 1626 connects to I-35, which provides convenient access to other
parts of Austin. However, I-35 during rush hour can be quite congested.

Manchaca
This unincorporated community 10 miles southwest of Austin experienced
development in the 1980s that brought growth and new residents. Its
approximately 4,000-plus residents reside on farm houses in the country
or in residential neighborhoods with homes of various sizes and styles.
Several of the homes are recently constructed, having been built in the
last 10 to 15 years.

EAST AUSTIN

Boundaries: North: intersection of Airport Blvd and I-35; East: Airport
Blvd; South: Town Lake; West: I-35

East Austin is an ethnically and culturally diverse part of the city that is home to the city's Hispanic and African-American communities. It has a rich heritage with many restaurants, local shops, and commercial enterprises. Whether it is a food store that is located within walking distance of residential areas or an establishment that provides services in Spanish, the businesses here are a part of the community. Several heavy manufacturing industries and the historically black Huston-Tillotson College are also located here. East Austin has had a reputation as a sketchy part of town.

As Austin has grown, the east side has become an attractive option because of its proximity to downtown and the University of Texas. Many developers see potential in an area that once attracted few homebuyers. Several new neighborhoods and subdivisions have gone up. It is not only new subdivisions that are attracting attention; older neighborhoods with historic homes are also garnering looks from potential buyers. In some instances, buyers are acquiring older residences as investment property, renovating and renting it out, or reselling it for a profit. New homes here are typically bought by young couples as starter homes. The increased interest in East Austin houses and apartments have boosted property values and rent, pricing out long-time residents and those with modest means. It has also meant the gentrification of a part of town that has an established sense of community and identity.

One of the up-and-coming areas in East Austin is **Govalle**. It is bounded roughly by Oak Springs to the north, Airport Blvd to the east, Town Lake to the south, and Webberville to the west. This neighborhood is an older, neglected neighborhood on the verge of revitalization. It is quite drab in some areas with warehouses located across from residential areas. However, some have found that its location near downtown and affordable housing makes it the perfect place to set up shop. Art galleries, nonprofit organizations, art studios, and a theater have all opened up on Tillery. The city's alternative weekly newspaper even named Govalle Austin's "Best New Bohemia" in 1994.

Riverside
The Riverside area is best known for the huge apartment complexes that cater to University of Texas and Austin Community College students. Though this part of town lacks the character and vitality of the central campus area, it offers cheaper rent and more spacious accommodations. Besides a few strip shopping centers in the area, there are few other notable structures in this neighborhood because most of it is undeveloped land. Riverside is mostly a low-income area that also features condominiums, government housing, and a few single-family residential homes. There are many outdoor recreational facilities such as the Pleasant Valley District Park, Colorado River Greenbelt, and a softball complex near Town Lake.

Web Site: www.ci.austin.tx.us
Area Code: 512
Zip Codes: 78702, 78722, 78741, 78617

Post Offices: Southeast Station, 4516 Burleson Rd; Del Valle, 2883 Hwy 71 E Del Valle; East Austin Station, 1914 E 6th St

Police Precinct: Austin Police Department: Central East Area Command, 512-974-5900, Southeast Area Command, 512-974-8201

Emergency Hospital: Brackenridge Hospital, www.seton.net, 601 E 15th St, 512-324-7000

Libraries: Austin Public Library: Terrazas Branch, 1105 E Cesar Chavez St, 512-472-7312; Cepeda Branch, 651 N Pleasant Valley Rd, 512-974-7372; Carver Branch, 1161 Angelina, 512-974-1010; Oak Springs Branch, 3101 Oak Springs Dr, 512-926-4453; Daniel E. Ruiz Branch, 1600 Grove Blvd, 512-974-7500

Adult Education: Austin Community College–Eastview Campus, www.austincc.edu/evc, 3401 Webberville Rd, 512-223-5188; Huston-Tillotson College, www.htu.edu, 900 Chicon St, 512-505-3000; Austin Community College – Riverside Campus, www.austincc.edu, 1020 Grove Blvd, 512-223-6000

Public Education: Austin Independent School District, www.austin.isd.tenet.edu, 1111 W 6th St, Austin, 512-414-1700

Community Publications: *Austin American-Statesman,* www.statesman.com; *Austin Chronicle,* www.austinchronicle.com; *Austin Business Journal,* www.bizjournals.com/austin

Community Resources: City Hall, 500 E Cesar Chavez St, 512-482-9407; East Austin Community Health Clinic, 211 Comal St, 512-972-4322; Rosewood-Zaragosa Community Health Clinic, 2802 Webberville Rd, 512-972-4792; Pan American Recreation Center, 2100 E Third, 512-476-9193; Metz Recreation Center, 2407 Canterbury St, 512-478-8716; Rosewood Recreation Center, 1182 N Pleasant Valley Rd, 512-472-6838; Pleasant Valley Sports Complex, 517 S Pleasant Valley; Ron Guerrero Colorado River Park, 8200 Grove Dr; Kreig Field Complex, 515 S Pleasant Valley; Montopolis Recreation Center and Park, 1200 Montopolis Dr, 512-385-5931

Public Transportation: Capital Metro, www.capmetro.org; *Bus:* 2, 4, 5, 6, 17, 18, 20, 21, 22, 26, 27, 37, 44, 100, 110, 127, 135, 137, 182, 300, 320, 331, 350, 411, 482, 486, 490, 499; *UT Shuttle:* NR, CP, BD, PL, DF, CR, PL, LS, NR, CP, BD, WL

DELWOOD, CHERRYWOOD, UNIVERSITY HILLS/WINDSOR PARK

Boundaries: DELWOOD (roughly): North: Hwy 290; East: Manor Rd; South: Manor Rd; West: Airport Blvd and I-35; CHERRYWOOD: North: Wilshire Blvd; East: Airport Blvd; South: Manor Rd; West: I-35; UNIVERSITY HILLS/WINDSOR PARK: Boundaries (collectively): North: US Hwy 290; East: US Hwy 183; South: 51st St; West: I-35

Delwood is a large neighborhood in East Austin that is composed of Delwood, Delwood II, Delwood III, and Delwood IV. The original Delwood stretches from 51st Street South to East 38th Street. It is known for magnificent ancient oaks and spacious yards.

Delwood II also has many large, beautiful trees. It is bounded by the old Mueller Airport to the north and to the east, Airport Blvd to the south, and I-35 to the west. The neighborhood contains remodeled post–World War II homes and an apartment complex. Residents here are a diverse group of young families and old-time homeowners of varied backgrounds. North of 51st Street, between Cameron and Berkman, is Delwood IV. It attracts mainly professionals who work near downtown.

The original Delwood is adjacent to the **Cherrywood** neighborhood, which includes the **French Place** subdivision, located between East 38th and 26th streets. Both Delwood and French Place have similar home prices and are popular with downtown professionals and individuals who want to be close to the University of Texas. Developed in the 1940s, French Place is one of Austin's more established neighborhoods, so homes here are relatively small, but in good condition. There are many old, eclectic homes that are colorfully painted with oddly shaped doorways. Most are two-bedroom, one-bath homes with wood flooring that are generally seen by many as good starter homes. In general, the neighborhood has a charming intown atmosphere. It attracts residents of diverse backgrounds and all ages. French Place's location near central Austin and its unique progressive atmosphere have made it an attractive residential area.

Cherrywood also includes the pricey **Wilshire Woods** subdivision, just off Airport Blvd. The area is full of lovely shaded and expansive yards.

From 51st to US Highway 290 is the neighborhood of **Windsor Park/ University Hills**. Homes here were built mainly during the 1960s and are more affordable than Delwood or French Place. This neighborhood is ideal for first-time buyers looking for a starter home.

Web Sites: www.ci.austin.tx.us, www.uhwpnp.info, www.delwood2.org, www. cherrywood.org, www.main.org/wwd1

Area Code: 512

Zip Codes: 78722, 78723

Post Offices: North Austin Station, 4300 Speedway, 512-453-2785; Northeast Austin Station, 900 Blackson Ave

Police Precinct: Austin Police Department, Central East Area Command, 512- 974-5900

Emergency Hospital: Brackenridge Hospital, www.seton.net, 601 E 15th St, 512-324-7000

Public Education: Austin Independent School District, www.austin.isd.tenet.edu, 1111 W 6th St, 512-414-1700

Library: Austin Public Library, University Hills Branch, 4721 Loyola Ln, 512-929-0551

Community Publications: *Austin American-Statesman*, www.statesman.com; *Austin Chronicle*, www.austinchronicle.com; *Austin Business Journal*, www.bizjournals. com/austin

Community Resources: City Hall, 500 E Cesar Chavez St, 512-482-9407; Dottie Jordan Recreation Center, 2803 Loyola Ln, 512-926-3491

Public Transportation: Capital Metro, www.capmetro.org; *Bus:* 23, 26, 37, 137, 161, 300, 320, 485, 499, 990; *UT Shuttle:* CR

SOUTH AUSTIN

South Austin is the area south of the Colorado River that is bounded by the lake on the north, I-35 on the east, Ben White Blvd on the south, and

Barton Creek on the west. It is not just a geographic location but refers to a specific community with a strong identity. Back in the 1980s, before the influx of out-of-towners and money changed Austin, its unique character was more pronounced. For many years South Austin was defined as that part of the city where an odd mix of hippies, Bubbas, blue-collar workers, and Hispanics lived side by side. South Austin residents were typically of moderate income and lower in economic status than residents on the other side of the Colorado River. The general stereotype was that South Austin was blue collar and North Austin was white collar professionals. These differences created a friendly rivalry between South and North Austin, though it has been much diluted with the growth of the city and the arrival of new residents. The high point of this rivalry occurred in the 1980s, when the two sides decided to settle their differences through a tug of war contest along the banks of Town Lake. Hundreds of spectators showed up on the north and south banks of the lake to witness the north side yuppies battle the south side Bubbas by pulling on a giant rope that spanned the width of the river.

South Austin residents have been stereotyped as odd and eccentric—and proud of it. The predominant zip code for the area, 78704, is immortalized on a popular bumper sticker which best sums up this community: "78704—more than a zip code, a way of life." Though it is becoming increasingly gentrified, there are still traces of South Austin's offbeat character, as it continues to be a more bohemian, funky, alternative, and unconventional part of the city, attracting artistic types—the ones who like to make art out of recycled junk—activists, and just plain "weird" people. Many of the homes here are no longer affordable for many moderate-income residents. Its proximity to downtown has attracted many professionals, and homes here can cost as much as $200,000, which is comparable to homes in desirable north Austin neighborhoods. New trendy condos, townhomes, and apartments have sprung up alongside gourmet retailers like Central Market, while many of the residents have moved to more affordable accommodations in north Austin. Today, you are just as likely to find a yuppie consuming organic vegetarian cuisine as you are an aging hippie protesting the war (pick any war).

TRAVIS HEIGHTS/BOULDIN

Boundaries: TRAVIS HEIGHTS: North: Riverside Dr; East: I-35; South: Oltorf; West: South Congress Ave; BOULDIN: North: Barton Springs; East: South Congress; South: West Oltorf; West: S Lamar

Once you cross the bridge over Town Lake into South Austin, it seems less densely populated. Most of the population resides in Travis Heights and Bouldin, historic communities whose homes are in high demand because of their proximity to downtown and other attractions. The neighborhoods contain single-family residential homes that cost in the upper price range, multi-family units, and more modest accommodations that attract professionals and St. Edwards University students. The average home in **Travis Heights** is a small two-bedroom, one-bath bungalow with a brick or stone exterior that costs around $275,000. Most of the backyards are large, which have enabled many residents to expand their homes. There are also a few mansions in the western section of the neighborhood known as **Fairview Park**. It was named for the "fair view" of the city from the bluffs of the riverbank and was the first subdivision in Austin.

People are attracted to Travis Heights not only for its great location, but also for its quaint charm and hilly terrain surrounded by plenty of majestic and mature trees. The neighborhood is the site of some of the oldest live oak trees in Austin. Homes here are as distinct and unique as its residents: a diverse mix of families, artists, actors, professionals, and school teachers. Those who find a home here have the advantage or disadvantage, depending on the perspective, of living near some of the city's larger performance venues: Auditorium Shores, City Coliseum, and Palmer Auditorium.

Bouldin is located immediately west of Travis Heights. The two adjoining neighborhoods are divided by South Congress Avenue, which has great, quirky streetfront shops and restaurants. On the first Thursday of every month, shops stay open until 10 p.m. and hold events and activities. Homes here vary in size and style and do not prescribe to any specific architectural design. The houses here are in high demand because of its location near downtown. Prices here are similar to homes in the Travis Heights neighborhood. Bouldin also offers duplexes, townhomes, and apartments that are popular with university students. There are many parks, greenbelts, and a creek that runs through the neighborhood.

ZILKER AND BARTON HILLS

ZILKER and BARTON HILLS: Collective Boundaries: North: Town Lake; East: Union Pacific railroad; South: Loop 360; West: Barton Creek; DAWSON: North: Oltorf St; East: South Congress Ave; South: Ben White Blvd; West: South 1st St; GALINDO: North: Oltorf; East: South 1st St; South: Ben White Blvd; West: Union Pacific railroad

Zilker is best known for the park that is named after this neighborhood. The park contains the botanical gardens and even prehistoric dinosaur footprints. However, the most popular attraction in the park is the Barton Springs Pool. The pool is actually a natural spring with a natural rock and gravel bottom. It is larger than the average neighborhood pool, extending 900 feet. Barton Springs is by far the most popular swimming spot in the city. It is especially crowded during the hot Texas summers when residents look forward to dipping in naturally cold spring waters that constantly average 68 degrees. **Zilker Park** is located in the northern half of the neighborhood historically known as Barton Heights. It contains many plain homes with a few large estates between some of the smaller homes. Some of the homes in this neighborhood are colorfully painted, eschewing the muted earth tones that are found in newer developments around Austin. Residents here are an eclectic mix of artists, musicians, authors, political activists, families, and professionals who represent diverse racial backgrounds, ethnicities, and socio-economic levels. With all the changes occurring in Austin, Zilker is the neighborhood that still has that quirky South Austin vibe.

Barton Hills is located to the west of Zilker. This quiet neighborhood is located along Barton Creek and isolated from the commercial areas of South Austin. Unlike the other neighborhoods in South Austin, Barton Hills is rather average. You probably will not find too many unusual characters here. It is more of a family-oriented residential neighborhood where a playground is more likely to be spotted than an art piece created by the homeowner. Tree-covered hills and winding roads add natural beauty to Barton Hills. Its location near downtown, Barton Springs, and Zilker Park enhances its appeal. Home construction in Barton Hills spans from the 1940s to the 1980s, which has resulted in a variety of sizes and styles. Though most homes cost between $200,000 and $500,000, a few can be found around the $100,000 range. Another neighborhood to consider in the area is **Inwood Hills**.

Next to St. Edwards University, **Dawson** has been the target of gentrification and is becoming an increasingly fashionable place. Homes here do not ascribe to any general characteristic because they are all unique in design. The **Galindo** neighborhood borders Dawson and features similar types of housing.

Web Sites: www.srccaustin.com, www.bouldincreek.org, www.ci.austin.tx.us, www.main.org/znaweb, www.dawsonneighborhood.com, www.main.org/bhna

Area Code: 512

Zip Code: 78704

Post Office: South Congress Station, 3903 S Congress Ave

Police Precinct: Austin Police Department, South Central Area Command, 512-974-5700

Emergency Hospital: South Austin Hospital, www.southaustinhospital.com, 901 W Ben White Blvd, 512-447-2211

Library: Twin Oaks Branch, 2301 S. Congress #7, 512-422-4664

Adult Education: St. Edwards University, www.stedwards.edu, 3001 S Congress Ave, 512-448-8400

Public Education: Austin Independent School District, www.austin.isd.tenet.edu, 1111 W 6th St, 512-414-1700

Community Publications: *Austin American-Statesman*, www.statesman.com; *Austin Chronicle*, www.austinchronicle.com; *Austin Business Journal*, www.bizjournals.com/austin

Community Resources: www.firstthursday.info; Seton Kotzmesky Health Center, 3706 S First St, 512-324-4940; South Austin Community Health Center, 2529 S First St,

512- 972-4722; Zilker Metropolitan Park, 2100 Barton Springs Rd; Barton Springs, 2101 Barton Springs Rd (located in Zilker Park), 512-476-9044; South Austin Recreation Center, 1100 Cumberland Rd, 512-444-6601

Public Transportation: Capital Metro, www.capmetro.org; *Bus*: 1L/1M, 14, 16, 27, 103, 101, 110, 127, 142, 328, 331, 338, 411, 470, 483, 484, 935, 984, 986, 987; *UT Shuttle*: PL

FAR SOUTH AUSTIN

Boundaries: (total) North: US Hwy 290 and 71; East: I-35 South: Austin city limits; West: MoPac

Many new neighborhoods and subdivisions have been constructed on the southernmost parts of Austin. They offer affordable housing and a child-friendly environment. The atmosphere here is quiet, relaxed, and in some instances almost like living in the country.

Neighborhoods here include:

- **Battle Bend**: Bounded by St. Elmo on the north, I-35 on the east, E Stassney Ln on the south, and S Congress Ave on the west, this quiet enclave, surrounded by trees and lush greenery, feels more like a small town than a neighborhood that is only minutes from the lights and noise of downtown Austin. Residents are mostly working class families, but also include retirees.
- **Cherry Creek**: This neighborhood is just off Brodie Ln in southwest Austin, between Davis and Slaughter on the north/ south boundary, Manchaca Blvd on the east, and Mopac on the west. Development began in the 1970s and there is still ongoing new home construction. It is a rather large community with several subdivisions. The area is covered by large oaks and winding streets. Several major roads that pass through Cherry Creek provide easy access to other parts of Austin. Homes are relatively affordable at $130,000–$200,000.
- **Tanglewood Forest**: A racially diverse community with many children, it features mostly small, single-story homes and a few duplexes and apartments.
- **Shady Hollow**: This neighborhood is on the edge of Austin in an unincorporated area of the city. Brodie Ln, the only major thoroughfare in and out of the neighborhood, runs through it, with Squirrel Hollow on the north, Doe Run on the east, El Dorado Trail on the south, and Lost Oasis Hollow on the west. The neighborhood was established in the early 1980s and features large front and back yards, and huge trees that shade the neighborhood. It remains popular because of good neighborhood schools and the close community atmosphere. Residents can get to central Austin via Brodie Ln to Mopac,

Slaughter Ln to I-35 or William Cannon Drive, or US 290/ Highway 71.

- **City of Sunset Valley**: Incorporated in 1954, Sunset Valley maintains a small town rural atmosphere while being surrounded by Austin. It is surrounded by Austin on the southern and western side, Barton Creek Wilderness Park on the north, and Westgate Rd on the east.

In addition, new construction of moderately priced homes can be found at these subdivisions:

- **Buckingham Estates**
- **Maple Run**
- **Oak Park**
- **Park Ridge**
- **Silver Stone**
- **Fairway Ridge**

Web Sites: www.ci.austin.tx.us, www.sunsetvalley.org, www.ourshadyhollow.com

Area Code: 512

Zip Codes: 78745, 78748, 78739

Post Offices: Mockingbird Station, 7310 Manchaca Rd; Manchaca Station, 780 W FM 1626, Manchaca

Police Precinct: Austin Police Department, South Central Area Command, 512-974-5700

Emergency Hospital: South Austin Hospital, www.southaustinhospital.com, 901 W Ben White Blvd, 512-447-2211

Libraries: Manchaca Road Branch, 5500 Manchaca Rd, 512-447-6651; Pleasant Hill Branch, 211 E William Cannon Dr, 512-974-3940

Public Education: Austin Independent School District, www.austin.isd.tenet.edu, 1111 W 6th St, 512-414-1700

Community Publications: *Austin American-Statesman*, www.statesman.com; *Austin Chronicle*, www.austinchronicle.com; *Austin Business Journal*, www.bizjournals. com/austin

Community Resources: City Hall, 301 W 2nd St, 512-974-2220; Battle Bend Park, 4600 Suburban Dr; Williamson Greenbelt, 4618 E William Cannon Dr; Stephenson Preserve, 7609 Longview Rd; Dittmar Rec Center, 1009 W Dittmar Rd, 512-441-4777; Mary Moore Searight Metropolitan Park, 907 Slaughter Ln; Circle C Metropolitan Park, 6301 W Slaughter Ln

Public Transportation: Capital Metro, www.capmetro.org; *Bus:* 1L/1M, 3, 10, 16, 101, 103, 110, 127, 201, 311, 328, 331, 333, 335, 338, 436, 451

SOUTHEAST AUSTIN

Boundaries: North: US Hwy 71; East: US Hwy 183; South: Unincorporated/Colton Blvd; West: I-35

Southeast Austin is largely undeveloped open space containing many parks and greenbelts, including one of the area's most scenic parks, McKinney Falls State Park. Though there are single-family residential homes here, southeast Austin contains predominantly apartments and low-income housing, most of which were built in the 1970s. There have been major changes to this part of Austin in the past decade. The new Austin Bergstrom airport opened up next door in 1999. In addition, technology company Advanced Micro Devices opened a facility here in 1995.

Some parts of southeast Austin, such as around Dove Springs, have a run-down look. Neighborhoods here are:

- **Wagon Crossing**
- **Silverstone**
- **Franklin Park**
- **Yarrabee Bend**
- **Williamson Creek**
- **Peppertree Park**
- **Onion Creek Plantation**
- **Kensington Park**
- **Indian Hills**

ONION CREEK

Boundaries: North: River Dunes; East: River Plantation; South: Pinehurst; West: I-35

Onion Creek is a gated country club community located next to I-35 in an unincorporated area outside of Austin. This quiet community provides an ideal relaxing atmosphere. It is surrounded by beautifully landscaped golf courses and 24-hour private security. One would expect exclusive communities like this to be composed of wealthy retirees, but Onion Creek has also attracted young professionals without children who want to be near central Austin and the airport. Of course, the advantage of being in a country club setting is access to a premier golf course. In this case, the Onion Creek Golf Course is actually part of the Senior PGA Tour. One of the biggest advantages of living in Onion Creek is its proximity to spectacular McKinney Falls State Park.

This neighborhood was developed in the 1970s, but contains many new fancy homes. However, there are also some older, modest-looking homes that do not resemble what one thinks of as the typical country club residence.

Web Site: www.ci.austin.tx.us
Area Code: 512
Zip Codes: 78744, 78747
Post Offices: Southeast Station, 4516 Burleson Rd; Manchaca Station, 780 W FM 1626, Manchaca
Police Precinct: Austin Police Department, Southeast Area Command, 512-974-8201
Emergency Hospital: Brackenridge Hospital, www.seton.net, 601 E 15th St, 512-324-7000

Library: Austin Public Library, Southeast Austin Community Public Library, 5803 Nuckols Crossing Rd, 512-462-1452

Public Education: Austin Independent School District, www.austin.isd.tenet.edu, 1111 W 6th St, 512-414-1700; and Del Valle Independent School District, www.del-valle.k12.tx.us, 5301 Ross Rd, Del Valle, 512-386-3000

Community Publications: Austin American-Statesman, www.statesman.com; Austin Chronicle, www.austinchronicle.com; Austin Business Journal, www.bizjournals.com/austin

Community Resources: McKinney Falls State Park, 5808 McKinney Falls Pkwy, 512-243-1643; Dove Springs District Park, 5801 Ainez Dr; Williamson Creek Greenbelt, 4618 E William Cannon Dr; Roy Kizer District Park and Jimmy Clay Golf Course, 5400 Jimmy Clay, 444-0999; Onion Creek District Park, 6900 Onion Creek Dr (contains leash-free dog park); Onion Creek Greenbelt, 7001 Onion Creek Dr; Springfield Park, 6300 E William Cannon; Marble Creek Greenbelt, 6500-6800 William Cannon

Public Transportation: Capital Metro, www.capmetro.org; Bus: 1L/1M, 27, 48G, 101, 127, 201, 311

NORTH AUSTIN

North Austin offers affordable housing options near the high tech corridor and downtown Austin. It is also located near fine shopping and other top-notch amenities. The area is surrounded by naturally beautiful scenery. Many of the new apartment complexes in the northernmost parts of Austin cater to young professionals who mostly work in the tech industry. Families are also moving to North Austin because of the quality school districts in the area.

WELLS BRANCH/SCOFIELD/MILWOOD/WALNUT CREEK

LAMPLIGHT VILLAGE AND GRACY WOODS/GRACY FARMS

Wells Branch is in far north Austin, centrally located near major freeways that provide convenient access to downtown and other parts of the city. This quiet community is also near many of the area's high tech employers and the city's fine shopping districts. Homes were built from the 1980s to the present and their eras of construction are reflected in their size and price. Predictably, older homes are smaller and in the lower price range, starting at around $90,000, while newer homes can measure over 3,000 square feet and cost around $250,000. One of the reasons families choose this neighborhood, aside from its location and affordable housing, is its location within the well-regarded Round Rock School District. Unlike most Austin neighborhoods, water and sewerage are not provided by the city but by a municipal utility district that operates as a political subdivision to provide utility and sewer service by levying property taxes.

Just south of Wells Branch is the large master-planned community of **Scofield**. The neighborhoods here have a suburban character with plenty of convenient shopping nearby, including major retailers such as Super Target, Super Wal-Mart, Kohl's, Home Depot, Lowes, and various chain restaurants. Many of the homes here are fairly new and were constructed between 1992 and 2002 by a handful of national homebuilders. They vary in size from average one-story residences to large two-story homes that can cover up to 4,000 square feet. There are many major employers close by, including Dell, IBM, Samsung, Austin Diagnostic Center, UT Balcones Research Center, National Instruments, and Time Warner.

Within Scofield is the working class neighborhood of **Lamplight Village**. It is bounded by Magazine Street on the north, Wells Branch on the east, West Parmer Lane on the south, and Tomanet Trail on the west. An older neighborhood within a sea of new development, Lamplight Village has been around for about 30 years, dating back to when the area was still a rural spot outside Austin. Now, the neighborhood is part of the city; it was annexed 10 years ago. The homes are, on average, single-story brick homes with the garage featured prominently in front of the house. They are plain and modest compared to homes in the surrounding new subdivisions and neighborhoods such as Scofield, but very affordable, with most of them under $150,000.

Milwood is an older suburban community that dates back to the 1970s. The typical street here contains evenly spaced lots, neatly trimmed lawns, wide winding streets, and cul de sacs. Strip shopping centers occupy some of the area outside of the residential neighborhoods. The average home here is more affordable than in Scofield, though a large part of it has to do with the fact that Milwood homes are generally older and do not have the huge square footage of some Scofield homes. Prospective buyers will mostly find smaller one-story residences that make great starter homes. However, newer residences can be found in the northernmost corner of Milwood, near RM 620. Like Scofield, it attracts families that work near the tech companies. Parmer Lane is a minute or two outside the neighborhood and connects to MoPac, which leads to the high tech corridor.

The **Walnut Creek** area includes the **River Oaks** and Gracy Woods neighborhoods. **Gracy Woods/Gracy Farms** is an ethnically and socio-economically diverse neighborhood. The surrounding greenbelt and mature trees insulate Gracy Woods and create a pleasant, quiet neighborhood atmosphere. Gracy Woods features affordable starter homes in the mid $100,000s that are conveniently located near the major high tech employers and other amenities in the area.

Web Sites: www.wcna-austin.org, www.gracywoods.org, www.main.org/rona, www.main.org/lvana, www.milwoodna.com

Area Code: 512

Zip Codes: 78728, 78727, 78753, 78758

Post Offices: McNeil Station, 14005 McNeil Rd; North Park Station, 1700 W Parmer Ln, Suite 620; Bluebonnet Station, 1822 W Braker Ln; Town North Station, 8557 Research Blvd, Suite 124

Police Department: Austin Police Department, North Central Area Command, 512-974-5500

Emergency Hospital: North Austin Medical Center, www.northaustin.com, 12221 Mopac, 512-901-1000; Round Rock Medical Center, www.roundrockhospital.com, 2400 Round Rock Ave, Round Rock, 512-341-1000

Libraries: Wells Branch Community Library, www.wblibrary.org, 15001 Wells Port Dr, 512-989-3188; Austin Public Library: Milwood Branch, 12500 Amherst Dr, 512-339-2355; Little Walnut Creek Branch, 835 W Rundberg, 512-836-8975

Adult Education: Austin Community College, Northridge Campus, www.austincc.edu, 11928 Stonehollow Dr, 512-223-4000

Public Education: Round Rock Independent School District, www.roundrockisd.org, 1311 Round Rock Ave, Round Rock, 512-464-5000 (Wells Branch); Pflugerville Independent School District, www.pflugervilleisd.net, 1401 W Pecan, 512-594-0000 (Scofield and tiny portion of Wells Branch)

Community Publications: *Austin American-Statesman*, www.statesman.com; *Austin Chronicle*, www.austinchronicle.com; *Austin Business Journal*, www.bizjournals.com/austin

Community Resources: Wells Branch Municipal Utility District, www.wellsbranchmud.com; Wells Branch Community Center, 2106 Klattenhoff; Katherine Fleischer Park, 2106 Klattenhoff; Balcones District Park, 12017 Amherst Dr; Far North Austin Community Health Center, 928 Blackson, 512-972-4170

Public Transportation: Capital Metro, www.capmetro.org; *Bus:* 1M/1L, 142, 174, 240, 243

NORTHEAST AUSTIN

This part of the city, especially in the areas on the outlying parts of town, has experienced a great deal of growth in the past decade. Previously an undeveloped and largely rural area, its untapped land and relatively cheap property prices have attracted the development of new, very affordable to high-income single-family residential homes all the way out to the City of Manor. There are also some horse farms in this quiet, recently settled part of Austin that borders the countryside. In addition, many business parks and companies have built new office space here, especially along Texas Highway 290.

MANOR

Ten years ago, Manor was an unassuming small town six miles outside of Austin along US Highway 290 that most people passing through would not have given much thought to, save for the local high school located along the highway. Even during the 1980s and 1990s, when other cities surrounding Austin were experiencing rapid residential growth and development, Manor remained unaffected. However, in the past decade many new subdivisions, office parks, and other commercial businesses have begun to occupy the area between Manor and Austin. Manor itself has experienced a slight increase in its population. Despite the increasing suburbanization of the area around it, Manor is still a small town, but located near the conveniences of a big city.

Web Site: www.cityofmanor.com

Area Code: 512

Zip Code: 78653

Post Office: Manor Station, 109 Burnet St N, Manor

Police Department: Manor Police Department, 201 E Parsons St, Manor, 512-272-8177

Emergency Hospital: North Austin Medical Center, http://northaustin.com, 12221 Mopac, 512-901-1000

Library: Manor Public Library, www.main.org/mpl, 601 W Carrie Manor St, Manor, 512-278-0882

Public Education: Manor Independent School District, www.manorisd.net, 312 Murray Ave, Manor, 512-278-4000

Community Resources: City Hall, 201 E Parsons St, Manor, 512-272-5555; Manor Chamber of Commerce, www.manorchamberofcommerce.com, 810 Caldwell St # B100, 512-272-5699; Manor Community Health Center, 600 W Carrie-Manor, Manor, 512-272-8881

HARRIS BRANCH, COPPERFIELD/ NORTH OAKS/WOODCLIFF

HARRIS BRANCH

If you are traveling along US Highway 290 into Austin, one of the first neighborhoods you will encounter is Harris Branch. This new residential neighborhood between Austin and Manor was developed in the 1990s. It features brick homes in various sizes that usually cost around $150,000. Its location along US 290 and proximity to technology companies make it an attractive option for individuals seeking affordable housing near work.

COPPERFIELD/NORTH OAKS (WALNUT CREEK AREA)/WOODCLIFF

The **Copperfield** neighborhood is popular with families looking for a very affordable home in a good public school district. At one time it was not as attractive as it is today, but as Austin has grown, more and more people are seeking out neighborhoods like Copperfield. Major employers that have moved into the area, such as Dell Computers, Samsung, and Applied Materials, have also created interest in this neighborhood. The median home price here is about $117,000, which is half the price of the homes closer to town. There have also been several new brick, stone, and masonry homes constructed in recent years.

North Oaks is separated from Copperfield by Walnut Creek to the north. The creek generates fertile soil, which has contributed to the large trees along its banks. This is a quiet neighborhood with winding streets and plenty of affordable housing that was mostly built in the 1960s and 1970s. It is popular with individuals who are employed at nearby technology companies. A drawback to living in North Oaks is that homes here use septic systems instead of a regular sewer line because it is an un-annexed neighborhood. However, it is trying to get annexed by Austin, so that it can receive city services.

Woodcliff is a quiet residential neighborhood located southeast of North Oaks on the other side of Dessau Rd. It is a neighborhood full of winding roads, hills, and trees, that overlooks the Big Walnut Creek Greenbelt to its east.

Other nearby neighborhoods and communities are:

- **Harris Ridge**: Bounded by Dessau Rd on the north, Weatherford Rd to the east, Josh Ridge to the south, and Harris Ridge Blvd to the west. Located in the far northeast corner of Austin at the edge of the city limits, this neighborhood is surrounded by vast amounts of undeveloped land.
- **Dessau**: This community, 11 miles northeast of downtown Austin, is named after a town in Germany.
- **Windermere**: Located in the nearby town of Pflugerville, this typical suburban neighborhood has an active homeowner's association.
- **Chimney Hills**: A small neighborhood right outside the Austin city limits along US Highway 290 and surrounded by open land on the north and east and the Walnut Creek Greenbelt on the west.

Web Sites: www.ci.austin.tx.us, www.main.org/copperfield, www.main.org/chnna
Area Code: 512
Zip Codes: 78752, 78753, 78754
Post Offices: Gmf Austin Station, 8225 Cross Park Dr; Northeast Austin Station, 900 Blackson Ave
Police Precinct: Austin Police Department, Northeast Area Command, 512-974-5500
Emergency Hospitals: North Austin Medical Center, http://northaustin.com, 12221 Mopac, 512-901-1000; Round Rock Medical Center, www.roundrockmedicalcenter. com, 2400 Round Rock Ave, Round Rock, 512-341-1000
Library: Austin Public Library, St. John Branch, 7500 Blessing Ave, 512-974-7570
Public Education: Independent School District, www.pflugervilleisd.net, 1401 W Pecan, Pflugerville, 512-594-0000
Community Publications: *Austin American Statesman*, www.statesman.com; *Austin Chronicle*, www.austinchronicle.com; *Austin Business Journal*, www.bizjournals. com/austin
Community Resources: City Hall, 301 W 2nd St, 3rd Floor, 512-974-2200; Northeast Austin Community Health Center, 7112 Ed Bluestein Blvd, 512-972-4622; Walnut

Creek Metropolitan Park, 12138 N. Lamar Blvd; Big Walnut Creek Greenbelt, 2611 Park Bend Rd
Public Transportation: Capital Metro, www.capmetro.org; *Bus:* 15, 135, 325, 392, 440, 485, 935, 990

PFLUGERVILLE

Incorporated in 1965, the town's name hints at its German heritage, which is strong in central Texas due to the many immigrants who settled in this region during the 1800s. However, current residents come from all over Texas and the United States and represent many heritages and backgrounds. Founded by German settlers in the 1860s, Pflugerville has grown from a town of 4,000 in 1990 to over 26,000 residents today.

Pflugerville is a quiet bedroom community with plenty of open land. In some areas, it feels like the country. Though there are older neighborhoods within the town, large portions of it were recently built by a handful of corporate builders. It is obvious that until recently some areas were undeveloped land or rural areas.

Pflugerville was one of the first communities to rapidly grow during the technology boom years. Hit hard by the tech bust of the 1990s, many homes were put up for sale. Despite the numerous unoccupied homes, new construction continued. Low mortgage rates and an upswing in the economy have helped the housing market here recover. There are currently new homes being built in Pflugerville. Signs with the names of various homebuilders are posted throughout the town to point people in the right direction.

Web Site: www.cityofpflugerville
Area Code: 512
Zip Code: 78660
Post Office: Pflugerville Station, 301 Heatherwilde Blvd, Pflugerville
Police Department: Pflugerville Police Station, 1611 E Pfennig Ln, Pflugerville, 512-251-4004
Emergency Hospital: Seton Pflugerville, www.seton.net, 200 N Heatherwilde Blvd, Pflugerville, 512-324-5350
Library: Pflugerville Community Library, 102 10th St, Pflugerville, 512-251-9185
Public Education: Pflugerville Independent School District, www.pflugervilleisd.net, 1401 W Pecan, Pflugerville, 512-594-0000
Community Publications: *Pflugerville Pflag*
Community Resources: City Hall, 100 E Main St, Pflugerville, 512-990-4363; Greater Pflugerville Chamber of Commerce, www.gpcc.pflugerville.tx.us, 101 S 3rd St, Pflugerville, 512-251-7799; Pflugerville Council of Neighborhood Associations, www.pfcona.org; Pflugerville Community Development Corporation, www.pfdevelopment.com, 100 W Main, Comerica Bank Building, Pflugerville, 512-990-3725; Pflugerville Pfamily Resource Pages, Pflugervillepfamily.com; Pflugerville Community Health Center (Rural), 15822 Foothill Farms Loop, Pflugerville, 512-251-6094

NORTHWEST AUSTIN

Northwest Austin is one of the most beautiful and scenic areas of the city. Tree-covered hills create a blanket of green up and down the landscape that features canyons, winding roads, and exposed limestone rocks that tower over freeways. The area is characteristic of the natural beauty of the Texas Hill Country. A significant deer population resides in the hills and it is not unusual to catch a deer bolting across the street or to see one munching on the front yard. The topography of the area makes it ideal for hiking and there are many trails here for that purpose.

The far northwest part of Austin is also known as Silicon Hills because of the many high tech companies such as IBM, Motorola, 3M, Dell, and other, smaller businesses located here. A downturn in the tech industry in the late 1990s slowed down Austin's economy, but it generally has not reduced the popularity of the housing here. Part of the reason for this is the quality public schools and school districts such as Round Rock. In addition to good schools, northwest Austin offers upscale single-family residences and new high-end apartments and townhomes. This suburban area has easy access to work, shopping, restaurants, and outdoor recreation. Some of Austin's best shopping is in northwest Austin.

BALCONES WEST/CAT MOUNTAIN/NORTH CAT MOUNTAIN/NORTHWEST HILLS

The neighborhoods here are mostly upper-income developments with single-family residential homes, townhomes, duplexes, and apartments. Balcones West/Cat Mountain and Northwest Hills are located about a 10-15 minute drive from downtown and near fine dining and shopping at the Arboretum.

One of the city's most impressive neighborhoods is **Cat Mountain**. Developed in the late 1970s and 1980s, homes here vary from single-story with minimal setbacks from the street to large residences on expansive lots. Cat Mountain homes cost anywhere from over $200,000 to the millions. Some of the houses on the western edge of the neighborhood have great views of the Colorado River and the Loop 360 Bridge. The neighborhood is great for residents with boats due to its proximity to the river. **North Cat Mountain** is separated from Cat Mountain by open land. It has similar environment, homes, and home prices to Cat Mountain.

To the north of Cat Mountain is **Northwest Hills.** Homes here are around $300,000 to $400,000, which is about the same as the average home in Cat Mountain. UT students inhabit most of the apartment complexes on Far West Blvd, which offer more affordable units than near campus. The university bus shuttle stops in front of apartment complexes on Far West Blvd, Hart Lane, and Wood Hollow Drive. **Balcones West** is directly north of Northwest Hills and features homes in the same price range.

THE ARBORETUM/GREAT HILLS/
BALCONES/SPICEWOOD SPRINGS

The **Arboretum** is an affluent area in northwest Austin that is named after a shopping and dining center of the same name. The beautiful landscape that characterizes northwest Austin is even more pronounced here. The hills seem steeper, the trees more abundant, the roads more sharply curving, and the canyons deeper. The Arboretum is known as a prime shopping area. Everything is available here from high end retailers to everyday shops and big box stores. One thing it lacks is an abundance of original and unique stores as can be found in central Austin. You are more likely to find Costco, Best Buy, and Banana Republic than you are a boutique store. Likewise, the dining here, which is mostly concentrated along US-183, is more chain restaurants like Macaroni Grill and Outback Steakhouse than a mom and pop restaurant. However, several local eateries (Brick Oven Pizza, Rudy's Bar-BQ, Poky Joe's Bar-BQ), though franchises, are a departure from the clutter of national chain restaurants on US-183. In this suburban area, the businesses and residences have been well incorporated into the natural surroundings, creating a charming atmosphere.

Great Hills is one of the most attractive and desirable neighborhoods in Austin. Located in the beautiful landscape of northwest Austin, it is also near major freeways that provide easy access to Downtown and other parts of the city. The streets here are wide, smooth, and winding. Power lines are buried underground so canyon views and vistas of the surrounding area are unobstructed. Great Hills is conveniently located near several grocery stores, banks, dry cleaners, movie theaters, and other amenities. In the heart of the neighborhood is the Great Hills Golf Course. There are several large apartment complexes and some townhomes, especially closer to US-183 on Jollyville Rd and Great Hills Trail, where the city bus and university shuttle have stops. Homes here are mostly custom built, two-story traditional-style homes with brick or stone exterior. They start in the upper $200,000s, but typically cost between $320,000 and $450,000. While development began as early as the 1970s, most of the homes were built in the 1980s. The neighborhood continues to develop, but at a much slower pace.

Some of the new and recent home construction is in the area above the Great Hills northern boundary. Jollyville Road contains many large apartment complexes and a few townhomes. Some of the apartments are built on challenging hills and have great canyon views. These are not typical of the older Austin apartments. In general, they tend to be larger complexes that incorporate the surrounding environment into the layout of the complex, resulting in beautiful grounds. Several apartment complexes are designed not merely as a place to live, but also as a lifestyle center with onsite laundromats, tennis courts, basketball courts, pools, hiking trails, picnic areas, and volley pits. They tend to attract professionals and older college students with families. Rents at these higher-end apartments are more expensive, but there has been over-construction of rental units in the city, so some of these may rent for a bargain.

Other subdivisions and neighborhoods in the Great Hills area include the **Mesa Hills/Mesa Park** neighborhood bounded by Duval Rd on the north, MoPac on the east, Braker Lane on the south, and US-183 (Research Blvd) on the west, and the **Balcones Woods** subdivision immediately below Mesa Park.

In **Balcones/Spicewood Springs** the neighborhoods are mostly inhabited by retired individuals, who moved here when these communities first opened in the 1970s. However, young professionals are replacing the retirees, who are moving on to other communities. Nevertheless, the quiet and idyllic landscape, plus its proximity to two golf courses, still attracts retirees. The homes here are usually custom built on large lots. Balcones and Spicewood Springs are located on the western edge of Austin, and include the **Balcones Village, Balcones Greenes, Balcones Hills** and **Balcones Estates** subdivisions.

Web Sites: www.main.org/bca, www.balconeswoods.org, www.northwesthills.org, www. ci.austin.tx.us

Area Code: 512

Zip Codes: 78759, 78731

Post Office: Chimney Corners Station, 3575 Far West Blvd

Police Precinct: Austin Police Department, Northwest Area Command, 512-974-5500

Emergency Hospital: Seton Northwest Hospital, www.seton.net, 11113 Research Blvd, 512-324-6000

Library: Austin Public Library, Old Quarry Branch: 7051 Village Center Dr, 512-345-4435

Public Education: Austin Independent School District, www.austin.isd.tenet.edu, 1111 W 6th St, 512-414-1700

Community Publications: *Austin American-Statesman*, www.statesman.com; *Austin Chronicle*, www.austinchronicle.com; *Austin Business Journal*, www.bizjournals. com/austin

Community Resources: North Cat Mountain Greenbelt, 6704 Cat Creek Trail; Beverly Scheffield Park, 7000 Ardath St

Public Transportation: Capital Metro, www.capmetro.org; *Bus*: 19, 151, 339, 982, 983, 984, 986, 987; *University Shuttle*: PRC, FW

FAR NORTHWEST AUSTIN

In addition to large homes, far northwest Austin has many apartment complexes, some of which are fairly new. The newer complexes command higher rent, especially those in a scenic setting. There is also a fair share of luxury apartments that cater to young professionals who desire spacious accommodations with all the amenities, but are not quite ready to move into a house yet. Stone and masonry exteriors are ubiquitous on buildings, houses, and apartment complexes in this area.

CANYON CREEK

Canyon Creek is a nice quiet neighborhood surrounded by the beautiful scenery of northwest Austin. Highlighting the natural splendor of this area is the Balcones Canyonland Preserve, which borders the eastern part of the neighborhood. It is easy to see why residents here think that this is one of the prettiest neighborhoods in Austin.

This is a family-friendly neighborhood where good schools are a priority for many of the residents. Not to worry, the schools here are some of the best in the city and in the top Round Rock public school district and Leander school district. In addition, residents are only a few minutes' drive away from Silicon Hills, where many of the tech industries, including Dell, 3M, Motorola, and IBM, are located.

Homes here vary from the low $200,000s to $500,000. The neighborhood features a park with a children's playground, junior Olympic swimming pool, volleyball court, tennis court, and basketball court. There is also a baseball diamond, football field, and soccer pitch at Trailhead Park.

Other neighborhoods and subdivisions here are:
- **Glen Lake**
- **Long Canyon**
- **Jester Estates**
- **Barrington Oaks**

AVERY RANCH

This affordable suburban community is geared toward families in differing income brackets. Homes in this master-planned community are divided into several neighborhoods and subdivisions according to price range. Oak trees have been planted to line the streets and to provide a soft edge to the neighborhood's aesthetic appeal. Like many other new residential communities, it has its own recreation center and sports complex. But what really makes it stand out are hiking and biking trails, an 18-hole golf course, and an outdoor amphitheatre.

Web Sites: www.canyoncreeknews.com, canyoncreek.net, www.greathills.org, www.bvshoa.com, www.ci.austin.tx.us, www.main.org/mpna, www.glenlakehoa.org, www.longcanyon.org, www.averyranch.com

Area Code: 512

Zip Codes: 78759, 78726, 78750, 78717

Post Offices: Balcones Station: 11900 Jollyville Rd; Bluebonnet Station, 1822 W Braker Ln; McNeil Station, 14005 McNeil Rd

Police Precinct: Austin Police Department, Northwest Area Command, 512-974-5500

Emergency Hospitals: Seton Northwest Hospital, www.seton.net, 11113 Research Blvd, 512-324-6000; Urgent Care Plus, www.urgentcareplus.com, 12701 Ranch Rd 620, 512-233-1260

Library: Austin Public Library, Spicewood Springs Branch, 8637 Spicewood Springs Rd, 512-258-9070

Public Education: Austin Independent School District, www.austin.isd.tenet.edu, 1111 W 6th St, 512-414-1700 (parts of Great Hills); Round Rock Independent School District, www.roundrockisd.org, 1311 Round Rock Ave, Round Rock, 512-464-5000 (parts of Great Hills, parts of Canyon Creek, Balcones Village/Spicewood Springs, and Avery Ranch); Leander Independent School District, www.leanderisd.org, 512-434-5000 (parts of Canyon Creek and Avery Ranch)

Community Publications: *Austin American-Statesman*, www.statesman.com; *Austin Chronicle*, www.austinchronicle.com; *Austin Business Journal*, www.bizjournals. com/austin

Community Resources: City Hall, 500 E Cesar Chavez St, 512-482-9407; Great Hills Pickfair Community Center, 10904 Pickfair Dr, 512-401-8119; Bull Creek Parks, 6701 Lakewood Dr

Public Transportation: Capital Metro, www.capmetro.org; *Bus*: 19, 151, 383, 392, 983, 984, 986, 987; *University Shuttle*: PRC

WILLIAMSON COUNTY

Williamson County is divided into two geographical regions by the Balcones Escarpment. The western half of the county is part of the Western Plains and has hilly brushland, while the eastern half is part of the Coastal Plains, which is lower in elevation and more flat. Southwestern Williamson County has seen rapid growth in the past 15 years. Most of the development occurred in the 1990s when the technology industry was riding high. Major technology-related companies relocated here, spurring residential and commercial development. Previously a rural area, small towns have turned into bedroom communities and new communities are being created in open land.

CEDAR PARK AND LEANDER

Cedar Park, a bedroom community in southwestern Williamson County, has become one of the fastest growing communities in the Austin area and among the top fastest growing in Texas. Its population has more than tripled from a population of under 10,000 to over 30,000 residents today. Most of the growth occurred during the tech boom of the 1990s. Cedar Park is located near many of the area's technology companies, where many of its residents work. It has a very educated population, with approximately 83% of its residents having attained at least a bachelor's degree. Families are attracted by the affordable homes and public school district, while young professionals choose to live here because of the job opportunities. In addition, retirees also find peaceful and scenic communities like Cedar Park the ideal place to enjoy their retirement.

The typical home here is quite affordable at prices between $130,000 and $150,000, though they can range from $100,000 to over $500,000.

The community also offers many new apartments that vary from basic accommodations to luxury rentals. Other options include condos and townhomes. Cedar Park also has many older neighborhoods primarily near its southern boundaries. Affordable homes and jobs are not the only reason people move to Cedar Park. Some prefer a quiet, laid-back atmosphere where they can spend their free time golfing, trail walking, boating, or engaging in other outdoor activities. Crystal Falls, River Place, Lago Vista Country Club, Highland Lakes Country Club, and Point Venture are all public access golf courses that are located near Cedar Park. Subdivisions here include: **Forest Oak**, **Cypress Creek**, **Cypress Bend**, **Shenandoah**, **Lakeline Oaks**, **Carriage Hills**, **Gann Ranch**, and **Buttercup Creek**.

Though Cedar Park prides itself on its rural atmosphere and some areas still have that country charm, it has become quite developed in the past decade. The area along Highway US 183, a major thoroughfare, is highly developed and looks like any other suburban community. Strip shopping centers, fast food, chains, gas stations, and other conveniences occupy both sides of the highway.

Leander first began as a settlement called Bagdad in the 1850s. It was renamed Leander after the Austin and Northwestern railroad was built in the 1880s and the populations shifted closer to the railroad tracks. Like Cedar Park, Leander is surrounded by natural beauty and tranquil country charm. This community is even more removed from the urban lifestyle than Cedar Park. It sits on the edge of the Hill Country, whose characteristics are reflected in the rolling hills, lakes, deer, and free-roaming wild fowls.

Leander has also grown rapidly in recent years from a small town of a few hundred residents to a bedroom community with a population of approximately 20,000.

Residences here include single-family residential homes, new construction homes, townhomes, and apartments. There are also a few bed and breakfasts that operate in the area.

Leander is less developed than Cedar Park. There is still plenty of open space, which gives the town its country atmosphere. A significant deer population resides in the more rural and suburban areas of Austin, so it is not unusual for residents here to encounter or see deer. One of the best times of the year to witness the beauty of the hill country is in spring. Wildflowers—mostly bluebonnets and Indian paintbrush—turn the surrounding hillside into blankets of red and blue, among other colors. There are many scenic drives in the area, including Leander itself, to view the flowers.

Web Sites: www.ci.cedar-park.tx.us, www.ci.leander.tx.us
Area Code: 512
Zip Codes: 78613, 78641
Post Office: Cedar Park Station, 500 E Whitestone Blvd, Cedar Park; Leander Station, 801 S Hwy 183, Leander

Police Departments: Cedar Park Police Department, 911 Quest Pkwy, Cedar Park, 512-259-3600; Leander Police Department, 200 West Willis St, Leander, 512-528-2800

Emergency Hospital: Round Rock Medical Center, 2400 Round Rock Ave, Round Rock, 512-341-1000

Libraries: Cedar Park Public Library, 550 Discovery Blvd, Cedar Park, 512-259-5353; Leander Public Library, www.leander.lib.tx.us, 1011 South Bagdad Rd, 512-259-5259

Adult Education: Austin Community College – Cypress Creek Campus, 1555 Cypress Creek Rd, Cedar Park, 512-223-2000

Public Education: Leander Independent School District, www.leanderisd.org, 512-434-5000

Community Publications: *Hill Country News*, www.hillcountrynews.com

Community Resources: Cedar Park City Hall, 600 North Bell Blvd, Cedar Park, 512-258-4121; Cedar Park Chamber of Commerce, www.cedarparkchamber.org, 1490 E Whitestone Blvd, Bldg 2, Suite 180, Cedar Park, 512-260-7800; Williamson County, www.wilco.org, 512-943-1100; Leander City Hall, 200 W Willis St, Leander, 512-259-1709; Greater Leander Chamber of Commerce, www.leandercc.org, 103 N Brushy, Leander, 512-259-1907

Public Transportation: Capital Area Rural Transportation (CARTS – door to door service, requires advance appointment); Capital Metro Special Transit Service, www.capmetro.org/riding/sts.asp (for disabled individuals who qualify under the Americans with Disabilities Act)

ROUND ROCK AND GEORGETOWN

The **City of Round Rock** is best known as the corporate headquarters of Dell Computers. Dell and other computer-related industries have contributed to its growth in the last decade from a small town 16 miles outside of Austin to a major bedroom community. Many of the homes and neighborhoods in this city are new construction. One of the main reasons people move here is because of its highly regarded school district. I-35, which passes through Round Rock, provides easy access into Austin. However, be warned that traffic can be heavy near the downtown Austin section of the interstate during rush hour.

Neighborhoods and subdivisions inside Round Rock include:

- **Round Rock West**: an older subdivision established in the late 1970s that is one of the popular neighborhoods here.
- **Vista Oaks**: located off 1431 between I-35 and Parmer Ln, it features mostly brick and stone homes.

Georgetown is perhaps best known for the retirement village, Sun City, located in the far northwestern corner of this city. However, before it was a retirement hot spot and even before it was a bedroom community, Georgetown was a small rural agricultural town with its own long established history and identity. Established in 1848, this historic community is located 25 miles north of Austin along the San Gabriel River. It is the county seat of Williamson County and home to Southwestern University. Like all the other cities in Williamson

County, Georgetown has grown rapidly due to the high tech industry in the northern Austin/Williamson County area. Many of the homes here are new residential developments. They include retirement communities such as Sun City and luxury golf course communities like Cimarron Hills. Georgetown's rural location, surrounded by open land on all sides, provides peaceful and beautiful country living. It is one of the reasons that the city is popular with retirees and snow birds. The city also attracts its fair share of young families looking for an affordable home in a safe, quiet community to raise the kids.

The border between Travis and Williamson County contains several communities that were once small independent towns but have been absorbed into suburbs or neighborhoods of Austin.

- **Anderson Mill**: (more northwest than north) about sixteen miles northwest of Austin in Williamson County. Formerly a small mill town started by Thomas Anderson, It is now a bedroom community of Austin.
- **Jollyville**: a small unincorporated area in southwest Williamson County. It is also the name of a suburban community in north Austin.
- **Cypress Creek**: bounded roughly by Cypress Creek Rd (FM 182) to the north, El Salido Pkwy to the west, and Clay Dr to the east.

Web Sites: www.ci.round-rock.tx.us, www.vistaoaks.org, www.main.org/amna, www.cypresscreekhoa.org, www.georgetown.org

Area Code: 512

Zip Codes: 78664, 78681, 78750, 78729, 78262, 78628, 78626, 78627

Post Offices: Round Rock Station, 2250 Double Creek Dr, Round Rock; Round Rock West Station, 797 Sam Bass Rd, Round Rock; Georgetown Station, 2300 Scenic Dr, Georgetown; Andice Station, 15255 Ranch Rd 2338, Georgetown

Police Departments: Round Rock Police Department, 615 E Palm Valley, Round Rock, 512-218-5500; Williamson County Sheriff's Office, 508 S Rock St, Georgetown, 512-943-1300; Austin Police Department, North Central Area Command, 512-974-5500; Georgetown Police Department, 809 Martin Luther King, Jr., Georgetown, 512-930-3528

Emergency Hospitals: Round Rock Medical Center, www.roundrockhospital.com, 2400 Round Rock Ave, Round Rock, 512-341-1000; Georgetown Healthcare System, 2000 Scenic Dr, Georgetown, 512-943-3000

Libraries: Round Rock Public Library, 216 E Main, Round Rock, 512-218-7000; Georgetown Public Library, www.georgetownpubliclibrary.org, 808 Martin Luther King Jr., Georgetown, 512-930-3551

Adult Education: Southwestern University, www.southwestern.edu, 1001 E University, Georgetown, 512-863-6511; Austin Community College, Round Rock Higher Education Center, 1555 University Blvd, Austin, 512-716-4000; Austin Community College, Georgetown Center-Georgetown High School, 2211 N Austin Ave, Austin, 512-930-0989

Public Education: Round Rock Independent School District, www.roundrockisd.org, 1311 Round Rock Ave, Round Rock, 512-464-5000

Community Publications: *Round Rock Leader*, www.rrleader.com; *Austin American-Statesman*, www.statesman.com

Community Resources: City Hall, 221 E Main, Austin, 512-218-5400; Round Rock Chamber of Commerce, www.roundrockchamber.org, 212 E Main St, Round Rock, 512-255-5805; Neighborhood Association of Southwestern Williamson County, www.naswc.org; Georgetown Chamber of Commerce, www.georgetownchamber.org, 100 Stadium Dr, Georgetown, 512-930-3535

LAKE SOUTH REGION

Around Lake Travis are several small towns and waterfront communities where there has been considerable new home construction in recent years. The area offers peaceful, quiet neighborhoods that sometimes feel more like a weekend vacation spot than an actual neighborhood.

STEINER RANCH, LAKEWAY, AND SPICEWOOD

Steiner Ranch is a unique master-planned community that incorporates the area's natural beauty with its residential homes. Over 800 acres have been set aside as a nature preserve for migratory birds and other wildlife. Known as the Steiner Ranch Preserve, it is part of the Balcones Canyonland Preserve. This environmentally conscious design provides residents scenic views and beautiful vistas of the Texas Hill Country.

Families are attracted here because of the safe, quiet environment and schools, while many others choose it to be near the high tech companies where they work. In fact, many of the new residents here are software engineers employed at nearby 3M, Tivoli Systems, or Dell. It is distinguished in many ways from many of the new communities and neighborhoods in far north and northwest Austin by its design, location, and amenities. Not many communities in the area can boast of having a lake next door where residents can dock their boat. Nor do many communities have neighborhoods located within a private gated country club community. Inside the gates of The University of Texas Golf Club are some of this community's newest neighborhoods, such as Canyon Gate, Eagles Glen, Hunters Green, and Woodland Hills. They contain luxury homes on private streets with the golf course as a wonderful backdrop.

When development of Steiner Ranch began over 10 years ago, the area was pretty isolated and residents would have to drive several miles to reach the grocery store. Since then, stores and other conveniences have moved into the area.

The **City of Lakeway** is a planned development located approximately 20 miles northwest of Austin and 6 miles west of Mansfield Dam on the shores of Lake Travis. It was established in the 1960s on the site of a former ranch as a unique community that blended a relaxing, country lifestyle into a suburban community. The city has a breathtaking landscape that features meadows, hills, wooded acres, and limestone cliffs that drop down to the valley and stretch out to Lake Travis. Lakeway's scenic beauty and leisurely pace of life is reflective of the Texas Hill Country environment. It is a popular place for a vacation home, timeshare, weekend condo, or retirement home and ideal for those who enjoy fine living on the lakefront. In addition to retirees and weekend homeowners, it also has many families. In general, it is an upper-middle-income to wealthy community.

One out-of-the-way community to consider is **Spicewood**. This town is located farther southwest of Lake Travis off of Highway 71. It is a recreational destination for water sports, fishing, and hunting. This natural oasis has an abundance of spring-fed creeks, cypress trees, and springs. The most magnificent is Krause Springs with its 30-foot limestone cliffs lined with ferns, moss, and other vegetation that empty out into a pool of water. The new subdivision of Cypress Hill is located here.

Web Sites: http://cityoflakeway.com, steinerranch.com, http://steinerranchhoa.org/
Area Code: 512
Zip Codes: 78732, 78734
Post Office: Lake Travis Station, 2110 Ranch Rd 620 S, Lakeway
Police Department: Lakeway Police Department, 104 Cross Creek Dr, Lakeway, 512-314-7590; Travis County Sheriff, www.tcsheriff.org, 512- 974-0845
Emergency Hospital: Seton Northwest Hospital, www.seton.net, 11113 Research Blvd, Austin, 512-324-6000
Library: Lake Travis Community Library, www.laketravislibrary.org, 3322 RR Hwy 620 S, Austin, 512-263-2885
Public Education: Lake Travis Independent School District, www.laketravis.txed.net, 3322 RR 620 S, Austin, 512-533-6000 (Lake North & South areas); Leander Independent School District, www.leanderisd.org, 512-434-5000 (Steiner Ranch)
Community Publication: *Lake Travis View*
Community Resources: City Hall, 1102 Lohmans Crossing, Lakeway, 512-314-7500; Lakeway Civic Connection, www.lakeway.org, 105 Cross Creek, Suite 2, Lakeway; Lake Travis Chamber of Commerce, www.laketravischamber.com, 1415 Ranch Rd 620 S, Lakeway, 512-263-5833

LAKE NORTH REGION

Like the Lake South region, the area north of Lake Travis features lakefront living that includes recreational activities such as fishing and boating right at residents' doorsteps. It, too, has many top-quality golf courses.

VOLENTE, LAGO VISTA, AND JONESTOWN

Volente is a nice unincorporated community in the country with hill and lakeside views. New homes here can be expensive and cost around half a million. Volente homes are largely custom built on land purchased by the owner for residential construction. This has resulted in a neighborhood with a mish mash of McMansions, vacation cabins, and average, single-family, residential homes. Some of the homes are on large acreage, surrounded by trees. The area is more akin to a small weekend vacation destination than a residential neighborhood. There are few commercial stores around, but plenty of wildlife, peace, and quiet. Most of the residents are young techies or retirees.

A lakeside resort community that was originally developed in the 1960s, **Lago Vista** is also a budding residential community. It is located within pristine country landscape and lakeview vistas, approximately 45 minutes from downtown Austin.

Jonestown is one of the Lake Travis area's gorgeous lakeside communities. Jonestown was a rural community until the 1990s when growth and development really took off. While most of its citizens are retirees, it has attracted many young families who commute to work in northern Austin or southwest Williamson County.

A park and ride, where commuters can park their cars at a bus station and take the bus into Austin, is located in both Jonestown and Lago Vista.

Web Sites: www.volente.org, http://citylagovista.homestead.com,
Area Code: 512
Zip Codes: 78641, 78645
Post Office: North Lake Travis Station, 8027 Bronco Ln, Lago Vista
Police Department: Lago Vista Police Department, 7207 Bar-K Ranch Rd, 512-267-7141; Travis County Sheriff, www.tcsheriff.org, 512- 974-0845
Emergency Hospital: Seton Northwest Hospital, www.seton.net, 11112 Research Blvd, Austin, 512-324-6000
Libraries: Lago Vista Community Library, 5803 Thunderbird, Suite 40, Lago Vista, 512-267-3868; Jonestown Community Library, 18649 FM 1431 #10A, Jonestown, 512-267-7511; Lake Travis Community Library, www.laketravislibrary.org, 3322 Hwy 620 S, Lake Travis, 512-263-2885
Public Education: Lake Travis Independent School District, www.laketravis.txed.net, 3322 RR 620 S, Austin, 512-533-6000
Community Publication: *Lake Travis View*
Community Resources: Lago Vista City Hall, 5803 Thunderbird, Lago Vista, 512-267-1155; Lake Travis Chamber of Commerce, www.laketravischamber.com, 1415 Ranch Rd 620 S, Lakeway, 512-263-5833; Jonestown Chamber of Commerce, www.jonestownchamber.org, 18700 FM 1431, Suite A, Jonestown, 512-267-5577; Jonestown Community Health Center, 18649 Hwy 1431, #12A, Jonestown, 512-267-3256
Public Transportation: Capital Metro, www.capmetro.org, *Bus:* 214

INDEX

Addicks 150-151
Addicks/Barker 150-51
Addison 47-48
Addison Circle 48
Aldine 175
Alief 154-158
Allandale 208-209
Allen 55-56
Allen Parkway 123, 130
Arboretum, The 20, 233-234
Arcadia Park 39-40, 110
Arlington 64-65
Arlington Heights 78-82, 86
Astrodome/Reliant Center 136
Atascocita 179
Avery Ranch 236-237
Azle 112-113

Balch Springs 44-45
Balcones 233, 235
Balcones West 233
Barker. *See* Addicks/Barker
Barnett Shale 75
Barton Creek 210-212, 215, 221-223
Barton Hills 222-223
Battle Bend 224
Bay Area 185-188
Bayou Place 122
Bayshore 184-185
Baytown 181-183
Bear Creek 148
Beckley Estates 34
Bedford 66-67
Bee Cave,Village of 212-214
Bellaire, Ft. Worth 95-96
Bellaire, Houston. *See* City of Bellaire
Bellaire Park North 88-89
Belmont 15-16, 19
Benbrook, City of 83-85
Bent Tree 30-31
Bentley Village 105-106
Berkeley Place 92-93
Beverly Hills Addition 34
Bishop Arts District 34
Bluebonnet Hills 95-96
Bluffview 26-27

Bouldin 221-222
Boulevard Oaks 136
Braeburn 155
Braeswood Place 137
Brentwood 208-209
Brentwood Hills 103-104
Briar Forest 147-148
Briargrove 143-144
Bruton Terrace 38
Bryan Place 17-18
Bryker Woods 203, 205-206, 208
Buckingham 51
Buckner Terrace 38
Buffalo Bayou 118, 122-125, 128, 138, 145-147
Bunker Hill Village 146
Burleson 114-116
Bush Intercontinental Airport 174, 178

CBD. *See* Central Business District
Camp Logan 119, 140-141, 146
Camp Mabry 207
Candlelight 167-169
Candleridge 99-100
Canyon Creek 235-237
Carol Oaks 101-102
Carrollton 28, 30-31, 47-51? 63
Casa Linda 21
Casa View 21
Castle Court 131
Cat Mountain 233
Cedar Hill 59-61
Cedar Park 237-239
Cedar Springs 11-12
Cedars, The 36, 38
Cedars Crest 35
Centerville 41
Central Austin 197-209
Central Business District (CBD) 75-79
Champion Forest 170
Channelview 183-184
Chapel Creek 87
Cherry Creek 224
Cherrywood 219-220

Chimney Hills 231
Cinco Ranch 149-150
Circle C 216
City of Bellaire 132-135
City of Benbrook 83-85
City of Katy 149-150
City of Lakeway 241-242
City of Sunset Valley 225
City Place 212
Cityplace 11
Cityview 88-89
Clarksville 204-206
Clear Lake 186-188
Clear Lake Shores 189-190
Cloisters 22
Cobblestone Square 105
Cochran Heights 17, 19
Cockrell Hill 39-40
Colleyville 71
Colonial/Bellaire 95-96
Colony, The 56-57
Como 79-81
Cooke's Meadow 105-106
Coppell 50-51
Copperfield 171-172
Coronado Hills 18
Country Day Estates 84
Cow Town 74
Crestview 208-209
Crestwood 79-80, 140-141
Crowley 113-114
Cultural District 78-79
Cypress 169
Cypress Hill 242

Dallas 5-74
Dalworthington Gardens 61, 65-66
Dawson 222-223
Deep Ellum 12-14
Deer Park 180-182, 216
Dell 34
Delwood 219-220
DeSoto 59-61
Dessau 231
Diamond Hill Area 107
Lockwood/Dixon Branch 22
Downtown (Austin) 197, 200
Downtown (Dallas) 6-7, 10
Downtown (Fort Worth) 75, 78-79
Downtown (Houston) 119, 122-126
Duncanville 59-61

East Austin 217-219

East Dallas 12-19
East End 127-128
East Ft. Worth 101-107
East Houston 127-130
Eastchase 106-107
Eastern Hills 101-102
Eastside 118
Eastwood 129
Edwards Aquifer 210, 214
El Lago 186-188
El Tivoli Place 34
Elmwood 34
Energy Corridor 148-149
Entertainment district/s 7, 11, 13,
     16-18, 20, 23, 28, 30, 75, 97,
     107, 197
Euless 66-67
Buckner Terrace/Everglade Park 38
Everman 115-116
Exposition Park 36-37
Exurbs 47, 54

Fair Park 36-37
Fairfield 171-172
Fairmount 92-95
Fairview 55-56
Fairview Park 222
Far North Dallas 28-30
Far North Fort Worth 110-111
Far Northwest Austin 235-237
Far South Austin 224-225
Farmers Branch 48-49
Fifth Ward 125
Fireside 39
Firestone/Upper West Side 75
First Ward 124-125
Flower Mound 68-69
Forest Hill 115-116
Forest Hills 21
Forest Park 94-95, 97
Fort Bend County 158-166
Fort Worth 74-117
Fort Worth Stockyards 74
Fossil Creek 110
Fourth Ward 124-125
French Place 220
Friendswood 194-195
Frisco 54-56
Frisco Heights 94

Galena Park 183-184
Galindo 222-223

Galleria 28, 118, 133, 140, 142-144, 153
Galveston 191-192
Galveston Bay 181, 187
Galveston County 189-193
Garden Oaks 167-168
Garland 40-41, 44
Gastonwood 18
Gay community 12, 130
Georgetown 239-241
Gleannloch Farms 170-172
Glen Brook 128
Glenn Heights 61
Glenshire 153-154
Govalle 218
Gracy Farms 227-228
Gracy Woods 227-228
Grand Lakes 149
Grand Prairie 63-64
Grandview 212
Grapevine 69-70
Great Hills 233-234
Greater Fondren Southwest Area 153
Greenland Hills 17, 19
Greenspoint 173-175
Greenway Plaza 138-140
Greenville 16-17
Gulfgate 129

Haltom City 73-74
Hampshire 101-102
Hancock 200-202
Handley 101-103
Harris Branch 230
Harris Ridge 231
Haslet 116-117
Hawthorne Park Estates 88
Hedwig Village 146-147
Heights 126-127
Highland 209
Highland Park 23-24
Highland Park. See also Park Cities
Highland Village 138-139
Hillcrest 79, 216
Hillcrest Addition 80
Hillshire Village 146-147
Historic districts/neighborhoods 10, 14-16, 18, 20, 32, 33, 37, 60, 93-95, 103, 109, 204
Historic West Austin 203-206
Hollywood/Santa Monica 18
Hospital District, Fort Worth 92, 97
Houston 118-195

Humble 178-180
Hunters Creek 146-147
Hurst 66-67
Hyde Park 131, 202-203

Idylwood 128-129
IM Fields. See Intramural Fields
Inner Loop 119-141
International Center 11
Intramural Fields 203
Inwood Forest 167
Inwood Hills 223
Irving 61-63

Jacinto City 183-184
Jersey Village 169-170, 172
Jester 212
Jewish community 36-37, 152
John T. White 105
Johnson Space Center. See NASA
Joint Naval Reserve Base 84-85
Jones Plaza 122
Jonestown 242-243
Junius Heights 15

Katy 149-150
Katy Area 149-150
Keller 72-73
Kemah 189-190
Kessler Park 33
Kidd Springs 32
Kiest Park 35
Kingwood 179-180
Klein 170
Knox-Henderson 11

La Marque 192-193
La Porte 184-185
Lago Vista 242-243
Lake Arlington 102
Lake Austin 206-207, 210-211
Lake Cliff 32
Lake Dallas 57
Lake Highlands 22-23
Lake North Region 242-243
Lake Olympia 164
Lake South Region 241-242
Lake Travis 212, 241-243
Lake Worth 111-113
Lakeside 112-113
Lakeway 241-242
Lakewood 20-21
Lakewood Heights 18

Lamplight Village 227-229
Lancaster 59-61
Las Colinas 62-63
Las Vegas Trails 87-88
League City 190-191
Leander 237-239
Lewisville 57
Lindale Park 128
Linkwood 137
Little Forest 21
Lochwood 22
Lockheed Martin Plant 85
Lost Creek 87-88
Lower Greenville 16-17

M Streets 17-19
Magnolia 173
Magnolia Park 127-129
Manchaca 217
Manor 229-230
Mansfield 116
Mason Park 128
McKinney 55-56
McKinney Avenue 10
Meadowbrook 101-102
Meadows Place 158-162
Meadows West 88-89
Medical Center 135-137
Memorial 145-148
Memorial Park 140-141, 145
Memorial Villages 146-147
Memorial West 148
Mesa Hills 234-235
Mesa Park 234-235
Mesquite 44-45
Metrocrest 47-51
Metroplex, The 5
Meyerland 151-152
Mid-Cities 61-73
Midtown 123-124
Milwood 227-229
Mira Vista 88-89
Missouri City 163-165
Mistletoe Heights 93-94
Mont Del 84
Montgomery County 176-178
Monticello 79-80
Montrose 130-132
Morgan's Point 185
Mt. Bonnell 207
Mountain View 40
Munger Place 15
Murphy 58

Museum District 135-136

Naaman 41
NAS Joint Reserve Base. See Joint
    Naval Reserve Base
NASA 118, 186-187
Nassau Bay 187
National Register of Historic Places
    15-16, 33, 36-37, 69, 93, 125-
    126, 204
Naval Air Base 90-91
Neartown 131
Norhill 127
North Austin 227-229
North Cat Mountain 233
North Dallas 23-28
North Hi Mount 79-80
North Houston 173-180
North Houston Ship Channel Area
    183-184
North Oak Cliff 31-34
North Oaks 230-231
North Richland Hills 71-72
North Shore 183
North Suburbs 47-57, 116
North University 201
Northcrest 81-82
Northeast Austin 229-232
Northeast Dallas 19-23
Northeast Houston 178-180
Northline 173-174
Northside 107-108
Northwest Austin 232-237
Northwest Fort Worth 111-113
Northwest Hills 233
Northwest Houston 166-173
Northwood Hills 29-30

Oak Cliff 31-35
Oak Cliff Gateway 32
Oak Forest 167-168
Oak Hill 215-216
Oak Lawn 11-12
Old Braeswood 132-135
Old East Dallas 14-19
Old Enfield 203-204
Old Historic West Austin. See Historic
    West Austin
Old Lake Highlands 22
Old West Austin 204-205
Onion Creek 226-227
Outer Loop 142-151
Overton 95, 97-99

Oyster Creek 164

Pantego 65-66
Park Cities 23-26
Park District 78
Park Glen 110
Park Hill 97
Park Ridge 94, 225
Parkdale 38
Pasadena 180-183
Pearland 193-195
Pecan Grove Plantation 166
Pecan Park 128
Pelican Bay 112-113
Pemberton Heights 204
Pflugerville 232
Piedmont 38
Piney Point 147
Plano 52-54
Platinum Corridor 49
Pleasant Grove 38
Pleasant Mound 38
Preston Center 27
Prestonwood 30-31
Prospect Heights 94

Quail Valley 164

Ravinia Heights 34
Red Bird 40
Reliant Center 136
Rice Military 140-141
Rice University 135-137
Rice Village 133-134
Richardson 41, 51-52
Richland Hills 71-72
Richmond 165-166
Ridglea 81-83
Ridglea Country Club Estates 82-83
Ridglea Hills 82-83
Ridglea North 82-83
Ridgmar 85-86
River Oaks 90-91, 138-139, 228
River Place 211-212
Rivercrest 81-83, 144
Riverside 108-109, 218
Riverside Terrace 129
Riverway Terrace 38
Rock Island 109-110
Rollingwood 213-214
Rosedale 207-208
Rosemont 99-100
Rosenberg 165-166

Round Rock 239-240
Rowlett 46
Ruthmeade Place 34
Ryan Place 92-93
Ryanwood 101-103

Sachse 58
St. Thomas University 130
Samuels Avenue 109-110
San Leanna, Village of 217
Sandy Oaks 105-107
Sandybrook 105
Sansom Park 111-112
Scofield 227-229
Scyene 38-39
Seabrook 187-188
Seagoville 39
Second Ward 124-126
Seminary 99-100
Sendera 216
Shady Hollow 215, 224
Sharpstown 154-158
Shenandoah 177-178
Shoreacres 185
Sienna Plantation 164-165
Silver Ridge 87-88
Sixth Street 197
Sixth Ward 125-126
South Austin 220-224
South Boulevard/Park Row Historic
    District 37
South Dallas 35-38
South Fort Worth 92-101
South Hi Mount 80
South Loop area 136-137
South Oak Cliff 35
South Shore Harbour 190
Southampton 136
Southeast Austin 225-227
Southeast Dallas 38-39
Southgate 100, 136
Southlake 70-71
Southside Place 132-135
Southwest Austin 214-217
Southwest Dallas 39-40
Southwest Houston 151-158
Southwest Seminary 99-101
Southwestern Baptist Theological
    Seminary 99-100
Southwestern Suburbs, Dallas 59-61
Spicewood 241-242
Spicewood Springs 233-235
Spring 175-176

Spring Branch 148
Spring Creek 29-30
Spring Valley 147
Stafford 158-162
State Thomas Historic District 10
Steiner Ranch 241-242
Stella Link 137-138
Stevens Park 33
Stockyards 107-108
Stonegate 97-99
Sugar Land 162-163
Summerfields 110
Sundance Square 75-78
Sunnyvale 46-47
Sunset Heights 80, 127
Sunset Hills 34
Sunset Valley 225
Swiss Avenue 16

Tanglewood (Fort Worth) 97-99,
    143-144
Tanglewood Forest 224
Tarrant County 64-74, 90, 112, 115-
    116
Tarrytown 206-207
Taylor Lake Village 187-188
TCU Area 94-99
TCU Campus 94-98
TCU. See Texas Christian University
Tejas Trails 87-88
Texas Christian University 89, 94-99
Texas City 192-193
Texas Medical Center 135-138, 193
Texas Southern University 125, 128-
    129
Theater District 118-119, 122, 124,
    133
Third Ward 125-126
Thomas Place 80
Timbergrove West 127
Tomball 172-173
Travis Country 210-212
Travis Heights 221-222
Turtle Creek 11-12

University Area 200-202
University Hills 219-220
University Oaks 129
University of Houston 125, 128-129
University of Texas 200-202
University Park 24-26
University Park. See also Park Cities
Universtiy Park Village 97

University Place 96-97
University West 96-97
Upper Greenville 17
Upper Kirby 138-140
Upper West Side 75-78
Uptown (Dallas) 10-12
Uptown (Houston) 142-144
Urbandale 38

Valley Ranch 62-63
Vickery Place 15
Victory Lakes 186, 190-191
Victory Park 11
Village of Bee Cave 212-213
Village of San Leanna 217
Villages, The 146-147
Volente 242-243

Walnut Creek 227-231
Wards 124-126
Warehouse District 197-200
Washington Terrace 129
Watauga 73-74
Webster 186, 188
Wedgewood 99-100
Wells Branch 227-229
West Austin 210-214
West Campus 200-210
West Central Austin 207-209
West End 7, 11
West Seventh Street 78-79
West University Place 132-135
West Village 10, 134
Westbury 153-154
Westchase 144-145
Westcliff 97-99
Western Hill 87-88
Westlake Hills 213-214
Westland 87-88
Westover Hills 86
Westpoint 87-88
Westwood 154-158
Westworth Village 89-90
Wheatley Place 37
White Lake Hills 103-105
White Rock Lake 19-23
White Settlement 91-92
Williamson County 237-241
Willow Lake 98-99, 104
Wilshire Heights 18-19
Wilshire Woods 220
Wilson Historic District 16
Windermere 231

Windsor Park 219-220
Winnetka Heights 33
Woodcliff 230-231
Woodhaven 103-105
Woodland Heights 127
Woodlands 176-178
Worth Heights 99-100
Wylie 58
Wynnewood North 33

Zilker 222-224

RELOCATION TITLES

MOVING WITH KIDS?

Look into *The Moving Book: A Kids' Survival Guide*.

Divided into three sections (before, during, and after the move), it's a handbook, a journal, and a scrapbook all in one. Includes address book, colorful change-of-address cards, and a useful section for parents.

Children's Book of the Month Club "Featured Selection"; American Bookseller's "Pick of the List"; Winner of the Family Channel's "Seal of Quality" Award

And for your younger children, ease their transition with our brand-new title just for them, *Max's Moving Adventure: A Coloring Book for Kids on the Move*. A complete story book featuring activities as well as pictures that children can color; designed to help children cope with the stresses of small or large moves.

GOT PETS?

The Pet Moving Handbook: Maximize Your Pet's Well-Being and Maintain Your Sanity by Carrie Straub answers all your pet-moving questions and directs you to additional resources that can help smooth the move for both you and your pets.

"Floats to the top, cream of the crop. Awesome book; I'm going to keep one on the special shelf here." – Hal Abrams, Animal Radio

NEWCOMER'S HANDBOOKS®

Regularly revised and updated, these popular guides are now available for Atlanta, Boston, Chicago, London, Los Angeles, Minneapolis–St. Paul, New York City, San Francisco Bay Area, Seattle, and Washington DC.

"Invaluable ...highly recommended" – Library Journal

If you're coming from another country, don't miss the *Newcomer's Handbook® for Moving to and Living in the USA* by Mike Livingston, termed "a fascinating book for newcomers and residents alike" by the *Chicago Tribune*.

Introducing NEWCOMER'S HANDBOOKS® NEIGHBORHOOD GUIDES!

This new series provides detailed information about city neighborhoods and suburban communities, helping you find just the right place to live. More locations to come!

FIRST BOOKS

6750 SW Franklin Street
Portland, Oregon 97223-2542
Phone 503.968.6777 • Fax 503.968.6779
www.firstbooks.com

READER RESPONSE

We would appreciate your comments regarding this first edition of the *Newcomer's Handbook® Neighborhood Guide: Dallas–Fort Worth, Houston, and Austin*. If you've found any mistakes or omissions or if you would just like to express your opinion about the guide, please let us know. We will consider any suggestions for possible inclusion in our next edition, and if we use your comments, we'll send you a free copy of our next edition. Please mail or fax this response form to:

Reader Response Department
First Books
6750 SW Franklin, Suite A
Portland, OR 97223-2542
Fax: 503.968.6779

Comments: _____

_____

_____

_____

_____

_____

_____

_____

Name: _____

Address: _____

_____

_____

Telephone: (   ) _____

Email: _____

6750 SW Franklin, Suite A
Portland, OR 97223-2542
USA
P: 503.968.6777
www.firstbooks.com